the logic of the price system

the logic of the price system

paul b. trescott

professor of economics and history
southern methodist university

mcgraw-hill book company

new york   st. louis   san francisco   düsseldorf   london
mexico   panama   sydney   toronto

the logic of the
price system

Library of Congress Catalog Card Number 76-102456

65140

1234567890 MAMM 79876543210

This book was set in News Gothic by The Maple Press
Company, and printed on permanent paper and
bound by The Maple Press Company. The designer
was Paula Tuerk; the drawings were done by John
Cordes, J. & R. Technical Services, Inc. The editor
was Sonia Sheldon. Sally R. Ellyson supervised the
production.

preface

This book is intended as a text for undergraduate courses in microeconomic theory for students who have already received some instruction in principles of economics. There are many texts available on this subject; why have another? To be sure, I have presented the materials with singular clarity and simplicity, but I suspect the other authors would, if pressed, confess to similar convictions about their own efforts.

The title of this book reflects two ways in which it is a differentiated product. It is a study of the *logic* of the price system, but does not attempt to be empirical and descriptive. A lack of realism is not something to boast about in itself, but it is a concession to another objective. This book gives more emphasis than most to the logic of relationships involving the entire economic *system:* the allocation of resources and the distribution of income especially. Many authors have explained individual bits and pieces of economic theory without conveying any real idea of how they are connected to each other. Fitting the pieces together has its cost, however, in that the pieces must be kept relatively simple. For those who wish them, descriptive case-study materials exist in abundance. I have avoided attempting to incorporate them, fearing they would present a distraction. Art is long and life is short; students have their hands full in mastering even the minimum elements of the tool kit of economic theory in the customary one-semester course, and they will, one hopes, have ample exposure to description of real firms and real industries elsewhere.

The expositional approach is an attempt to use the optimal degree of mathematics. The structure of economic theory is unavoidably mathematical, but the structure of the student mind all too frequently is not. Most existing texts either use too little mathematics or too much. The traditional verbal-geometric approach is inadequate for the multivariate relationships so central to the analysis, and the geometry is very vulnerable unless the diagrams are derived from mathematical functions. At the opposite extreme, the full mathematical treatment, even if conceptually valid, is pedagogically not appropriate for the vast majority of the customers taking the course.

The mathematical level employed here stresses repeated use of the simple first derivative. This is the minimum degree of mathematics required to cope with the subject, and it yields an enormous payoff relative to the effort involved. Emphasis is placed on specific illustrations with specific numbers, which are keyed into the verbal explanations, tables, and diagrams. Experience suggests this approach works well with the student who has had a course in calculus but has never been able to see how to use it. Further, the amount of calculus employed in this book can be learned ad hoc by many students, and I have tried to make the use of the derivative as nearly self-explanatory as one can without making a full attack on limit theory.

The mathematical level employed is essential to the content, since the relationships explored typically involve more than two variables. This is particularly true of the production function, which is probably the central integrating element in the entire presentation. Because of their simplicity and ease of mathematical manipulation, Cobb-Douglas production functions are the main form of illustration. By working from a production function, such standard constructs as cost functions and factor-productivity functions can be derived and not merely contrived.

The mathematical notation is geared to the mathematically unsophisticated. I have not used partial-derivative notation even where it would be more appropriate and have stuck to the old-fashioned da/db form of writing derivatives. Capital letters A, B, and so on, are used consistently to denote products; lower-case letters a, b, and so on, to denote inputs. The same letter which identifies the classification is likely to be used to represent the number of units in the examples. The inelegance of the notation will probably annoy readers who have some real mathematical facility. My feeling is that good mathematicians will have an easier time reading bad notation than will bad mathematicians trying to cope with "good" notation of the sort employed in much of the literature.

At any rate, emphasis is on the manipulation of the mathematics, not merely contemplation. Numerical examples in the text are worked out in considerable detail and are followed up by problems at the ends of many of the chapters. Answers and discussion of some of these appear in the back of the book.

Early drafts of this material were prepared while I was serving as visiting professor at Thammasat University, Bangkok, Thailand. The response of my Thai students encouraged me to proceed with the chosen approach. I received valuable criticism from two Bangkok colleagues, W. David Maxwell and H. Peter Gray, both of whom read substantial portions of the manuscript. Lengthy sections were inflicted on my students in Economics 415 at Miami University, who responded in a sporting way with both criticism and encouragement. The structure of Chapter 7 was inspired by a set of simulation exercises developed by Prof. Herbert Fraser. To these and many others, my sincere gratitude.

paul b. trescott

contents

1

what economic analysis
is about

The central concern of economics is the production, distribution, and consumption of goods and services. The economist's concern with these matters gives him an interest in such matters as money and prices, labor, wages, and employment, international trade and finance, government finance and other areas of public policy, and a great variety of matters relating to the structure and functioning of business enterprise.

The subject matter of economics overlaps with subjects studied by engineers, by students of business administration, by sociologists, and by many other specialized disciplines. The distinctive feature of economics is its central core of analysis—*economic theory*—which finds applications to many diverse areas of subject matter. Economics is not a mere accumulation of descriptive information. Economic theory provides a logical, organized framework which helps to explain how one thing relates to another. Economic theory is concerned with interdependencies, with probable relationships of cause and effect.

Yet, at the same time, economics is concerned with people. The noted British economist Alfred Marshall stated that "Economics is a study of mankind in the ordinary business of life; it examines that part of individual and social action which is most closely connected with the attainment and with the use of the material requisites of wellbeing."[1]

welfare and productivity

Economics deals with subjects which greatly affect people's material well-being— their economic welfare. The welfare of human beings depends in considerable degree on the amount of goods and services which they have the opportunity to consume—basic necessities such as food, clothing, and shelter, and amenities such as recreational facilities and the products of artistic and cultural skill. A large proportion of mankind has always lived in conditions of material poverty—conditions which subject them to continuing physical discomfort and condemn them to lead lives far too "nasty, brutish, and short."

For a society as a whole, the ability to consume depends on the ability to produce—on the amounts of food, clothing, housing, etc., which can be turned out. We must be careful of the way we use the words "produce" and "production." We shall wish to use the concept of production to include the rendering of *services* which may themselves be intangible. Productive activity is that which creates or increases utility, where utility refers to anything people find enjoyable or desirable. The farmer or manufacturer may apply processes which transform products from less useful to more useful forms. Middlemen and transport media help transfer goods from places where they are less wanted to places where they are more wanted, and many productive services, such as those of teachers or physicians, may create utility directly without being embodied in a specific product.

Differences in productivity account for differences in the wealth of nations, the great disparity between "rich" nations like the United States and "poor" ones such as India. What are the reasons for such wide differences in productivity?

resources: the factors of production

Whether a nation's economy produces goods and services in abundance depends first of all on the available *productive resources,* or *factors of production.* Labor— human effort of all kinds—is by far the most important of these resources. The most important source of high productivity in the modern world is a labor force of high quality—physically strong and healthy, intelligent and well educated, well motivated and responsible, skilled and experienced both in technical matters and in the ability to work together effectively.

---

[1] Alfred Marshall, *Principles of Economics,* 9th ed., New York, Macmillan, 1961, p. 1.

Productivity also depends on *natural* resources in the broadest sense. These include such endowments of the earth as soil fertility and mineral deposits, but extend also to climate and topography.

A third category of productive resources consists of *capital goods*—man-made instruments of production. Capital goods take on a variety of forms—machinery and equipment, buildings, and even the inventories of goods in the process of production and distribution. The farmer's tools and livestock, the merchant's goods on hand, the railroad's roadbed and rolling stock—all are capital goods.

technology and organization

The productivity of a society also depends on how effectively the available productive resources are used. This is partly dependent on the level of *technological achievement*. As improvements in science and engineering are adapted to methods of farming, manufacturing, transportation, etc., it becomes possible to obtain more output from the same amount of resources.

The effectiveness of resource use also depends on *organization*. Important problems of organization occur within individual productive units, whether private business firms or government agencies. More effective techniques of administration make possible greater productivity. However, some crucial problems of organization occur at a higher level: they involve the pattern of organization of economic activity for the society as a whole.

The problem of organization is closely related to *specialization*. Ever since the time of Adam Smith, economists have stressed that specialization—division of labor—can greatly increase the productivity of an economic system. Instead of attempting to produce all the things he wishes to consume, each worker can restrict himself to a narrower range of functions. In this way, he can develop greater skill and efficiency in performing those functions. Similarly, land and capital goods can gain in efficiency through specialization. Individual land tracts can be used for those products to which their climate and soil conditions are best suited. Capital goods can be designed to achieve degrees of strength, temperature, precision, and control not possible with unspecialized hammers, lathes, or shovels.

In thinking of specialization, it is well to remember that, generally, *resources have alternative uses*. This is particularly true of human labor, which is remarkably adaptable. The manpower which goes into farming could be employed in building a house or in transporting goods to market. The tract of land which is used to pasture cattle could be the site of a house or store.

scarcity

Central to economic theory is the problem of *scarcity*. Economic goods and services are scarce, in the sense that they are not available in sufficient amounts to give everyone all he would choose to consume at a price of zero. If something is so abundant that we can have all we want without paying for it, then it is not scarce economically. The air we breathe is, under ordinary circumstances, not scarce. But when the natural atmosphere is too thin (in a jet airliner at 30,000 feet), or too hot or too polluted (in smog-ridden Los Angeles), the principle of scarcity comes into operation. People are willing to pay for higher pressure, or lower temperature, or purification.

Several aspects of scarcity deserve emphasis, as follows:

1. Economic goods and services are scarce *relative to people's desires* for them. To use a time-honored example, there are more good eggs than bad eggs, but it is good eggs which are scarce. Why? Because it is the good eggs which people desire to consume.

2. The scarcity of economic goods and services arises from the scarcity of resources used to produce them. Labor, land, and capital goods exist only in limited amounts. Perhaps the ultimate limitation is that of human time and effort. Each of us can expect only a limited life span, and the amount of that which we are willing to devote to work is only a small proportion of the total.

3. There may appear to be individual economic goods or services which are not scarce. One sometimes hears that there exists a surplus of some commodity— wheat or rubber, for instance. Usually this means that the supply is sufficient to cause a decline in the price, to the annoyance of producers of the commodity. Only if its price falls to zero can a commodity be considered exempt from the principle of scarcity. And if the resources which produce it—for example, the land, labor, and capital needed to produce rubber—can be transferred to the production of something else, the price of rubber cannot (except very temporarily) fall to zero.

4. It is not likely that the principle of scarcity will be overcome merely by increasing the productivity of the economy. Admittedly, it should be possible to fulfill completely people's desire for any one specific commodity. But as long as resources have alternative uses, there will remain some unfulfilled need to which they can be devoted. And if all desires for consumption were fulfilled, there would remain the desire to work less long and less hard.

5. However, the principle of scarcity might be overcome if people were willing to be contented with modest standards of consumption and found some positive enjoyment in work. These are not impossible conditions. Some religious faiths teach that contentment is to be found in the limitation of desires. However, the vast majority of the world's population have not accepted the ascetic philosophy.

choice

Economic theory is primarily concerned with decisions involving choice. The necessity for choice arises directly from the principle of scarcity. Because economic resources are scarce, we cannot have everything we want. The more labor, land,

and capital goods we devote to production of bread, the less we have left for shoes. The more time we spend in such enjoyable activities as eating, sleeping, gossiping, and going to the movies, the less we have to spend on activities which earn the income which we enjoy spending. For the society as a whole, the choices emphasized by economic theory are those involving the *allocation of resources*. Resource allocation refers to decisions concerning how the labor, land, and capital goods of the society are to be employed—what products are to be produced and in what quantities, and what methods of production are to be used.

The existence of scarcity also raises a conflict of interest among consumers: the more I consume, the less of the economy's scarce output remains for you. For the society as a whole, this problem gives rise to another area of choice—choice relating to the *distribution* of goods and services among competing consumers. "Who is going to get what?" becomes a major corollary question to "Who is going to do what?"

maximization and constraint

When individual consumers or business firms make their decisions, they are guided by some sort of goal or objective. In economic theory, we express the guiding principles underlying choice by asserting that each household or firm is trying to *maximize* something. The use of a maximization assumption is most easily understood in the case of business firms, where we usually assume that business decisions are aimed at maximizing profits. It is not so easy to construct a counterpart for the decisions of households; these cannot be reduced to anything so quantitative as profits. The essential assumption regarding household behavior is that people have some conception of their self interest and act in such a manner as to promote that self-interest. This need not mean that people are chiefly motivated by greed and acquisitiveness. It does tend to mean that they are interested in their own material well-being (along with a lot of other things) and will act to further their material well-being in some situations.

Whatever people maximize, they act under constraints; that is to say, their range of feasible choices is limited. For individual households and business firms, the most apparent constraint is imposed by limited purchasing power, the budgetary constraint. Expenditures are limited by the availability of funds from income, from previously accumulated wealth, or from credit. For the society as a whole, the effective constraint on consumption is imposed by productivity and its ultimate determinants: resources, technology, and organization.

equilibrium

The notion of *equilibrium* is closely linked with the notion of maximization. Each economic participant is regarded as being in equilibrium when he has achieved a position of maximization consistent with the existing condition of the economic environment. If the participant has not achieved a position of maximization, we assume he will adapt toward such a position. Thus our analysis of business firms assumes that a firm is in equilibrium when it is making the greatest profit possible, given the condition of costs, demand, and market structure.

Our discussion will frequently involve identifying conditions under which equilibrium will exist for entire groups of transactors. However, equilibrium implies a condition of completion and fulfillment which is not very applicable to the world of experience. Good economists recognize this; they are not infatuated with analysis of equilibrium positions as such, but rather recognize that the equilibrium concept is essential to analyze *dis*equilibrium. For this purpose, one needs to emphasize the adjustment process by which a condition of disequilibrium tends to resolve itself.

substitution

Much of our analysis deals with the response of production or consumption patterns to changes in the prices confronting the producers or consumers. Some initial equilibrium pattern is identified, a change in price is then assumed, and a new equilibrium pattern is then identified. This response of producers and consumers to changing prices almost always can be expressed in terms of *substitution*. Substitution may involve a decision by a buyer to purchase more of one product and less of another. For example, business firms substitute among inputs by using more capital equipment and less labor. Less familiar, but no less important, are substitutions made by sellers. Business firms may decide to substitute one line of output for another. Individual workers may decide, in effect, to substitute one occupation or employment for another. Substitutions tend to follow a systematic pattern. Buyers tend to substitute against an item which has risen in price, to buy less of it and more of the substitutes. On the other hand, sellers tend to substitute in favor of an item which has risen in price. That is, business firms will be drawn toward increased production of items which have risen in price; workers will be drawn toward occupations which have become more remunerative, etc.

market behavior

The study of choices under conditions of scarcity, which we are about to undertake under the name of economic theory, generally concentrates attention on people's behavior in "the marketplace." Thus we shall deal primarily with situations in which people earn money incomes through the sale of the services of their labor or their property to business firms and use those incomes to buy the consumption goods and services which they want from business firms. However, many people do not live this way. In some countries there are many farm households, for example, which are basically self-sufficient. Such families are not exempt from the problems of scarcity and choice—far from it. Economic analysis can be applied to the actions of the self-sufficient farm family, but such application is neither common nor very useful. Economic theory is particularly concerned with questions of *interdependence*, with the manner in which the self-interested activities of each person in society affect the others. The genuinely self-sufficient farm family has little effect on other members of the society, and is little affected by them.

A society probably cannot achieve a high level in economic productivity without departing from self-sufficiency and accepting the principle of specialization. In the self-sufficient farm household, decisions about what work to perform are directly related to the consumption desires of the household. But when work becomes specialized, a separation is introduced between consumption desires and decisions about what work to perform. The individual performs work which does not directly yield goods and services which he wants to consume.

A society organized on the basis of specialized activity in production is immediately confronted with two very large problems:

1. The necessity for exchange. There must be some means whereby individual producers can dispose of their specialized productions and receive in exchange the goods and services they desire—which are in turn the results of the specialized production of vast numbers of other persons.

2. The necessity for organization and guidance. Each person working in an economy based on specialization needs some guide or directive to inform him what to do. Some system must exist which provides guidance on what products need to be produced, and in what relative quantities. There must be some basis for deciding what methods of production are to be employed, and for matching up the available workers with the work which needs to be performed. One possible way of providing such guidance is by some central authority, which plans and administers the production pattern of the economy. But a form of guidance can also be achieved without central control, through the operation of the price system and the market mechanism. How such guidance can arise, and how well it functions, are among the major topics of this book.

money

Whether centrally controlled or not, an industrial economy organized on the principle of specialization cannot function efficiently without the use of money and a price system. Money provides the most efficient basis for exchange. Producers sell their goods for money, which they then use to buy the things they want. Without money, it would be necessary to exchange one kind of product for another directly. The result would be a cumbersome and inefficient process of barter and swap. By the use of money, individuals can separate more thoroughly their activities as producers from those as consumers.

Money is also the indispensable common denominator of exchange in its role as the unit of account (the unit in which prices are stated). By having all prices expressed in a common unit of account, choices are greatly facilitated. Each consumer can compare the costs of different products and choose the products which he thinks will yield him the most enjoyment for a given expenditure. The common denominator of money greatly aids business efficiency as well. By expressing both costs and revenues in a common monetary unit, the business firm can arrive at a single measure of profit, which serves as a guide to decisions concerning inputs and outputs.

Because of its extensive use in the exchange economy, money may become a misleading "veil" which hides from individuals some important economic realities. For the individual household, the availability of money—purchasing power from income, wealth, and credit—appears as the constraint which limits consumption and real income. However, for the society as a whole, the real constraint lies in the scarcity of resources and the limitations of their organization. Admittedly there may be times when a scarcity of money causes undesired idleness in resource use; workers who want income may be unemployed when they could be producing the equivalent of the goods they so urgently desire. But creation of money is no panacea for the "niggardliness of nature," the brute fact of scarcity as it confronts the majority of the world's population.

microanalysis and related matters

Economic theory deals primarily with the behavior of business firms and individuals in a market economy, characterized by specialization and exchange, using money as a unit of account and a medium of exchange. Consequently, much attention is directed to the behavior of individual decision-making units within the economic system, chiefly business firms and households. This part of economic theory is often referred to as *microanalysis*. It utilizes a microscope, so to speak, to study economic activities "in the small." The subject is grounded on the notion that the behavior of each unit can be interpreted in terms of maximization. However, the main emphasis in economic analysis is not on describing or explaining the actual behavior of individual households or business firms. Instead, the analysis identifies certain inherent regularities in such behavior and uses them to draw out consequences. For example, in much of our exposition the "business firm" is really a logical construct designed to help explain the reaction of prices and quantities of input and output to changes in the various elements of the economic environment. Many important conclusions of the analysis are not "micro" at all, but relate to the society as a whole: to the pattern of production, the efficiency with which resources are used, the distribution of real income, and the effects of growth, taxes, and international trade opportunities. (There is an important area of economic analysis termed *macroanalysis*, or the theory of income and employment, which concentrates on the causes and consequences of the flow of money expenditures through the economy. Such topics are not substantially dealt with in this volume.)

price theory

It is common among professionals to refer to microanalysis as *price theory*. Descriptively, this term has some merit. Much of the material which follows deals with the manner in which individual household and business decisions are conditioned by prices, and with the manner in which prices, in their turn, respond to individual decisions. Prices serve as one of the most important organizing elements in a free-market economy. Nevertheless, to refer to this area of economics as price theory is misleading in two major respects. First, we will develop only a theory of *relative* prices; that is, the price of one commodity or service compared with another. The theory of absolute prices, expressed in specific monetary units, is to be found in macro-, or money-flow, analysis.

Second, to refer to this area of economics as price theory implies that the explanation of price determination is a matter of vital concern in itself. This is not so, as generations of bored students can testify. The analysis of prices is useful because it facilitates the analysis of *quantities* of inputs and outputs, quantities which describe the real income of the members of a society and which relate intimately to its resource allocation, economic efficiency, and economic welfare.

economic efficiency and economic welfare

In discussing the use of maximization postulates, we observe that individual households and business firms *care* about the outcome of their decisions. A household prefers one pattern of consumption to another, a business firm prefers one method of production to another. In an interdependent, market economy, the decisions which individual units undertake, each following its own preferences, have extensive consequences for the welfare of all the members of the society.

We are accustomed to speaking of the *efficiency* with which a given business firm operates. However, it is also possible to speak of the efficiency of the economic system as a whole. For the entire economy, economic efficiency means getting the most output out of the available productive resources. Viewed in these terms, increased efficiency can be a means to increased welfare. Our study of the logic of a market economy is therefore not merely concerned with how it functions, but also how well it functions.

scarcity, efficiency, and choice—a graphic view

Much of the subject matter with which we will deal in this book is intrinsically mathematical in its underlying structure. Where possible, we attempt to develop these ideas through several styles of exposition—through words, through examples based on simple arithmetic, through more general algebraic statements, and through graphs.

In economic analysis, graphs exploit the two-dimensional quality of the printed page to express relationships between two variables. One variable is measured horizontally, increasing from left to right. The other is measured vertically, increasing from bottom to top. Each point on the graph represents a combination of two numbers, one measured by the horizontal distance, the other by the vertical. We say that each point represents an ordered pair of numbers, with the horizontal coming first.

In Figure 1-1 is represented a concept which does much to illustrate the problems of scarcity and choice. It is called a *production-possibilities curve*. Imagine that the economic system can turn out only two commodities, beef and cloth, each of which is relatively homogeneous. The existing supply of labor, land, and capital goods sets a limit to the amount of each product which can be produced, the precise location of the limit depending on technology and organization. Suppose the economy devoted all its resources to cloth; with the best feasible

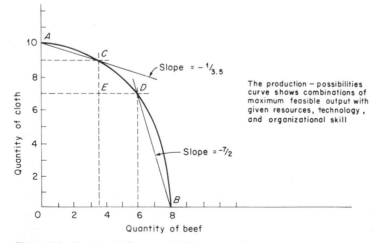

The production — possibilities curve shows combinations of maximum feasible output with given resources, technology, and organizational skill

Figure 1-1 The production-possibilities curve.

technology and organization, the maximum annual output might be 10 million square yards, which we measure vertically in the diagram. Since there are no resources left to produce beef, this output of 10 million square yards of cloth is associated with zero tons of beef, defining a point on the diagram marked A.

However, resources have alternative uses. By transferring all resources into the production of beef, there is some maximum annual output which could be achieved with the best feasible technology and organization—say 8 million tons. This joins in an ordered pair with the zero output of cloth to give us the point B.

Assuming that this society is dependent on its own production, it is not likely that people will want to consume *only* cloth or *only* beef. They are more likely to wish some combination of both. Somewhere between A and B there must lie a whole set of points which identify feasible combinations of cloth and beef which can be produced with the existing resources and technique. Such a set, or locus, of points has been drawn as a curve which bulges outward away from the origin, or zero point. If we start from point A, we can explain this curve (which we call a production-possibilities curve) as being generated by a process of *output substitution*, or transfer of resources from cloth to beef.

Some resources are very poorly suited to cloth production, but will be very productive for beef. This is especially true of tracts of land. If we start transferring such misused resources out of cloth and into beef, we move to the right from point A. At first we gain much output of beef, while the sacrifice of cloth is very slight. The curve is almost horizontal. However, before long the withdrawal of resources begins to reduce the output of cloth. Thus the curve bends downward as we move further to the right. The further we move, the greater the quantity of cloth we are obliged to give up in order to obtain an additional unit of beef. Eventually, of course, the curve becomes very steep and may be vertical by the time it reaches point B. The last resources to be transferred out of cloth are those which are most productive in cloth and least productive in beef.

The points on the curve represent the different combinations of cloth and beef which the society can produce with its limited resources. Because resources have alternative uses, the society can vary the relative amounts of the two products and increase one by reducing the other. Such variation is a form of substitution. To increase the output of one product requires a reduction in output of the other. In a fundamental sense, the *cost* of the added output of one product is the amount of the other which must be sacrificed. In such a view, cost is often called *opportunity cost;* one opportunity or option has been sacrificed in order to pursue another.

In terms of the production-possibilities curve, the marginal opportunity cost of a product can be expressed by the *marginal rate of substitution*. This is simply the amount of one product which the society must give up in order to obtain an additional unit of the other, moving from one point to another on the production-possibilities curve. It is arbitrary which way we move along the curve, but in order to use consistently a concept which will recur many times in the pages which follow, we will adhere to this rule: always put in the top half (numerator) of the fraction the change in the variable which is measured vertically. In Figure 1-1, the marginal rate of substitution can be expressed as Δ cloth$/\Delta$ beef, where the symbol delta (Δ) stands for a finite change in the variable specified.

Now the slope of a straight line drawn in a coordinate system such as this one is defined as the ratio between a change in the vertical dimension divided by the change in the horizontal. It follows, then, that the marginal rate of substitution between any two points on the production-possibilities curve is equal to the slope of a straight line drawn through these two points. Consider a movement along the curve from A to C. A shift of resources reduces the output of cloth by 1 million units, but increases beef output by 3.5 million units. The marginal rate of substitution is 1/3.5, which is also the slope of the line drawn between these points. (Actually the slope is $-1/3.5$. However, since we will in general know whether curves are sloping up or down, we will often leave out plus and minus signs associated with direction of slope. We wish to emphasize absolute values.)

Students of calculus may observe that the marginal rate of substitution can be expressed at any point on the production-possibilities curve as the derivative dC/dB of the function $C = P(B)$ defined by the production-possibilities curve. It is measured by the slope of a line tangent to the curve at that point. A fuller discussion of functions, derivatives, and their application to economic theory is given in Chapter 2.

As we move to the right, shifting more resources out of cloth and into beef, the absolute value of the marginal rate of substitution increases: that is, we have to give up increasing amounts of cloth to obtain any given increment of beef. From D to B, for instance, the society must relinquish 7 million units of cloth to obtain 2 million added units of beef, a ratio of 3.5 to 1. The increasing marginal rate of substitution here illustrates a general property of the economic system: the opportunity cost of each product tends to increase as the output of that product increases (with a given supply of factors and state of technology).

Why does the marginal rate of substitution increase? Why does the production-possibilities curve bulge outward from the origin? The reason is that the productive resources are not perfect substitutes for each other, and each individual resource tends to be better suited for one product than for the other. Land and labor are not perfect substitutes for each other, and land is more important in beef production than it is in cloth production. A full demonstration of how the production-possibilities curve can be derived, and what determines its shape, will be offered in Chapter 16.

The production-possibilities curve represents the limits imposed on output by the fact of scarcity. The society cannot obtain *more* than the combinations specified by the curve. However, if things are not well managed, it may find itself with *less*. If inferior technology is used, or if the pattern of organization is inefficient, or if resources are left unemployed, the society may find itself at some point like E, falling short of its maximum potential.

Over a period of time, one would expect the production-possibilities curve to shift outward. The quantity of labor and capital may increase, technology may improve, and economic organization may become more efficient. Our diagram is drawn for one particular point in time, and does not show such shifts.

The curve between A and B (and the points like E which lie inside it) represents the *area of choice* open to the society. Any combination of cloth and beef lying on or inside the curve is technically feasible to produce. The society's problem is to choose which combination will actually be produced. In some societies, such decisions are made by some central authority. In others, such output choices emerge as the result of a vast number of production and consumption decisions made by individual business firms and households. At this point, we merely wish to emphasize that ordinarily the members of the society *care* about the outcome. Most assuredly they do not wish to be totally deprived of either commodity, to starve or to shiver. Thus output combinations like C or D are likely to be preferred to A or B. However, whether there is one combination that is better than the others is a question which we shall reserve for later investigation. Likewise, we will try to show what sort of output choice can be expected to occur in a free-market economy.

In a diagram it is possible to show the production possibilities for combinations of only two commodities. For a real economic system, the range of production possibilities would extend to combinations involving thousands and thousands of specific products. It is possible, using input-output analysis, to obtain rough estimates of the production possibilities for any economy for a number of classes of commodities—for instance, 100. Our diagram should be regarded merely as a two-dimensional representation of a very multidimensional phenomenon.

summary

Every economic system is confronted by scarcity of economic goods and services, and of the productive resources available to them. Because of scarcity, every society is obliged to make choices concerning what products to produce, how to produce them, and who is to get them. Economic analysis deals with the choice patterns of individuals, business firms, and entire societies, in economic situations where specialization and exchange are extensive. Since resources have alternative uses, the society must devise some means for allocating them into specific functions and end-products—for deciding who is going to do what. Economic analysis helps us understand how this process takes place in a market economy using money and prices. It may also help us understand how *well* it is done, and to evaluate alternative methods of carrying out the same process.

The production-possibilities curve shows the output choices open to a society, given the condition of resources and technology. Along such a curve, increased output of one product can be obtained only by giving up some of another product. This "opportunity cost" can be measured by the marginal rate of substitution.

TERMS AND CONCEPTS

Each chapter contains terms, phrases, concepts, and analytical devices with which you must become familiar. At the end of each chapter we will present a list of those which have been introduced in that chapter. Be sure you can define or identify each and understand its relationship to the analysis.

1. Production and productivity
2. Productive resources
3. Scarcity
4. Allocation of resources
5. Maximization
6. Microanalysis
7. Production-possibilities curve
8. Marginal rate of (output) substitution

QUESTIONS AND PROBLEMS

Explain each of the following in terms of the general notion of scarcity:

1. The government of the United States concerns itself at great length about the problem of surplus agricultural production, particularly of wheat, corn, and cotton.

2. In many towns of the American northeast, there are many black-walnut trees. Each year they produce thousands of nuts which fall to the ground. Each nut is surrounded by an outer, pulpy hull which, when green, makes an ugly brown stain on the skin of a person touching it. The nutshell is very hard. The kernels of the nuts are delicious and fetch a good price in stores, but most nuts are not harvested.

3. Since the capacity of the human stomach is limited, there is a limit to the amount of bread which consumers would wish to consume. As agricultural and baking technology improve, it should be possible to eliminate the problem of scarcity in relation to bread.

4. It is sometimes claimed that a major problem of modern economic systems is to find jobs for all the people who want them.

a general view of the market economy

To understand something about the complex world of economic affairs, it is necessary to start with a simplified view. Let us imagine that we are dealing with an economy in which there is widespread specialization, in which exchange is conducted through the use of money, in which productive resources are privately owned, and in which individuals are substantially free to work, produce, buy, and sell as they choose. These conditions constitute what we will refer to as a *market economy*.

We can view the market economy as consisting of two categories of decision-making entities, or units, namely business firms and individual households. The activities of production and distribution are carried on by business firms, which employ the services of productive resources for these purposes. Households are the ultimate "owners" of all productive resources; in particular, they are the source of the available supply of labor. Households are also the consuming units of the economy; the ultimate purpose of economic production is to provide the households with goods and services for consumption.

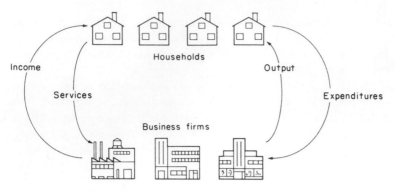

Figure 2-1 The flow of income, output, and expenditures.

These two types of economic entities are linked by a network of market relation-ships which involve buying and selling, the transfer of money and of goods and services. This network is shown in Figure 2-1. Note that it leaves out of account such real-world phenomena as government transactions and international trade. We will ignore both of these in the bulk of this work, but each will receive attention after we have analyzed the theory of a self-sufficient, private-market economy. In the real world business firms carry on much of their buying and selling with each other, and some households sell services directly to other households. Neither of these is stressed in Figure 2-1. In the subsequent analysis we will deal primarily with a simplified conception of business firms as if they bought their inputs from households and sold their output to households. This is a conception which is more nearly valid for the economy as a whole than it is for any individual firm.

Despite these oversimplifications, Figure 2-1 displays some important ideas which have relevance to the real world. One of these is the notion of circularity. Figure 2-1 suggests that two kinds of flow are taking place, in opposite directions. One consists of a flow of money expenditures, moving from business firms to households in payment of wages, rents, and other factor incomes, and back to businesses in the form of expenditures for currently produced goods and services. The second is a flow of real inputs and outputs, originating in the ser-vices rendered by labor and productive property to business firms, and culmin-ating in the output of real goods and services for consumer purchase. In the study of macroeconomics, one would concentrate on the behavior of the aggregate stream of money expenditures and on the manner in which aggregate output and employment are affected by it. Our interests, however, lie with the other stream, the flow of real inputs and outputs.

the world of supply and demand

A century ago critics contended that all that was necessary to develop an econo-mist was to catch a parrot and teach it to say "Supply and demand." The element of truth in this gibe is that much of economic analysis (as we shall develop it here) consists in showing how various problems can be interpreted in terms of supply and demand. However, supply and demand are usually only organizing concepts which help us to focus our thoughts.

It may be helpful at this point to speak not so much of supply and demand but of buyers and sellers. The word "demand" expresses what buyers do; it refers to the amount of some commodity which buyers are prepared to take under a given set of conditions. The word "supply" expresses what sellers do; it refers to the amount of some commodity which sellers are willing (and able) to furnish under a given set of conditions. An understanding of the actions of buying and selling is central to an understanding of demand and supply.

Each of the component units of the economic system appears both as buyer and as seller. Business firms are the sellers of currently produced goods and services, but are buyers of the services of labor and productive property. Households are the buyers of the final production of the system, but are the sellers of services of labor and property. Further, each unit's activity as a buyer is constrained by its success as a seller, which determines the amount of income available for spending. This feature of economic life could be identified by a horizontal line through the middle of Figure 2-1. However, we want also to emphasize the different types of markets in which demand and supply interact. As a first step, consider Figure 2-1 to be divided by a vertical line through the middle. The left side of the diagram can be regarded as representing a set of markets for resources, the factors of production. Here business demand interacts with household supply to determine prices of productive resources—rates of wages, interest, and rents—and consequently to influence the distribution of total income among individual households. The right side of the diagram represents the set of markets for the output of goods and services. Here the demand of households interacts with the supply from business firms to determine prices of final goods and services.

These supply and demand forces determine not only the prices of goods and services, but their *quantities* as well. The interplay of decisions to buy and sell produces in the economy a determinate pattern of inputs by business firms, and of incomes and consumption patterns by households. Since the decisions of business firms and households are influenced by the prices at which they can buy and sell, we speak of their actions as being influenced by the *price system*, which simply refers to the price aspect of a market economy.

In a market economy, people's actions guided by the price system result in a particular pattern of resource allocation, in which are determined such important social questions as who is going to *do* what and who is going to *get* what. Because the members of the society *care* about what things they consume, the workings of the market economy and the price system are of great importance to their economic welfare. We must inquire whether the market economy and the price system help the society to achieve a high degree of economic efficiency, or whether they do not. In the process, we will try to develop an idea of what constitutes an efficient use of productive resources, and by what means efficiency can be improved.

decisions and choices

Our analysis is rooted in the behavior patterns of individual households and business firms, studied under conditions of abstraction and simplification. In particular, our analysis is based on the study of choices which decision-making units make in their buying and selling activities.

In the analysis of *demand*, we study the behavior of buyers. Buyers can be thought of as shopping around in an effort to get the most for their money. Their activities as buyers are constrained by their limited incomes and other sources of purchasing power. Consuming households must select from a wide variety of possibilities the specific items they will purchase. In so doing, they are guided by their psychological tastes and preferences. They are also guided by the prices which must be paid for individual items. When one commodity falls in price, people tend to substitute it for others, and buy more of it. A decline in the relative price of pork is likely to lead consumers to buy more pork and less of its close substitutes such as chicken or fish.

Business firms must also make decisions as buyers. They must decide what persons to employ, and how much labor, raw materials, and other inputs to purchase in any time period. In making its purchase decisions, the business firm is guided by considerations of profit. It will choose inputs and methods of production which are technically efficient and productive, but it, too, will be influenced by the prices of different input items. There is usually more than one way to produce any given product. The various kinds of inputs are, to some degree, substitutes for each other. Within limits, the firm can substitute machinery for labor, or steel for cement or wood. When substitution possibilities exist, firms will tend to use more of any input which falls in price relative to the others. Thus price is always a consideration in guiding the decisions of buyers. The lower the price of one item becomes, the more attractive it becomes to buyers, who are trying to get the most for their money. Sellers are also confronted with choices for which prices furnish guidance. Sellers are in general trying to get the most in return for what they sell. Thus high prices will tend to attract, and low prices repel, the sellers of goods and services.

Households are confronted with decisions about selling the services of their productive resources. This is merely an elaborate way of describing such down-to-earth decisions as what sort of occupation one should attempt to follow or where and for whom one should work. Owners of land and capital must also make decisions about how these resources shall be used. To be sure, both workers and property owners tend to maintain patterns of custom and tradition. This should not obscure the fact that the *opportunity* for change is available and that some people do change.

Sellers of productive resources desire to obtain income, but it would be absurd to say that this is their only desire. Most workers have definite preferences for the kind of work they do, the kind of firm for which they work, and the location of their work. Nevertheless, if we hold these elements constant, it remains true that workers will be guided by the incomes yielded by different kinds of work. If two jobs are identical except in pay, people are going to prefer the better-paying position.

The choices confronting business firms as sellers are wider and more obvious. Business firms must decide what things they are going to sell. This will mean, for many, deciding what things to produce and precisely what specifications to select. A firm must decide not merely that it will make furniture, but specifically what items (e.g., chairs, or desks, or both) and precisely what sizes, shapes, and designs.

Because of its desire to earn profits, the business firm is strongly influenced by prices. It will be attracted toward the production and sale of those products for which the prospective selling price is high *in relation to the cost* of production and distribution. The cost, in turn, depends on the prices which have to be paid for productive services, and on the efficiency of technology and organization by means of which inputs are converted into output. The business firm's decisions as buyer and as seller are closely interrelated, and we will attempt later to show how these can be viewed as part of one general decision-making pattern based on profit considerations.

competition and prices

In the foregoing, we have spoken of the way in which a given configuration of prices influences the buying and selling decisions of households and business firms. But there is an influence operating in the other direction as well—the buying and selling decisions of firms and households also help to determine the level of individual prices.

Sometimes this influence is direct and apparent. We usually think of a merchant or storekeeper as being able to set the price he will ask for the things he sells. But we know also that if he sets his asking price too high, people will not buy from him. A seller's control of price is always limited by the fact that he cannot force people to buy from him. His opportunity to charge a high price depends on the effectiveness of *competition*. If there are other sellers offering the same product at a lower price, buyers will find out about it. Then a high price asked by one seller will lead buyers to substitute other sources of supply.

Suppose, however, there are no other sources of supply—that one seller has a *monopoly* of a product or service. If buyers want the product, they must meet the monopolist's price. He has a greater opportunity to charge a high price. Even so, he cannot *force* people to buy the product; they may choose to do without it.

When the number of sellers is large, and each is small relative to the total market, the individual seller will find that he does not have much ability to charge a high price and still sell goods in a very large quantity. However, if the number of firms is small and each is relatively large, competition may not be very vigorous or effective. Even if there is not a monopoly, firms are more likely to engage in *collusion* when they are few in number and large in size. This means that they may meet together and agree on prices they will ask.

The behavior of individual business firms differs depending on the sort of competitive environment in which they find themselves. Different environments are referred to as *market structures;* they are identified by differing conditions relating to the number of firms, their relative size, the ease with which newcomers can enter a trade or business, and the extent to which the products offered by one firm are similar to or differentiated from those of another. We will explore the analysis of market structures in a later part of this study.

We have spoken of the extent to which an individual seller can control his selling price, looking primarily at the product market (right side of Figure 2-1). There may, of course, also be price control by buyers—particularly when the buyers are business firms. However, we must be careful not to exaggerate the extent of such control. The individual farmer, in virtually every country of the world, feels himself to be helpless in setting prices and believes that he is confronted with powerful middlemen who possess arbitrary power in setting the prices they will pay for farm products. In reality, however, there are generally many individuals and firms operating as middlemen. Competition is intense. The individual farmer can usually find several possible buyers for his products. Competition among the middlemen keeps the prices they offer from falling very far below what the middlemen themselves can sell the products for.

The individual wage earner also feels himself to be helpless in the determination of wages. Certain job opportunities are available, and it appears that employers set the wage rates to suit themselves. But again the power of individual employers may be rather limited. A firm which offers very low wages will find it can obtain very few workers, and those perhaps not very efficient. Competition can operate to keep wages high, provided that the workers are productive and efficient and that the number of firms is sufficiently large so that workers have some real choice of employments.

pure competition

In dealing with market structures, as in many things, it is helpful to postulate a situation which, though not very realistic, is simple to analyze. Once we have dealt with it, we can introduce more and more elements of realism. Our starting point will be a set of market conditions termed *pure competition*.

Let us assume that the number of buyers and sellers of each product is very large and that there is no differentiation between the product of one seller and that of another—i.e., the product is homogeneous within each industry. All buyers and sellers are assumed to have extensive knowledge of market conditions. It is further assumed that collusion is not possible and that people are free to enter or leave a given business or occupation without restrictions such as permits, licenses, etc. These conditions are approximately fulfilled in markets for many agricultural products, but are less common in manufacturing or trade.

Under conditions of pure competition, the individual buyer or seller is so small as to have no effective influence on the price of what he buys or sells. Further, because everyone is assumed to know what is going on, the prices charged by the various sellers of a given product will tend toward uniformity. Each buyer or seller will feel himself confronted with a going market price which is "out there" and beyond his control. A seller who asks more than the going price will not find any buyers; they can all buy on better terms from someone else. However, since each seller is small, he can sell all he wants to sell at the going price. Therefore he has no motive to charge less than the market price. Individual buyers are in a comparable position. They can obtain all they want at the going price, but nothing below it.

the interplay of supply and demand

We have introduced the assumptions of pure competition at this point because they help to clarify the operations of supply and demand. Under pure competition, individual buyers and sellers have no direct influence on price. Each participant in the market is a "price taker" rather than a "price maker"; he must accept the price as "given" and beyond his own control. What is within his control is the volume of business he wants to do at the going price. The individual consumer is free to decide the quantity of each product he will buy at the going price. The business firm is free to decide how much of any given product it will offer for sale and how much of each input it will purchase under the prevailing price conditions. Individual households can decide how many members will go to work at prevailing wage circumstances and perhaps how much time they will spend at their jobs. In all these decisions, households and firms adjust their behavior to a *given* set of price conditions, on the basis of their psychological preferences or profit expectations. However, for the economic system as a whole, prices are very much *not* "given." When we adjust our level of analysis to the economy as a whole, it is prices which are being "caused" by the interplay of buying and selling activity.

It is one of the fundamental propositions of economics that in a competitive market, the price of any commodity tends toward the level at which the supply is equal to the demand. More accurately, this means the price at which the quantity which suppliers wish to sell is equal to the quantity which buyers wish to buy. This is referred to as the *equilibrium price*.

In equilibrium, each individual transactor has achieved a position where he is doing as well for himself as is possible, given the conditions confronting him. In addition, the behavior patterns of all the transactors are mutually consistent, so that, for instance, the output decisions of producers as a group are consistent with the purchase decisions of consumers as a group. Should the quantity demanded exceed the quantity offered, some transactors are *not* doing as well for themselves as they think possible. As buyers attempt to obtain the quantities they desire, some will tend to bid the price up, rather than be content with the quantities originally available. Sellers will be pleased to raise price and also to increase output. If the quantity offered for sale were to exceed the quantity demanded, the selling price would tend to fall. Some sellers would be willing to accept a lower price rather than be limited to the existing volume of sales; buyers would be willing to increase their purchases only if offered a lower price.

Here, as in most cases of equilibrium, much of our analysis is really concerned with what happens if equilibrium does *not* exist. As a rule, to explain why one set of conditions constitutes an equilibrium, assume that set of conditions does not prevail, and see what adjustments would occur.

The interplay of supply and demand, of desires to sell and to buy, will tend to produce in each market an equilibrium price and an equilibrium quantity. The process will operate in markets for factors of production as well as for products. Payments for the services of land, labor, and capital will provide the incomes of consumer households. As the process of equilibration takes place throughout the economy, there emerges a definite composition of total output, as well as a corresponding pattern for the inputs of factors of production. We want to know more about this pattern: What characteristics is it likely to have? Will it be a pattern which utilizes the scarce resources efficiently? What difference would it make if elements of monopoly were introduced?

In the chapters which follow, we will be attempting mainly to develop in much greater detail the analysis of supply and demand and the manner in which they interact. As a first step in this process, we will consider some refinements of terminology and exposition which help to give greater precision to these concepts.

functions and schedules

Our analysis of supply and demand will be greatly facilitated if we regard them as functions or schedules. A *function* is a mathematical expression indicating the relationship between the quantity of some dependent variable and the quantities of other, independent variables. A functional relation need not imply anything about causation; it merely asserts that for a given set of values of the independent variables, there exists some particular value for the dependent.

The relationship between the area of a square and the length of its side is an example of a simple function. For every number one might assign to the length of the side, there corresponds a number which represents the area. The area function can be expressed algebraically in this form:

$$A = s^2$$

Once we have this general equation, we have a rule which enables us to determine the area corresponding to any specific value of s.

Algebraic equations expressing one variable in terms of others are examples of functions, and we will make use of such equations extensively. However, not all functions can be expressed by specific equations.

In economics, a functional relationship between only two variables is often referred to as a *schedule*. This reflects the fact that it is easy to make a table in which the related values of the two variables are placed side by side. For instance, it would be easy to make such a table for the area function noted above, which could look like this:

Side	Area
0	0
1	1
2	4
3	9

When the function can be represented algebraically, that is usually the most convenient way to write it. Further, the algebraic statement makes it clear whether the function is continuous—that is, whether it holds for fractional values of the variables. However, there are many relationships which cannot be expressed in simple algebraic form. Such literal schedules as a railroad time-table or a list of the dates of Easter in several years represent a kind of function which really needs tabular presentation. We will have much occasion to speak of demand and supply schedules, in which we associate with each possible price a quantity which buyers will purchase (demand) and a quantity which sellers will offer for sale (supply).

A functional relationship between two variables can also be represented by a graph. Each point represents a combination of the two variables, one measured vertically and the other horizontally. Economists tend to use the phrase *demand curve* to mean the same thing as *demand schedule*, referring to the same functional relationship between two variables.

Often we deal with functional relationships in which we do not know the specific equations or schedules but can identify some characteristics of functional interaction. We can use a more generalized kind of functional notation for cases where the specific form of the relationship is not specified. Letting A stand for the notion of the area function of a square, it would be correct to write

$$A = A(s)$$

as a way of saying area (A) is a function of length of side (s). The latter notation does not tell us anything about the actual content of the area function. It merely states that there is a functional relation between A and s. Subsequently we shall see that there are ways of specifying some attributes of a function even when one cannot assign a specific algebraic formula to the function itself. In particular, it is often possible to specify what kind of *changes* will occur to the dependent variable for a given change in the independent variable(s).

the demand function

Many of the important relationships which we will be dealing with can be expressed as functions. To illustrate, consider the demand for a product by consumers. In a demand function, the dependent variable is the quantity of the product (measured in some sort of physical unit) which people will purchase during a given period of time (a month, a year). If we were considering the demand for pork, we would want a function expressing the number of pounds of pork which consumers would buy during a given period of time. The chief independent variables, determining the quantity of pork purchased, would include consumers' incomes, the prices of pork and of other products, and the state of consumers' psychological tastes, preferences, and expectations. Probably the quantity of pork purchased would rise as people's incomes went up. Quite likely the quantity would fall if pork prices rose relative to other prices. Changes in the prices of other commodities might have either positive or negative effects.

We might write a general functional statement for the demand for any commodity A in such form as this:

$$Q_{DA} = D(Y, P_A, P_B, P_C, \ . \ . \ .)$$

We let Y stand for incomes, P_A for the price of A, and P_B, P_C, etc., for the prices of other commodities. We could include a term in the function to stand for consumer tastes, but since this is not an easy item to quantify, we might prefer to leave it out of the explicit function, and instead to understand that the entire function as written would be valid only for one particular set of consumer tastes.

Estimates of demand functions for specific commodities have been derived from statistical records of quantities purchased and related variables. For example, one study derived the following expression for the demand for beef in the United States during the years 1922–1941:[1]

$$X_1 = 90.814 - 1.850X_2 + 0.0832X_3 - 0.415X_4$$

where X_1 = beef consumption per capita, lb

X_2 = beef price at retail, deflated by index of consumer prices

X_3 = disposable income per capita, deflated by index of consumer prices

X_4 = pork consumption per capita, lb

From this equation we can infer that consumption of beef tended to vary inversely with the price of beef (X_2), directly with incomes (X_3), and inversely with consumption of pork (X_4).

It is possible to derive a schedule from a function of several variables by specifying values for all but one of the independent variables. For instance, given a general demand function for beef containing such independent variables as incomes and prices of several related products, we might specify values for income and for all prices except that of beef itself. Then we could isolate a demand schedule showing how beef purchases would vary with changes in the price of beef, other things remaining unchanged.

derivative of a function

Economics is full of problems involving changes or increments. In particular, we are frequently interested in the sensitivity of one variable to changes in another. How much does cost change when output is increased? What happens to the quantity of pork purchased when people's incomes rise? The change in the dependent variable of a function associated with a small change in one of the independent variables can be expressed by the *derivative of the function*. Given a functional relation $y = f(x)$, the derivative (often written dy/dx) expresses the change in y associated with a very small change in x.

Where a function is expressed as a specific algebraic equation, mathematical rules often permit us to obtain an equally specific expression for the derivative. For our illustrations, it will be sufficient to deal only with the most elementary of these. Suppose we have an algebraic expression in the form cx^n, where c is a coefficient, x is a variable, and n is an exponent of x. Such an expression is a function of x, and we could write $f(x) = cx^n$. The first derivative of the function is as follows:

$$\frac{df}{dx} = cnx^{n-1}$$

[1] Mordecai Ezekiel and Karl A. Fox, *Methods of Correlation and Regression Analysis*, 3d ed., New York, Wiley, 1959, pp. 200–201.

That is, we find the derivative by multiplying the coefficient c times the exponent n times the variable x with its exponent reduced by one. For example, let us consider a function y such that $y = 5x^3$. Here the coefficient c is 5 and the exponent n is 3. By the formula, the derivative dy/dx would be

$$15x^2 \qquad \text{that is} \qquad 5 \cdot 3 \cdot x^{3-1}$$

This expression is also a function of x. To find the derivative at a specific point, we substitute some given value for x. When $x = 10$, for example, the derivative would be 1,500. A small change in x at that point would be associated with a change in y which would be 1,500 times as large. If we increase x from 10 to 10.01, y increases by 15.*

Since finding the derivative requires manipulation of exponents, it is useful to review the mathematical conventions for writing exponents. The ordinary exponent indicates how many times the variable is multiplied by itself; thus $x^3 = x \cdot x \cdot x$.

When the exponent is unity, it is customarily omitted; thus $x^1 = x$.

Roots of the variable can be expressed by fractional exponents; thus $\sqrt{x} = x^{1/2}$, $\sqrt[3]{x} = x^{1/3}$, and $\sqrt[3]{x^2} = x^{2/3}$.

Inverse expressions of the variable can be expressed by negative exponents; thus $1/x = x^{-1}$, and $1/x^2 = x^{-2}$.

When we multiply terms containing x, we add the exponents; thus $x^2 \cdot x^3 = x^5$; and $x^{1/3} \cdot x^{2/3} = x$.

When we raise an x term to a power, we multiply exponents; thus $(x^2)^3 = x^6$; and $(x^3)^{1/2} = x^{3/2}$.

A variable with an exponent of zero is equal to 1; thus $x^0 = 1$.

When a function is expressed by a polynomial, we can take the derivative of each term separately and add them together to obtain the derivative of the function. Suppose we have a total cost function

$$TC = 10Q - 5Q^2 + Q^3$$

where Q represents the quantity of output produced by a firm. The first derivative of this function represents the change in total cost associated with a small change in output, which we will later define as *marginal cost*. We can find the value of this derivative by taking each expression separately, multiplying the coefficient times the exponent times the variable with its exponent reduced by one. The operations

---

* Actually, the derivative is mathematically accurate only when the change in x is infinitely small. As soon as a finite change in x is used, the derivative gives an approximate answer. In our example, the increase in y is actually 15.015005. The approximation is off by less than 1 percent.

are as follows:

$$10 \cdot 1 \cdot Q^{1-1} = 10$$
$$-5 \cdot 2 \cdot Q^{2-1} = -10Q$$
$$1 \cdot 3 \cdot Q^{3-1} = 3Q^2$$

Adding the three terms gives this expression for marginal cost:

$$MC = 10 - 10Q + 3Q^2$$

At any specific output, the specific value of marginal cost is obtained by substituting a number in place of Q. For instance, at an output of 2, marginal cost would also be 2 (i.e., $10 - 20 + 12$). A small increase in output would raise the total cost by an amount double that change in output. Raising output from 2 units to 2.01 units would thus raise total costs from 8 to about 8.02.

The simple cases of derivative analysis presented here represent only a beginning, but they offer a large payoff to the student of economics. A large part of economic analysis can be illustrated with relatively simple functions with simple derivatives. Applications of the derivative are suitable in cases where we would use the word "marginal." Marginal cost, marginal revenue, marginal product, marginal propensity to consume—all can be represented as derivatives of some kind of function.

maximization

The emphasis on marginal analysis, and the prominence of the derivative, stem largely from the importance of maximization postulates in economic analysis. Economists want to know what behavior patterns result if buyers or sellers act to maximize or minimize some variable which can be expressed as a function. The derivative of a function is zero at the point where the function reaches its maximum or minimum. (However, not all points with zero derivatives are maximum or minimum points, so this technique of identification must be used with care.)

Consider again the total cost function introduced above. By dividing through by output (Q), we obtain an average cost function, as follows:

$$AC = 10 - 5Q + Q^2$$

We may wish to find the output at which average cost is minimized. For this operation, we can determine the derivative of the average cost function and set it equal to zero. Thus

$$\frac{dAC}{dQ} = -5 + 2Q = 0$$
$$5 = 2Q$$
$$Q = 2.5$$

Average cost will be at its minimum when output is 2.5 units—assuming that the output units are divisible. Note that the derivative of the constant (10) is zero.

When we have a function containing more than one independent variable, we may be interested in its partial derivatives. The demand function characteristically contains several independent variables: income, price of the product, prices of other products. To isolate the change in quantity associated with a change in one such variable, we must choose specific values for the other independent variables, substitute them into the functional equation, and thus reduce it to a simple function with only one independent variable. We can then obtain the derivative of the simple function. This entire operation identifies a partial derivative of the more complex function. Often we are dealing with functions which are not expressed in precise equations. We may still be able to identify important characteristics of the functions in terms of derivatives. For instance, given a general demand function $Q_{DA} = D(Y, P_A, P_B, \ldots)$, one might specify that the partial derivative $\partial Q/\partial Y$ was positive, meaning that people would buy more of the product as their income increased. And one would expect that $\partial Q/\partial P_A$ would be negative, as people would buy less of product A at a higher price.

elasticity

It is only a short step from the derivative or marginal value of a function to the concept of elasticity. Derivatives or marginal relationships show the ratio of changes in two variables. *Elasticity* expresses a ratio between *proportional* or percentage changes in two variables which are functionally related. The difference is important. However, it is relatively simple mathematically to move from the derivative of a function to its elasticity. For instance, given a demand schedule, in which Q (quantity demanded) is expressed as a function of P (price), the proportional change in quantity can be expressed as $\Delta Q/Q$ and the proportional change in price is $\Delta P/P$. Dividing the first by the second yields

$$e = \frac{\Delta Q/Q}{\Delta P/P} = \frac{\Delta Q}{\Delta P} \cdot \frac{P}{Q}$$

If we make the change in P very small, the ratio of the delta terms simply becomes the derivative, and the elasticity of demand is expressed by $e = (dQ/dP)(P/Q)$.

geometry of functions and derivatives

A function expressing one variable in terms of another can often be shown as a line or curve on a graph. It is often desirable to be able to draw the curve corresponding to a function which is expressed in equation form. This can usually be done by choosing specific values for one variable and solving the equation for the corresponding value of the other variable.

For example, to graph the function $y = x^2$, one would choose some values for x and solve for the corresponding values of y, in this manner:

x	y
0	0
1	1
2	4
3	9
4	16

Each pair of numbers is then plotted as a point on a graph, as shown in Figure 2-2. Then a curve is drawn through them, as smooth and continuous as possible.

The derivative of a function has a useful geometric relation to the curve of its "parent" function: it is equal to the slope of a tangent drawn to that parent curve (which is equal to the slope of the parent curve itself). In the function just drawn, when $x = 3$, $dy/dx = 6$. A tangent drawn to the curve at that point will intersect the base at the point where $x = 1\frac{1}{2}$. Its slope is measured by the ratio of its vertical change (between 0 and 9) to its horizontal change (between $1\frac{1}{2}$ and 3) and is therefore 9 to $1\frac{1}{2}$, or 6.

Any function in the form $y = a - bx$ (where a and b are constants) in which the x term has an implicit exponent of 1 is called a *linear* function and will produce a straight line on a graph. A straight line has the same slope at all points, reflecting the fact that the derivative of a linear function is a constant.

summary

A market economy can be viewed as a circular flow of inputs and outputs, of income and expenditures, among households and business firms. Each unit

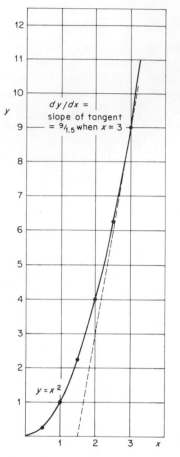

Figure 2-2 Curve of the function $y = x^2$.

participates in the economic process as a buyer, and tries to get the most value for its money. Each unit also participates in the process as a seller, and tries to find the most rewarding selling opportunities. Viewed individually, households and business firms adapt their buying and selling activities to the prices which confront them. Viewed collectively, these buying and selling activities determine prices. We analyze this influence in terms of supply and demand, which can be regarded as functions, or schedules. The demand function relates quantity purchased to such independent variables as incomes, prices, and preferences. The supply function relates the quantity supplied to price and to costs. In a competitive market, price tends to the level where demand and supply are equal. Supply and demand interactions extend through the product and factor markets of the economy and lead to a particular pattern of resource allocation, production, and consumption.

TERMS AND CONCEPTS

1. Market economy
2. Price system
3. Equilibrium price
4. Market structure
5. Pure competition
6. Supply function, supply schedule
7. Demand function, demand schedule
8. Function, derivative

QUESTIONS AND PROBLEMS

Answers to parts of selected problems are given in the back of the book.

1. Assume that the production-possibilities curve for a society can be represented by this equation: $40A + 25B - AB = 400$ (where A and B represent the quantities of two commodities).
   (a) Draw the production-possibilities curve.
   (b) Suppose the economy suffered from a depression and did not use all
   its resources. Locate a point in the diagram which might represent such
   a situation.
   (c) Calculate the marginal rate of substitution between $A = 10$ and $A = 9$,
   and compare it with MRS between $A = 1$ and $A = 0$.
   (d) Suppose capital formation and technical improvement increased the
   economy's production potential. Indicate how this could be shown in
   the diagram.

2. Find the derivative dy/dx for each of the following functions:
   (a) $y = 10x$
   (b) $y = 10x + 20$
   (c) $y = 10x + 20 + 5/x$ (*Hint:* use negative exponent)
   (d) $y = \sqrt{10x}$ (*Hint:* use fractional exponent)
   (e) $y = 5x^3 - 12x^2 + 4x - 2$

3. Find the specific numerical value of dy/dx in each of the functions in Problem 2 when $x = 10$. Illustrate the meaning of the derivative by relating it to
   the effect on y of an increase in x from 10 to 10.1.

4. Draw the graphs corresponding to functions in Problems 2a and 2d. Draw
   the tangent to each at the point where $x = 10$, and illustrate that the
   slope of the tangent equals the value of the derivative as calculated in
   Problem 3.

the theory of demand:
the individual consumer

Demand relates to the behavior of buyers. A demand function relates the quantity of any product which buyers will buy to such determining influences as incomes and prices. A demand schedule (or its geometric counterpart, a demand curve) relates the quantity demanded of some product A to the price of A, assuming other demand determinants to remain fixed.

Some aspects of the structure of demand relationships are shown in Figure 3-1. Our starting point will be the analysis of household demand for consumer goods, and we shall examine the manner in which individual households adjust their purchases of individual commodities to varying conditions of incomes, tastes, and prices. Next we shall examine the market demand for any given product (such as pork). The *market demand* is simply the aggregation of demand by all the individual households in the economy. From market demand we can move, in turn, to the demand situation confronting the individual producer of a specific product such as pork. This demand situation is determined partly by the condition of market demand for that product and also by the competitive relationship among the firms producing that product.

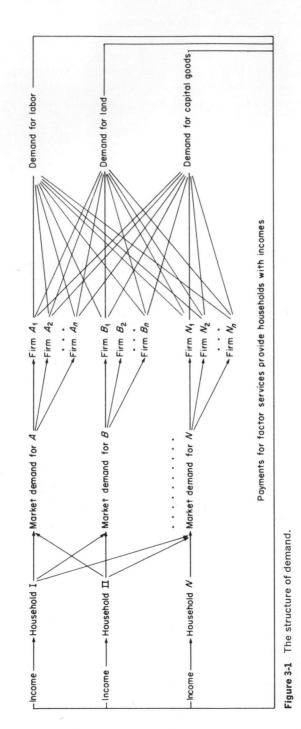

Figure 3-1 The structure of demand.

The final step in the linkage of demand consists of the demand by each producer for the services of factors of production. This is regarded as a *derived demand*, since productive services are purchased not because they yield utility or pleasure directly to the buyer, but for the contribution they make to turning out things demanded by consumers. Demand for livestock feed, therefore, will depend in part on the consumer demand for livestock products such as pork.

demand by the individual household

In studying the behavior of individual consuming households, we need to understand the concepts of scarcity, choice, and maximization. By *scarcity* we mean that each household has access to only a limited amount of purchasing power, chiefly from income. By *choice* we mean that a wide variety of specific products and services is available from which to make a selection. We use the term *maximization* to imply that consumers have a set of desires and preferences about what they consume—some combinations of goods and services appear preferable to others.

The bases for diversity in consumer tastes are many. The facts of biology influence dietary and clothing requirements. In most societies, however, social factors exert an important influence. These may be embodied in custom and tradition, perhaps with a religious sanction: the Hindu thinks so highly of the cow that he will not eat beef, while the Moslem has such a low opinion of the pig that he will not eat pork. In western industrial societies, consumer preferences are more volatile, a fact which partly reflects the influence of advertising. It would be a mistake to claim that consumer tastes are fixed and unchanging. We merely assume that at any given time each consumer acts as if he had a scale of preferences among goods and services. Ordinarily, his behavior would imply that different combinations are ranked as more strongly preferred or less desirable, with limiting cases where two combinations appear equally desirable.

Further, we assume that, other things being equal, the consumer prefers more of a commodity to less of it. Given a choice between two collections of goods, one collection A containing more of each commodity than the other collection, the consumer will choose collection A. Even if collection A contains more of only one item, but the same amounts of the other items, the consumer will prefer it. For more advanced analysis, one would wish to modify this assumption to allow for cases of satiation, where the consumer has enough of one item and would not take more for his own use even as a gift.

Our assumption that people prefer more stuff to less stuff does not tell us how people would choose among two combinations each of which contains more of some items than the other. If collection A contains more bread but less potatoes than collection B, we have no way of knowing which will be chosen. We merely say that the consumer's preferences will determine whether one is preferred to the other, or possibly that they will appear equally desirable.

systematic analysis of demand—indifference curves

To give some precision to the analysis of demand by individual households, economists employ a geometric device known as an *indifference curve*. This is a way of giving graphic representation to the preferences of the consumer and to the behavior which he undertakes on the basis of those preferences. In Figure 3-2, the vertical axis measures the number of pounds of pork, and the horizontal, the number of pounds of chicken. Two diagonal lines have been drawn. Along each line lie points representing combinations of pork and chicken purchased per month. Thus the point A_1 represents 2 pounds of pork and 1 pound of chicken.

What can we say about the consumer's preference among the six combinations we have identified? Our general rule tells us that he will prefer more stuff to less stuff. This can easily be applied to points along one of the diagonal lines. The point A_2 represents more stuff than A_1 because it represents more pork *and* more chicken. Point A_3 represents even more than A_2. We conclude that when comparing points lying along such a straight line, the consumer will prefer a point lying further from the origin.

Can we say anything about comparisons between A points and B points? Sometimes we can. Comparing A_2 with B_1, for instance, we find that A_2 represents more pork than B_1, and that both represent the same quantity of chicken. Thus A_2 represents more stuff than B_1 and therefore will be preferred. By the same reasoning, B_2 is preferred to A_1. Even less effort is required to see that B_3 is preferred to A_1, and that A_3 is preferred to B_1. However, our rule does not tell us whether the consumer would prefer A_1 to B_1, or A_2 to B_2, or A_3 to B_3. These comparisons

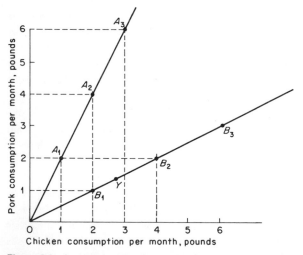

Figure 3-2 A consumer-preference system.

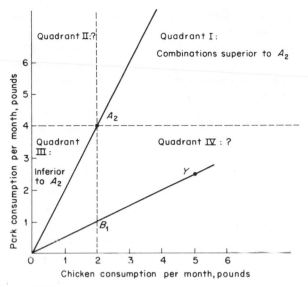

Figure 3-3 A consumer-preference system.

involve more of one but less of the other commodity. And the choices, or orderings, between such pairs reflect the subjective preferences of the consumer.

To separate cases where preference is clear from those where it is not, consider the point A_2 in Figure 3-3. The horizontal and vertical lines through A_2 divide the surrounding points into four quadrants. All combinations represented by points in quadrant I are preferred to A_2, since they contain more of both commodities. All points in quadrant III represent combinations less preferable than A_2, since they contain less of both items. Points on the dotted lines above or to the right of A_2 represent superior combinations, since they contain more of one item than A_2 but the same of the other. Points on the dotted lines below or to the left of A_2 are inferior combinations, containing less of one item and the same amount of the other.

What about the combinations represented by quadrants II and IV? Our initial assumption does not tell us whether these will be preferred or not. If our consumer were both very self-conscious and very cooperative, we might simply ask him to describe his preferences. For instance, we could ask him to express his preference between the point A_2 and the various points along the B line. If we assume that pork and chicken can be bought in any amounts, then every point along B represents a real combination. At first, moving up the B line from the origin, its combinations will clearly be less preferable than A_2. But sooner or later the consumer will reach a point such as Y, above which he finds the combinations on the B line preferable to A_2. Very likely he cannot identify the point Y

exactly but can only approximate it as moving from the two less ambiguous extremes. Nevertheless, it exists as a limit, or range, of his preferences.

If the point Y can be established, we say it represents a point of indifference, as compared with A_2. By a similar means we could locate a point of indifference compared with A_3. But what about all the points which do not lie on either line A or B? We must imagine our diagram to contain not merely two, but a very large number of such diagonals. And we must imagine that it is possible to identify not merely one, but a whole family of points of indifference which go along with A_2. Conceptually this step is shown in Figure 3-4. Here we show a larger number of diagonals, on each of which we have established points of indifference compared to A_2. We can connect these several points with a line, and the curve which results is called an *indifference curve*. This simply means that the consumer is indifferent with respect to the points on the curve. The various commodity combinations on the curve appear equally desirable to him. However, it may be easier to remember that the indifference curve is a *boundary line*. All points lying above the curve (that is, further out from the origin) are definitely preferred to those lying below it (that is, closer to the origin).

Typically, we will draw indifference curves with the sort of shape shown in Figure 3-4—that is, somewhat hyperbolic. The specific shape depends on the substitutability between the products concerned. The limiting case, where two products are regarded as perfect substitutes by the consumer, is shown in Figure 3-5a. Here the indifference curve becomes a straight line. If the consumer regards white eggs and brown eggs as identical, one combination of ten eggs is as good as another. Figure 3-5b describes an opposite extreme, where two commodities are consumed in fixed proportions.

In the normal case, however, we expect the curve to slope in such a way that it bulges toward the origin. This bulge arises from the fact that, typically, products

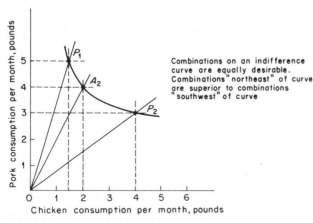

Combinations on an indifference curve are equally desirable. Combinations "northeast" of curve are superior to combinations "southwest" of curve

Figure 3-4 A consumer indifference curve.

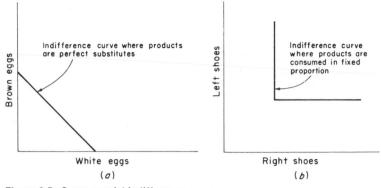

Figure 3-5 Some special indifference curves.

are not perfect substitutes for one another. Imperfect substitutability is reflected in a decreasing marginal rate of substitution as one moves along the indifference curve. Given an indifference curve relating products A and B, the marginal rate of substitution indicates the decrease in A associated with a unit increase in B as one moves along the curve.

The marginal rate of substitution (MRS) can be calculated between two points on an indifference curve. In such a case it is defined as the ratio $\Delta A/\Delta B$, where the deltas represent finite changes in the variables measured vertically (A) and horizontally (B). On the diagram, the MRS between a pair of points is simply the ratio between the vertical movement and the horizontal as one moves along an indifference curve.

Consider the points P_1, A_2, and P_2 in Figure 3-4. As the consumer moves from P_1 to A_2, he is willing to reduce his consumption of pork from 5 pounds to 4 pounds in order to increase his chicken consumption from 1.5 pounds to 2 pounds. Mathematically, we take the ratio of these changes and find that the marginal rate of substitution is $1.0/0.5 = 2$. However, in moving from A_2 to P_2, our consumer is willing to give up only 1 pound of pork in order to obtain an additional 2 pounds of chicken. The marginal rate of substitution calculated between these points has fallen to one-half.

As a general rule, the marginal rate of substitution decreases as one moves along the indifference curve from left to right. The marginal rate of substitution of pork for chicken decreases as the quantity of pork falls and the quantity of chicken increases. The more we have of a given commodity, the less of others we are willing to give up in order to get an additional unit of that commodity. This condition is reflected in the fact that typically a family consumes a substantial number of different commodities, rather than just one or two.

The marginal rate of substitution can also be defined as the derivative of the function represented by any given indifference curve. If we represent the points on the curve by an equation in A and B, it can always be solved for A in terms of B.

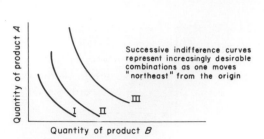

Figure 3-6 An indifference map.

From that we can take the derivative dA/dB. This gives us a marginal rate of substitution at a specific point on the indifference curve. The derivative at any point is equal to the slope of a line tangent to the indifference curve at that point.

To illustrate, suppose we have an indifference curve defined by the equation $AB = 100$. This can be solved for A to yield $A = 100/B$ $(=100B^{-1})$. Taking the derivative, we obtain $dA/dB = -100B^{-2} = -100/B^2$. We can find the value at any specific value of B by substitution. If $B = 5$, for instance, the derivative is -4. A straight line drawn tangent to the curve at the point where $B = 5$ (and $A = 20$) would have a slope of -4; that is, for every unit moved to the right, the line would descend 4 vertical units.

Geometrically, the decreasing MRS is represented by the increasing flatness of the indifference curve as one moves further to the right. Mathematically, it is represented by the fact that the absolute value of the derivative $(100/B^2)$ becomes smaller as the value of B increases. (We typically ignore the sign of the derivative and measure increases and decreases in relation to its absolute value.)

Just as we can (conceptually) create an indifference curve by utilizing an infinite number of diagonals, so we can derive a whole family of curves corresponding to the points along each diagonal. Theoretically, there is an indifference curve passing through every point in the diagram. However, we wish to show only a limited number. Figure 3-6 shows a family of indifference curves. By our assumptions, we know that any point on curve III is preferred to any point on curve II (remember the boundary characteristics).

The *indifference map* enables us to give some sort of precision to the idea that the consumer has a set of preferences. In effect, this set represents an *ordering* of all possible consumption choices, ranking each one in terms of the others as preferred, indifferent, or not preferred. Such a set of preferences may be referred to as a *preference function* (or, sometimes, as a *utility function*).

Mathematically, the preference function can be generalized to refer not merely to two commodities but to any number of commodities. One can also bring in any other uses which the consumer makes of his limited income—for instance, acquisition of cash, repayment of debts, acquisition of income-bearing assets of varying descriptions.

But surely it is not very reasonable to expect that a consumer could tell us, on casual request, how he would order all conceivable combinations of the thousands of commodities from which he can choose. However, it is not necessary that the consumer's preference function be a deliberate and conscious set of notions. All we require is that the consumer behave as if he were acting in accordance with such a preference schedule.

equilibrium of the consumer

The indifference map or preference function merely gives representation to the psychological preferences of the consumer. It does not tell us which combinations of things he will actually choose. His actual choice will depend on the amount of money he has to spend and on the prices he has to pay for the products. These represent the constraints imposed on him. If we assume that he will spend his income on two products A and B (representing a much larger actual range of choice) and that their prices are specified, the options available to the consumer are identified. They are shown in Figure 3-7. We assume that he has $100 to spend on A and B combined and that the prices of A and B are $4 and $5, respectively. From this information we can construct a line showing all the combinations of A and B he can purchase under these conditions. We might call this a *consumption-possibilities curve*, or *budget line*.

If the consumer spends his entire budget on product A, he can obtain 25 units of it and none of B. If he spends the $100 on B, he can buy 20 units of it and none of A. Each of these possibilities is identified by a point on one of the axes, and a straight line connecting them will identify all the combinations of A and B which will cost the consumer $100. For example, the line would pass through the combination representing 10 units of A (costing $40) and 12 units of B (costing $60). Algebraically, the line can be represented by the equation $4A + 5B = 100$. For any value of prices and income (Y) the budget equation takes the form $A \cdot P_A + B \cdot P_B = Y$. Since A and B have implicit exponents of unity, the budget line is a straight line. Its slope, which is the same at every point, is the ratio of vertical change to horizontal

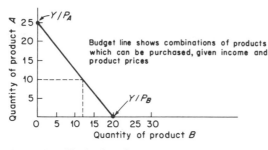

Figure 3-7 The budget line.

change moving along the line. By inspection this can be perceived to equal 25 to 20 (the ratio of the intercepts) or 5 to 4. The vertical intercept represents $Y/P_A = {}^{100}\!/_4 = 25$. The horizontal intercept represents $Y/P_B = {}^{100}\!/_5 = 20$. For any value of income and prices, therefore, the ratio of the intercepts will be $(Y/P_A)/(Y/P_B) = P_B/P_A$. The slope is equal to the inverse ratio of the prices. [1]

Here as in most such cases we will assume that the quantities of the products are fully divisible. Fractional units can be obtained, as would be the case with food items sold by weight. The slope of the budget line shows the amount of one product one has to give up in order to buy one more unit of the other while keeping the total expenditure constant. In our example, one can add 1 unit of B to his consumption by relinquishing 1.25 units of A. Note that this slope is the same at any point on the line. Furthermore, we could construct another line with the same slope for any other income which we wished to analyze. Such a family of budget lines would all be parallel for a given set of prices of A and B.

Given the range of *choice*, defined by the range of commodities and prices, and the *constraint* imposed by a limited income, what combination of products will achieve *maximization*—that is, put the consumer in the most highly preferred position? By definition, the solution is that combination of A and B which enables him to reach the highest indifference curve touched by the budget line. And the highest indifference curve will be the one to which the budget curve is *tangent*— that is, the one it barely touches, but does not cross. The solution is shown in Figure 3-8. Bear in mind that there are an infinite number of indifference curves, and that through any point in the diagram an indifference curve can be constructed.

---

[1] The slope of the budget line is also the derivative dA/dB of the implicit budget function

$$A = \frac{Y - B \cdot P_B}{P_A} = \frac{Y}{P_A} - \frac{B \cdot P_B}{P_A}$$

Since both Y and P_A are treated as constants, the term Y/P_A has a zero derivative with respect to changes in B. Therefore $dA/dB = (-)P_B/P_A$.

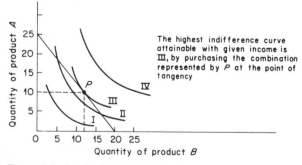

Figure 3-8 Equilibrium of the consumer.

It follows, then, that for every curve like II, which is crossed by the budget line, there exists a curve like III, which is higher, and to which the budget line is merely tangent. (This solution assumes, as we will do consistently, that the indifference curves are smooth and continuous and do not have waves and wiggles in them.) It should be apparent from Figure 3-8 that no point on the budget line lies *above* indifference curve III; thus the consumer can do no better for himself than that combination at which tangency occurs (roughly 10 units of A and 12 units of B). Given his preferences, this is the combination which the consumer would choose. We call it his *equilibrium position*.

Two curves which are tangent to each other have the same slope at the point of tangency. We have already established definitions for the slopes of the two curves. The slope of the indifference curve reflects the (subjective) marginal rate of substitution, an aspect of the consumer's preference pattern. The slope of the budget line reflects the (inverse) ratio between the prices of the two commodities. It follows, therefore, that in the equilibrium position of tangency, the subjective marginal rate of substitution must be equal to the (inverse) ratio of prices of the two commodities.

an algebraic example

For students familiar with elementary geometry and calculus, the following example may help in fixing these notions. No diagram is furnished; it would be useful for you to try to construct one.

Imagine that the consumer has a preference pattern which can be represented by a family of rectangular hyperbolas with the general formula $A \cdot B = k$, where A and B are the amounts of the two commodities and k is any constant. There exists such a hyperbola for every value of k, and consequently an infinite number can be drawn.

Let us now assume that the consumer has $50 to spend, and that A costs $1 and B $2. What is the optimum amount of each for him to buy? We can solve this by finding a point on the budget line at which the derivatives of the indifference curve and budget line are equal. The equation for the budget line may be written $A + 2B = 50$, which can be solved for A to yield $A = 50 - 2B$. The derivative of this is $dA/dB = -2$. Ignoring the minus sign, this is simply P_B/P_A.

Each indifference curve is identified by an equation $AB = k$, which can be transformed into $A = k/B$, or kB^{-1}. Taking the derivative we obtain $dA/dB = -kB^{-2}$, or $-k/B^2$. Setting the derivatives equal to each other, we obtain $-k/B^2 = -2$, or $k = 2B^2$. Now we know that $k = AB$. Thus $AB = 2B^2$, or $A = 2B$ at the equilibrium point. Substituting this into the budget line equation, we obtain $B = 12.5$. At this point $A = 25$ and $k = AB = 312.5$. The derivative of the indifference curve at this point is $-312.5/156.25 = -2$, which is also the derivative of the budget equation. Thus indifference curve and price line are tangent at the point representing 25 units of A and 12.5 units of B. This is the most strongly preferred commodity combination which can be purchased with an income of $50.

response to changes in income

The indifference-curve analysis provides a means for giving systematic description to the way in which the consumer responds to changes in the conditions which confront him. We will deal first with changes in his income, then with changes in prices.

Figure 3-9 reproduces a set of indifference curves. In addition, it contains a family of parallel budget lines. Each of these corresponds to a given amount of income. The higher the income, the further the corresponding budget line lies from the origin. We assume the prices remain constant; therefore budget lines are parallel to each other.

On each budget line, there is one point at which tangency is achieved with an indifference curve. This point represents the preferred manner of allotting that income between the two commodities. Conceptually, we can locate the tangency points for all levels of income and connect them with a continuous curve. This locus of tangency points we call an *income-consumption curve*. It reflects the way in which consumption of A and B responds to changes in the consumer's income when prices remain unchanged.

If we use simple assumptions, we can derive an algebraic expression for an income-consumption curve. Suppose a consumer's indifference map is identified by the expression

$$AB^2 = k \qquad \text{(where } k \text{ can be any constant)}$$

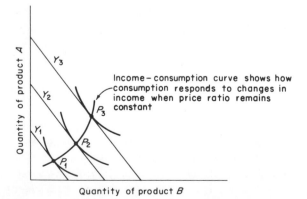

Income–consumption curve shows how consumption responds to changes in income when price ratio remains constant

Figure 3-9 The income-consumption curve.

The MRS is obtained by taking the derivative; thus

$$MRS = \frac{dA}{dB} = (-)\frac{2k}{B^3} = \frac{2A}{B}$$

The equilibrium position is identified by setting this equal to the inverse price ratio:

$$\frac{2A}{B} = \frac{P_B}{P_A}$$
$$2A \cdot P_A = B \cdot P_B$$

Solving for A in terms of B yields

$$A = B\left(\frac{P_B}{2P_A}\right)$$

For any given values of the two prices, this defines a straight line in a diagram showing combinations of products A and B. Given the condition that $Y = A \cdot P_A + B \cdot P_B$, this expression identifies consumption at each level of income. In this special case, consumption of the two products would increase by equal proportions if income increased. However, the more realistic prospect is that shown by Figure 3-9, where the proportion between the products changes as income changes. Studies of consumer spending patterns indicate that the proportion of income spent on foods typically declines, and the proportion spent on housing, recreation, and personal care increases as income goes up.

When one considers individual items of consumption, it is entirely possible that there are some for which the quantity purchased will actually go down when the consumer's income rises. Such so-called inferior goods have usually consisted of staple food items, such as rice or potatoes, which constitute the main dietary component at low incomes. When incomes rise, people prefer to buy more of higher-cost sources of calories. Similarly, a person's consumption of bus rides might decline when he achieved enough income to own an automobile.

reaction to changing prices

We can use indifference-curve analysis to describe the manner in which consumption changes in response to variations in the price of a commodity. As we shift the price of commodity B through various possible levels, we must change the slope of the budget line accordingly. The vertical intercept remains fixed (since we have not changed the price of A). But for every price of B, a different ray can be drawn. Income is assumed to remain constant. Refer to Figure 3-10.

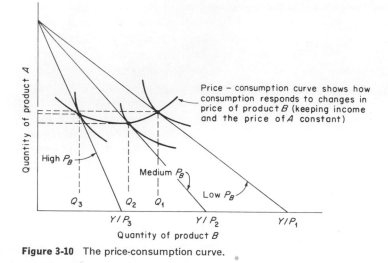

Figure 3-10 The price-consumption curve.

The higher the price of B the less of it can be purchased with a given outlay. Consequently, as the price of B increases, the budget line intersects the horizontal axis closer and closer to the origin, and its slope becomes steeper and steeper. At the low price P_1, consumption of B is large, at Q_1. An increase in price to P_2 shifts the budget line toward the origin and yields the quantity Q_2, and so on. With different plausible shapes of indifference curves, one might obtain either higher or lower sensitivity of quantity to changes in price.

Conceptually, we can locate the tangency positions corresponding to all possible prices of B. Connecting these tangency positions with a line, we obtain a *price-consumption curve*. The equilibrium commodity combination corresponding to any price of B is found where the appropriate budget line intersects the price-consumption curve.

Figure 3-10 also can be used to analyze the effect on the quantity of A which results from changes in the price of B. We note that a fall in the price of B from P_3 to P_2 produces a net reduction in purchases of A. However, a further reduction from P_2 to P_1 yields a net rise in purchases of A, which would become greater if we reduced the price of B still further, judging from the upward tilt of the price-consumption curve at the right edge.

substitution effects and income effects

The effect on consumption of a change in one price can usefully be divided into two components. The first is the *substitution* effect. An increase in the relative price of any commodity tends to cause consumers to reduce the quantity of it which they purchase, and to shift to substitutes. The other component is the *income* effect of the price change. An increase in the price of a commodity reduces the consumer's purchasing power; thus his real income is reduced, and probably his consumption also.

In Figure 3-11 we show the effects of an increase in the price of B from P_1 to P_2. The total effect of the price change is to move the consumer's equilibrium position from x to z, reducing his purchases of B and increasing those of A.

The substitution effect of such a price increase is measured along a given indifference curve. It measures the consumption change which is attributable to a change in relative prices. We can identify the substitution effect along the original indifference curve by finding on it a point y at which the slope is equal to that of the new budget line. The point y can be identified by drawing an imaginary budget line parallel to the new budget line but tangent to the original indifference curve. This budget line, drawn as a broken line, would result if the consumer were compensated for the rise in the price of B by being given just enough income to keep him on the original indifference curve.

In Figure 3-11, the movement from x to y provides a measure of the substitution effect. Because of the shape of indifference curves, substitution effects always work in the direction of reducing the consumption of the item which has risen in price.

The income effect of a price change results from a movement from one indifference curve to another. The higher price of B has reduced the real income of the consumer by an amount which can be measured by the distance between the broken budget line and the new actual budget line based on P_2. His shift from y to z is in response to the income effect, and it causes him to reduce his consumption of both commodities. However, income effects might operate to increase purchases of one commodity at the expense of another.

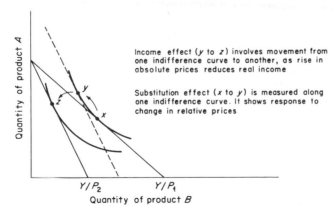

Income effect (y to z) involves movement from one indifference curve to another, as rise in absolute prices reduces real income

Substitution effect (x to y) is measured along one indifference curve. It shows response to change in relative prices

Figure 3-11 Income effect and substitution effect of a price change.

There is an essential ambiguity in separating the income and substitution effects, since we have a choice which of the two to calculate first. If we took the income effect first, then the substitution effect would be measured along the lower indifference curve. Ordinarily the two will not yield identical results. For the uses to which we will put the analysis, however, it will not matter.

The relative size of the substitution effect can be expressed in terms of the *elasticity of substitution*. This is defined as the proportional change in the ratio of the quantities of two products, divided by the proportional change in the marginal rate of substitution between them (or, assuming equilibrium conditions, divided by the proportional change in the ratio of their prices). The concept is an awkward one to use, and we will not use it at this point; therefore details of calculation will be postponed. However, if two products are close substitutes, the elasticity of substitution between them will be high, and a given proportional change in the ratio of their prices will lead to a large proportional change in the ratio of their respective quantities. It is necessary to move a long distance along a (relatively flat) indifference curve to reach a point where the marginal rate of substitution equals the new price ratio. On the other hand, low elasticity of substitution means that the products are not close substitutes. The relative consumption of the two does not change much when the ratio of their prices alters. The indifference curve bends sharply; thus its slope changes rapidly and it is not necessary to move very far along the curve to reach a point where the marginal rate of substitution equals the new price ratio.

Both the income and substitution effects tend to reduce the consumption of product B as its price rises. Under what circumstances will this decrease in quantity be large, relative to the price increase? Consumption of B will decline more, for a given price increase, the closer the substitution between A and B. The higher the elasticity of substitution (and the flatter the indifference curves), the larger will be the substitution effect of an increase in P_B. The income effect will depend on two matters. If the consumer is spending a large proportion of his income on B, a rise in its price will tend to have a large effect on his real income. Thus consumption of B will tend to fall more, for a given increase in P_B, the larger the proportion of his budget devoted to B. Second, the income effect depends on the extent to which the indifference curves change shape as one moves from higher to lower. The proportional division of a high income among individual products is not usually the same as the proportional division of a lower income.

from indifference curves to demand curves

The indifference-curve analysis has the advantage of dealing explicitly with the interdependence between the consumption of one commodity and another. The prices of individual commodities appear implicitly, through the construction of the budget lines. For the analysis of price and output determination, however, we want to make use of a demand schedule, in which the consumption of one commodity is treated explicitly as a function of its price. Geometrically this is represented by a demand curve in a diagram which shows price on the vertical axis and quantity horizontally.

An individual's demand curve for any given commodity A can be derived from his indifference map, given his income, tastes, and the prices of other commodities. In Figure 3-12, we have drawn an indifference-curve diagram, showing the response to price change of the quantity of commodity A purchased. However, the diagram embodies one minor change. Instead of letting the vertical axis measure one specific commodity, we can let it represent all other commodities (and other dispositions of money as well, if we wish). As a shortcut we can simply treat the vertical axis as representing a certain sum of money, provided the prices of all other commodities are given. We can let the price of "everything else" be represented by an index of the "price level."

The upper part of the diagram shows what happens to consumption as we lower

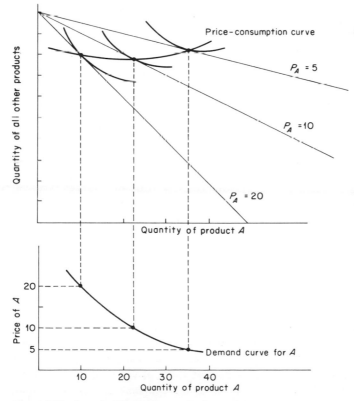

Figure 3-12 From indifference map to demand curve.

the price of A. The tangency points move further to the right. Each of these tangency points provides us with information to locate a point on the demand curve, shown below. The upper diagram shows that at a price of 20, the consumer buys 10 units of A. This enables us to locate the first point in the lower diagram, using the same horizontal distance (both diagrams measure units of A horizontally) and setting the vertical distance equal to the price of 20. Similarly, we find that at a price of 10, the consumer will buy 22 units of A. And so on. Conceptually, we can do this for every possible price, and in that manner fill in all the points along the demand curve.

We can also derive a demand schedule algebraically. Assume the consumer's indifference map follows the formula $A \cdot B = k$, where k represents any constant. For any income Y and prices P_A and P_B, we have the following:

1. Budget equation: $A \cdot P_A + B \cdot P_B = Y$; therefore $A = (Y - B \cdot P_B)/P_A$.
2. Indifference map: $A \cdot B = k$; therefore $dA/dB = -k/B^2 = -A/B$.
3. Equilibrium condition: $dA/dB = P_B/P_A$.

Substituting condition 2 (and dropping the minus sign) we obtain $A/B = P_B/P_A$; therefore $A = B \cdot P_B/P_A$.

We now have two equations expressing A and can set them equal, obtaining

$$\frac{B \cdot P_B}{P_A} = \frac{Y - B \cdot P_B}{P_A}$$

Eliminating the redundant P_A term and solving yields $B = Y/2P_B$. A similar solution method will yield $A = Y/2P_A$. Each expression is a demand schedule expressing quantity purchased as a function of income and price of product. The quantity of A demanded varies directly with income and inversely with its price. Our special assumptions produce hyperbolic demand functions which are independent of each other; that is, quantity of A demanded is not affected by P_B. Such independence would not normally happen.

other dimensions of household behavior

Indifference-curve analysis can also be applied to household behavior in the sale of productive services. Each household has some choice about the amount of labor services it chooses to sell, and this amount depends partly on the expected pay. Leisure time can be treated as a commodity. Decisions about labor can be regarded as a choice between leisure and other commodities. Devoting more time to work sacrifices leisure in favor of more income and more of the other commodities. Reducing labor time provides increased leisure but decreases ability to consume other commodities.

Because many of us think of the 5-day, 40-hour work week as standard for wage earners, we may overlook the wide opportunities available for changing the number of hours worked, particularly over a longer period such as a year. By self-employment, by "moonlighting" (taking a second, perhaps part-time job), by taking opportunities to work overtime, and by varying the number of work days through vacation or absenteeism, most people have quite a wide range of options toward annual work hours. The options are even broader for a family group containing several persons.

The indifference curves relating leisure and goods would have a relatively normal shape, as Figure 3-13 indicates. We assume the physical maximum of annual working hours for one person is 5,000 (remember that $16 \times 365 = 5,840$) and define leisure time as 5,000 minus work time. Assume the wage rate is initially $3 an hour.

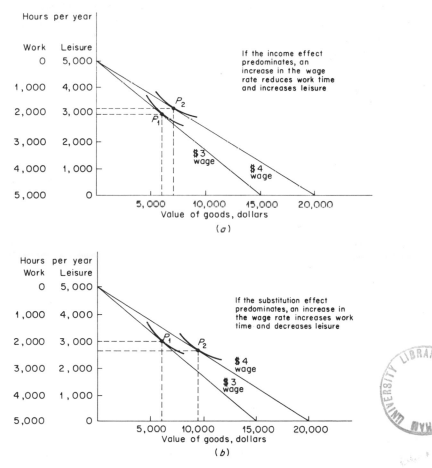

Figure 3-13 Wage level and supply of labor.

By working all the time, our consumer could earn $15,000 worth of goods; his budget line connects that point on the horizontal axis with the vertical point representing 5,000 hours of leisure and no goods at all. His chosen position, however, is to con-sume $6,000 of goods and 3,000 hours of leisure, working 2,000 hours.

Suppose the wage rate were to rise to $4. His maximum consumption of goods is now increased to $20,000; the new, flatter budget line links that horizontal point with the maximum leisure point of 5,000. The increase in the wage rate now makes leisure more expensive; the substitution effect would tend to make people consume more goods and less leisure, working longer hours. But the higher wage raises income and moves the consumer to a higher indifference curve. The income effect would tend to increase his consumption of leisure and thus decrease the amount of labor time offered. In Figure 3-13a, the income effect predominates, and he works less at the higher wage. If the substitution effect predominated (Figure 3-13b), the higher wage would draw forth increased labor (and decreased leisure).

One implication of the foregoing is that income is itself the outcome of deliberate choices by each household concerning work versus leisure. Earlier we treated income as the constraint on purchases of goods. Figure 13-3, however, suggests that the real constraint is some measure of income-earning potential, such as maximum potential working hours. Ownership of property needs to be considered also. In recent years, economists have become accustomed to thinking of all potential sources of income as varieties of wealth. Capacity to supply labor services can be expressed in terms of human wealth, and capacity to supply property services represents nonhuman wealth. Viewed in these terms, the constraint on both income and consumption is the household's wealth. Specific values for both income and consumption result from the confrontation among prices, wealth, and preferences.

utility and all that

For many years economists presented the theory of household behavior as a process of maximizing "utility." Utility was variously defined to mean pleasure, satisfaction, or some related psychological quality. It was treated both as a motive behind consumption decisions and also as the psychological sensation resulting from consumption. Individual commodities were said to be subject to diminishing marginal utility, so that the more one already had of a commodity, the less utility he would derive from an additional unit.

The utility concept had many defects. If economists attempted to identify it precisely, they could find no counterpart consistent with respectable psychological evidence or analysis. If they left it vague, utility analysis became mere tautology, saying in effect that "people do what they do." The "law" of diminishing marginal utility, usually illustrated by examples involving short-run physical satiation of biological needs (the twentieth ice cream cone is less enjoyable than the nineteenth, even on a hot day), cannot be generalized to all commodities, if treated purely as a relationship between consumption and psychological enjoyment.

In truth, the valid elements of marginal utility analysis have largely been absorbed, and greatly clarified, by the indifference-curve approach. Instead of the one-at-a-time implication of marginal-utility analysis, indifference-curve analysis keeps before us the idea of substitution among many commodities. Instead of a dubious law of diminishing marginal utility, we have a much more defensible principle of diminishing marginal rate of substitution. We do not know nor greatly care whether the marginal enjoyment from a commodity decreases as we consume more of it; we are fairly certain that the consumer will be the less willing to give up other things for an additional unit of that commodity, the more of it he is already consuming.

The law of diminishing marginal utility was used to "explain" the principle that demand curves slope down. A better explanation utilizes the income and substitution effects explicitly. Even so, one may wish at times to revert to the idea of diminishing marginal utility as a kind of shorthand way of referring to the conditions which make demand curves slope down.

Viewed as a measure of psychological sensation, utility became a foundation for early welfare economics. A socially optimum situation could be achieved, the argument went, if the total utility of the population were maximized. In its extreme form, the view never got very far, since utility proved not amenable to measurement (even if the aggregation had been meaningful). In more moderate form, however, a concern for utility still underlies modern welfare economics.

The simple premise of welfare economics is that each individual has some sort of utility function or preference function, of the sort depicted by an indifference map (but extended to all relevant commodities, not just two). The higher the indifference curve he achieves, the better off he is. Since the indifference curves are merely indications of his preference, this notion of "better off" simply says that "people ought to get what they want." This is not a very profound basis for social philosophy, but it has a lot to recommend it, and is certainly the attitude of most economists toward people other than their own students and children.

Modern welfare economics does not involve the sort of aggregation required to deal with the "total utility" of the society. It does not evaluate different distributions of income, since it argues that there is no valid basis for comparing the enjoyments received by one person with those of another. It does follow a suggestion advanced by the Italian economist Vilfredo Pareto, who pointed out that it is sometimes possible to move one person to a higher indifference curve without moving anyone else to a lower one and that this should always be done when possible. From these suggestions, economists have given the term *Pareto optimum* to a situation in which it is *not* possible to move any person to a higher indifference curve without moving someone else to a lower one.

equalizing marginal rates of substitution

One application of Pareto optimality can be illustrated in terms of the indifference-curve analysis as we have explained it. The underlying idea can be stated in this way: Pareto optimality requires that the marginal rate of substitution between any pair of commodities be the same for all consumers. If some people are consuming combinations of goods such that the MRS is not uniform for all, it will be possible by rearranging consumption patterns to move some people to higher indifference curves without moving anyone to a lower curve and without changing the quantity and composition of output.

To prove one situation is optimal, we usually show that deviations from it are less than optimal. In Figure 3-14 we illustrate indifference maps for two consumers, Joe and Sam. They are the only survivors of a shipwreck and have just swum ashore. Joe has managed to salvage eight cans of applesauce and four cans of beans; Sam has two cans of applesauce and twelve cans of beans. We assume that with this initial distribution of stocks of goods, Joe's MRS (dA/dB) is $\frac{1}{4}$ and Sam's MRS is 4.

Indifference maps involving two separate transactors can often be analyzed by a *box diagram,* of which Figure 3-14 is an example. Joe's situation is shown in the orthodox position, with zero at the lower left and quantities of goods measured from bottom up (applesauce) or from left to right (beans). Sam's situation, however, is shown by reversing the arrangement so that his zero point is the upper right-hand corner, and his holdings are measured from top down (applesauce) or

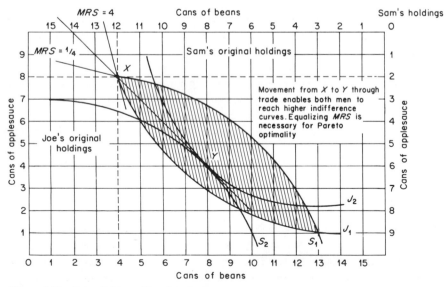

Figure 3-14 Potential benefits of exchange.

from right to left (beans). The size of the box is determined by the total stocks on hand; thus it is 16 units wide and 10 units high. The point X identifies their initial stocks, which put them on the indifference curves J_1 and S_1. Following these two indifference curves down and to the right, we find they bound a football-shaped area (shaded). Each point in this area represents a distribution of the existing stocks of commodities which would put each of our heroes on a higher indifference curve. To exploit this possibility, they can agree to swap at some mutually accept-able ratio of exchange. Suppose they agree to trade one for one. We can show this by a straight line with a slope of -1 drawn through point X; this line is equivalent to a budget line. Trading moves both of them downward to the right; both reach higher indifference curves until they come to point Y. Here tangency exists between the price line and each man's indifference curve; thus the indifference curves are tangent to each other. Given the ratio of exchange, the combination represented by Y is the best they can agree on; it is a point of Pareto optimality. The movement from X to Y was a process of equalizing the marginal rates of substitution between the two men. Originally they were $\frac{1}{4}$ and 4; at Y both are equal to unity. Joe now has four cans of applesauce and eight of beans, a combination he prefers to the original one. Sam's situation has also improved.

Our analysis does not identify the equilibrium trading ratio itself; mutually advantageous trade could occur at any ratio between the original MRS values of $\frac{1}{4}$ and 4. However, only the points where the indifference curves are tangent to each other represent positions of Pareto optimality. Of course, our analysis does not rule out the possibility that one of our heroes will overpower the other and take the entire supply—but that is precisely the kind of "transaction" which contradicts the Pareto condition.

In a market economy, where there is one ruling market price for each commod-ity, equalization of MRS comes about automatically, as each consumer individually adjusts his consumption pattern to the same price ratio. Under such conditions, there is no possibility for swapping existing commodities in a manner which could move some people to a higher indifference curve without moving others to a lower one.

The same opportunity for two parties to gain from trade when their marginal rates of substitution are initially unequal is an important element in the theory of international trade. We will explore it further in Chapter 18.

summary

This chapter presents the technical details involved in describing the behavior of the individual consumer. We can represent the state of his tastes and preferences by an indifference map, in which each indifference curve connects various com-modity combinations which are equally preferable. The constraints imposed by income and prices are represented by a budget line, showing the different combinations of the commodities which can be purchased with a given amount of money at a given set of prices. The best combination which a consumer can buy with any given income is found at the point of tangency between the appropriate budget line and an indifference curve. At this point, the (subjective) marginal rate of substitution between commodities is equal to the (inverse) ratio of their prices. By imposing different parallel budget lines on the consumer's indifference map, we can trace his response to changing incomes, with prices unchanged. By changing the slope of the budget line but keeping one intercept fixed, we can trace his reaction to a change in the price of one product, while income and other prices remain unchanged. The latter reaction can be expressed as a combination of substitution effect and income effect. From the points traced out when one price is changed we can derive the points on a conventional demand curve, expressing the quantity purchased of one commodity as a function of its price, with a given income and set of other prices.

Modern welfare economics assumes that a person is better off to the extent that he achieves a higher indifference curve. If people's existing consumption patterns do not represent identical marginal rates of substitution, it is possible to move some people to higher indifference curves through readjusting consumption patterns without moving anyone else to a lower curve.

TERMS AND CONCEPTS

1. Indifference curve, indifference map
2. Marginal rate of substitution (along a consumer indifference curve)
3. Budget equation
4. Income effects, substitution effects of price change
5. Pareto optimum
6. Box diagram

QUESTIONS AND PROBLEMS

1. In Chapter 1 we drew a production-possibilities curve which bulged outward from the origin. In this chapter, our consumer indifference curves are drawn with their bulge going *toward* the origin. Explain the difference. Suppose a set of consumer indifference curves bulged outward from the origin. What sort of behavior and feelings would this imply?

2. Assume a consumer's indifference map is identified by the general equation $2A + AB = k$, where k may be any constant. Find a general expression for the marginal rate of substitution dB/dA on such an indifference curve. Use it to derive an expression for the demand function for B in terms of

income (Y) and the price of B. If income is $1,000, what is the demand schedule for B?

3. Draw a set of indifference curves relating leisure and goods, similar to Figure 3-13, and show how to derive from it a supply schedule of labor hours worked as a function of the wage rate (assuming prices of goods remain unchanged).

4. It is a logical impossibility for one indifference curve to cross another in the indifference map of an individual consumer. Explain why.

5. Our indifference curves are drawn on the assumption that the consumer prefers more of any product to less of that product. Suppose, however, that the consumer reaches a point where additional units of one commodity yield him no additional pleasure or satisfaction. What would happen to indifference curves in such an area on his indifference map? Illustrate graphically.

6. It is logically possible that a consumer may increase his consumption of a commodity in response to an increase in its price, without any change in other prices, his tastes, or his income. Explain what such behavior must imply in respect to income and substitution effects. Draw an illustration.

7. "Increasing the price of things he has to buy is equivalent to reducing the consumer's income." Discuss and illustrate geometrically.

the theory of demand: market demand

the market demand function

In Chapter 3 our analysis of consumer behavior identified a number of influences upon the quantity of some product A which a consumer would purchase. These same considerations will be relevant in determining quantity purchased by all consumers considered in the aggregate. We consider in turn psychological tastes and preferences, incomes, the price of the product, and the prices of other products.

1. Tastes and preferences. Ultimately consumers buy things because they want them. We do not investigate *why* they want them. Welfare economics assumes that consumer preferences are important, and that economic welfare is enhanced to the extent that people get more of what they want.

2. Income. The individual consumer tends to consume a larger amount of goods and services the higher his income is. However, he does not always consume the same things at a higher income. Some "inferior" goods may be consumed less as income rises.

When we investigate a market demand function to include income, we must take into account the distribution of income as well as its aggregate amount. People's tastes differ, and a change in the distribution of a given aggregate income might change purchases of individual items. Mostly we will assume that the proportional distribution of income does not change much, and consider increases and decreases in total income as involving most people in a similar manner.

3. The price of the product. A strong conclusion from indifference-curve analysis is that the quantity of a product demanded varies inversely with its price, other things being equal. Much of the impact comes through the substitution effect, but this is usually reinforced by an income effect operating in the same direction.

4. Prices of other products. Here again income and substitution effects are relevant. An increase in the price of B tends to reduce the consumer's real income and in that manner may depress his purchases of A. However, if A and B are substitutes, he may consume more of A to take the place of B. Note that income and substitution effects tend to work in opposite directions in the relation between price of B and consumption of A.

Some products are complementary—that is, they tend to be consumed together. Some examples are tires and gasoline, cigarettes and matches, bread and butter, corned beef and cabbage. A change in price of one complementary product may affect the consumption of the combination. If product C is complementary with A, a rise in the price of C may decrease consumption of both A and C. Such a decrease would reflect lack of substitution between A and C, a normal income effect, and perhaps substitution of another combination for that of $A + C$.

5. Other determinants. In addition to income, demand may depend on the existing wealth and assets of consumers. Assets can be a source of purchasing power, and thus might stimulate higher demand. On the other hand, purchases of durable items may be depressed to the extent that consumers are well supplied with them already (houses, autos, furniture, appliances, etc.).

Credit may be a source of purchasing power, and demand for goods may be affected by changes in interest rates and credit conditions. On the other side, changes in interest rates and other specifications of savings assets may affect the proportion of total income used for consumption as compared with saving.

Expectations of future prices and incomes can influence current consumption. People who expect their income to rise rapidly and soon may decide to consume now, even if they must borrow to do so, rather than postpone enjoyments. Expected price increases can spur more rapid purchases, particularly of durable items which can be bought now and used later.

Most of the considerations under heading 5 will not be discussed in detail.

Rather, we concentrate on the demand functions expressing quantity demanded of A as a function of income, the price of A, and prices of other products, the shape of the entire function being dependent on a particular condition of psychological tastes and preferences.

As an oversimplified representation, the demand function for product A might be represented by a form such as the following:

$$Q_{D_A} = \frac{Y}{P_A} + P_S - \frac{P_C}{5}$$

where Y = income

P_A = price of product A

P_S = price of substitute product

P_C = price of complementary product

If we specify a value for each of the independent variables, we identify one particular quantity of A demanded. The entire equation represents one particular configuration of tastes and preferences. A change in tastes could shift the entire function.

the demand schedule

If we specify values for income and for other prices, we can transform the demand function into a demand schedule, expressing the quantity of A demanded as a function of the price of A. Suppose income were \$500, P_S were \$25, and P_C \$10. Our demand schedule would then be $Q_{DA} = 500/P_A + 23$. Geometrically, this would produce a curve of hyperbolic shape. Along a given demand schedule, quantity demanded varies inversely with price.

A change in any of the other elements of the demand function would tend to shift the entire demand schedule. The entire schedule would increase if there were

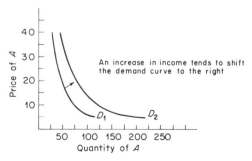

Figure 4-1 A shift in demand.

an increase in income, or an increase in the price of the substitute product, or a decrease in the price of the complementary product. Figure 4-1 compares the original demand schedule with its new value if income were to increase from $500 to $1,000. A change in tastes could shift the demand schedule even if income and prices remained the same.

The phrase "change in demand" should be used only to refer to shifts in the entire demand curve. When considering the effect of a change in the price, with a given demand curve, one can only speak of changes in the quantity demanded.

elasticity of demand

It is often useful to have some measure of the sensitivity of the dependent variable in a function to changes in an independent variable. In economics, such sensitivity is often measured as elasticity, a relation between the *proportional* change in one variable and the corresponding *proportional* change in another.

In analyzing the demand function, we can calculate an elasticity measure to correspond to each of the possible independent variables. We consider first the price elasticity of demand, which measures the sensitivity of quantity demanded to changes in the price of the product, taking as given income, tastes, and prices of other products.

Price elasticity of demand is defined as the ratio between the proportional change in quantity and the proportional change in price. It can be measured between two points on a demand schedule (*arc* elasticity), in which case it involves finite differences in price and quantity, or it can be measured at a given point on a demand schedule (*point* elasticity), using the derivative to measure the rate of change. We will discuss these two approaches in succession.

Elasticity calculated between two points on a demand schedule can be represented by this formula:

$$\frac{\Delta Q/Q}{\Delta P/P}$$

Since quantity moves in the direction opposite to price along a demand schedule, the price-elasticity coefficient commonly has a minus sign. This is sometimes omitted, and the price-elasticity coefficient treated as an absolute number. If the quantity demanded is highly sensitive to changes in price, the elasticity coefficient will be large, and we say that the demand schedule is highly elastic. If quantity purchased is relatively insensitive to changes in price, the elasticity coefficient will be small. If it is less than unity, we say that the demand schedule is inelastic.

By using a simple numerical demand schedule, we can illustrate the calculation of price elasticity.

Price	Quantity Purchased
$10	1
9	2
8	3
7	4
6	5
5	6
4	7
3	8
2	9
1	10

We can calculate an elasticity coefficient between any two points on the schedule. Take the first two points, corresponding to prices of $10 and $9. We need to determine the percentage change in price involved in a reduction from $10 to $9, and the percentage increase in quantity involved in going from 1 to 2. Intuitively, one tends to identify the first as a 10 percent decrease and the second as an increase of 100 percent. However, it is preferable to have a measure of elasticity which is reversible—that is, which will give the same result going from 9 to 10 or from 10 to 9. Such a measure can be obtained if we calculate percentage changes from the average of the initial and terminal values.

In our example, we are better advised to calculate the percentage change in price on the *average* of $10 and $9, and the percentage change in quantity on the average of 1 and 2. Our calculations then come to this:

$$\Delta Q = 1$$
$$Q = 1.5$$
$$\Delta P = 1$$
$$P = 9.5$$

The percentage change in quantity then becomes 1/1.5, and the percentage change in prices is 1/9.5. Dividing the latter into the former yields a coefficient of elasticity of 6.33.

Now consider the elasticity between the prices of 6 and 5. The average price here is 5.5. The quantities purchased are 5 and 6; these also average 5.5. As a consequence, we will find that the percentage change in price, 1/(5.5), is the same as the percentage change in quantity. Thus our elasticity coefficient equals 1 between these two points.

Price-elasticity of demand can be measured at a point on the demand curve. The derivative dQ/dP measures the change in quantity associated with a small change in price; all that is necessary is to introduce a factor which will adjust to proportional changes. We want to obtain the equivalent of $(dQ/Q)/(dP/P)$, which can most conveniently be expressed as $dQ/dP \cdot P/Q$.

Consider the demand schedule represented by the equation $Q = 11 - P$ (the same schedule we used numerically above). Suppose we want to determine the elasticity at the point where $P = \$5$, and $Q = 6$. The derivative $dQ/dP = -1$, and $P/Q = \frac{5}{6}$. Thus the elasticity coefficient at that point is $(-)\frac{5}{6}$.

graphic representation

Elasticity of demand at a point can easily be illustrated graphically. In Figure 4-2 a demand curve is shown. We wish to find a geometric expression for the elasticity at point E, where price is measured by OP and quantity by OQ. The derivative dQ/dP is measured by the *inverse* of the slope of a tangent to the demand curve at point E. (It is inverse because the slope measures dP/dQ, the price being the vertical variable.) We draw the tangent to intersect the price axis at A and the quantity axis at B. The slope of the tangent is measured by OA/OB, and its inverse is therefore OB/OA. Because triangle AEP is similar to ABO, $OB/OA = PE/PA$. We want to multiply this by the ratio of price to quantity, which is given by OP/OQ. By construction, $PE = OQ$, so we can write OP/PE as a measure of the price-quantity ratio.

To determine elasticity, we want to multiply the measure of the derivative dQ/dP by the price-quantity ratio.

$$\frac{PE}{PA} \cdot \frac{OP}{PE} = \frac{OP}{PA} = e$$

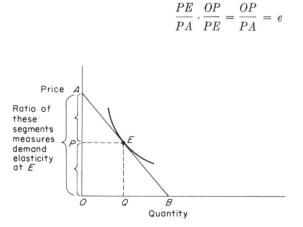

Figure 4-2 Geometry of demand elasticity.

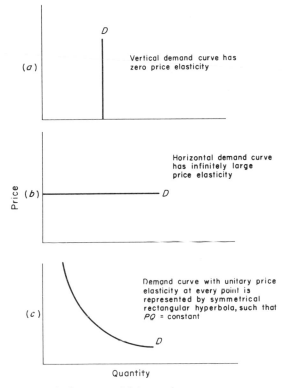

Figure 4-3   Some special demand curves.

The ratio so derived is a convenient measure of elasticity, since it is the ratio of the two segments into which price divides the vertical line OA.

It is also useful to know the geometric representations of certain specific elasticity conditions. Figure 4-3 illustrates the following cases:

1.   A demand curve of zero price elasticity is represented by a vertical line. Quantity purchased is constant regardless of price (as illustrated by Figure 4-3*a*).

2.   A demand curve of infinite elasticity is represented by a horizontal line. Buyers will take any quantity offered at the specified price, but nothing at any higher price. We will find this demand curve useful in analyzing the position of an individual seller in a purely competitive market (Figure 4-3*b*).

3.   A demand curve of unitary elasticity throughout is represented by a rectangular hyperbola which is asymptotic to the axes (Figure 4-3*c*).

an elasticity function

It is sometimes useful to derive a function expressing the price elasticity of an entire demand schedule. Since straight-line demand schedules are often useful and manageable illustrations, we examine some of their elasticity properties. The general expression for a straight-line demand curve is $Q = a - bP$, where a and b are positive constants and $a > bP$. In terms of P, $P = (a - Q)/b$.

The general expression for price-elasticity of demand is $(dQ/dP) \cdot (P/Q)$. The derivative dQ/dP of a straight-line demand curve is always $-b$, but we will ignore the minus sign to concentrate on the absolute value of the elasticity coefficient. Demand elasticity is thus $b(P/Q)$; and since P varies inversely with Q, this expression tells us that elasticity will vary directly with P and inversely with Q. The demand schedule will have unitary elasticity at the point where $Q = bP$.

The straight-line demand schedule has a different elasticity at every point, even though its slope (derivative) is constant. The variation appears in the ratio P/Q.

By substitution in the expression P/Q we can express demand elasticity as a function of P or of Q:

$$\frac{P}{Q} = \frac{P}{a - bP} = \frac{a - Q}{bQ}$$

$$e = b \cdot \frac{P}{Q} = \frac{bP}{a - bP} = \frac{a - Q}{Q} = \frac{a}{Q} - 1$$

revenue of sellers

Some of these propositions are illustrated in Table 4-1, which reproduces the arc-elasticity values for whole-number price and quantity entries of a particular straight-line demand schedule. The price elasticity is different at each point and declines steadily as price falls and quantity rises.

In Table 4-1 we also show the total expenditure of buyers at each price-quantity combination. Total expenditure is simply price multiplied by quantity; further, it is identically equal to the total revenue which sellers would receive at such a price-quantity combination.

The movement of total revenue in response to changes in price and quantity is closely related to the price elasticity of demand. In the upper section of the table, reduction in price leads to such a large increase in quantity demanded that total expenditure increases. However, at the range where unitary elasticity prevails, the changes in price and quantity are exactly offsetting, and total expenditure remains constant at $30. Below that point, the proportional increases in quantity are smaller than the price reductions; therefore, the total expenditure decreases

TABLE 4-1

Price	Quantity Demanded	Price Elasticity of Demand (Arc Elasticity)	Total Expenditure (Total Revenue of Sellers)
$10	1		$10
		6.33	
9	2		18
		3.40	
8	3		24
		2.14	
7	4		28
		1.44	
6	5		30
		1.00	
5	6		30
		0.69	
4	7		28
		0.47	
3	8		24
		0.29	
2	9		18
		0.16	
1	10		10

as price is reduced. The relationships may be summarized as follows:

1. When price elasticity of demand is higher than unity, total expenditure (total revenue) varies *inversely* with price. A seller confronted with a demand curve of high elasticity would be able to increase his total revenue by reducing his price.

2. When price elasticity of demand is unity, the total expenditure on the product is constant when price changes.

3. When price elasticity of demand is less than unity, total expenditure (total revenue) varies *directly* with price. A seller confronted with an inelastic demand curve can increase his total revenue by raising his price.

determinants of price elasticity

Whether a commodity has a high price elasticity of demand depends chiefly on whether there are close substitutes for it. If consumers regard chicken and pork as close substitutes, an increase in the price of chicken (pork price unchanged) will cause a substantial reduction in purchases of chicken. Any commodity which has close substitutes will have a high price elasticity of demand.

Income effects will also affect price elasticity of demand. This is particularly true for a commodity on which people spend a relatively large proportion of their incomes. A change in the price of such a commodity would produce a relatively large change in the real income of consumers, which could in turn substantially affect the quantity they purchased of the commodity in question.

If a commodity has no close substitutes and has a low price in relation to average consumer income, then it is likely to have a low price elasticity of demand.

other types of demand elasticity

In addition to price elasticity of demand, it is useful to make use of the concepts of *income* elasticity and *cross* elasticity. Income elasticity of demand measures the sensitivity of the quantity of some product demanded to changes in consumer incomes. The numerical coefficient of income elasticity is the percentage change in quantity demanded divided by the percentage change in income. It is typically positive. High income elasticity of demand means that the *proportion* of income spent on the given commodity increases as income goes up. Luxury items are typically in this category. Income elasticity of demand can be negative; there are always some specific commodities of which people consume smaller absolute amounts as their incomes rise. Such situations typically reflect the availability of somewhat more costly but more desirable substitutes.

Cross elasticity of demand refers to the influence which changes in the price of one product A have on the amount demanded of some other product B. The numerical coefficient of cross elasticity is the ratio between the proportional change in the quantity demanded of B and the proportional change in the price of A. Where the two products are substitutes, the cross-elasticity coefficient will tend to be positive and large. That is, an increase in the price of pork will lead to a substantial increase in the quantity of chicken consumed. If complementarity is strong between commodities, then the cross-elasticity coefficient may be negative. An increase in the price of one may lead to a decrease in the consumption of the other.

indifference-curve analysis of elasticities

It is relatively easy to infer from a consumer's indifference map whether his price elasticity and income elasticity of demand for a product are greater than, equal to, or less than unity. Consider first price elasticity of demand. We have seen that if his price elasticity of demand for a product A is high, he will spend more money on it at a lower price. This means he will spend *less* money on other commodities, and since their prices are unchanged, he will purchase a smaller *quantity* of other commodities as the price of A declines. This situation is shown in Figure 4-4. If we

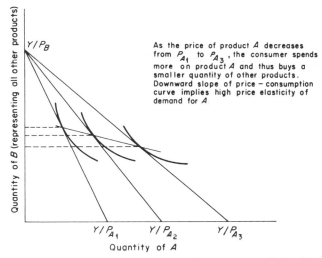

As the price of product A decreases from P_{A_1} to P_{A_3}, the consumer spends more on product A and thus buys a smaller quantity of other products. Downward slope of price – consumption curve implies high price elasticity of demand for A

Figure 4-4 Indifference-curve analysis of price elasticity of demand.

measure the quantity of product A horizontally and the quantity of all other prod-ucts (composite) vertically, a high price elasticity of demand for A is associated with a downward-sloping price-consumption line. By similar reasoning we can infer that if a consumer's price elasticity of demand for A is less than unity, he will spend less money on A as its price declines and thus purchase a larger quantity of other products. Thus the price-consumption line would be upward sloping. Now determine for yourself how to illustrate the case where the price elasticity of demand for A has a coefficient of unity.

Figure 4-5 illustrates income elasticity of demand.

This time we measure the quantity of product A vertically and the quantity of B (representing a composite of all other products) horizontally. At an income of $500 a month, the consumer buys a combination represented by point x. A straight line drawn from the origin to x has a slope equal to the ratio between the quantities of A and B. If income were to rise to $1,000, consumption would shift to point z. A straight line from the origin to z is flatter than the original line to x; the ratio of quantities A/B is thus shown to be smaller at z than at x. Since prices of A and B are unchanged, a decrease in the quantity ratio A/B means that the consumer is spending a smaller proportion of his income on A and a larger proportion on B. Thus the income elasticity of demand for A is below unity. Another identification of this condition would be to extend a straight line through points z and x; it would intersect the vertical axis before the horizontal. Test your understanding by con-structing an indifference map to illustrate unitary income elasticity of demand for A.

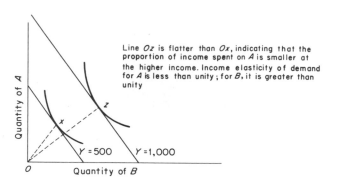

Figure 4-5 Indifference-curve analysis of income elasticity of demand.

The indifference-curve analysis of elasticities helps to show that the three types of elasticity are interrelated. A product which has close substitutes will tend to have a high price elasticity of demand; in addition, cross elasticities between it and its substitutes will tend to be high. Both will reflect high elasticity of substitution, reflecting in turn the relatively flat slope of individual indifference curves. Income elasticities, however, reflect the differing slopes and relative locations of successively higher indifference curves. These same considerations will be relevant to the income effects of a price change.

applications of the elasticity concepts

Demand elasticities have a number of important applications in economic analysis which deserve mention here; some will be developed more fully later. Business managers need to concern themselves with demand elasticities. The price policy of the firm can be guided toward greater profits if the price elasticity of demand for the product can be identified. Sales forecasting can be improved if the firm can anticipate changes in prices of substitute products and the relevant cross elasticities. Similarly, analysis of income elasticity of demand can help in forecasting the response of sales to expected increases in consumer incomes.

Demand elasticities are important to many questions of social and political importance. One of the central problems puzzling observers of industrial countries for the past two centuries has been the impact of technical change and capital formation on employment opportunities. Ever since the time of the Industrial Revolution, some people have expressed alarm that a nation's ability to produce might tend to outrun its ability to consume. However, so long as the principle of scarcity continues to hold good and people's desires remain infinitely expansible, there should be no problem of general overproduction. But such reassurance cannot be offered for each specific industry.

And when the problem is posed for a specific industry, the impact of technical change and capital formation depends on the price and income elasticities of demand for the product, particularly the former. Technical progress enables an industry to produce more cheaply and thus to sell at a lower price. If demand has a high price elasticity, a small price reduction may lead to a sufficiently large increase in quantity purchased so that employment opportunities are increased, rather than decreased. This was the case in the American automobile industry in the first two decades of the twentieth century. A high income elasticity will help matters along, since it is likely that a society in which technical progress is occurring will have rising income levels.

If price and income elasticities of demand are low, however, technical progress may cause unemployment or depress producer incomes. This has been the case in agriculture and in mining in many western countries. Prices of agricultural products have fallen, in relative terms, but consumers have not responded very much. Rising consumer incomes have not brought large increases in food consumption. Low elasticities of demand make the adjustment to technical progress much more difficult. In recent years, increasing output and inelastic demands have depressed prices of many farm products and other raw materials.

Some other problems for which elasticity analysis is useful are these:

1.   Suppose a group of workers forms a labor union. How much ability will they have to obtain higher wages? What will happen to product price and to employment opportunities?

2.   Suppose a tax is imposed on some commodity. What effects will this have on its price? How will the burden of the tax be distributed, as between consumers of the product, and producers?

3.   Suppose a country is confronted with a deficit in its balance of international payments. Would it be a useful measure to devalue the monetary unit internationally?

demand schedules confronting producers

The condition of demand is one of the most important elements in the economic environment in which producers operate. Indeed, it is useful to emphasize here just what a market demand schedule would tell the producers of a commodity (if they had some way of knowing what it was). Each of the following statements is a useful way of putting the matter:

1.   The market demand schedule shows the quantity of the product which producers as a group would be able to sell at any given price.

2.   The market demand schedule shows the price which producers as a group would receive if they placed on the market any given quantity of the product.

3.   The market demand schedule can be used to determine the total sales

revenue which producers as a group would receive for any given quantity of the product placed on the market.

When we come to analyze the behavior of the individual firm, we need to consider more than merely the market demand for a product as a whole. There exists as well, for each seller, a demand schedule *for his own output,* which may differ quite a bit from the market demand schedule facing all producers as a group. The difference arises because the demand confronting the individual seller is conditioned by the state of competition in the market.

In general, the price elasticity of demand depends on the existence of substitutes. The price elasticity of the demand schedule confronting the individual seller depends on the alternatives which are available to buyers. If one seller is in competition with hundreds of others, all offering the same products, then the demand schedule confronting the single seller will be one with high price elasticity. If he raises his selling price, buyers will go elsewhere. We use these considerations to analyze the limiting case of pure competition, in which the number of sellers is very large, each offers the same product for sale, and no one seller is large enough to exert an appreciable influence on the market price. In that case, the demand schedule confronting the individual producer possesses infinite price elasticity, regardless of the elasticity of the market demand for the product as a whole. Geometrically, the demand curve facing the individual seller is a horizontal line located at the going market price.

The other limiting case is also easy to establish. If there is only one producer of a commodity—a monopoly—then the demand schedule confronting him is the same as the market demand schedule for the product as a whole.

Thus the elasticity of the demand schedule confronting the individual seller depends on his size in relation to the total market. The smaller his share, the higher the price elasticity of his own private demand schedule. However, that elasticity also depends on whether the products his competitors sell are identical with his or are differentiated in some way. To the extent that differentiation exists, demand elasticity will tend to diverge from infinity. There may be many sellers of a product, but if they are located at different points, this will give each one some range within which he can adjust the price.

Bear in mind that the price elasticity of the demand schedule facing the individual seller determines how his total revenue will respond to changes in selling price. If the demand for his product is inelastic, then he can increase his total revenues by raising the price. If the elasticity is high, then he may choose to lower the price. However, if the elasticity is infinite, he will have no reason to lower his price, because he will be able to sell all he desires to offer at the going market price. Of course, the individual producer may not be able to determine with any precision the price elasticity of demand for his output. However, trial-and-error adjustments in his output and price can give him some notion of elasticity, at least within some limited range. Further, his price policy will depend not only on demand conditions, but also on the state of his costs. In due time we will show how his most profitable position can be determined on the basis of cost and revenue considerations.

demand for productive factors

To conclude our present discussion of demand, let us consider briefly the demand by producers for factors of production. Just as each consumer may be said to have a demand schedule for any given product, relating the quantity purchased to the price, so each firm has a demand schedule for any given factor of production— services of a given type of labor, capital goods, or land.

We have already noted that demand by producers for productive resources is a *derived* demand. The producer wants to purchase productive services not because of the direct contribution which they make to his enjoyment of consumption, but because of the contribution they make to production of things which he expects to sell at a profit. Just as demand for consumption goods depends on their *utility*, so demand for productive resources depends on their *productivity*—their contribution to the output and revenue of the firm. The strength of a firm's demand for any productive factor depends on the quality of the services rendered by the factor, on the strength of customer demand for its products, on the technology of production, and on the quantity and quality of other factors available either as substitutes or complements.

Typically, a firm's demand curve for any productive service is downward sloping —that is, the higher the price of the service (other things being equal) the less the firm will buy. One reason for this is the existence of opportunities for substitution. Other inputs are available which can perform more or less the same functions. The higher the price of one, the greater the incentive to use another. Downward-sloping demand for a factor also results because demand curves for products are typically downward sloping. Increase in price of a factor of production may make the product more expensive and cause the public to buy less of it, meaning less output and less factor employment. It follows from these considerations that the price elasticity of demand for a factor tends to be high if there are close substitutes for it, or if the demand for products in which it is extensively used is also highly elastic.

Market demand for any factor of production is the aggregation of the demands for it by all individual firms in the economy. Typically, factors of production are used in more than one industry. Indeed, if we deal with broad categories such as land, labor, and capital goods, we may find that all firms in the economy are competing buyers of such resources.

The interaction of business demand for each type of productive service with the supply forthcoming from households yields a set of prices and quantities in markets for labor and property which are the basis for the payment of money incomes from firms to households. And these incomes are, in turn, one determinant of the consumer demand for individual products. As is so often the case, an element which we take as given at one stage of the analysis turns out to be a dependent variable in another.

summary

If we assume some determinate pattern of the distribution of income, there will be a market demand function expressing the quantity of any product A which all buyers will attempt to buy. The shape of the demand function reflects the tastes and preferences of consumers; the terms of the function will typically show that quantity demanded varies directly with income and with the prices of substitute products, and varies inversely with the price of A and prices of complementary products.

Holding the other variables constant, one can derive a demand schedule expressing quantity demanded of A as a function of the price of A. This is graphed as the conventional (downward-sloping) demand curve. A change in tastes, income, or other prices could shift the entire demand schedule (curve).

The sensitivity of quantity demanded to changes in its determinants can be expressed by elasticity measures. Price elasticity of demand is a ratio between proportional change in quantity demanded and proportional change in price. High price elasticity tends particularly to arise where close substitution exists. Income elasticity compares proportional change in quantity demanded with proportional change in income. Cross elasticity relates proportional change in quantity of A demanded with proportional change in price of another product B. Positive cross elasticity reflects a substitution relationship.

The demand schedule confronting each producer is determined partly by the market demand for his product and partly by the degree of competition (the market structure) of the industry in which he operates. His pricing policies will depend on the price elasticity of the demand schedule which confronts him. Each producer also has a demand schedule for each factor of production.

TERMS AND CONCEPTS

1. Demand function
2. Demand schedule, curve
3. Complementary products
4. Price elasticity of demand
5. Income elasticity of demand
6. Cross elasticity of demand

QUESTIONS AND PROBLEMS

1. Suppose that a monopolist is currently operating at a specific price-output position. He suspects that the demand schedule for his product is inelastic at that position. What action could he take to increase his profits? Explain.

2. Let the market demand schedule for a product be defined by the equation $Q = 20 + 100/P$.
   (a) Draw this demand curve.
   (b) Calculate the point elasticity coefficient at $P = 5$.
   (c) Illustrate the geometric representation of this elasticity calculation.
   (d) Calculate the arc-elasticity coefficient between $P = 5$ and $P = 6$.

3. Distinguish between a change in demand and a movement along a given demand schedule. Explain the chief causes of each.

4. Even though the market demand schedule for a product may have a low price elasticity, an individual producer of that product may find himself confronted with a highly elastic demand schedule for his own output. How is this possible?

5. Prove that in any consumer indifference map in which the income-consumption curve is a straight line passing through the origin, the income elasticity of demand for each commodity is equal to unity.

6. Derive a general expression for price elasticity of demand in terms of Q for each of the following demand schedules:
   (a) $Q = 100 - 5P$
   (b) $Q = 1,000/P$
   (c) $Q = 10,000/P^2$

7. If two products are neither substitutes nor complements in the usual sense, they will still tend to have negative cross elasticity toward each other. Why? What will determine how great the cross elasticity is?

interaction of supply and demand

We use supply and demand concepts as an organizing device to explain the determination of the price of a product or service and the quantity bought and sold. In this chapter we present a brief introduction to the theory of supply and its interaction with demand. In the chapters which follow, both topics will be developed much more fully.

Let us recapitulate a few basic principles. Demand refers to the behavior of buyers. A demand function relates the quantity of a product which consumers will purchase to such determinants as consumer incomes, the price of the product, and the prices of other products. A demand schedule (or curve) refers to that sub-division of the demand function in which quantity purchased is expressed as a function of price. The typical demand curve is downward sloping and much of its character can be expressed in terms of the price elasticity of demand. Changes in consumer tastes, incomes, or the prices of other products can lead to shifts in the entire demand curve.

supply schedules

Supply refers to the behavior of sellers. A supply schedule expresses the way in which quantity offered for sale depends on the price which sellers receive. It is used to describe sellers' reactions to changes in demand. The supply schedule is expressed geometrically as a supply curve, with the horizontal dimension of each point representing the quantity supplied at each possible price (vertical dimension).

We shall consider first the supply schedule for a consumer product and concentrate our attention on the activities of *producers* of goods and services, using the term to include not only farmers, manufacturers, and others who "make" things, but also firms engaged in transportation, wholesaling, retailing, and other services which are productive in the sense that they add utility. Later we will shift the emphasis to the supply schedules of factors of production. We limit our analysis of supply schedules at this point to market situations of pure competition, where there are numerous buyers and sellers, each one too small to exert any appreciable influence on prices.

The supply schedule of a product depends on costs. Sellers cannot afford (at least for very long) to sell a product for less than its cost per unit (including some normal return on the capital and labor of the owners of the firm). If price were below average cost, some producers would curtail or cease production of the product. If price were above average cost, more producers would be attracted into the industry. Adjustments of this sort tend to make product price equal to average cost.

The cost per unit of producing and distributing any product depends on the technology and organizational skill which go into the processes of production and distribution. Technology and organizational skill help to determine the physical quantities of inputs required for any given quantity of output. Unit costs also depend on the prices which have to be paid for those inputs and on the supply schedules relating input prices to the quantities employed. The supply schedule for a product is constructed on the assumption of a given condition of technology and organizational technique and a given set of supply conditions for inputs. A change in technology, or a shift in the supply schedule of an input, could result in a shift of the entire product supply schedule or curve.

The unit cost of a product may also depend on how much of the product is produced. The larger the output which an industry produces, the larger the quantity of inputs it requires, and very possibly the higher the prices which must be paid to obtain those inputs. In addition, the physical efficiency of the industry—the output obtained per unit of input—may depend on the size of the industry.

If the population of firms is taken as fixed, and if each operates with a given quantity of durable capital assets, short-run changes in output will take place only by varying the quantities of labor, materials, and other variable inputs. Such changes in output will encounter diminishing returns, and costs per unit will tend to rise as output increases.

In the long run, changes in output can occur through changes in the number of firms and through variations in the stock of durable capital as well as other inputs. The effect of output change on costs will depend mainly on how input prices are affected by changes in industry output. If the industry is a relatively small buyer of inputs, their prices may be unaffected by variations in the industry's purchases. In such a case, the industry may be able to expand output without encountering rising unit costs. This situation is described as one of *constant costs*. The phrase does not mean that costs are unchanging over time, but merely that changes in industry output do not alter the average cost of producing a unit of the product.

More commonly, we would expect that long-run unit costs would rise with higher industry output. The basic reason is that productive resources are scarce and have alternative uses. As one industry expands production, it needs to draw resources away from other sectors of the economy. The more it draws, the higher will go the price it must pay to obtain the inputs, and thus the higher the cost of producing a unit of the product. Such a case is called one of *increasing costs*. The phrase does not mean that costs necessarily increase over time; it merely means that the higher the output the industry produces the higher the unit cost of production will tend to be. We will treat this situation as the normal case.

It is conceivable that the physical efficiency of production may be affected by changes in industry output. It is conceivable, for instance, that there may be sources of increased efficiency which arise from the expansion of the industry as a whole but which are external to the individual firm. Such "external economies of scale" should not be confused with once-and-for-all improvements in technology or managerial skill, however. The latter have been important historically, but it is not likely that the former will be of great importance. We will generally assume that the physical efficiency of production of an industry is not affected by the size of industry output.

elasticity of supply

The sensitivity of quantity supplied to changes in price is expressed in terms of elasticity of supply. The coefficient of elasticity is equal to the proportional change in quantity supplied divided by the proportional change in price. The calculation is similar to that used in determining price elasticity of demand, except that here we use the price-quantity relationships embodied in the supply schedule. (Also, the elasticity coefficient of a downward-sloping demand curve emerges with a minus sign, though we have tended to ignore this and have dealt with its absolute value.)

Elasticity of supply can be calculated between two separate points on a supply schedule (arc elasticity). In calculating arc elasticity, we calculate proportional changes on the average of the two points, not simply one or the other. Elasticity of supply can also be calculated at a single point, using the derivative of the supply curve in the expression $dQ/dP \cdot P/Q$. The higher the coefficient of elasticity, the more sensitive is the quantity supplied to changes in price. If the coefficient of elasticity is greater than 1, a given increase in price will bring forth a more-than-proportional increase in quantity. If the coefficient is unity, the proportional changes in price and quantity are equal. If the coefficient is less than unity (inelastic supply), the proportional change in quantity is less than the proportional change in price.

In the short run, an industry's supply curve typically slopes upward because of diminishing returns. Increasing output with a given endowment of durable capital assets usually leads to reduced efficiency and rising unit costs as output rises. The elasticity of the short-run supply curve depends on the degree to which this sort of decrease in efficiency is encountered. The more extreme the decrease, the less elastic the short-run schedule will be.

The elasticity of the long-run supply schedule depends on how unit costs respond to changes in industry output brought about through changes in the number of firms and in all their inputs. If input prices are not affected by changes in industry output, the industry's long-run supply schedule will tend to be infinitely elastic. The more input prices are pulled up by increases in this industry's output, the less elastic the industry's supply schedule will be. Note that this input-price response reflects the elasticity of supply of the inputs. The long-run elasticity of supply of a product depends heavily on the long-run elasticity of supply of the inputs used in making it.

When we analyzed elasticity of demand, we found that it was closely related to substitution. Price elasticity of demand tends to be high for products which have close substitutes. A small change in price of one product can lead to large shifts among close substitutes. Now we will stress that elasticity of supply is also closely related to substitution. Sellers can make substitution in what they offer for sale. Often business firms produce many products which use very similar raw materials, equipment, and manpower skills. Different items of furniture would be a good example. If the selling price which can be obtained from one item of furniture rises, other things remaining unchanged, the firm can easily shift its operations to produce more of that item. Thus high elasticity of supply tends to accompany a situation of high substitutability by producers.

Similar considerations apply to sale of productive services by households. Each household can substitute one kind of labor services for another by developing new skills and interests. Shifting employment from one industry to another may also be regarded as a form of job substitution by households. The more readily labor and other productive services make such shifts, the higher the elasticity of supply of the products involved will tend to be.

There is thus a general relation of great importance: wherever there exists a high degree of substitutability, there tends to be a high elasticity. Where buyers regard products as close substitutes for each other, demand tends to have a high (price) elasticity. Where sellers are able to make substitutions easily in what they produce and sell, elasticity of supply tends to be high.

geometry of supply

Figure 5-1 illustrates some possible supply curves. Where unit costs remain the same in face of increases in output, the result is a flat supply curve which has infinite elasticity (5-1a). At the opposite extreme, a product the quantity of which cannot be varied would have a zero elasticity of supply, shown by Figure 5-1b.

However, as with demand curves, one must not be hasty about inferring elasticity from slope. Consider Figure 5-1c. Here we have drawn a family of supply curves, all straight lines coming through the origin. Despite the differences in slope, all these supply curves have the same elasticity, namely unity.

Figure 5-2 illustrates a method of finding a geometric expression for elasticity of supply, comparable to the one we derived for elasticity of demand. As before, we want an expression for $dQ/dP \cdot P/Q$. To find elasticity at point E, we draw a tangent to the curve at that point, extending it to intersect both axes. dQ/dP is the inverse of the slope of the tangent. Thus, $dQ/dP = AQ/OP$. The price-quantity ratio is

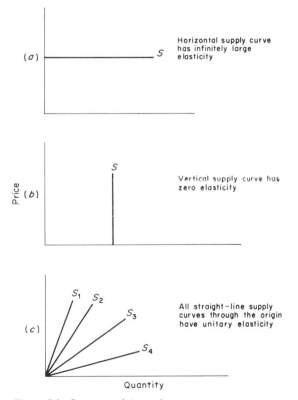

Figure 5-1 Some special supply curves.

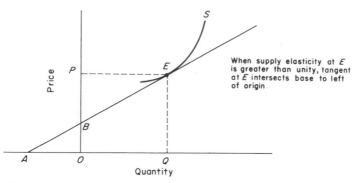

Figure 5-2 Geometry of supply elasticity.

expressed by OP/OQ. Multiplying, we obtain $OP/OQ \cdot AQ/OP = AQ/OQ$, which is thus one measure of elasticity. By construction, $OQ = PE$, so $AQ/OQ = AQ/PE$. Because triangles AQE and BPE are similar, $AQ/PE = QE/PB$. By construction, $EQ = OP$. Therefore, elasticity is represented by OP/BP or by AQ/OQ.

When the elasticity is greater than 1, the tangent intersects the horizontal axis to the left of the origin. When elasticity is less than 1, the tangent intersects the base to the right of the origin. Thus a tangent going through the origin would be associated with unitary elasticity, since OP and BP would be the same.

Elasticity of supply can be calculated from an algebraic supply schedule by use of the derivative formula $e = (dQ/dP)(P/Q)$. To illustrate its use, we examine the elasticity properties of simple supply schedules passing through the origin. Such supply schedules can be represented by the expression

$$Q = aP^n \qquad \text{where } a \text{ and } n \text{ are positive}$$

The derivative of such an expression will take the form

$$\frac{dQ}{dP} = anP^{n-1}$$

The ratio P/Q can be expressed (by substitution) as

$$\frac{P}{Q} = \frac{P}{aP^n} = \frac{1}{aP^{n-1}}$$

Multiplying to obtain the elasticity, we obtain

$$e = \frac{dQ}{dP} \cdot \frac{P}{Q} = anP^{n-1} \cdot \frac{1}{aP^{n-1}} = n$$

Thus the elasticity of a supply schedule passing through the origin is equal to the exponent of the price term in the function. A straight-line supply schedule in the form $Q = aP$ would have an elasticity of unity regardless of the value of the coefficient a.

equilibrium and disequilibrium

In Chapter 2, we stated that the market for a product would be in equilibrium at that price which would equate the quantity demanded by buyers with the quantity offered by sellers. Geometrically, the equilibrium price and quantity are located at the point where the demand curve intersects the supply curve.

An equilibrium position is a state of rest, where forces making for change are mutually offsetting each other. If the system is at the equilibrium position, it tends to remain there. In the market for a consumer product, equilibrium conditions relating to the buyers are met when each buyer is purchasing that quantity of the product corresponding to a tangency position between an indifference curve and a budget line. Each consumer has succeeded in equating the subjective marginal rate of substitution between this product and others with the relevant ratios of product prices.

Equilibrium among producers exists when each has adjusted the variables under his control to achieve the maximum potential profit. Further, in a purely competitive industry, the number of firms reaches equilibrium only when revenues are just sufficient to cover costs, including a normal return to capital and entrepreneurship.

Equilibrium is thus closely related to maximization. To identify equilibrium, we typically identify the maximization position of each participant, and specify various market-clearing conditions such that their relationships with each other are mutually consistent. To identify supply-demand equilibrium, we assume that a single uniform price exists for all buyers and sellers and that the quantity which the buyers demand at that price is equal to the quantity which the sellers provide.

In equilibrium, pressures toward change are mutually offsetting. Buyers would be happier with a lower price, but they do not want to accept a smaller quantity. Sellers would prefer a higher price, but are not prepared to accept a reduction in sales volume.

Now equilibrium is not the normal state of most participants of the economic process in the real world. To stop one's analysis with a mere description of equilibrium is not only unrealistic, but neglects the purpose to which equilibrium analysis is most usefully put. Equilibrium is an essential ingredient in the analytical method of *comparative statics*. On the basis of a set of initial data, we identify an initial equilibrium situation E_1. Then we introduce a disturbance, usually by changing one of the original assumptions. A new equilibrium, E_2, then emerges, and the change from E_1 to E_2 is regarded as a measure of the impact of the disturbance. The analysis is static in that it neglects the time path of the system's adjustment to the disturbance. The technique of comparative statics is illustrated in the following two sections.

adjustment to change in supply

One of the principal uses of a demand curve is to show how price and quantity respond to shifts in the supply schedule. Shifts in supply result from changes in cost, which may in turn arise from changes in technology or in the prices of productive factors. If unit costs fall, suppliers will tend to offer a larger quantity at any given price. The entire supply curve shifts to the right.

The impact of an increase in supply depends on the price elasticity of the demand curve. The higher the elasticity, the greater the impact on quantity relative to price. In Figure 5-3, an initial equilibrium situation is shown at point E, with price P_1 and quantity Q_1. Now assume the supply curve shifts to the right to S'. The two demand curves represent alternative possibilities; they illustrate how impact would depend on the elasticity of demand. The curve D_1 has a lower elasticity at point E. The given shift in supply would cause a substantial drop in price, to P_3, while the increase in quantity to Q_2 would not be large. By contrast, if the reaction went along D_2, the increase in quantity sold would be greater and the price decrease less.

A shift in supply tends to move price and quantity in opposite directions. Increased supply, as in Figure 5-3, raises quantity but lowers price. Decreased supply lowers quantity but raises price. The higher the elasticity of demand, the greater the relative response of quantity and the smaller the relative response of price to a shift in supply.

Price elasticity of demand also determines the impact of a supply shift on the total revenue of sellers. If price elasticity of demand exceeds unity, total revenue of sellers will rise in response to an increase in supply. The proportional increase in quantity will be greater than the proportional decrease in price. If price elasticity of

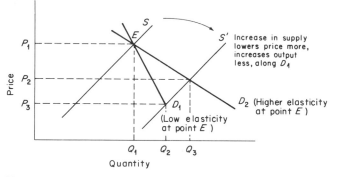

Figure 5-3 A shift in supply.

demand is low, however, an increase in supply will lower sellers' revenue, since the proportional decrease in price will be greater than the proportional increase in quantity. (Change in sellers' total revenue is not the same as change in sellers' profits, however, which depend on costs as well as revenue.)

The analysis we have just offered illustrates a point made in Chapter 4: the impact of technical improvement on the output of an industry (and its employment) is heavily dependent on the elasticity of demand for the product. Agricultural products are commonly in the predicament illustrated by the inelastic demand curve D_1.

adjustment to shift in demand

One of the chief purposes of a supply curve is to show how output and price respond to shifts in the demand schedule for a purely competitive industry. Shifts in the demand schedule may arise from variations in consumer tastes, incomes, or the prices of other products. The impact of a shift in demand will depend on the elasticity of the supply schedule. To illustrate the significance of different supply elasticities, we contrast short-run and long-run impacts. Supply elasticity is typically lower in the short run, when number of producers and capital of the industry are assumed not to change, than in the long run, when greater opportunities for expansion or contraction are available. In Figure 5-4, a competitive industry is assumed to be initially in equilibrium at P_1, Q_1, with demand equal to both short-run and long-run supply. The demand curve then increases, shifting to the right. Both price and output increase. In the short run, lower elasticity of supply is reflected by greater increase in price, and smaller increase in quantity, than ultimately prevail when long-run equilibrium is achieved. The short-run output response is carried out by existing firms with existing facilities. Price is driven up sufficiently that new firms are attracted into the industry, bringing about the further increase in output from

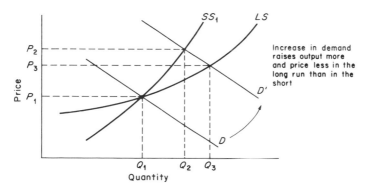

Figure 5-4 A shift in demand.

Q_2 to Q_3, and bringing price down sufficiently that only "normal" profits are being earned.

Shifts in the demand schedule cause price and quantity to move in the same direction. The higher the elasticity of the supply schedule, the larger the proportional change in quantity relative to price. Total expenditure and total sellers' revenue always change in the same direction as the shift in demand.

This is not nearly an adequate analysis of the cost-price-profit relationships underlying the supply behavior of a competitive industry. Those will be developed more fully in the chapters which immediately follow this one.

disequilibrium

Comparative statics, as embodied in the preceding paragraphs, may leave unexamined some rather crucial questions. Is there any reason to expect the system to be in equilibrium to start with? What happens if it is not in equilibrium? If an initial equilibrium is disturbed, what will be the timing of the adjustment pattern?

Some of these questions are answered by discussion of *stability conditions*. An equilibrium position is said to be stable if departures from it tend to be self-correcting. To put it less formally, if the system is not at the equilibrium position, it will tend to go there. How this happens is worth investigating in each specific case; however, we consider only brief illustrations here.

Suppose a disequilibrium exists in the form illustrated by Figure 5-5. At price P_1 and output Q_1 the sellers would just be covering costs; unfortunately the quantity is not what buyers want at that price. If sellers persist in producing Q_1 they will find unsold inventories piling up. Sellers will tend to attack this problem by curtailing production and lowering price. These actions will move the system toward the equilibrium position.

Another pattern of disequilibrium is illustrated by Figure 5-6. The initial price and

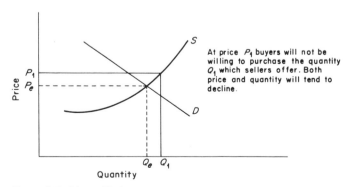

Figure 5-5 Disequilibrium of supply and demand.

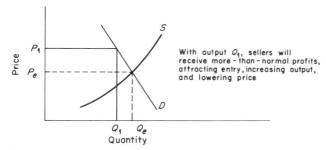

Figure 5-6   Another disequilibrium of supply and demand.

quantity are mutually consistent for buyers, who are just willing to buy Q_1 at price P_1. However, at that price and output sellers would be receiving revenues more than sufficient to cover costs. High profits would tend to attract more firms and elicit more output. This expansion would cease only when the price had been brought down equal to average cost (including a normal profit).

When the price is above the equilibrium level, there is typically an excess of supply over demand. The excess supply leads to adjustments in price and quantity which move the system toward the equilibrium values. If the price is below the equilibrium level, there tends to be an excess of demand, which tends to force up price and quantity.

statics and dynamics

Such stability conditions usually insure that adjustment from disequilibrium will move in the right direction. Further, analysis in terms of short-run and long-run supply schedules, as in Figure 5-4, brings in at least some semblance of a time dimension. However, one might well wish to know more about the time pattern of the adjustment. How rapidly will the system move toward the equilibrium position? How will the speed of adjustment relate to the magnitude of the disequilibrium? Analysis in which the time dimension is explicitly specified is termed *dynamic analysis*.

Dynamic analysis is much more difficult than static analysis and we will not attempt to do much with it. However, one example will help to illustrate how it may yield different results from the static approach. Agricultural commodities often have a definite planting period during which most of the inputs are committed. The crop must then ripen through a period of some months, and eventually it is harvested. The amount of inputs committed during the planting season sets an outside limit on the amount of production which will be possible, although of course actual output will depend on random influences such as weather. Such a seasonal

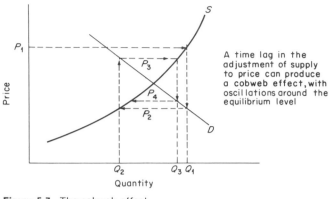

A time lag in the
adjustment of supply
to price can produce
a cobweb effect, with
oscillations around the
equilibrium level

Figure 5-7 The cobweb effect.

pattern creates the basis for a particular set of lagged responses among supply, demand, and price.

To illustrate this, let us assume that in any period t_1 there exists a price P_1, which is the basis on which input decisions are made by producers. However, a time lag then ensues, during which time the crop ripens. The crop is not harvested and marketed until period t_2, when it is sold for whatever it will bring; this produces a new price P_2 which is the basis for the next set of planting decisions. Such a market may easily be subject to perpetual disequilibrium, as shown in Figure 5-7.

Suppose for some reason the initial price P_1 is higher than the equilibrium level. As a result, producers turn out a large output Q_1 which is sold for whatever it will bring. To find the price at which Q_1 will sell, we must find the point on the demand curve lying directly above Q_1. This proves to be the very low price P_2. Because P_2 is so low, producers now cut back on their output plans for the following year, and output is reduced to Q_2. This limited output pushes the price up to P_3, which is above the equilibrium level and calls forth (after delay) output Q_3. And so on.

As we have drawn the figure, the market is at least getting closer to the equilibrium position, although the adjustments always overshoot. However, if we have a sufficiently high elasticity of supply and low elasticity of demand, we may find that the market is "explosive"—that is, the price and output become further and further removed from the equilibrium, instead of approaching it.

The example is oversimplified in one sense; presumably the producers would eventually begin to anticipate price changes, and not adjust output mechanically to the price of the past season. But there is plenty of evidence that something like this process does take place with some agricultural products.

For reasons which should be obvious from the diagram, this sort of adjustment is referred to as a *cobweb effect*. It exists in a world of dynamic analysis, in which a time pattern of adjustment is specified.

The cobweb effect results because the system overshoots its mark—it overcompensates for disequilibrium. Under such conditions, the equilibrium concept itself becomes of rather limited usefulness. To define a dynamically self-correcting system, it may be necessary to specify how the system reacts to disequilibrium. One could specify that if the price is above the equilibrium level, it will fall during the first time period by a certain fraction of its excess. (Or one could specify the pattern in terms of quantities.) Suppose the actual price were $11, the equilibrium price $10, and the adjustment pattern such that the price would fall each week by one-half of its excess over the equilibrium price. Assuming an unchanged equilibrium value, the actual price would approach the equilibrium value asymptotically, passing through the weekly values of $10.50, $10.75, $10.875, etc. Case studies of actual market adjustments would reveal some in which adjustments are rapid and others where they are very slow.

Analysis of the time path by which an actual position approaches a desired position has come to occupy an important place in quantitative studies of economic magnitudes. In this book, however, we will restrict our attention mainly to comparative statics. This restriction enables us to focus on the logical structure of the system. But the timing of adjustment, which is largely an empirical question, is clearly essential when one attempts to apply the analysis to real-market situations.

supply and demand in factor markets

Pricing and allocation of factors of production also occur under the influence of supply and demand schedules. Demand for services of a factor is a derived demand, derived from a demand for the final output which the factor's services help to produce. There is at any time a downward-sloping schedule representing business demand for any factor service. More will be purchased at a lower price, partly because of substitution among factors, partly because lower cost will tend to lead to higher output.

The individual characteristics of factors of production show up in peculiar features of their supply curves. For instance, the total supply of land is, for all practical purposes, fixed. This means that it is completely inelastic. Thus the price of a piece of land (or the rent which will be paid for its use over a limited period of time) will depend on the state of demand. This situation is illustrated by Figure 5-8. Should the demand for land increase, perhaps because of a demand for housing or for farm products, the annual rental value would be pushed up, but the quantity available would not change.

The supply schedule of labor is, of course, limited by the existing size and composition of the population. In addition, the proportion of available people who are willing to work may vary according to the wage offered. A higher wage may call forth more labor, or less. The outcome can be analyzed in terms of the choice between income versus leisure. Raising the wage rates makes leisure more costly and should lead to a substitution effect in favor of work plus income and away from

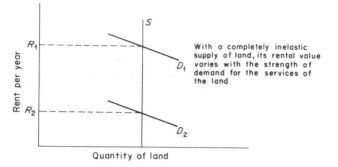

Figure 5-8 Completely inelastic supply of land.

leisure. However, the income effect may produce the opposite result. The higher wage makes it possible to earn any given income with less work. A household might choose to take its higher real income in the form of more leisure, receiving the same money income as it did before.

Variations in labor supply may particularly come about through variations in the number of family members who work. When wage rates are low, there may be strong pressure for all family members to find employment—men, women, and children—to ward off starvation. At higher wage rates, the family can afford to keep the children in school and the wife at home. The result may be a "backward-sloping" supply curve for labor, at least as wages rise from the very low level.

The market for capital services is too complicated to deal with here. We observe merely that the supply of capital involves two separate elements, one being the cost of production of real capital goods, such as machinery and buildings, and the other being the cost of capital funds available for investment.

The interaction of business demand and households' supply in markets for productive services yields a pattern of prices and quantities. This pattern has double significance. First, it establishes the *allocation of resources* in the economy—the assignment of specific productive inputs to their specific occupations. In the process emerges the pattern of methods of production to be employed. Second, the market adjustment results in a pattern of *distribution of income* among households. The income received by each household reflects the quantities of productive services supplied, either by labor or by ownership of property, each weighted by the price received for it.

It is useful to stress the formal similarities between product markets and factor markets. Because the latter are the source of personal incomes, they tend to be a focal point for intense emotional considerations; this sometimes leads to defective analysis and ill-considered public policies. At the same time, however, there are differences between product and factor markets that are worth noting.

It is not unreasonable to think of products as homogeneous, but homogeneity is not a characteristic of land tracts nor particularly of human beings. For this and other reasons, the equilibration of supply and demand may not proceed as dependably in factor markets—particularly the market for labor. In markets for many products, the opportunity to exercise repetitive choice facilitates shopping around, learning from experience. Factor markets often involve relatively long-term commitments involving substantial uncertainty. The opportunity to benefit from one's mistakes by learning how to avoid repeating them is not so easily available.

intermediate products

In the real world, a large proportion of the inputs purchased by business firms consist of the output of other business firms. A manufacturing firm may purchase raw materials, electric power, transportation services, and other inputs from other business firms. A retail store may find that the greatest part of its costs is expenditures at wholesale for the products to be resold in the store. Correspondingly, a large part of the demand for output of some firms arises from sales to other firms, rather than to final consumers. Products sold from one firm to another are called *intermediate products*.

In the chapters which follow, discussion of the individual firm and industry will be stated in terms of the broader concept of inputs rather than the narrower concept of factors of production. The theory of demand by business firms is valid for inputs generally, and applies to both intermediate products and to factors of production. On the supply side, the same analysis can be applied to products sold to final consumers and to intermediate products.

summary

A supply schedule or curve expresses the quantity of a product offered by sellers (in a competitive market) as a function of the price they receive. The supply schedule of a product reflects the relation of unit costs to the quantity produced by the industry. The unit-cost relationship in turn reflects the technical conditions of production and the supply conditions of the inputs used in the product. A short-run supply curve, with a fixed number of firms and a fixed stock of capital goods, would tend to slope up because of diminishing returns. A long-run supply curve for an industry would tend to slope up if the inputs used by the industry have upward-sloping supply curves in that industry.

In a competitive market, price and quantity tend toward a level at which supply and demand are equal. The equilibrium position contains no inherent tendency to change; but if the system is out of equilibrium, a process of adjustment will move it toward equilibrium. Static analysis concerns itself with a comparison of equilibrium positions, and perhaps with the general nature of the adjustment process, but does not fully investigate the time path of adjustment. Dynamic analysis, in which time is treated more explicitly, is used for analysis of disequilibrium situations such as those represented by the cobweb effect.

The demand curve indicates how price and quantity will respond to a shift in supply. The lower the price elasticity of demand, the greater the relative response of price, rather than quantity, to a shift in supply. With inelastic demand, an increase in supply will decrease the total revenue of sellers. If demand is elastic, such an increase in supply will raise quantity proportionately more than it lowers price, and sellers' revenue increases.

The supply curve indicates how price and quantity will react to changes in demand. The lower the elasticity of supply, the greater the relative response of price, rather than quantity, to a shift in demand. The elasticity of supply of a product tends to be higher in the long run, when the number of firms can change, than in the short run, when the number of firms and their stock of capital are constant.

TERMS AND CONCEPTS

1. Supply schedule, curve
2. Comparative statics
3. Elasticity of supply
4. Dynamic analysis
5. Equilibrium
6. Cobweb effect

QUESTIONS AND PROBLEMS

1. Given a supply curve defined by the equation $Q = 4P - 20$,
   (a) Draw the supply curve.
   (b) Calculate the point elasticity of supply at $P = 10$.
   (c) Draw the geometric expression of elasticity of supply at that point.
   (d) What happens to elasticity of supply along this supply curve as the price rises? Derive a general expression relating the elasticity of this supply schedule to the price of the product.

2. Given the supply and demand curves defined by these equations:

$$\text{(Supply)} \quad Q_s = 6P - 40$$

$$\text{(Demand)} \quad Q_d = \frac{100}{P} + 10$$

   (a) Draw the curves.
   (b) Find the equilibrium price and quantity.

(c) Calculate the point elasticities of supply and demand at the equilibrium point.

3. What is wrong with the wording of this sentence: "An increase in demand raises price, but an increase in price reduces demand." Rephrase this in a more nearly correct manner.

4. Draw a typical supply and demand diagram showing equilibrium price and quantity. Now illustrate how the effects of each of the following could be shown in such a diagram:
   (a) An increase in consumer incomes
   (b) An improvement in technology
   (c) A decrease in the price of a product which buyers regard as a close substitute for this one

5. "Quantity bought must equal quantity sold. Therefore supply and demand are always equal." Comment.

the production function

An economic system can be looked upon as a means for transforming the scarce productive resources of the society into goods and services to meet the consumption needs and desires of the people. This transformation, or production, may involve changes in the physical characteristics of things, or merely changes in their location, ownership, and other attributes. And of course much production consists of services not embodied in any tangible products—services of doctors, lawyers, entertainers, teachers, policemen, and judges.

How well the economic system performs its function depends in large measure on the terms of this transformation—that is, how efficiently the system transforms its available resources into goods and services for consumption. In a market economy, this transformation is carried on mainly through the efforts of business firms. The decisions made by business firms play a major role in the process by which the economy as a whole determines what products to produce and in what amounts, how to produce them, and who shall receive them. The efficiency with which business firms operate strongly influences the efficiency with which the entire economy performs its function.

The incentive which leads the individual firm to seek efficiency is the search for profits. In fact, in our analysis we will generally assume that business firms attempt to maximize their profits. We will investigate the meaning and limitation of this assumption subsequently.

Briefly, the profits of a firm are the difference between revenues and costs. Thus concern for profits leads to efforts to obtain high revenue and maintain low costs. The desire for revenues reflects itself in the decisions of the firm about *what* to produce, and how much. The firm must determine which products it will produce and settle the details of styles, quality, size, color, etc. In making such decisions, it will obtain some guidance from the apparent demand for each class of product, as a determinant of the price at which any given quantity can be sold.

The firm is also concerned with its costs. It attempts to keep costs low by purchasing its inputs as cheaply as possible and attempting to substitute low-cost for high-cost inputs. In addition, it attempts to be efficient, in the sense of getting the greatest possible output out of any given combination of inputs.

technology, organization, and efficiency

In considerable degree, the firm's quest for efficiency takes the form of concern for *organization* and for *technology*. The most important aspect of organization, in a firm of any considerable size, is the proper use of *people*, through what is often termed *personnel management*. Every person is a unique bundle of skills, aptitudes, motivations, memory, and other characteristics. Part of personnel management consists of matching up jobs with people in such a way as to make the best of each person's positive attributes. Furthermore, efficiency may depend on how effectively people can work together. This will lead to concern for the proper choice of foreman and supervisors, and for many other aspects of group relationships. Effective management will seek methods for giving the workers strong motivations to perform their tasks well and to look for better ways of doing things. The subject of personnel management is a substantial academic discipline in itself, incorporating elements of psychology, physiology, and business administration. Economic theory as such does not explore it very far, but rather takes as given the existing state of personnel practices and other organizational practices among business firms.

Problems of organization shade gradually over into the second area we wish to identify—*technology*. Technology is concerned primarily with the physical aspects of the production process itself. In a large firm, technology is the domain of engineers —people trained in the application of physics, chemistry, and biology to productive operations.

But the vast majority of business firms the world over are not directly involved with very complicated technology. They are farms or stores or other small enterprises involved in fairly simple operations. For them, technology may be largely a combination of tradition and manual skill.

Formally, however, the carpenter considering the most efficient method to build a table, and the engineers designing a petroleum refinery or steel mill are dealing with similar problems. In considerable degree, these problems are both questions of technical efficiency, which can be expressed either as trying to obtain the greatest (or best) output from a given quantity of inputs, or trying to produce a given output with the smallest quantity of inputs.

Economics takes a great interest in technology. Economists have attempted to explain the conditions under which technological progress takes place, and to explore the relation of technical progress to the size of business firms, their relation to each other, and the broader social environment within which innovation takes place. In addition, economic analysis has a great concern for clarifying the general concept of efficiency. The individual business firm desires to produce any given output in the cheapest possible manner. Technical efficiency, as we have defined it above, helps to achieve this result. But it is a mistake to assume that engineers alone can guide a firm to optimum efficiency without resorting to economic analysis. For it seldom happens that a firm is choosing between processes where the quantities of inputs and outputs are the only concern. Often one needs to know their *costs* as well. One electrical generator may turn out more kilowatt hours of electricity per ton of coal burned than another, but if the first generator costs more to buy than the second, the firm must weigh the added costs against the added efficiency. This is essentially an economic question, and it is the sort of problem which we will be exploring at length before long.

the production function

A large part of managerial effort is devoted to deciding how to get the greatest output from a given collection of inputs. For economic analysis, however, we will assume that the skills of managers, personnel experts, and engineers have settled these matters, so that for each specific batch of inputs, there is one best output which the firm can and does obtain. The same quantity of output might be obtained from many different input combinations, but there is one unique output quantity associated with any unique input combination. On these assumptions, we can express the input-output relationship as a *production function*. The production function identifies the quantity of output associated with each combination of the various inputs. Initially we will concentrate on the production function of an individual firm. Later we will consider production functions for an industry and for the economic system as a whole.

A firm's production function is valid only for a given state of technology and organizational skill. A change in technology or in management effectiveness could cause the entire production function to shift. The production function also depends on the *quality* of the inputs employed. The amount of output which can obtained from a given amount of labor will depend, for instance, on the quality of the labor force, as reflected in skill, education, experience, motivations, etc. For analysis, we must assume no change in the quality mix of the inputs on which the production function is based.

Generally the relation between inputs and outputs is positive—that is, an increase in the quantity of inputs usually results in an increase in output. However, economists want to know more precisely how output responds to changes in inputs. They have dealt with this question in two dimensions: scale and proportionality. In considering scale, one considers what happens to output if all inputs are increased in the same proportion. In considering proportionality, one considers what happens to output if the quantity of one input is changed while the quantity of the others is held constant.

The distinction between scale and proportionality is useful because there are likely to be differences in the attitude of the firm toward variations in the quantity of different inputs to achieve a desired change in output. Some inputs lend themselves better than others to short-run variation. One extreme is represented by utilities such as electricity or water, where the rate of use can be varied not merely from day to day, but from minute to minute. The opposite extreme may be represented by inputs of the services of durable capital assets, where a complex process of design and construction may be necessary to enlarge the stock of those assets. Facilities of a chemical plant, petroleum refinery, or steel mill would illustrate these problems. Considerations of this sort lead us to assume that (in the short run) each firm's inputs can be classified as either variable or fixed and that changes in output will be initially carried out by changes in the employment of the variable inputs only.

However, the speed with which the firm *can* change its employment of different inputs is not the only basis for the distinction between long and short run. The really *long* aspect of long-run decisions concerns the planning period involved in the firm's decision—the length of future time which the firm needs to consider. Here the element of ownership or long-term contractual commitment is crucial. When services alone can be purchased, the firm may be free to act on the basis of a very short time horizon. Additional electricity or public transportation services can be used to increase output next week without great concern for what the firm expects for the following week or the following year.

However, if the firm can increase its employment of input services only by increasing its stock of some durable asset such as buildings or machinery, then a long-term commitment is involved. The asset purchase may be profitable only if the firm can use the input services not merely next week, but for many weeks thereafter. Thus purchase of durable assets is regarded as a long-term matter because the firm will have to consider the long-run prospects for revenue and cost before deciding that such a purchase is worthwhile.

Individual firms can, of course, evade such problems by leasing durable assets to acquire their services when wanted. This merely shifts the problem around, however, since capital goods will not be available unless someone has been willing to assume the risks and responsibilities of paying for their production.

Traditionally, labor has been regarded as a variable input, since firms could and did hire or dismiss workers in the short run. However, in many occupations the firm has in fact an implied contractual obligation to keep most of its workers unless something drastic happens. Tenure for educators is a formal recognition of a kind of long-term employment commitment which exists informally in many other areas. Where hiring a worker is so regarded, employers are more likely to keep long-run considerations in view in making employment decisions.

To sum up: we assume that in the short run, the firm treats some of its inputs as fixed and some as variable, and makes output changes only through changes in the variable category. In the long run, however, all inputs are regarded as variable. And the length of the short and long runs may depend not merely on the speed with which input changes can be made but on the length of the time horizon over which expectations are relevant to the input decision.

the problem of scale

Viewed in the above terms, what we are looking for is a conception of a long-run production function. Such a function would tell us the quantity of any given product A which could be obtained with each possible combination of inputs $a, b, c, \ldots, n$. Both output and inputs have a time dimension: that is, our production function describes output per unit of time (a week, a month), and the inputs must also have a time dimension—so many man-hours of labor, for instance.

We assume that each firm will achieve technical and managerial efficiency. Whatever the inputs employed by the firm, it will use them in a manner which yields the largest possible output obtainable from that input combination. This means, for instance, that each person employed by the firm is assigned to the proper task. Since a large part of the responsibility of business management is to achieve technical and managerial efficiency in the use of a given input mix, we are sweeping aside a very large problem area by our assumption that the firm does this job well. We will, however, attempt to analyze the firm's choice of inputs; our assumption here is merely that the firm uses effectively whatever inputs it does decide to use.

Because of technology, production functions will differ from one industry to another and will change over time. Can we say anything about their general character? To analyze the properties of scale, we start at some positive point in the function, from a given input-output situation, and find out what happens to output when *all* inputs are increased in the same proportion. One would naturally suppose that the output would increase by the same proportion. We say that in such a situation, the firm is subject to *constant returns to scale*. We will argue that the situation of constant returns is indeed what one normally expects to find. However, departures from constant returns may occur because of lack of divisibility of inputs.

Because men and machines come in units not subject to fractionalization, it is argued, firms are likely to be subject to *economies of large-scale operations*. At a small size, the firm cannot achieve as great a degree of specialization as it might at a larger size. Doubling all the inputs may, therefore, cause a greater than doubling of the total output. Economies of scale are particularly likely to appear in industries using highly specialized and intricate capital equipment. Steel, chemicals, automobiles, petroleum refining, and electricity generating are examples of industries subject to large economies of scale arising from use of specialized capital equipment. The term *increasing returns to scale* is also applied to situations where a given proportional increase in all inputs generates a larger proportional increase in output.

Improved opportunity for specialization is the most commonly cited explanation for increasing returns to scale. The potential for specialization is generally defined by the stocks of inputs available to the firm: the number of workers, the value of capital assets, etc. However, some economists feel that it is more appropriate to identify the production function in terms of flows of input services. These flows have a time dimension—man-hours of labor rather than number of men employed. It is not necessary to employ a large quantity of man-hours to achieve a high degree of labor specialization. One thousand man-hours of labor may reflect the work of 10 men for 100 hours each, or 1,000 men working 1 hour each, or 60,000 men working 1 minute each. The potential for specialization inheres in the number of men, rather than the number of man-hours.

If the production function is viewed in terms of flows, therefore, it might display constant returns to scale over a very considerable range. Theoretically, a firm which produces one automobile could be as efficient as General Motors by employing a comparable number of workers and leasing a comparable batch of equipment for a minute or two. The example is sufficient to demonstrate the limits of this approach. The ability of firms to obtain capital services without owning stocks of capital depends on the willingness of others to own those stocks and lease out their use. Market imperfections, uncertainty, and risk may cause this to be an inferior alternative when done on a small scale. More important, the effective managerial operation of a firm requires some continuity of input stocks over time. One really needs to have many of the same people coming to work tomorrow as today. Each human being is unique, and particularly each experienced employee has a large accumulation of memory and reflex which enables him to function productively. Some minimum input of factor-service flow therefore appears necessary to achieve the benefits of specialization in factor stocks. There exists some organizational or managerial constraint on the divisibility of factor services. Whether we stress factor stocks or flows, it seems reasonable to assume that there are economies of scale in any kind of production up to some point, but that constant returns will hold for a considerable range as output further increases. The actual range of increasing returns may differ greatly from one industry to another, reflecting differences in technology and management practice.

decreasing returns to scale

We must also ask, is there any limit to the range of constant returns as the firm grows very large? A common answer is that beyond some point a firm becomes so large that managerial difficulties arise. Either the firm will begin to suffer from difficulties of coordinating and controlling a huge organization or it will have to increase the proportion of its personnel devoted to managerial activity. This can be illustrated by the concept of *span of control* used in the study of administration. Suppose that for every ten workers, the firm needs one supervisory employee at a higher administrative level. As the number of primary workers increases, the number of supervisory workers increases, and so does the proportion. When the firm has 100 production workers, it reaches a new level and needs a man to supervise the ten supervisors. As the base of the pyramid widens, its height increases and the ratio of supervisory to operative personnel increases. However, the assumption about fixed proportions may not be a valid one.

In any case, it is apparent from American experience that firms may grow to very large size without loss of efficiency. General Motors is notoriously more efficient than its competitors in the automobile industry, and similar conclusions could be drawn about such large firms as Du Pont or Proctor and Gamble. On the other hand, size is no guarantee of efficiency, either, as U.S. Steel and the Pennsylvania Railroad would illustrate.

We will argue, with perhaps a rather flimsy basis, that the typical production function ultimately encounters diseconomies of scale, but that this encounter may occur at an output which is very large. Our scale pattern, therefore, is one in which economies of scale are present in the low range of output, constant returns over a considerable intermediate range, and decreasing returns at some large level.

Economies of large-scale operation appear in industries where very sophisticated technology is embodied in highly specialized capital goods. By contrast, such important sectors as agriculture, retailing, and services do not display extensive economies of scale. This is apparent in the fact that the vast majority of producers in these categories are small, yet are able to compete successfully.

proportionality: the law of diminishing returns

In the short run, the firm is likely to find it inexpedient to change all inputs proportionally. Thus, short-run changes in output generally alter input proportions. What happens to output when we change some inputs, while holding constant the quantity of other inputs? One of the most famous generalizations in the history of economic thought was developed to deal with this question: it is the *law of diminishing returns*. One way of stating it is as follows: if we increase the quantity of one (variable) input while holding constant the quantity of another (fixed) input, the output will probably increase, but the increments of output (per unit of variable input) will tend to decline. To put it another way, the additional output yielded by an additional unit of variable input tends to become smaller as the quantity of variable input increases.

The law of diminishing returns was developed by British economists in the early nineteenth century to analyze the response of food production to increases in population and labor supply. The law has generally been interpreted to treat land as the fixed input. However, its validity arises from the general fact that productive resources are not perfect substitutes for each other. There are unique kinds of productive contribution associated with each factor of production: soil fertility and location, for instance, with land; memory and intelligence with labor; strength and precision with machinery; and so on. Increasing only some of the inputs may mean imbalance in these productive contributions, with diminishing returns as the consequence.

We will assume that the principle of diminishing returns is always valid *as a tendency*. However, there may be an initial phase in the production function where diminishing returns does not hold, where increases in one input are accompanied by increasing increments of output up to a point. This can occur at very small quantities of the variable input, when the quantities of fixed inputs are large. In particular it is likely to occur if the production function displays economies of scale. Given the quantity of land and capital embodied in a steel mill or petroleum refinery, for instance, the first increments of labor may well show increasing returns. There is some minimum quantity of labor required for efficiency. However, if we keep on increasing the labor input while holding the others constant, beyond some point diminishing returns will set in, and the increments of output (per unit of labor) will tend to decline.

Closely related to the principle of diminishing returns is the concept of the *marginal physical product* of a variable input. This is defined as the change in the quantity of output associated with a change in the quantity of one (variable) input, other inputs remaining constant. Given the production function, we can derive a schedule of marginal physical product for any variable input. One way of stating the law of diminishing returns is to say that the marginal physical product of any input tends to decline as the quantity of the input is increased.

illustration: a hypothetical production function

We can illustrate some of these properties of the production function by an algebraic and numerical example. Imagine a production function expressed by this equation: $Q = 10 \sqrt{ab}$, where Q represents the physical quantity of output, and a and b represent the physical quantities of two inputs.[1] The production function

---

[1] This functional form, which we will use extensively, is an example of the so-called *Cobb-Douglas function*. A more general form is $Q = ka^x b^y$, where x and y do not necessarily add up to unity.

tells us that if we multiply the quantity of input a times the quantity of input b, take the square root of their product, and multiply by 10, the result will equal the quantity of output. Input a might represent man-hours of labor, and input b machine-hours of some capital equipment. From this function, we can calculate the quantity of output associated with each combination of inputs. We assume the function is continuous, and that it is meaningful to speak of fractional units of input and output. This assumption is defensible because input and output quantities have a time dimension. A firm cannot employ half a man, but it can use half a man-hour. It may not be meaningful to produce a half-car, but the production may average half a car per day, per hour, or per minute.

Table 6-1 illustrates some of the specific input-output combinations implied by this production function. The numbers along the edges represent the quantities of inputs, while each number in the body is the quantity of output resulting when we combine the horizontal quantity of a with the vertical quantity of b. For instance, to find the output which can be obtained by combining 5 units of labor with 3 units of capital, move to the right to the fifth column, then move down to the fourth row. There we find the output identified as 38.73 units (that is, $10 \sqrt{15}$). We can use this function to illustrate the effects of changing all inputs in proportion—the scale properties of the function. This can be done through an elasticity approach. We can compare the percentage change in output with the percentage change in inputs, keeping constant the proportion between the inputs. Let us call this the *scale elasticity*. If the elasticity coefficient is greater than 1, the function displays increasing returns to scale. If the coefficient is less than unity, there are decreasing returns to scale, and if the coefficient is unity, constant returns.

This elasticity can be determined between two points, using the arc-elasticity approach and basing percentage changes on the average of the two values. It can also be determined by using the derivative at a single input-output point. Since all inputs change in proportion, we can express the elasticity coefficient in terms of

TABLE 6-1 OUTPUT YIELDED BY SPECIFIED INPUT COMBINATIONS†

Units of Capital Input (b)	Units of Labor Input (a)					
	0	1	2	3	4	5
0	0	0	0	0	0	0
1	0	10.00	14.14	17.32	20.00	22.36
2	0	14.14	20.00	24.49	28.28	31.62
3	0	17.32	24.49	30.00	34.64	38.73
4	0	20.00	28.28	34.64	40.00	44.72
5	0	22.36	31.62	38.73	44.72	50.00

† In accordance with a hypothetical production function $Q = 10 \sqrt{ab}$ (rounded to two decimal places).

any one of the inputs. It could be written

$$\frac{\Delta Q/Q}{\Delta a/a} \quad \text{or as} \quad \frac{\Delta Q/Q}{\Delta b/b} \quad \text{since} \quad \frac{\Delta a}{a} = \frac{\Delta b}{b}$$

Choosing the first and converting to derivative form yields $(dQ/da)(a/Q)$. Let $b = ka$, where k is the constant expressing the initial input proportion. The production function then reduces to

$$Q = 10 \sqrt{ka^2} = 10a \sqrt{k}$$

The derivative at any specific point is expressed by the following:

$$\frac{dQ}{da} = 10 \sqrt{k}$$

The ratio a/Q is always equal to $\frac{1}{10} \sqrt{k}$. Multiplying the two expressions together yields an elasticity coefficient of unity. Thus the function under study displays constant returns to scale. This is also illustrated by the central diagonal of Table 6-1, representing outputs resulting when $a = b$. Output changes in the same proportion as input.[2]

diminishing returns

Our hypothetical production function also illustrates the tendency toward diminishing returns. Choose some level of one input to be considered fixed—for instance, let $b = 3$. As the quantity of labor input is increased, the increments of output become successively smaller. In Table 6-1, we can calculate the marginal physical product of labor for finite, whole-number changes by subtracting the successive figures along the row corresponding to $b = 3$. The first unit of labor increases output by 17.32 units, the second unit of labor adds 7.17 to output, and so on. These decreases in the marginal physical product of labor reflect diminishing returns.

We can also calculate an expression for the schedule of labor's marginal physical product by taking a derivative of the production function itself. When $b = 3$, the resulting short-run production function becomes $Q = 10 \sqrt{3a} = 17.32a^{1/2}$. The

---

[2] A function in the form $Q = a^m b^n$ is said to be *mathematically homogeneous*, which means that it possesses the same scale properties throughout. The scale elasticity coefficient is equal to the sum of the exponents $(m + n)$. Our illustration employs a function equivalent to $Q = 10a^{1/2}b^{1/2}$, with exponents summing to unity. This special case is termed a *linear homogeneous function*.

schedule of marginal physical product of a is the derivative of this function, as follows:

$$MPP_a = \frac{dQ}{da} = (17.32)(\tfrac{1}{2})(a^{\frac{1}{2}-1}) = \frac{8.66}{\sqrt{a}}$$

With this formula, we can calculate the marginal physical product of a at any given quantity of a. Observe that the marginal physical product will vary inversely with the size of a. Thus the function displays diminishing returns throughout.

Although for simplicity we will generally deal with production functions containing only two inputs, it would be possible to extend this form of function to cover any number of inputs, as follows: $Q = Ka^n b^m \cdots x^g$, where $a, b, \ldots, x$ represent the inputs and K is some constant.

summary

The production function expresses the quantity of a product which can be obtained from a given combination of inputs, assuming a given pattern of technology and organizational skill. Observing the behavior of output when all inputs are varied by the same proportion, we can establish whether the production function displays increasing, constant, or decreasing returns to scale. Increasing returns, or economies of large-scale operation, may occur where there are indivisibilities in some inputs, such as machinery, so that greater specialization occurs at larger scales. If inputs are divisible, however, constant returns to scale are likely to occur.

The typical production function is subject (beyond some point) to the law of diminishing returns. That is, if the quantity of one input is increased while the quantities of other inputs remain constant, the increments of output will decline. Such increments of output can be termed the marginal physical product of the variable input.

TERMS AND CONCEPTS

1. Production function
2. Technical efficiency
3. Returns to scale
4. Law of diminishing returns
5. Marginal physical product
6. Cobb-Douglas function

QUESTIONS AND PROBLEMS

1. Assume a production function defined by the equation $Q = 5\sqrt{ab}$, where a and b are the quantities of two inputs.
   - **(a)** Calculate a 5×5 table showing the quantity of output associated with every integral input combination of a and b, accurate to two decimal places.
   - **(b)** Use the table to illustrate the difference between diminishing returns to a factor and returns to scale.
   - **(c)** Letting $a = 4$, calculate the marginal physical product of b between the points representing integral values of b (1, 2, 3, 4, 5).
   - **(d)** Using the derivative method, find a general expression for the marginal physical product of b when $a = 4$.

2. Explain the economic reasons why a firm might encounter increasing returns to scale (economies of large-scale operation). How are these reasons related to the divisibility of inputs?

3. What kind of returns to scale would be associated with each of these production functions? Determine the scale elasticity of output in each case.
   - **(a)** $Q = ab$
   - **(b)** $Q = \sqrt[3]{ab}$
   - **(c)** $Q = 20ab - a^3 - b^3$ (*Hint:* Let $a = b$ and find an expression for the scale elasticity, or use the arc-elasticity approach.)

implications of the production function: a simple model

The amount of output which an economic system can obtain from its scarce productive resources is obviously a major influence on economic welfare. In order to illustrate the importance of the production function and to introduce some additional ideas of economic interdependence, we devote this chapter to a simple model of an economic system. It will provide some review of the supply and demand analysis of preceding chapters, as well as a foretaste of what will be coming up later when we talk about the determination of wage rates.

We assume an economic system which produces only one product, "food," which comes in bushels. Consumers desire as much of this commodity as they can obtain. Food is produced by land and labor; we ignore capital as a productive factor for the time being. All labor is assumed to be of the same quality, and individual workers are assumed to be indifferent to all aspects of their work except the income it yields them, which is paid in a quantity of the product.

The land tracts in the society are assumed to fall into five grades, which we will designate by the letters A through E. Each grade has a unique productivity schedule,

TABLE 7-1

Man-years of Labor	Land Grade				
	A	B	C	D	E
	Bushels of output per tract				
1	50	60	70	80	90
2	96	117	136	156	175
3	140	170	197	227	256
4	182	218	252	289	330
5	218	261	299	347	399
6	243	294	340	396	462
7	263	323	373	441	513
8	278	347	399	476	552
Number of tracts in each grade	100	80	60	40	30

given in Table 7-1. The output per year on each tract of land is determined by the amount of labor employed on it. Technology is assumed to remain unchanged.

Two aspects of the productivity table deserve immediate comment. First, we have assumed that the productivity pattern is subject to diminishing returns throughout. As we increase the labor on a tract of land, the total output increases, but the *increments* of output decrease. Second, we have presented the data in the table only for integral values of the labor input, as if it could not be divided. For this illustration, we will proceed as if the only feasible outputs were those shown in the table. However, in reality, the labor input could be varied continuously to produce outputs between those shown in the table.

self-sufficiency

To commence the conjectural history of our imaginary society, let us imagine that each family in the society owns one tract of land and farms it on a self-sufficient basis. The total number of families is equal to the number of tracts, namely 310. To simplify the bookkeeping, we will assume that one man does the basic farm work for each family and ignore the likelihood that all members of the family might help with the labor. If you prefer, assume that the women and children perform household activities which do not affect the output of food.

On each tract of land, the total output is shown by the first figure in the table—that is, the result of applying one man-year of labor. Each tract of quality E produces 90 bushels, each tract of B 60 bushels, etc. The total output of the society is calculated by multiplying the output of each tract in a given grade by the number of tracts in that grade, then adding the totals.

In this scheme of things, some families are better off than others. Some have as much as 90 bushels, others as little as 50. Why? Not because of differences in their work, for we have assumed that the amount and quality of labor are the same for all. No, the differences in income reflect simply the fact that some land is better than other land. Inequality in property ownership is, in this illustration, the basis for initial inequalities of real income.

Now we are ready for a momentous social change. Let us suppose that the idea becomes accepted in this society that it is proper for some people to work for others as farm laborers in exchange for a wage, paid in units of the product. Of course, such an arrangement is purely voluntary on both sides. This means that no one will offer to hire himself out as a laborer unless he can increase his income in that manner (compared to what he could earn as a self-sufficient farmer). And no one will employ laborers unless they add more to total output than the amount of the product which has to be given to them for wages.

introduction of a labor market

To make the operation of the labor market as simple as possible, we will assume that conditions of pure competition prevail. This means that every worker and every employer treats the wage rate as being beyond his own control, as "given" by market forces. We also assume that sufficient knowledge of market conditions prevails so that there will tend to be one wage rate, uniform for all workers throughout the society. We assume that the market will tend toward an equilibrium wage at a level which will equate the number of jobs available with the number of people seeking jobs. Each employer believes himself able to hire as many people as he wants at the going wage rate, which rate is not affected by his decisions. He has no incentive to offer more than the market rate of wages, but will not be able to hire any workers for less. The workers perceive that jobs are available at the equilibrium rate; they have no incentive to accept less but cannot effectively demand more, since no employer need pay a higher rate than the equilibrium level.

The data which we have are sufficient to enable us to prepare a set of market supply and demand schedules for labor. These are in turn built up from the decisions of individual workers and landowners. Consider first the decisions by individuals as to whether they would hire out or not. We have already assumed that each is indifferent to all features of his employment except the income (in bushels of food) which it yields. Consider a man who owns a tract of land in category A. He can obtain 50 bushels of food by working his own land. If he is offered a job for wages at 40 bushels, he would not wish to take it. But if the wage offered were 60 bushels, he would be willing to hire out. And we will assume that if the wage offered were 50 bushels, he would be indifferent.

Thus the supply of persons willing to hire themselves out for wages can be determined by looking at the number of tracts of land in each grade and at the productivity of one man on each tract. At any wage less than 50 bushels, no workers will be available. As soon as the wage reaches 50, the 100 men with land of the lowest grade become available. At 60, they are joined by 80 more from category B. And so on. The supply of labor becomes an upward-sloping function of the wage offered: as the wage rises, more workers become available, although they enter only at specific points on the wage scale (not a realistic assumption, as you are well aware, but it simplifies the arithmetic).

demand for hired labor

The landowner who is trying to decide about hiring workers must figure out whether he will be better off if he does so. With more workers, he can produce more output. But he must pay the workers with some of the product. We will assume that he is trying to maximize his own real income—that is, obtain for himself the largest possible amount of the product. We have already assumed that he has no direct control over the wage which he pays; that is "given" by the market. His decision, then, reduces to one of quantity—how many men to employ?

The landowner can approach the problem through some sort of marginal analysis. That is, he can compare the addition to output which an extra worker would produce with the added cost which the worker's wage would entail. If the increase in output is greater than the wage, then the employer will benefit from adding the extra man.

Consider the owner of a tract of land in category E. With no hired workers, he can produce 90 bushels. If he hires one man (we assume each landowner continues to work himself), he can increase his output to 175. The hired worker adds 85 bushels to the output. If the wage required to obtain the hired worker is less than 85, the landowner will gain by employing him. If the wage is greater than 85, the landowner will find his income reduced if he hires the man. And if the wage is equal to 85, the landowner will be indifferent whether to employ the man or not.

He can apply the same consideration to a second hired worker. By adding a second man, output is increased from 175 to 256—an increase of 81 bushels. If the wage were lower than 81, it would be advantageous to hire two men. If the wage were higher, the second man would not be worth hiring. If the wage were equal to 81, the landowner would be indifferent.

marginal productivity

In the foregoing, we have attributed to the landowner the use of one of the most important concepts of economic analysis—the notion of marginal productivity. More specifically, our illustration involves the concept of the *marginal physical product* of labor. The marginal physical product of any input is defined as the change in the quantity of total output associated with a change in the quantity of one input, other inputs remaining unchanged.

For any given tract of land, it is possible to calculate a schedule of marginal physical productivity. This is done by calculating the change in output which results from the successive addition of each extra man. The calculation for a tract of land in category E would be performed as shown in Table 7-2. Notice that the numbers representing marginal physical product are placed between the lines representing total output. Marginal physical product can be calculated for both increases and decreases in inputs. Thus the marginal product of the sixth worker tells us that we increase total output by 63 bushels if we add him, or decrease total output by 63 bushels if we dismiss him.

Because of the law of diminishing returns, the marginal product of labor decreases as more labor is added. Indeed, it is convenient to use this as a definition of diminishing returns. Note well that the decreases in marginal physical product result entirely from increases in the *quantity* of labor (relative to land or some other fixed factor). In our example, we have assumed no differences in the quality of individual workers. It would, therefore, make no difference which individual is the first worker or the fourth worker. Indeed, we would be more accurate to speak of the marginal product of having four workers instead of three. By a similar line of reasoning, the total output of the farm would fall by 63 bushels if the number of workers were reduced from four to three, regardless of which worker was dismissed.

In the real world, of course, some differences in labor productivity do result from differences in quality. Even so, the productivity of each worker depends on how many workers there are, relative to other productive resources.

Marginal productivity concepts are the basis for the *demand schedule* for any factor of production. In our example, the demand for hired workers by any farm can be determined directly from the schedule of the marginal physical product of

TABLE 7-2

Labor Input	Total Output	Marginal Product
0	0	
		(90)
1	90	
		85
2	175	
		81
3	256	
		74
4	330	
		69
5	399	
		63
6	462	
		51
7	513	
		39
8	552	

TABLE 7-3

Number of Hired Workers	Output	Wage Cost	Net Landowner Income
0 (owner alone)	90	0	90
1	175	70	105
2	256	140	116
3	330	210	120
4	399	280	119
5	462	350	112

labor. The hiring decision can always be expressed in terms of the marginal physical product and the wage, as follows:

If the marginal physical product exceeds the wage, add a man.
If the wage exceeds the marginal physical product, dismiss a man.

If the firm follows these rules, it will always tend towards the same equilibrium employment: it will add workers until it reaches the point at which the marginal physical product is equal to the wage.

We can illustrate this with category E land again. Suppose the going wage rate is 70 bushels. The landowner could calculate his net income position for different numbers of hired workers as shown in Table 7-3.

TABLE 7-4

Number of Hired Workers	Marginal Physical Product	Wage at Which That Number of Workers Would Be Hired	Wage	Number of Workers Demanded
1	85	81–85	85	0–1
2	81	74–81	82–84	1
3	74	69–74	81	1–2
4	69	63–69	75–80	2
5	63	51–63	74	2–3
6	51	39–51	70–73	3
7	39	39 or less	69	3–4
			64–68	4
			63	4–5
			52–62	5
			51	5–6
			40–50	6
			39	6–7
			38	7

By this sort of comparison of output and cost, the landowner can ascertain that his net income would be maximized by hiring three workers. He cannot control the wage, but he can decide the most advantageous number of persons to employ. This is the same result he could have reached by marginal productivity analysis. The marginal physical product of the third worker was 74, so he is worth adding. By employing a third man, the employer raises his own income by the difference between marginal physical product and wage ($74 - 70 = 4$). Beyond this point, however, the marginal product falls below the wage. To add a fourth hired worker would add only 69 bushels to output, which would cause the landowner to lose net income of 1 bushel.

If each landowner follows the marginal-product rule (implicitly or explicitly), then the marginal-product schedule on each tract of land can be used to derive a demand schedule for labor on that tract. The derivation is shown in Table 7-4 (using land grade E again to illustrate).

market demand schedule for labor

A demand schedule of the type shown in Table 7-4 can be constructed for each tract of land in the economy. The market demand for hired labor can then be derived simply by adding together the demand schedules for the individual tracts of land. If you have understood the foregoing, you should be able to make this derivation yourself. To give you some help, we will derive one point on it for you. Then take your pencil and try to calculate the others. When you are finished, compare your results with those drawn in Figure 7-1.

To calculate points on the aggregate demand schedule, it is useful to have a table showing the marginal productivity schedules for the different grades of land, as shown In Table 7-5. Let us try to establish the point on the market demand

TABLE 7-5

Hired Workers	Marginal Products on Land of Grade				
	A	B	C	D	E
1	46	57	66	76	85
2	44	53	61	71	81
3	42	48	55	62	74
4	36	43	47	58	69
5	25	33	41	49	63
6	20	29	33	45	51
7	15	24	26	35	39
Number of tracts	100	80	60	40	30
Workers demanded at wage 55	0	80	120–180	160	150

schedule corresponding to a wage of 55 bushels. First, we need to determine how many hired workers would be demanded on each grade of land. We can do this by reading down the marginal productivity schedule until the figure drops below 55. We have drawn lines across each column where this occurs. By rapid inspection, we see that there will be a demand for 1 hired worker on each tract in category B, for either 2 or 3 workers on each tract of land in category C, for 4 workers on each tract of category D, and for 5 workers on each tract of category E. Since there are 80 tracts of grade B land, a total of 80 workers will be demanded for those tracts. Similarly, we total the number demanded on each other category. The results, shown along the bottom of the table, add up to the total number of hired workers demanded at wage 55, namely between 510 and 570. (The range results from the fact that 55 is a *point of indifference* for grade C; landowners in that grade wish to employ any number from 120 to 180.)

By a similar method, we establish the other points on the demand schedule. The result is shown in Figure 7-1. Because of the discontinuities in the figures, we end up with what mathematicians call a step function rather than a continuous curve of the sort which we drew in previous chapters. As in much of this chapter, the particular shape of the curve should be regarded as a concession to numerical simplicity.

Our demand schedule possesses one property of importance and probable general validity: it is downward sloping. This means that the number of jobs available varies inversely with the (real) wage rate. This result follows directly from the principle of diminishing returns. Later on, when we analyze the demand for labor

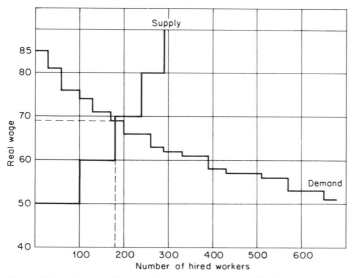

Figure 7-1 Labor-market supply, demand, and equilibrium wage.

in a more complex society, we will still argue that the individual firm has a down-ward-sloping demand curve for labor, or for any other factor of production.

equilibrium

In Figure 7-1, we have brought together the market demand and supply schedules relating to hired labor. The supply schedule is an upward-sloping step function, with the steps coming at points corresponding to the self-sufficiency outputs which workers can obtain on their own land. Behind this lies the general proposition that the willingness to work (or to supply any factor of production) depends on the alternatives available. In the real world, the alternative might be leisure; here we have assumed it is self-employment.

Equilibrium will occur where supply and demand are equal: that is, where the two curves cross in the diagram. This occurs at a wage rate of 69, at which level a total of 180 hired workers are employed. At any higher wage, the number of jobs would fall below the number of available workers, and the wage would fall. At any lower wage, the number of workers would be less than the number of vacancies, and the wage would be bid up.

The equilibrium position has a number of noteworthy aspects. First, observe how many things have been determined. Not only has it produced a determinate outcome for the wage level and number of hired workers, but in addition decisions have been made which determine the total output of the economy and the choice of a particular pattern of resource allocation. By their decisions concerning the number of workers to employ, the landowners have also adopted a particular output target. And in the shift from self-sufficiency to a labor market, the economy as a whole has changed its method of production and has altered its allocation of resources. Previously, the prevailing pattern was one in which each person cultivated his own tract of land. Now, with hired labor being used, some tracts of land have several workers on them, while other tracts have been withdrawn from production. The same quantity of land is available, but less of it is being used than before. Finally, in addition to these dimensions of the outcome, we find also that a new pattern has emerged with respect to the distribution of income.

Let us compare more closely the state of affairs when the economy was divided into self-sufficient farms, and the situation after introducing the labor market and arriving at the equilibrium wage. With a wage of 69, who works for whom and where? Clearly our hired workers are drawn from the low-productivity tracts of land. Owners of land in grades A and B find it advantageous to work for wages. Owners of land in grade C continue to cultivate their own land. They can earn an income of 70 by doing so, and thus will not themselves work for wages. On the other hand, they cannot benefit by hiring workers, as the wage of 69 which they would have to pay is higher than the marginal product of hired labor on their land (that is, 66).

Owners of the highest-grade lands, in categories D and E, do find it advantageous to hire workers. Owners of grade D land hire 2 workers each, providing a total of 80 jobs. Owners of the best land, grade E, hire at least 3 workers each, and some hire 4, since 69 is a point of indifference to them. All told, the 180 hired workers are deployed so that 80 of them work on grade D land and 100 on land of grade E. (On grade E land, twenty farms employ 3 workers each and ten farms employ 4 workers each).

effects on total output

Let us see what effects this reallocation of labor has had on the total output of the economy. Initially, each tract of land was in use. Now only the land in grades C, D, and E is used, but much of it is cultivated more intensively. The behavior of output can be followed in Table 7-6.

The result of the reallocation of labor is that the total output of the economy has been increased substantially, from 19,900 under self-sufficiency to 23,870 with a labor market. This result is not just a random accident, but a systematic result of an allocation based on considerations of wage and marginal productivity. The increase in output occurred because the labor market tended to draw workers out of employments in which their marginal productivity was low and into employments where marginal productivity was high. Suppose the first worker moved out of land of category A and went to work on category E. His withdrawal at one end caused output to fall by 50, which was his marginal product on land grade A. By adding his labor on land grade E, output could be increased by 85. Of course, as more workers are shifted, the gains become smaller. The additions to output on the good land decline, because of diminishing returns, while at the other end, workers are shifting out of better land. Eventually, a point is reached beyond which no further advan-

TABLE 7-6

| Land Grade | Output Before | | | Output After | | |
	TRACTS	PER TRACT	TOTAL OUTPUT	TRACTS	PER TRACT	TOTAL OUTPUT
A	100	50	5,000	100	0	0
B	80	60	4,800	80	0	0
C	60	70	4,200	60	70	4,200
D	40	80	3,200	40	227	9,080
E	30	90	2,700	20	330	6,600
				10	399	3,990
Total			19,900			23,870

tageous shifts can be made. Our position of labor market equilibrium is such a position. No further reallocation is possible which would further increase output. And this sort of maximum position has a very important formal property, which can be expressed this way: *Given the existence of factors of production which are individually homogeneous in quality, the maximum output of the economy is achieved when each factor is allocated among alternative uses in such a way that its marginal product is the same in every use.* This principle of the equalization of marginal products is a central concept in the analysis of economic efficiency. Later on we will want to refine it a bit; here we state it merely in terms of marginal physical products.

The theorem has an obvious corollary: If a factor is allocated in such a way that its marginal product is *not* the same in all uses, the total output of the economy can be increased by moving that factor out of the employment in which its marginal product is lower and into an employment where its marginal product is higher.

In our numerical example, there are discontinuities in the figures, and the marginal products are not literally equalized throughout. They are merely close. However, no reallocation is possible which would increase total output. If we moved one man from land grade E to grade D, we would reduce output by 69 bushels on grade E in order to gain only 62 bushels on D. A shift from C to E would cost 70 bushels in order to gain 69. And so on.

Our analysis not only establishes a standard for an efficient allocation of resources, but implies that a free and competitive market will tend to bring about such an allocation. Such a result clearly follows from our assumptions: that there is a single, uniform wage, that it equates supply and demand, and that each firm employs a sufficient number of workers to equate the marginal physical product of labor to the wage. But we have not established that markets meeting these conditions exist in the real world. In that sense the most critical questions are still to be explored.

With due allowance for discontinuities, we can observe an important property of our equilibrium wage rate: *It is equal to the marginal physical product of the entire labor force.* Indeed, this is the only outcome consistent with our assumption that the equilibrium wage equates supply with demand. A wage higher than the marginal physical product of the entire labor force would leave unemployed some people seeking hired employment. And a wage below the marginal physical product of the entire labor force would cause landowners to attempt to add more hired workers than would be available.

the distribution of income

The same process which determines the volume of production and the allocation of resources also settles the distribution of income. Again it is useful to compare "before" and "after"—that is, the state of affairs under self-sufficiency and that

TABLE 7-7

Land Grade	Income Before	Income After
A	50	69
B	60	69
C	70	70
D	80	89
E	90	123

under the competitive labor market. In Table 7-7 we show the per capita incomes of the owners of land in different grades. The owners of poor-grade lands A and B benefit because the wage they receive is substantially above what they earned as self-sufficient farmers. The owners of high-grade lands D and E benefit because they can hire workers at a wage which is less than the *average* productivity of the workers. The owner of grade D land is able to increase his output by 147 bushels by hiring two men, to whom he must pay 138 bushels in wages. The owner of grade E land is able to increase his output (over the self-sufficiency level) by 240 bushels, of which he must pay 207 in wages.

Is this result fair? This is not a question which can be answered by economic analysis. Questions of fairness and justice, like all judgments involving goodness or badness, can only be dealt with by the use of value judgments, and value judgments cannot be established by any purely scientific, logical, or objective means.

Here we will merely point out that income distribution has been influenced by a combination of two forces. First, the introduction of a labor market has equalized incomes insofar as they are derived from labor alone. The people who were stuck with land in category A have now been given a chance to work on the high productivity land and to share in the benefits of its high productivity.

Indeed, the emergence of an equilibrium wage rate gives us the basis for assigning (imputing) a value to *labor* services and *labor* income for all members of the work force. Since all persons are assumed to furnish labor of identical quality, it follows that each has the same marginal product, namely something close to 69 bushels. This is the marginal product of the labor of the richest landowner; it is the amount by which his output would decline if he decided to cease working.

If each person's labor income is 69, it follows that anything earned beyond that represents an income received because of the ownership of land. In fact, we will call this part of income the *implicit rent* derived from the land, even though it does not represent an actual payment from lessee to lessor in the legal or institutional sense. Implicitly, at least, the owner of land in grade C receives a rent of 1 bushel, the owner of land in grade D a rent of 20 bushels, and the fortunate owner of land in grade E, a rent of 54 bushels. Some land is not worth cultivating: namely, land on which the marginal product of labor is below the equilibrium wage rate. Such land yields no rent; thus the owners of land in grades A and B derive no income from them. (This is not very realistic, of course; presumably they could still use the land to live on, and to raise a garden and some livestock for their own use.)

This is not the place to attempt to develop a complete theory of rent. Nevertheless, it is apparent that the implicit rents yielded by the different grades do reflect differences in their productivity. And while we have not introduced buying and selling of land into our analysis, one may assume that the selling prices of different tracts of land would tend to bear some proportional relationship to the rents which could be derived from owning them.

increase in labor force

Let us suppose that the population of our hypothetical society is increasing. Since the quantity of land is fixed in supply, there must occur some changes in the pattern of property ownership. For instance, existing tracts of land might simply be subdivided among the heirs of a family. At the other extreme, something like primogeniture might be observed, by means of which land tracts would remain undivided in the possession of one heir (the eldest son) of the family, while the other children would be obliged to make some other provision for themselves.

Obviously it will be a matter of some importance to the distribution of income whether land ownership continues to be widespread or is concentrated. For illustrative purposes, we will concentrate on the case where land ownership is not subdivided. There are several reasons for choosing this possibility. In particular, it enables us to introduce into our model a group of landless persons. It corresponds to the historical trend which has occurred in some important western countries, such as England. And it would also apply to a situation where population growth occurred through immigration.

We assume that our production function remains the same, and that the number of persons owning land is unchanged, at 310, but that an additional 100 persons enter the labor force—persons who do not own any land and are dependent entirely on wages for their livelihood. We will assume these landless persons are willing to work for whatever wage they can obtain. Thus the supply schedule of hired labor will be shifted to the right by 100 workers at any given wage rate. Figure 7-2 illustrates this shift.

Since the productivity schedules have not shifted, the demand schedule for hired workers is unchanged. It is also shown in the diagram. Because of the increase in supply, the labor market is not in equilibrium at the former wage of 69. Quantity supplied exceeds quantity demanded, and consequently the wage rate tends to fall. With lower wage rates, owners of good land are willing to employ more men. We assume that a new equilibrium wage eventually emerges, one at

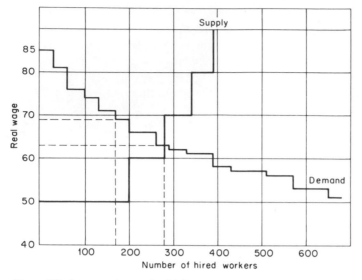

Figure 7-2 Increase in supply of labor.

which the quantity of hired workers demanded is equal to the quantity supplied. This new wage rate will be equal (or very close to) the marginal physical product of the enlarged labor force. Because of the law of diminishing returns, the increase in labor force pushes the society down to a lower level of marginal product, and the wage is lower than before.

Specifically, the addition of 100 workers drives the wage rate down from 69 bushels to 63. At that level, there will be 280 workers seeking work. Of these, 60 will work on land of grade C, 80 on grade D, and the remaining 140 on land of grade E.

The extent to which the wage must fall in order to increase employment opportunities depends on the *elasticity of demand* for labor. The increase in jobs from 180 to 280 represents a percentage increase of about 43.5, while the decrease in wage which brought it about was from 69 to 63, or about 9 percent. The coefficient of elasticity between these points on the demand schedule has, thus, a numerical value of nearly 5.0, which is quite high. As a result of the high elasticity of demand, the total amount of wages paid increases. Had the elasticity coefficient been less than unity, total wage payments would have decreased.

What determines the elasticity of demand for labor? In our example, it depends on the character of the productivity schedule, particularly on the degree to which diminishing returns operates. The more sharply the marginal physical product declines with increased labor input, the lower the elasticity of demand for labor would be.

TABLE 7-8

Land Grade	Output Before			Output After		
	TRACTS	PER TRACT	TOTAL OUTPUT	TRACTS	PER TRACT	TOTAL OUTPUT
A			0			0
B			0			0
C	60	70	4,200	60	136	8,160
D	40	227	9,080	40	227	9,080
E	20	330	6,600	20	462	9,240
	10	399	3,990	10	399	3,990
Total			23,870			30,470

total output and its distribution

With more workers available to cultivate the fixed supply of land, total output increases. Workers are added to tracts in grades C, D, and E. The before and after output pattern is as shown in Table 7-8. The total output increases by 6,600 bushels. However, we have increased the number of workers (hired and otherwise), from 310 to 410. This means that the output per worker has declined from 77 bushels, on the average, to slightly over 74 bushels. This is a reflection of the principle of diminishing returns.

This reduction in income is by no means evenly spread. Table 7-9 shows what happens to the incomes of owners of various grades of land as a result of the rise in population and the fall in wages. Here is a fine state of affairs! The rich are getting richer and the poor are getting poorer. The reasons for the divergence are not hard to identify. Those who are dependent on wages suffer a decline in incomes. But those who own better grades of land are in a position to benefit by being able to buy labor more cheaply. As a result, their incomes increase.

TABLE 7-9

Land Grade	Income Before	Income After	Net Change
A	69	63	−6
B	69	63	−6
C	70	73	+3
D	89	101	+12
E	123	157	+34

Technically, this reflects the fact that the implicit rents on their tracts of land have risen.

classical economics

The sort of model and problem we have been discussing constituted an important element of so-called political economy as it existed in Great Britain in the first half of the nineteenth century. The Reverend Thomas R. Malthus argued that as long as wages were above the level required for subsistence, population would increase. Because of diminishing returns, output would not be able to increase in proportion to population; thus wages would be forced down to the subsistence level, by a process comparable to that in the example just concluded. His friend David Ricardo observed that the growth of population would tend to raise rents, so that the landlord class would be the chief beneficiaries of economic progress. Their forecasts of what would occur if population growth were not checked led many people to refer to economics as the dismal science. Malthus and Ricardo argued that in effect the real cause of mass poverty lay in overpopulation, and that the poor would be unable to improve their status until they were willing to limit their numbers.

It is not difficult to find countries in which the problem of overpopulation in the Malthusian sense is serious. However, many regions of the world have found ways of escaping it. One expedient has been to bring additional lands into cultivation. The great expansion of cultivated areas in the Americas helped absorb population growth in the nineteenth century. Furthermore, in western societies, population growth was slowed by decreases in birth rates, as families became increasingly willing and able to limit the number of children. However, a decisive element in averting the Malthusian disaster was the sustained improvement in technology, coupled with a massive increase in capital to embody it. In Europe and America agricultural output has increased more rapidly than population, creating political problems of surplus production.

In terms of our model, technological innovation would tend to raise the productivity of labor and shift the demand schedule to the right. Increased productivity would tend to raise income per capita and also the real wage. Of course the precise effect on income distribution would depend on the character of the technical changes. Labor-saving innovations might raise the average product of labor without raising the marginal product, while land-saving innovations might reduce the ability of landlords to obtain income from rents. Historically, technical change and capital growth benefited the wage-earning group on the average, but benefits were not certain or evenly distributed among industry or occupational groups.

summary

In this chapter, we developed a model of a simple economy utilizing two factors, land and labor, to produce one product. Beginning with self-sufficient production by each family on its own land, we introduced a competitive market for wage labor. The supply schedule for labor developed on the basis of what each person could earn on his own land. The demand schedule for labor developed from the schedule of its marginal physical productivity. The wage rate equated supply and demand at a level equal to the marginal physical product of the entire labor force.

The shift from self-sufficiency to hired labor increased the total output of the economy by shifting workers into areas where their marginal productivity was higher. Ultimately, in competitive equilibrium, maximum total output was reached where the marginal physical product of the labor force (assumed homogeneous in quality) was the same on every tract of land using labor.

In the process of reaching an equilibrium wage, the economic system also settled into a determinate pattern with respect to total output, the method of production (in the sense of how to match up tracts of land with workers), and the distribution of income. Imputing to each worker the going rate of wages, we could determine an implicit rent, representing the added income resulting from the ownership of good land.

An increase in the labor force, in the form of additional landless workers seeking wage employment, tended to lower the equilibrium wage rate, to an extent depending on the elasticity of demand for labor. Total output increased, but output per capita declined because of diminishing returns. Income inequality increased as wage earners suffered diminished incomes and owners of good land found their incomes increased by the opportunity to obtain labor more cheaply. Such a process of worker impoverishment through population growth played a large part in the gloomy outlook of English political economy in the nineteenth century.

However, in world economic history, the adverse effects of population growth and diminishing returns have been offset in some areas by technical innovation. If innovation raises the schedule of the marginal product of labor, the demand for labor tends to rise, and the equilibrium wage rate tends to be higher.

Our model is not a very realistic one. But quite a few of the conclusions have validity in the real world as well. The nature of marginal productivity and its relation to the demand for a factor of production, the principle of the equalization of marginal products, the simultaneous determination of the volume of output, the pattern of resource use, and the distribution of income, the imputation of income to rent and wages—all these are ideas which we will wish to develop further. You will find things much easier later if you study them attentively now, without being too annoyed by the lack of realism in the model.

TERMS AND CONCEPTS

1. Marginal physical product
2. Equilibrium real wage
3. Implicit rent

QUESTIONS AND PROBLEMS

1. Explain why the output of the economy in this model is maximized when labor is used in such a way as to equalize its marginal product in all uses.

2. Explain why the equilibrium real wage tends to be equal to the marginal product of the labor force.

3. The specific results of the model contained in this chapter depend on the numbers of people owning land of various grades. Using the same production function and other assumptions, run through the exercise again using the following values for the number of people owning land of each category:

   A 80
   B 70
   C 50
   D 20
   E 10

   Describe the economic situation under self-sufficiency and with a competitive labor market. Calculate the supply and demand schedules for hired workers and derive the equilibrium wage rate. Show how the hired workers would be employed at this rate. Compare the total output and income distribution under self-sufficiency with those under the competitive labor market.

4. Explain why the demand schedule for hired labor in this model is downward sloping.

5. Starting from the equilibrium position shown in Figure 7-1, assume that the members of the hired labor force decide to seek higher wages through trade-union activity.
   (a) What would happen if the workers on one farm tried to obtain higher wages through forming a union among themselves?
   (b) Suppose all the hired workers in the economy form a union. They demand an increase in wages from the existing level of 69 to a new level of 75. If they succeed, what economic consequences will follow? Why might the union have trouble holding its members?
   (c) Assume that the union undertakes to compensate any of its members who become displaced by the higher wage. It pays them the difference between their former income of 69 and their self-employment income if they are obliged to return to farming. The funds are raised by making a proportional assessment against the wages of the people who are still

being hired. What would the result be? What is the highest wage the union could obtain and still successfully use this sort of compensation system? What property of the demand schedule for labor determines the outcome?

(d) Suppose the labor union becomes so strong that it can compel the employers to accept an "all-or-none bargain." That is, each employer is free to hire no workers, if he chooses. But if he wants to hire any, he must employ the same number as he did in the competitive equilibrium, and pay each of them 75 bushels. What would the outcome be?

selection of least-cost input combination

In Chapter 6 we discussed the production function of the firm, expressing the physical relationship between input and output on the basis of a given condition of technology, organizational skill, and quality of inputs. The production function is a way of representing a range of choices open to the firm. The firm must decide what quantity of output to produce and what quantities of inputs to purchase.

At times, the production function may prescribe one unique set of inputs which must be acquired in order to produce a chosen output target. The firm may find itself obliged to maintain fixed proportions among inputs for technological reasons. The firm may be heavily committed to a specific design of capital equipment, under which each machine requires a fixed amount of manpower, raw materials, fuel, etc.

However, in the long run, firms usually have considerable opportunity to make substitutions among various inputs. To put it another way, the production function in the long run is more likely to present the firm with several possible ways of producing any given output. Such input substitutions can be made more easily when the firm is not committed to a particular design of capital equipment, but can vary the specifications. It may be necessary to change the form of machinery in order to vary the quantity of manpower, raw materials, and fuel required per unit of machinery.

We will concentrate our attention on simple and rather unrealistic long-run production functions which offer the firm opportunities for continuous substitution among inputs. The prototype of such a function is the one we introduced in Chapter 6, namely

$$Q = 10 \sqrt{ab}$$

where Q stands for the quantity of output, and a and b for the quantities of two inputs. Any specific quantity of output which the firm wants to produce can be produced in an infinite variety of ways, by varying the proportions of the inputs a and b. Consider the output of 50 units. Substituting for Q in the equation, we find that this output can be obtained from any input combination such that $ab = 25$. Indeed, we can construct a schedule showing the quantity of one input appropriate for any given quantity of the other input, for producing this output.

Input a	Input b
1	25
2	12.5
3	8.33
4	6.25
5	5

diagrammatic representation

Having expressed the long-run production function in numerical and algebraic terms, we will also find it useful to show it graphically. For this purpose, we use a device much like the consumer indifference curves employed in Chapter 3. Let the two axes represent quantities of two inputs. Find any point in the coordinate map representing a combination of positive values for the two inputs. Corresponding to that point there is some corresponding quantity of output, which can be determined from the algebraic formula. However, that same quantity of output can also be produced by other combinations of the inputs. We can (conceptually) identify all the different combinations capable of producing any given output, locate each one as a point in the diagram, and connect all these points with a curve. This we call an *isoproduct* curve, or *production isoquant*. The prefix "iso" means "same"; all points on the curve represent the same level of output.

To derive a production isoquant for the output of 100, we set our production function equal to 100, then insert a succession of values for one input and determine the corresponding values for the other. In carrying out this operation, it is useful to rewrite the equation so that a is expressed in terms of b. The transformation goes like this:

$$Q = 10\sqrt{ab}$$
$$100 = 10\sqrt{ab}$$
$$10 = \sqrt{ab}$$

Since we are restricting ourselves to positive values, we can square both sides, obtaining $100 = ab$, which reduces to $a = 100/b$. Note that the solution is a formula for a rectangular hyperbola.

Figure 8-1 shows the curves for outputs of 25, 50, 75, and 100. Since we have assumed that the production function is continuous, we could construct a similar isoquant through any point in the diagram.

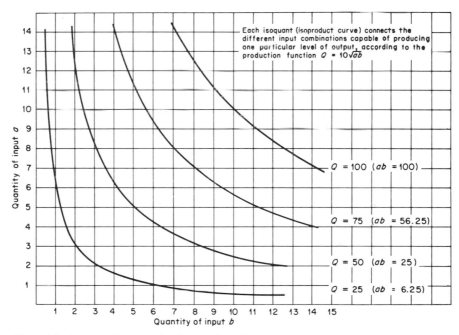

Figure 8-1 Isoproduct curves (an isoquant map).

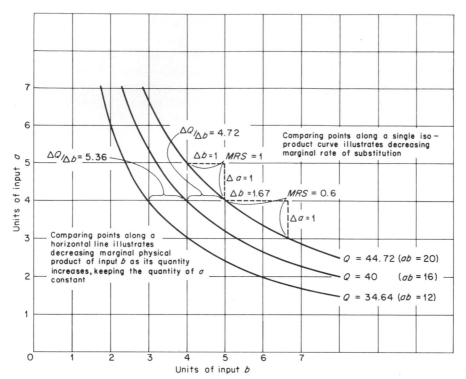

Figure 8-2 Marginal product and marginal rate of substitution.

input substitution

Isoproduct curves typically slope downward to the right. This reflects a process of substitution. As one input is reduced, the quantity of the other must be increased to keep output unchanged. Furthermore, the inputs are subject to a diminishing marginal rate of substitution for one another, because they are imperfect substitutes. By the marginal rate of substitution we mean the ratio of the changes in the two inputs involved in moving along a production isoquant.

The marginal rate of input substitution can be expressed either in terms of a finite movement from one point on an isoquant to another or as a property of the isoquant at a given point.

In Figure 8-2 isoquants are drawn through several adjoining integral values of a and b. Consider the isoquant representing 44.72 units of output (which joins all points which have the property that $a \cdot b = 20$). We can produce this amount of output with 4 units of a and 5 of b, or with 5 units of a and 4 of b. The marginal rate of substitution can be expressed as

$$\frac{\Delta a}{\Delta b}$$

Remember that we always put in the top of the fraction the variable measured on the vertical axis. Between the two points noted, the marginal rate of substitution is 1. (We ignore the minus sign.) To keep output constant when we reduce the input of a by 1 unit, we must increase the input of b by 1 unit. But if we continue along the isoquant and reduce the input of a from 4 to 3 units, we must add 1.67 units of b to keep output constant. The ratio between the increments is now 1 to 1.67, or 0.6. This is what we mean by a diminishing marginal rate of substitution. As the quantity of a is reduced, the substitution ratio declines. The less of a is being used, the more difficult it is to reduce the input of a still further.

The marginal rate of substitution can also be expressed by the derivative of the isoquant at a point. The equation for this isoquant is $a = 20/b$, and its derivative is $-20/b^2$ (although we usually disregard the minus sign). Obviously, as b increases (and a declines), the marginal rate of substitution declines. Decreasing MRS reflects the fact that the two inputs are not perfect substitutes for each other; that is, each one contributes something relatively unique to the productive process which cannot be completely matched by the other.

Geometrically, the marginal rate of substitution at a point on the isoquant is measured by the slope of a tangent to the curve at that point.

marginal physical product

We have already identified the marginal physical product (MPP) of an input as the change in quantity of output associated with a change in employment of that input, when the quantities of other inputs are held constant. In Chapter 7 we used extensively a measure of MPP derived between discrete points on a production function. This interpretation is illustrated in the left portion of Figure 8-2. The quantity of input a is taken as 4. With 3 units of input b, output is 34.64 units. Increasing the quantity of b by one unit adds 5.36 units to output. Adding a further unit of b raises output by 4.72 units.

The marginal physical product can also be expressed as the derivative of the production function with respect to one input when the other input is being held constant. Given a production function $Q = 10\sqrt{ab}$, the schedule expressing MPP_b would take this general form:

$$MPP_b = \frac{dQ}{db} = \frac{5a^{1/2}}{b^{1/2}}$$

When the quantity of input a is taken as 4, this expression reduces to $10/b^{1/2}$. These expressions indicate that the value of MPP_b varies inversely with the quantity of input b, as postulated by the law of diminishing returns.

Marginal physical product and marginal rate of substitution differ in respect to what varies and what is held constant. MPP is calculated holding one input constant and letting output vary in response to the other input. MRS is calculated by holding output constant and letting the two inputs vary in opposite directions. But MPP and MRS are closely related mathematically: at any given point MRS is equal to the (inverse) ratio of the marginal physical products of the two inputs, so that $da/db = MPP_b/MPP_a$. The marginal physical product of a is represented by dQ/da, and the MPP of b is dQ/db. Thus $MPP_b/MPP_a = (dQ/db)/(dQ/da)$. In determining the marginal rate of substitution, we want to keep output constant, so we consider the dQ elements as canceling out in top and bottom, leaving da/db, which is the MRS.

This relationship can be illustrated at the point where $a = 4$ and $b = 5$. The marginal rate of substitution da/db is $20/b^2 = \frac{4}{5}$. The marginal physical product of a is the derivative of $Q = 10\sqrt{5a}$, which derivative has the general value $11.18/\sqrt{a}$ and solves out to 5.59 when $a = 4$. The marginal physical product of b is expressed by the derivative of $Q = 20\sqrt{b}$. Thus $MPP_b = 10/\sqrt{b} = 4.47$ when $b = 5$. Putting them together, we obtain, $MPP_b/MPP_a = 4.47/5.59 = \frac{4}{5} = da/db$.

choice and efficiency

Our isoproduct curves reflect an economic fact of great importance: in the long run there are many different input combinations capable of producing any given output. Some of the possible ways have already been eliminated from the picture by assuming that the firm's production function consists of technically efficient ways of using any given input combination. Now the firm is confronted with a problem of *economic efficiency*, which cannot be solved with technical information alone. Technical efficiency enables the firm to obtain the maximum output from any given quantity of resources. In seeking economic efficiency, however, the firm is attempting to *produce any given output at the lowest possible cost.*

Which is the cheapest method of producing 100 units of output—twenty machines and five workers, or five machines and twenty workers? Or is it cheaper to produce with 10 units of each? We cannot determine this until we know the *prices* which the firm must pay for the respective inputs. For simplicity, we continue to assume that the firm operates in a purely competitive market for inputs. Thus it takes input prices as given and merely adjusts its quantity of inputs to them. On this assumption, given any set of input prices, it is fairly easy to determine which of a given set of input combinations is the cheapest. Try it on the three combinations in this paragraph, assuming that machinery services cost $1,000 per unit and labor services $100 per unit. Then reverse the prices.

A graphic approach is useful in describing the solution to the least-cost problem. In analyzing consumer behavior, we used the device of a budget line, which showed all combinations of two products which a consumer could purchase with a given sum of money. Similarly, with any given set of input prices, we can connect with an *isocost line* all the combinations of the two inputs which can be purchased with a given sum of money. However, we do *not* assume that the total expenditure of the firm is given. Total expenditure can only be determined after we have identified the most profitable level of output, after an analysis of revenue and costs. The set of input prices defines a whole family of isocost lines; we need more information to identify the one which will be most advantageous for the firm. Figure 8-3 shows a set of isocost lines corresponding to prices of $60 for a and $40 for b. With $240, the firm could buy 4 units of a, and none of b, or 6 units of b, and none of a. The intercept points are thus defined as $240/P_a$ and $240/P_b$. Dividing the vertical intercept by the horizontal gives the slope, which equals P_b/P_a (or $\frac{2}{3}$ in this case). Isocost lines representing other amounts of expenditure will be parallel, having the same slope.

Our diagram can now be used for quick comparison of the costs of different ways of producing any desired output. Consider the output of 24.5, represented by $ab = 6$. Starting in the upper left and moving along that isoquant, we cross a series of isocost lines representing successively lower total expenditures. With one unit of b and 6 of a, cost is $400. With 2 of b and 3 of a, total cost is $260. Eventually a point is reached where the isoquant is just tangent to an isocost line. This is where $b = 3$ and $a = 2$, with total costs of $240. If we continue beyond this point, decreasing a and increasing b further, we cross the isocost lines again, but now they represent successively higher expenditures. The tangent point is thus the least-cost method of producing 24.5 units of output.

We could also visualize the firm moving along an isocost line and seeing what amount of output could be obtained for a given expenditure. The tangency position with an isoquant represents the largest output obtainable for a given expenditure.

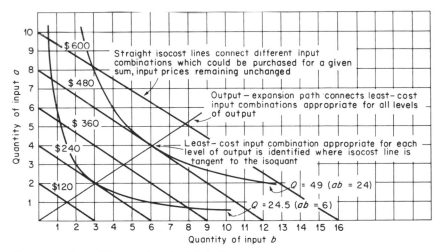

Figure 8-3 Isocost lines and cost minimization.

The point of tangency is a point at which the slope of the isocost line is equal to the slope of the production isoquant. Thus the marginal rate of input substitution is equal to the inverse ratio of the input prices. In algebraic terms, we can express this as $da/db = P_b/P_a$. The point which fulfills this condition represents the least-cost combination of inputs for producing that particular quantity of output.

The isoquant representing 24.5 units of output is represented by the equation $ab = 6$. The marginal rate of substitution is equal to the derivative da/db, which is $6/b^2$. Setting this equal to the price ratio of 2 to 3, we obtain $6 = 2b^2/3$, which yields $b = 3$. Since $ab = 6$, $a = 2$.

The equilibrium position can be described in another way. In equilibrium, if the firm relinquishes $1 worth of one input, it will have to add $1 worth of the other to keep output unchanged. If the firm is not employing the optimum input proportions, however, it can get rid of $1 worth of one input and keep output constant by adding less than $1 worth of another. If the firm were operating where $MRS = 1$, for instance, it could eliminate $1 worth of input a but keep output constant by adding $0.67 worth of input b.

The least-cost input combination can be identified in terms of marginal physical products. Specifically, the optimum input position of the firm will be one in which the ratio of the marginal physical products of any two inputs is equal to the ratio of their prices. This follows from the conditions we derived above. We have seen that the marginal rate of input substitution will equal the inverse ratio of input prices at the equilibrium position. Thus $da/db = P_b/P_a$. We know that the marginal rate of substitution is equal to the inverse ratio of the marginal physical products, thus $da/db = MPP_b/MPP_a$. Setting these two expressions equal to each other yields $MPP_b/MPP_a = P_b/P_a$ which can also be written $MPP_a/P_a = MPP_b/P_b$. The latter expression means that in order to minimize costs, the firm should adjust the quantity of each input so that a uniform ratio prevails between marginal physical product and input price. This condition can easily be extended to include any number of inputs.

The rules just described identify the least-cost combination of inputs appropriate for each feasible output. Each least-cost combination is represented by a point of tangency between an isocost line and an isoquant. If we connect all these tangency points, we identify an output-expansion path for the firm. Given the production function, the prices of the inputs, and the existence of pure competition in input markets, the firm will minimize costs if it operates on the output-expansion path. Efficient changes in output will be carried out by movement along the output-expansion path. Figure 8-3 illustrates an output-expansion path. The least-cost input combination for each output is located where the appropriate isoquant intersects the output-expansion path.

The output-expansion path can be identified algebraically when the production function is simple. To derive it from the production function $Q = 10\sqrt{ab}$, we square both sides and rearrange to obtain $a = Q^2/100b$. For any given value of Q, this expression has a derivative $da/db = (-)Q^2/100b^2$. Setting this equal to P_b/P_a (or $\frac{2}{3}$) and dropping the minus sign, we obtain

$$\frac{Q^2}{100b^2} = \frac{2}{3}$$

$$b^2 = \frac{3Q^2}{200}$$

Since $Q^2 = 100ab$, we substitute to obtain

$$b^2 = \frac{300ab}{200} \quad \text{and} \quad b = \frac{3a}{2}$$

This last expression relating b to a is an expression for the output-expansion path corresponding to the given production function and input prices. In this particular case it is a straight line (see Figure 8-3); that is, the optimum ratio between a and b is the same regardless of the quantity of output. With more complex production functions, this result would not necessarily occur.

We have not yet determined how much output the firm will produce. However, the points along the output-expansion path furnish the data from which we can derive a set of cost schedules to help us to identify the most profitable output for the firm. And once we have determined that output, we can refer to the appropriate point on the output-expansion path to find the combination of inputs suitable for producing that output at lowest cost.

change in input price

The location of the output-expansion path depends on the prices of the inputs. A shift in the price of one input relative to the other would cause the least-cost points to shift, and the entire output-expansion path would move. This is illustrated by Figure 8-4. We assume that the price of input b rises from \$40 to \$60. As a result, the isocost line representing \$240 shifts toward the origin, and becomes steeper in slope. The production isoquant $Q = 24.5$ no longer touches it. To find the least-cost method of producing that output, we must draw a new isocost line, with a slope representing the new price ratio (which is 1). This proves to be a line representing an expenditure of \$294, and it is tangent to the isoquant at the point where the firm would use equal amounts of the two inputs. At that point the slope of the isoquant (its derivative) is equal to unity.

The shift in the least-cost point occurs similarly on every other isoquant. As a result, the entire output-expansion path shifts to the left. What is being described is simply a process of input substitution. The firm initially settled upon an optimum

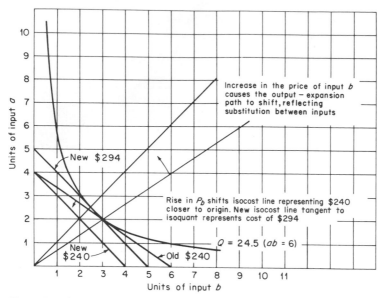

Figure 8-4 Change in input price.

input mix on the basis of one set of prices, and when the input-price structure shifted, the firm moved to a different input mix. The substitution has, as one would expect, worked against the input which has risen in price. For any given output, the firm will now use less b and more a than it would have done previously.

The magnitude of the potential substitution effect can be evaluated in terms of the concept of the *elasticity of substitution*. This is defined as the following ratio:

$$\frac{\text{Proportionate change in } a/b}{\text{Proportionate change in } db/da}$$

The upper term represents a proportionate change in the ratio of quantities of the two inputs. The lower term represents a proportionate change in their marginal rate of substitution. A change in input price would lead the firm to shift its input mix in order to bring the MRS into equality with the new input-price ratio. This elasticity coefficient indicates how large a shift in the input mix would result from any given (proportionate) change in input prices. A high coefficient of elasticity means a large substitution effect accompanying a given change in the ratio of input prices.

Of course, a rise in the price of input b has also the effect of increasing the cost of producing any given level of output. As we shall see, this is likely to cause changes in the total output of the firm. Thus it is likely to move from one production isoquant to another as well as exhibit substitution effects along any individual isoquant.

Indeed, just as we spoke of income effects and substitution effects in considering the effects of price changes on consumer purchases, so we will speak of output effects and substitution effects of changes in prices of inputs.

some complications

We have greatly oversimplified the problem of cost minimization to concentrate on the way in which producers tend to vary the mix of inputs in response to changes in their relative prices. In doing this we have assumed away one of the largest problems of day-to-day business management, which is getting the largest output from a given collection of inputs (the problem of technical efficiency). We have limited our analysis to conditions of pure competition, under which the prices of the inputs are not affected by changes in the quantity purchased by the individual firm. If the firm is confronted by upward-sloping supply schedules for inputs, more complex rules for cost minimization are required; these are discussed in Chapter 22.

There are also problems in defining the units of measurement for the inputs. Often these are expressed as some physical quantity multiplied by a time unit. We are accustomed to thinking of man-hours of labor; we could similarly speak of truck-hours of vehicle use, or acre-years of land. Such usage is fine as long as it corresponds to the basis on which inputs are paid for. If labor is paid by the hour, then a definite price attaches to the labor unit. However, if the workers are paid a monthly salary, it is much harder to identify the cost of a man-hour—especially the cost of adding an additional man-hour. If labor is remunerated on a piece-rate system, even greater problems are raised, since the wage ceases to be independent of the production function.

Inputs of the services of capital assets are particularly troublesome. Suppose the firm leases its trucks; a typical lease arrangement bases cost on both time units and use units: $10 a day plus 10¢ a mile. This reflects a basic condition which will also confront the firm which owns its trucks: their rates of depreciation and obsolescence depend on both time and use. The firm which owns its capital assets always incurs some interest cost, implicit or explicit, arising from the fact that capital goods must be paid for before they provide their services. The firm's costs for depreciation and maintenance will be mainly a function of truck-miles, while its interest cost (and perhaps part of depreciation) will be more a function of truck-years.

The cost-minimization decisions of the firm are rendered more difficult by considerations of this sort. In effect, the firm must decide what the optimum flow of capital-service inputs is, and also what the optimum stock of capital assets to hold is, where the stock and flow are not rigidly linked in fixed proportions.

Cost minimization is also complicated by situations of *joint production*, where a batch of inputs yields output of more than one product. Raising sheep produces output of meat and output of wool; cattle can be raised for meat and for milk. By modifications in methods of production, one can change the emphasis between outputs. The input mix of breed and feed which is best suited for dairy farming is not likely to be the best for beef production. It is still possible, at least on the conceptual level, to identify a least-cost input combination, but there may well be a different one for every combination of the outputs. Since the choice of outputs will be a function of their potential selling price, the final choice of input mix will only be determined as a part of a set of simultaneous decisions about output.

The problems of choosing an optimum livestock feed can be used to illustrate still more complexities. Suppose that the livestock raiser can identify several components of an adequate diet, such as vitamins, protein, and minerals, and wishes to feed each animal at least some minimum daily requirement. If dietary adequacy were defined solely in terms of calories, the conventional analysis would probably be adequate. But the effort to secure adequacy across a number of items, in cases where the criterion is chiefly the achievement of some minimum acceptable intake, typically cannot be expressed in terms of the marginal criteria we have used earlier in this chapter. For one thing, the diet problem typically involves "all-or-none" decisions. Items used in zero quantities do not necessarily meet the marginal conditions of least-cost analysis. Looked at another way, the diet problem means that the productivity or effectiveness of inputs cannot be reduced to a single quantitative element of output. And the criterion that the adequate diet must contain at least the minimum quota of each nutrient introduces a different sort of equation into the system of relationships.

The diet problem is a good example of the sort of managerial problem for which practical solutions can be obtained by linear programming, whereby the principles of matrix algebra can be used to identify a maximum or minimum solution involving constraints which make a problem beyond the scope of conventional marginal analysis.

summary

The long-run production function of the firm typically provides opportunities for substitution among inputs; that is, each output level can be reached by any one of several combinations of inputs. For two inputs, this relationship can be depicted by a set of isoproduct curves, or production isoquants, each of which connects the various input combinations capable of producing one specific output level. Such isoquants display a decreasing marginal rate of substitution; they become flatter as one moves further to the right, because of imperfect input substitutability.

The long-run least-cost combination of inputs for producing any desired output is found where the appropriate isoquant is tangent to an isocost line. At that point, the marginal rate of input substitution is equal to the (inverse) ratio of the prices of the inputs. Connecting all the tangency points (with a given production function and set of input prices) we obtain an output-expansion path showing the least-cost methods of producing all potential outputs. A shift in the relative prices of the inputs would cause a shift in the output-expansion path, as for each output the firm would tend to use less of the input which had become relatively more costly. In the real world, input substitution may occur in a discontinuous fashion, as firms shift from one process to another. Such shifts are more likely to occur in the long run, since they often involve changes in the form of capital equipment.

Having analyzed the least-cost method of producing each possible quantity of output, we still need to analyze the firm's selection of that output quantity which is most profitable. Before we can do that, we need to derive various measures of the firm's costs, an enterprise to which the next chapter is devoted.

TERMS AND CONCEPTS

1. Isoquant; isoproduct curve
2. Isocost line
4. Output-expansion path
5. Elasticity of substitution
3. Marginal rate of input substitution

QUESTIONS AND PROBLEMS

1. Assume a production function defined by the equation $Q = 5\sqrt{ab}$, where a and b are the quantities of two inputs.
   (a) Identify the expression for an isoquant representing an output of 25 units. Draw the isoquant. Derive a general expression for the marginal rate of substitution between inputs along this isoquant, and find the numerical value for MRS when $b = 4$.
   (b) Find the least-cost method of producing 25 units of output if the price of input a is $10 and the price of b is $5. Show the solution geometrically and algebraically. What is the total cost of producing 25 units if the least-cost input combination is used?
   (c) Using the same assumptions as in part (b), show how the least-cost input combination can be identified by using the marginal physical product schedules of the inputs. How does this approach relate to the one which uses the marginal rate of substitution?
   (d) Derive an expression for the output-expansion path, using the prices given for part (b). What would happen to the output-expansion path if the price of input a were to rise to $20? Show the shift geometrically.

2. Prove that for any production function in the form $Q = a^m b^n$ the output-expansion path will be a straight line, given the prices of the inputs.

9

the cost functions
of the firm

In the preceding chapter, we analyzed the firm's problem of identifying the least-cost method of producing each possible output. We first assumed that the firm would operate with technical and organizational efficiency, getting the largest possible output from any given combination of inputs. This assumption permitted us to identify a production function in which one unique quantity of output is associated with each possible combination of inputs. Under ordinary substitution opportunities, the firm would still have to choose (in the long run) among alternative ways of producing the same output. The least-cost input combination would be identified by equating the marginal rate of input substitution with the (inverse) ratio of the prices of the inputs. We shall use this information to explain the way in which the firm's input and output decisions would tend to be affected by changes in the prices (or supply conditions) of inputs and the price (or demand conditions) for its output.

what costs are

A firm's economic costs arise from the payments which it makes to obtain the services of inputs. Some of these inputs are intermediate products, purchased from other firms in the economy. And some are factors of production—labor, capital, etc. In this section, we make no distinction. Later we shall concentrate our attention on the ultimate factors of production.

By assuming that each firm is technically efficient and chooses the least-cost combination of inputs, we can identify one unique combination of inputs appropriate for each possible quantity of output (given the prices of inputs). This enables us to assign to any given output a unique measure of total cost. When this relationship is established for all possible outputs, it becomes a *total cost function* (or schedule) in which total cost is expressed as a function of the quantity of output.

In constructing the total cost function, we need to make explicit our assumption that *the cost of each input is equivalent to its market value*. We need an assumption of this sort to take care of situations in which accounting costs are not the same as economic costs. Consider the input of capital. If a firm uses borrowed funds, it incurs an accounting cost for interest on the loan. But if the firm uses capital provided by the owners, no such accounting cost is incurred. However, capital is a scarce resource, and it has an economic cost regardless of the source from which it is obtained. Our assumption is that capital must be assumed to have an *implicit cost* equal to its market "price" regardless of whether an explicit money payment is made by the firm or not. For the market price of capital we need some notion of a normal rate of interest or other return to capital; that is, some measure of what the owners of capital could have earned with it in another use. Unfortunately, this is not very precise and often cannot be measured in the real world. For our illustrations we will assume there is some sort of financial market and that a measurable rate of return exists on financial investments.

Divergence between accounting costs and economic costs may also arise in the cases of labor and land. Consider a self-employed shopkeeper. His income consists of the total net revenue of his shop. He does not receive any explicit wage. Nevertheless, his labor services impose an implicit cost on the firm, a cost equal to the market value of his labor—that is, the wage he could have earned by hiring himself out. Or consider the case of a farmer who owns his own land. He need make no explicit payment of rent for its use. Nevertheless, the land involves an implicit cost, equal to the amount of rent which the owner could have received by renting it to someone else. In the long run, factor services will be available only if they are paid as much as they could earn elsewhere. Thus implicit costs, like explicit costs, must be covered in the long run in order to obtain factor services.

the long-run total cost function

Corresponding to each output of the firm there is a single figure for total cost, provided we take as given the prices of the inputs and the technology and organizational skill of the firm which underlie the production function itself. In the following, we show how the total cost function can be derived.

We start with a production function which tells us the output which can be obtained from each combination of inputs; it is assumed to be $Q = \sqrt[3]{ab} = a^{1/3}b^{1/3}$. Second, we assume that the prices of the two inputs are \$40 for each unit of input a and \$10 for each unit of input b. On the basis of these data, the firm can determine the least-cost method of producing any given output. From this, it can determine the specific combination of inputs required for each level of output; by attaching prices to these, it can find a total cost figure.

Total cost consists of the expenditures for the inputs; the expenditure for each input is the product of quantity times price. In our example, total cost can be expressed as follows:

$$TC = a \cdot P_a + b \cdot P_b$$

We want to convert this into a function dependent on output Q. To make the conversion we can find expressions for the quantities of inputs a and b in terms of Q by setting the marginal rate of input substitution equal to the (inverse) ratio of input prices.

We can cube the production function and write it $Q^3 = ab$. Therefore $a = Q^3/b$ and $b = Q^3/a$. Treating Q as a constant, we can obtain the derivative da/db as follows:

$$\frac{da}{db} = (-)\frac{Q^3}{b^2}$$

Dropping the minus sign and setting the expression equal to P_b/P_a, we obtain $Q^3/b^2 = {}^{10}\!/_{40}$, which yields

$$b = 2Q^{3/2}$$

By a similar method, we set db/da equal to P_a/P_b and obtain

$$a = \frac{Q^{3/2}}{2}$$

Now we can substitute these values for a and b back into the total cost expression (along with the specific prices of a and b), deriving the following example of a total cost function:

$$TC = a \cdot P_a + b \cdot P_b = (40)\frac{Q^{3/2}}{2} + (10)(2Q^{3/2}) = 40Q^{3/2}$$

The expression $Q^{3/2}$ represents the square root of Q^3; multiplied by 40, this yields the total cost of that Q. In this function, total cost rises faster than output. One unit of output costs \$40; two units cost \$113. This result reflects the fact that this production function displays decreasing returns to scale. Had we used a production function in the form $Q = a^{1/2}b^{1/2}$, as we did in earlier chapters, total cost would have been a linear function of output, reflecting constant returns to scale. A production function subject to increasing returns would show total cost increasing less rapidly than output.

Our method of calculation helps to remind us that the total cost function for a competitive firm is based on given values for input prices and for the production function. A change in the price of an input would cause the total cost function to change in the same direction. A change in technology could also change the total cost function.

geometric representation

In Figure 9-1 the derivation of the total cost schedule is shown geometrically. At the top, where a production function and a set of input prices have been given, the least-cost combinations of inputs have been identified and connected by an output-expansion path. (The diagram does not reproduce the same production function or input-price data we used in the numerical example.) The total cost schedule is determined from the tangency points along the output-expansion path. Each of these tangency points has a pair of numbers associated with it. One number represents the total output at that point, the other represents the total cost. To draw total cost as a function of output (as in the lower diagram), we associate with each output (measured horizontally) the appropriate total cost (measured vertically). The upper diagram tells us that an output of 20 units is associated with a total cost of $75. Consequently in the lower diagram, we locate a point with a horizontal distance of 20 and a vertical distance of 75, and so on. (Note that the upper diagram is laid out in terms of inputs, and the lower in terms of outputs. Thus comparisons of distances on the two are meaningless.)

measures of unit cost

Once the total cost function has been derived, we are in a position to obtain some measures of cost per unit of output, measures which will be of great use in analyzing the most-profitable-output position of the firm. The two most common measures of cost per unit are *average cost* and *marginal cost*. Average cost is simply total cost divided by total output. Marginal cost is the *change* in total cost associated with a *change* in output. Marginal cost can be calculated for finite changes in output, in which case it is expressed as $\Delta TC/\Delta Q$. Marginal cost can also be calculated at a point on the total cost schedule; it is then simply the first derivative of total cost with respect to output (dTC/dQ).

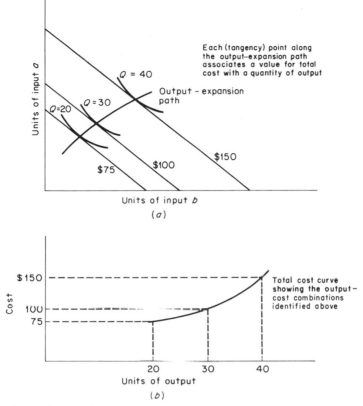

Figure 9-1 From isoquant map to cost curves.

In our example on page 143, we obtained a total cost function expressed by $TC = 40Q^{3/2}$. Dividing by Q gives us average cost, namely,

$$AC = \frac{40Q^{3/2}}{Q} = 40Q^{1/2}$$

Taking the derivative dTC/dQ of the total cost function yields marginal cost, expressed as follows:

$$MC = \frac{dTC}{dQ} = (3/2)\,(40Q^{1/2}) = 60Q^{1/2}$$

Observe that AC and MC expressions have the same exponent for the Q term; this result is typical of homogeneous production functions (scale elasticity the same

TABLE 9-1

Output (Q)	Total Cost (TC) ($10Q - 5Q^2 + Q^3$)	Average Cost (TC/Q)	Marginal Cost between Points ($\triangle TC/\triangle Q$)	Marginal Cost at a Point (dTC/dQ)
0	0			
1	6	6	6	3
2	8	4	2	2
3	12	4	4	7
4	24	6	12	18
5	50	10	26	35
6	96	16	46	58

throughout). A special case of this arises when the production function displays constant returns to scale and total cost is a linear function of output. If we have $TC = 5Q$, then

$$AC = \frac{5Q}{Q} = 5 \quad \text{and} \quad MC = \frac{dTC}{dQ} = 5$$

Average and marginal costs are both constant and are equal to each other.

It will be useful to consider an example which might arise from a nonhomogeneous production function. Suppose the total cost function is expressed as follows:

$$TC = 10Q - 5Q^2 + Q^3$$

Total cost for small integral values of Q would be as in Table 9-1. This cost function corresponds to our general conception of a normal shape. We assume that the typical production function shows an initial phase of increasing returns, but ultimately encounters decreasing returns to scale. This corresponds to a total cost function in which costs initially rise less rapidly than output, but eventually rise more rapidly.

In the table we have illustrated the calculation of average and marginal costs. Both conceptions of marginal cost are shown. The first one uses finite differences between successive levels of output. Each figure for marginal cost is shown *between* the two levels of output for which it is calculated. We also show marginal cost calculated as the derivative of the total cost function at points representing integral values of output. The first derivative of the total cost function is expressed by this equation:

$$MC = \frac{dTC}{dQ} = 10 - 10Q + 3Q^2$$

By substituting the successive integral values of Q (1, 2, . . . , 6) we obtain the value of the derivative at each point. The latter conception of marginal cost is somewhat more useful, since it can be calculated for fractional values and is itself a continuous function.

At any rate, the unit cost data in the table display certain patterns which are worthy of note. As output increases, average cost declines at first, levels off, then rises at an increasing rate. Marginal cost also declines, then rises. Further, it can be shown that marginal cost intersects average cost at the lowest level of average cost. To prove this, set equal to each other the algebraic expression for marginal cost (given above) and the expression for average cost. Average cost is

$$\frac{TC}{Q} = \frac{10Q - 5Q^2 + Q^3}{Q} = 10 - 5Q + Q^2$$

To find the point where the two measures of unit cost are equal, we solve the following equation for Q:

$$10 - 5Q + Q^2 = 10 - 10Q + 3Q^2$$
$$5Q = 2Q^2$$
$$Q = 2.5 \quad \text{(ignoring the irrelevant zero root)}$$

The two measures of unit cost are equal at an output of 2.5. By substitution, we ascertain that at that point they have a value of $3.75. We can prove this is the lowest point on the average cost function by showing that the derivative of average cost is zero at that point. The average cost function is $10 - 5Q + Q^2$, and its derivative is $dAC/dQ = 2Q - 5$. Since $Q = 2.5$, the expression for the derivative is equal to zero at that point.

We can also establish that if marginal cost is greater than average cost, average cost must be rising, and if marginal cost is less than average cost, average cost must be falling. The assumption $MC > AC$ is equivalent to the assumption that dAC/dQ is positive.

$$10 - 10Q - 3Q^2 > 10 - 5Q - Q^2$$
$$2Q^2 > 5Q$$
$$Q > 2.5$$

The first derivative of AC is $2Q - 5$. Clearly this will be positive if $Q > 2.5$. A similar proof can be used for cases where $MC < AC$.

If the production function continued to display increasing returns to scale as output increased, the unit cost curves would continue to slope downward, and marginal cost would lie below average cost (assuming a given set of input prices). And we have already noted that if the production function is subject to constant returns to scale, the average and marginal cost curves are flat and coincide with each other.

Because of the nature of the cost functions, it is always possible to use any one of them to derive the other two. For instance, given the average cost of any output, total cost is obtained by multiplying average cost times output. Total cost can also be obtained from marginal cost. If we know the marginal cost function or schedule, we can integrate this to find total cost. In Table 9-1, for instance, the total cost of any output can be obtained by simply summing the successive figures for marginal cost calculated between points. And when one has a (long-run) marginal cost function $MC(Q)$ algebraically defined, $TC_n = \int_0^n MC(Q)\, dQ$ for any output n. (For a short-run cost function, it is necessary to add fixed cost to the integral of MC to obtain total cost.)

graphic analysis of cost functions

Since cost can be expressed as a function of one variable, namely output, it is simple to represent cost functions graphically. We measure output horizontally and designate the cost corresponding to any given output vertically. Figure 9-2 shows the unit cost functions used in the preceding example. The U-shaped characteristic of average cost is one which we will assume to be general. Note that MC intersects AC at the lowest point on AC, and that AC is rising when MC is above it. Another general property is that the point of lowest MC is at a lower output and a lower value than the point of minimum AC.

short-run cost functions

In discussing the production function we observed that it is common to investigate the behavior of the firm on the assumption that it is already endowed with some

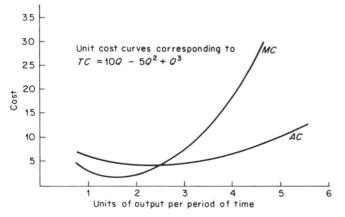

Unit cost curves corresponding to
$TC = 10Q - 5Q^2 + Q^3$

Figure 9-2 A set of unit cost curves.

quantity of fixed capital and is confronted, in the short run, with a decision of how much of some variable inputs to use. Presumably the firm treats some inputs as fixed because it is too costly to change them rapidly, or because of uncertainty that a change in output will be anything but short-lived. Typically the fixed input consists of some stock of productive assets, and quite possibly the firm can vary the use it makes of those assets. The number of trucks may stay constant, but the number of truck-miles can vary.

A short-run production function need not bear a simple relation to the long-run production function. When we lay out a long-run production function, we may be thinking of the capital input in relatively unspecified form, so that the firm might be using different kinds of capital equipment depending on the quantities of other inputs to be employed. Thus $20,000 worth of capital may be best embodied in a bulldozer if it is to be used with 2 men, but better used for picks, shovels, and wheelbarrows if it is to be used with 200 men. In the short run, not only the amount but the form of capital equipment may be fixed. The short-run production function in such a case need not bear any simple mathematical relation to the long-run function.

Despite this looseness of linkage, however, we will use the simplifying assumption that the short-run production function is a partial derivative of the long-run function. Given the prices of inputs, it is possible to determine a set of short-run cost functions corresponding to any short-run production function. Let us take a production function similar to one we used before. Let $Q = a^{1/3}b^{1/3}$. Now transform this into a short-run production function by setting $b = 8$ and holding it constant. The function then becomes $Q = 2a^{1/3}$. The total costs of the firm in the short run can now be divided into two categories. The costs of the fixed capital input (b) will be the same no matter what the firm produces. We call these *fixed costs*. They are fixed only in the functional sense of being unaffected by changes in output in the short run. The other category of costs consists of *variable costs*. These are variable in the functional sense: they change in response to changes in output. Our terminology has nothing to tell us about whether the various cost categories are stable over time.

Let us assume that the price of b is $100 and the price of a is $100. Table 9-2 shows some input-output choices open to the firm and the cost conditions associated with each. We observed previously that short-run production functions display diminishing returns to the variable input. This is evident in the function shown. The increment of input a required to raise output by 1 unit rises steadily throughout the table. This has direct consequences for the behavior of variable costs per unit. We have identified a category of *average variable costs* (AVC), defined as total variable cost divided by output. AVC rises steadily in Table 9-2, as does short-run marginal cost (SMC). Since the quantity of input b is constant, these cost increases reflect the increased expenditures on input a required to expand output by one unit. Diminishing returns are reflected in the increased increments of the variable input required to yield constant increments of output.

TABLE 9-2 HYPOTHETICAL SHORT-RUN COST DATA†

Units of Output (Q)	Units of Variable Input (a)	Total Variable Cost (TVC)	Fixed Cost	Total Cost (STC)	Average Variable Cost (AVC)	Short-run Average Cost (SAC)	Short-run Marginal Cost ΔSTC/ΔQ	dSTC/dQ
0	0	0	800	800.00				
							12.50	
1	0.125	12.50	800	812.50	12.50	812.50		37.50
							87.50	
2	1.000	100.00	800	900.00	50.00	450.00		150.00
							237.50	
3	3.375	337.50	800	1,137.50	112.50	379.17		337.50
							462.50	
4	8.000	800.00	800	1,600.00	200.00	400.00		600.00
							762.50	
5	15.625	1,562.50	800	2,362.50	312.50	472.50		937.50
							1,137.50	
6	27.000	2,700.00	800	3,500.00	450.00	583.33		1,350.00

† Since $Q = 2a^{1/3}$, we have implicitly $a = Q^3/8$. Our cost function $STC = 800 + 100a$ can be transformed by substituting for a to obtain $STC = 800 + 12.5Q^3$. The first derivative of this is $37.5Q^2$, which is used to obtain the values for marginal cost at the extreme right.

Since diminishing returns characterize the short-run production function generally, it follows that short-run cost functions are upward sloping, at least beyond some point. Short-run unit costs, average and marginal, tend to rise with output regardless of the shape of the long-run production function and long-run cost curves.

Because of the existence of fixed cost, short-run total cost is not zero at zero output. Fixed costs are generally associated with inputs of the services of durable capital assets. Such assets give rise to cost in the form of interest and depreciation allowances over the period in which the assets yield their services. If the asset depreciation is purely a function of time, a truly fixed cost results. To the extent that depreciation is a function of use, however, it is a variable cost. Another way to think of the distinction between fixed and variable costs is to regard variable costs as avoidable. Fixed costs cannot be avoided by producing zero output; they are sometimes called "sunk" costs.

The existence of fixed cost gives the short-run average cost (SAC) curve a pronounced U shape. SAC declines sharply as output increases from low levels, as the constant amount of fixed cost is spread over increasing output.

relation of short-run to long-run cost functions

Our purpose in developing long-run and short-run cost schedules is to use them to explain the input and output decisions of the firm. Briefly, the long-run cost schedules (combined with appropriate revenue considerations) are the basis on which the firm decides on the best stock of capital assets (and other related commitments extending into the future). Corresponding to the chosen capital stock is a particular point on the long-run average cost (LAC) schedule, representing the intended output Q^* which the chosen capital stock would be expected to produce.

Once the capital stock has been acquired, it identifies a set of short-run cost schedules. Each SAC has one point in common with the $LAC;$ the two are equal at output Q^*. At all other outputs SAC is larger than LAC. At output Q^*, the input mix which is being used in the short run is the same as that which achieves long-run cost minimization. Short-run changes in output necessarily depart from this long-run optimal input mix and thus necessarily impose costs higher than LAC.

To illustrate, consider the data used for Table 9-2. With a long-run production function $Q = a^{1/3}b^{1/3}$ and both input prices equal to $100, the optimum input mix uses equal quantities of the two inputs, and the long-run total cost schedule is $LTC = 200Q^{3/2}$. Table 9-2 indicates that the firm uses equal quantities of the two inputs in the short run to produce 4 units of output. The long-run and short-run production functions coincide at that point, and so must the corresponding cost functions. Solving the LTC schedule for $Q = 4$ yields $LTC = $1,600$, which equals the short-run total cost shown in Table 9-2.

If output is 3 units, LTC is $1,039 while STC is $1,139. If output is 5 units, LTC is $2,236 while STC is $2,363. Correspondingly we find that both SAC and LAC have the value $400 at output 4 but that SAC is above LAC at all other outputs. The SAC would be tangent to the LAC curve at the output of 4 units. Our LAC function would be $200Q^{1/2}$, which is upward sloping throughout. Thus the point of tangency will also be on the upward-sloping portion of SAC. This is reflected in Table 9-2, showing that SAC was lower at output 3 than at output 4 (actually the output which minimizes SAC is about 3.17 units).

It follows that tangency between SAC and LAC does not necessarily occur at the output which minimizes SAC. On a downward-sloping LAC curve, the tangency would occur at an output less than that which would minimize SAC. Only where LAC is flat does the tangency occur at the bottom of SAC.

In terms of our example, this may be stated as a paradox: the best plant size for producing 4 units of output is the one represented by 8 units of input b. But 4 units of output is not the most efficient output to produce with that plant.

geometric representation

The foregoing example was limited by our desire to show how cost functions are based on production functions. It yielded homogeneous long-run cost functions which are easy to manipulate mathematically but which do not correspond to our notion of the prototype cost pattern. For a geometric illustration, we assume that the firm's long-run cost schedules yield an LAC curve which is itself broadly

U-shaped. At low levels of output the production function displays increasing returns to scale, so LAC is downward sloping. Eventually LAC reaches a minimum, then begins to slope upward as diseconomies of scale are encountered. For mathematical simplicity the LAC curve is shown as symmetrical, though symmetry is not a likely economic outcome. The total cost functions are assumed to take the following values:

$$LTC = .25Q^3 - 40Q^2 + 2,500Q$$
$$STC_1 = Q^3 - 98.75Q^2 + 3,600Q + 2,000$$
$$STC_2 = .35Q^3 - 59.6Q^2 + 3,420Q + 4,000$$

As an exercise, calculate the corresponding average and marginal cost functions, which are shown in Figure 9-3. SAC_1 is tangent to LAC at 40 units of output, where LAC is downward sloping. Consequently SAC_1 is also downward sloping at output 40, reaching its minimum at about 50. Where the average cost curves are tangent, the marginal curves must cross. (Why?) Thus we find that $SMC_1 = LMC$ at output 40. Note that both lie below the average cost curves, as they must when the average cost curves are sloping downward.

By contrast, SAC_2 is tangent to LAC at 100 units of output, where both curves are upward sloping. Thus the tangency output is higher than the output at which SAC_2 is minimized (which is 86). $SMC_2 = LMC$ at output 100; since the average cost curves are upward sloping at this output, the marginal costs are higher than the average costs.

Potentially, one can construct a set of short-run cost functions for each possible value of the fixed input, so their possible number is unlimited. Among the possi-

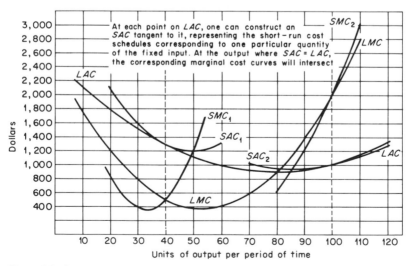

Figure 9-3 Long-run and short-run cost curves.

bilities, there will be at least one SAC curve which is tangent to LAC at the minimum point on LAC. The tangency will also be at the minimum point on the SAC curve, and the corresponding SMC and LMC curves will intersect at that same point. This case is illustrated in Chapter 10.

shifts in cost functions

The cost functions of the firm are dependent on the production function. Should the production function shift, as for example through a change in technology, the entire cost function would be altered. For a firm buying inputs in a competitive market, the cost functions also are based on a particular set of input prices. Changes in the prices of inputs would thus shift the cost functions.

When the production functions are simple, the cost functions can often be expressed in a form which makes it easy to analyze changes in input prices. Consider the data underlying Table 9-2, reflecting a short-run production function $Q = 2a^{1/3}$ and a fixed quantity of 8 units of b costing $100 per unit. The short-run total cost function would be

$$STC = a \cdot P_a + b \cdot P_b = \frac{Q^3}{8} P_a + 800$$

We could identify the impact of a change in P_a by finding the derivative $dSTC/dP_a$, which is simply $Q^3/8$. The impact of a change in P_a is thus larger, the larger the quantity being produced. At output of 4 units, for example, an increase in P_a by 1 cent tends to raise STC by about 8 cents.

The effect of a change in input price on long-run cost functions depends on the elasticity of substitution between the inputs. If the firm can easily substitute against the input which has risen in price, cost functions may not rise so much as if such substitution were not possible.

For a production function of the type represented by $Q = a^{1/3}b^{1/3}$, the total cost function can be expressed in this general form:

$$TC = 2P_a^{1/2}P_b^{1/2}Q^{3/2}$$

The elasticity of total cost with respect to a change in the price of an input is simply one-half. Be sure you can derive the cost function and demonstrate that this is its elasticity.

summary

Given the long-run production function and a set of input prices, the least-cost input combinations for the purely competitive firm are identified at the points of tangency between isoquants and isocost lines. These points of tangency define the output-expansion path, and from the points on it we can derive a schedule showing the long-run total cost for each level of output. From the total cost schedule we derive the most important measures of cost per unit of output, namely marginal cost and average cost.

Each point on the LAC curve of the firm represents some particular quantity of those inputs such as buildings and equipment which may be treated as fixed in quantity in the short run. A set of short-run cost schedules can be derived for each quantity of fixed inputs and the appropriate short-run production function. Each SAC curve is tangent to the LAC at one output and above it at all other outputs. Because of diminishing returns, the short-run unit-cost curves tend to be more sharply upward sloping than the long-run curves. Short-run costs can be classified as fixed or variable depending on whether they are functionally related to output.

The shape of the long-run unit-cost curves depends on the scale properties of the long-run production function (given the prices of the inputs.) The LAC curve slopes down with increasing output if the firm's production function displays increasing returns to scale. The LAC becomes horizontal where the firm experiences constant returns to scale and slopes upward where decreasing returns prevail. We assume the typical cost curve displays all three phases.

Marginal cost intersects average cost at the lowest level of average cost. If marginal cost is below average cost, average cost is falling, and if marginal cost is above average cost, average cost is rising.

The cost schedules are derived on the basis of a given set of prices for the inputs; thus a change in input prices would tend to shift the cost functions. Likewise, the cost functions are based on a given production function, reflecting a particular level of technology and organizational skill. A change in the production function would tend to shift the cost functions.

The analysis of cost derivation presented in this chapter applies mainly to a firm operating under conditions of pure competition. Later we will consider the case of a monopsonistic firm, which buys so much of an input as to affect its price. For the monopsonistic firm, cost schedules can be derived if one has the supply schedules of inputs, not merely their prices. Further, our cost analysis deals only with those costs associated with production. When we consider firms in imperfectly competitive markets, we shall recognize also other costs arising from such activities as advertising.

TERMS AND CONCEPTS

1. Total cost function, schedule
2. Implicit cost
3. Average cost

4. Marginal cost
5. Short-run cost schedule
6. Long-run cost schedule
7. Variable cost
8. Average variable cost

QUESTIONS AND PROBLEMS

1. Given a production function defined by the expression $Q = 2a^{1/3}b^{1/3}$ where a and b are the quantities of two inputs.
   (a) Derive equations for the production isoquants for $Q = 10$ and $Q = 20$ and graph them.
   (b) Assume that input prices are $P_a = 3 and $P_b = 2. Find the least-cost combination of inputs for producing 10 units of output. Derive a general expression for the output-expansion path and draw it in your diagram.
   (c) Derive an algebraic expression expressing total cost as a function of output, using the assumptions above. Do the same for average cost and marginal cost. Draw the three cost curves in a second diagram.
   (d) Comment on the shape of the cost functions and their relation to one another and to the scale properties of the production function.

2. Using the same production function as in (1) assume that the firm is operating with 8 units of a fixed input b, which has cost $4 per unit. Derive a short-run production function. Assuming the price of a is $8, calculate a short-run schedule for each of the following: total cost, average cost, marginal cost, total variable cost, and average variable cost.

3. Suppose a man is trying to decide whether it is cheaper to drive his car to work or to travel by bus. How could the distinction between fixed and variable costs facilitate the comparison? What difference would it make whether (a) he would own a car in any case and (b) depreciation of the car is purely a function of time rather than use?

4. Assume a total cost function has the form $TC = Q^2/2 + 100Q + 100$.
   (a) Explain why this can be recognized as a short-run cost function.
   (b) Calculate expressions for each of the following, and draw them: fixed cost, average fixed cost, variable cost, average variable cost, average cost and marginal cost.
   (c) Explain the shape of AVC and AFC.
   (d) Illustrate that $MC = AC$ at minimum AC.

5. It is possible that a short-run production function might generate a marginal cost schedule that was constant up to some capacity output, beyond which no expansion could take place, given the fixed input. Assuming fixed cost is $1,000, capacity output is 10 units, and marginal cost is $100 per unit up to capacity, derive and graph expressions for the corresponding schedules of total cost, average cost, and average variable cost.

10

input and output decisions
by the competitive firm

On the basis of its technical and organizational information and practices, a firm is able to develop a production function, showing the output which can be obtained from any combination of inputs. Given a set of input prices (assumed to be beyond the control of the individual firm) the firm is able to select that combination of inputs which provides the cheapest method of producing any given output. Combining all the least-cost points yields an output-expansion path, which can be translated into a set of cost functions. Knowing the inputs required for each output, the firm can develop a function which shows the total cost of each possible level of output. From this can be derived the measures of unit cost—average cost, marginal cost, and (for the short run) average variable cost.

In this chapter we proceed to the final step in the input-output decisions of the firm. This step is the selection of the profit-maximizing output itself and—implicitly—the selection of the profit-maximizing input combination to go with it. Profit is the excess of revenue over cost. We have already carried out the analysis of cost, and have a number of functions to show the relationship between costs and the output of the firm.

revenue schedules

Before we can complete analysis of profit maximization, we need to concern ourselves with the revenue side. We confine our discussion to revenue received from the sale of the firm's output. Each firm is confronted implicitly by some sort of demand schedule for its product. If the firm is in operation, one point on that demand schedule is defined by the actual price and output of the firm. Other points may not be known to the firm, although by trial and error adjustment over time it would be able to form some opinion about them.

Whether the demand schedule is known or not, it exists. And with it are associated a set of revenue schedules similar in derivation to the cost schedules we have been using. The total revenue schedule associates with each output the total revenue (price times quantity) which the firm can obtain from that output. The average revenue schedule expresses total revenue divided by output at each output level. Average revenue is simply equal to price, and the average revenue schedule is represented geometrically by the demand curve. Finally, *marginal revenue* is the change in total revenue associated with a change in output. It can be calculated between two different levels of output, in which case it is $\Delta TR/\Delta Q$. It can also be calculated at a point, in which case it is the first derivative of the total revenue schedule dTR/dQ.

The precise character of the firm's revenue schedules depends on the market structure in which it operates. In a purely competitive market, the individual firm has no appreciable influence over the price of what it sells. It can sell any desired quantity at the going market price. This means that the demand curve confronting the firm is perfectly horizontal at the level of the existing price. It has infinite elasticity.

Under such conditions, the revenue functions become very simple indeed. Since price is not affected by the firm's output, total revenue is simply proportional to total output. Average revenue is a constant, equal to the market price. Marginal revenue is also equal to the price.

However, if the firm were in an imperfectly competitive market, the demand curve confronting it would be downward sloping. Increase in output would cause the price to decline. Consequently the marginal revenue would be lower than the price.

The marginal revenue situation confronting the firm depends on the elasticity of demand for its output. The greater the elasticity of demand for the firm's output, the closer its marginal revenue comes to the price. The firm in pure competition confronts a demand schedule for its output which is of infinite elasticity. At this level, the marginal revenue schedule and the demand schedule confronting the firm become identical.

the profit-maximizing output

By bringing together marginal cost (MC) and marginal revenue (MR), we are in a position to identify the most profitable output of the firm. At any given output, MC can be compared with MR. MR measures the change in total revenue associated with a change in output. MC measures the change in total cost associated with a change in output. If MR exceeds MC, then the total profits of the firm will be increased by an increase in output. On the other hand, if MC exceeds MR, further expansion of output would reduce profits; the firm would gain by reducing total output.

It follows that the relationship of marginal cost to marginal revenue provides the firm with an important guide to its output decision. A firm following this guide will be led toward that particular point where its profits are the largest possible. That point will be, of course, the output at which marginal cost and marginal revenue are equal.

numerical illustration

To illustrate, we revert to a (long-run) cost illustration used in the preceding chapter, in which the total cost function is $TC = 10Q - 5Q^2 + Q^3$. We assume that the selling price of the product is $10. Table 10-1 compares various measures of costs and revenues. If we confine our attention to integral values of output, we can easily locate the point of maximum profit by comparing total cost with total revenue. The most profitable output shown in Table 10-1 is 3 units, with a revenue of $30, cost of $12, and profit of $18. The validity of the marginal conditions for the maximum-profit output can be observed by comparing marginal cost with marginal revenue. (As before, we have shown two measures of marginal cost.

TABLE 10-1

Output	Total Revenue	Total Cost	Profit	Average Cost	Marginal Cost Finite	Marginal Cost Deriva-tive	Marginal Revenue
0	0	0	0				
1	10	6	4	6	6	3	10
2	20	8	12	4	2	2	10
3	30	12	18	4	4	7	10
4	40	24	16	6	12	18	10
5	50	50	0	10	26	35	10
6	60	96	−36	16	46	58	10

The one to the left gives the simple differences in moving from one level of output to the next; the other gives the derivatives of the total cost function at specific output points.) The first unit of output adds $10 to revenue and $6 to cost; thus it contributes $4 to profit. The second unit adds only $2 to cost and thus raises profit by $8. The third unit adds $4 to cost and thus raises profit by $6. However, to expand from 3 to 4 units of output would add $12 to cost, only $10 to revenue; thus profit would be lower by $2.

The analysis implies that the firm could benefit by following these rules:

1. If MR exceeds MC, expand output.
2. If MC exceeds MR, reduce output.

Following these rules will normally move the firm closer to the maximum-profit position. If MR exceeds MC initially and the firm expands output, the expansion will tend to raise MC, while MR (for a competitive seller) remains constant. Eventually an output is reached at which $MR = MC$. By similar reasoning, if MC initially exceeds MR and the firm reduces output, the cutback will tend to lower MC, while MR remains constant. Output adjustment following the rule will again lead to an output where $MC = MR$.

Equality of MC with MR is a necessary condition for the profit-maximizing output, but not a sufficient condition. We must specify that at the equilibrium output MC must be rising more rapidly (or falling less rapidly) than MR—otherwise $MC = MR$ becomes a point of *minimum* profit! These "second-order" conditions for maximum profit are fulfilled in the conventional case where MC is rising and MR is constant or falling.

algebraic and graphic illustrations

At each level of output, profit is equal to total revenue minus total cost. Since we can express total cost and total revenue as functions of output, we can also identify a profit function which is simply the total cost function subtracted from the total revenue function. The derivative of the profit function is equal to the derivative of total revenue (which is MR) minus the derivative of total cost (which is MC). To maximize profit, we set the derivative of the profit function (π) equal to zero. Thus $d\pi/dQ = MR - MC = 0$. This condition can be achieved only if $MC = MR$.

In our illustration, the total cost function was $TC = 10Q - 5Q^2 + Q^3$. Taking the derivative of this yields us $MC = 10 - 10Q + 3Q^2$. When we set this equal to the marginal revenue of 10, we find that the most profitable output, assuming complete divisibility, is $3\frac{1}{3}$ units.

The profit function could be expressed as total revenue ($10Q$) minus total cost; thus $\pi = 10Q - (10Q - 5Q^2 + Q^3) = 5Q^2 - Q^3$. Profit is maximized when the

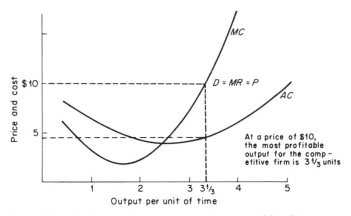

Figure 10-1 Profit-maximizing output for the competitive firm.

derivative of the profit function is equal to zero; thus we obtain $10Q - 3Q^2 = 0$, which yields $Q = 3\frac{1}{3}$, as before.

Figure 10-1 illustrates the relationship between unit cost and price for this firm. Since the firm can sell as much as it desires at the going market price of $10, we can draw a horizontal line at that price which represents the demand schedule confronting the firm and also the marginal revenue schedule which accompanies it. The most profitable output occurs where the marginal cost curve intersects the line representing price and marginal revenue. Note that the most profitable output is not necessarily the one for which average cost is lowest. At the maximum-profit output of $3\frac{1}{3}$, the total revenue of the firm is $33\frac{1}{3}$, which is equal to the area of the rectangle marked off by the price and quantity dimensions of the equilibrium position. Total cost is equal to average cost multiplied times output, shown as the area of the rectangle marked of by average cost ($AC = 4.44$ at output $3\frac{1}{3}$) times output. Thus profit, which is total revenue minus total cost, is measured by the rectangle between average cost and price extending horizontally to the output.

In addition to the marginal conditions for profit maximization, we must add an important proviso. In the long run, the price must be sufficient to cover average cost (including a normal return on capital) or the firm will cease to operate. By definition, capital can earn a normal return in other uses. If it cannot earn such a return in this use, it will be withdrawn.

long- and short-run costs

We are interested in identifying the firm's supply schedule of output—how much it will produce at any given price. Our analysis of costs and revenues puts us in a position to draw some conclusions about the firm's response to various prices.

Here we must distinguish between short-run and long-run adjustments. We will assume that the firm exists as a going concern and that it possesses some quantity of fixed factors, such as land and capital goods. The firm has already spent money for these and thus has certain fixed costs which exist regardless of whether the firm produces or not. Short-run changes in output are achieved by changing the quantity of certain variable inputs, such as labor and raw materials.

By contrast, long-run adjustments by the firm are made on the basis of conditions expected to prevail well into the future. Long-run adjustments involve changes in all inputs; thus they may involve changes in the firm's entire scale of plant and equipment.

We can construct long-run and short-run cost curves corresponding to these respective adjustment patterns. The long-run average cost reflects the lowest cost of producing each level of output when size of plant can be varied. The short-run average cost reflects the lowest cost of producing each level of output with some specific plant already in existence. There exists a separate set of short-run cost curves for each plant the firm might have; thus there will be an entire family of short-run curves to accompany a long-run curve. Figure 10-2 illustrates a possible long-run average cost curve and two of the short-run curves which might be associated with it. For each average cost curve there also exists a corresponding

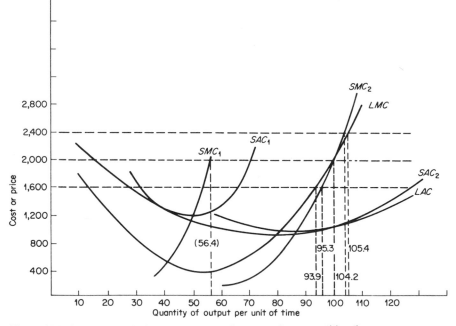

Figure 10-2 Long-run and short-run output adjustment by competitive firm.

marginal cost curve. In the diagram, the long-run average and marginal costs correspond to the total cost function $LTC = 0.25Q^3 - 40Q^2 + 2,500Q$. The short-run curves SAC_1 and SMC_1 correspond to the total cost function:

$$STC_1 = Q^3 - 98.75Q^2 + 3,600Q + 2,000$$

The short-run curves SAC_2 and SMC_2 correspond to the total cost function:

$$STC_2 = 0.35Q^3 - 59.6Q^2 + 3,420Q + 4,000$$

Note that the short-run average cost curves are tangent to the long-run average cost curves and that the marginal costs are equal at the output where the average costs are tangent (outputs of 40 for SAC_1, and 100 for SAC_2).

Assuming pure competition in markets for inputs, the shape of the long-run average cost curve reflects the economies or diseconomies of scale. We have assumed that the firm is subject to economies of scale in the lower range of output; this property is reflected in the downward-sloping portion of LAC. The curve is relatively flat in the output range 70–90, reaching its lowest at output of 80. Ultimately we assume that diseconomies of scale are encountered, so that the LAC curve slopes upward. If the firm is selling in a purely competitive market, it always has an incentive to achieve a plant of at least the size represented by the lowest point of LAC. However, it may take a firm a long time actually to reach such a size, because of limitations of finance or managerial considerations. If the economies of scale are extensive, individual firms may ultimately grow to be large relative to the market in which they sell—sufficiently large that the market ceases to be a purely competitive one. Our assumption that the long-run average cost curve ultimately turns up is a necessary one, therefore, if we are to analyze pure competition at all.

Suppose that our firm is initially producing with the plant represented by SAC_1 in Figure 10-2 and that the price of the product is $2,000. The most profitable output in the short run would be about 56.4 units. However, as a long-run objective the firm would wish to continue expanding plant and output until it reached the output where $P = LMC$, which would be 100 units. The plant which it would then have would be the one represented by SAC_2 and SMC_2, and it would be producing with both long- and short-run marginal costs equal to the price.

reaction to price change

If the price changes, the firm will tend to change its output—first on the basis of short-run costs, ultimately on the basis of long-run costs. The cost curves (and the functions underlying them) enable us to trace the output response of the profit-maximizing firm. Suppose the firm is producing 100 units of output, operating the plant corresponding to SAC_2 and SMC_2. Assume the product price rises to $2,400. In the short run the profit-maximizing output rises to about 104.2 units, where SMC_2 intersects the new price. The magnitude of this output response depends on the shape of SMC. The steeper SMC is, the smaller the short-run response of output to a change in price. The shape of the SMC curve reflects the extent of diminishing returns as the firm adds variable inputs to its fixed capital. In the long run, if the price remains at $2,400, the firm will wish to enlarge its plant, in order to reach an output of about 105.4 units. This long-run supply response depends on the steepness of the LMC curve, which is a reflection of diseconomies of scale. Expansion of the firm's plant will bring with it a new SMC curve to the right of SMC_2.

How long are the "long" run and the "short" run in a situation like this? The timing of output adjustments depends on two matters. One is the length of time required for the firm to make the output adjustment. Building a new factory may entail a lengthy "gestation period," while adding more workers and raw materials can be achieved more rapidly. Such considerations limit the adjustments which a firm can feasibly make in a given time. The other is the length of time over which the firm is forming expectations and making plans. If an increase in output is expected to persist over a long time, the firm's management will be more willing to incur the risks and commitments involved in additional fixed capital. If the management has no confidence that the increase will be sustained, they will be less willing to add fixed assets. Considerations of this type relate to the firm's *willingness* to make the output adjustments which are within the bounds of feasibility.

Suppose the firm is producing 100 units of output and the price falls from $2,000 to $1,600. Initially, the firm will reduce its output by moving back along the SMC_2 curve, which intersects the new price at an output of about 95.3 units. Ultimately it would reduce the scale of its plant, moving to the output of 93.9 where $LMC = $1,600. At this scale of operations, a new SMC curve would come into existence to the left of SMC_2.

The lowest point on the LAC curve occurs at an output of 80, where LAC is $900. If the firm is to continue operating in the long run, it must receive a price at least sufficient to cover long-run average cost (which includes a normal return on the capital of the owners). This is equivalent to saying that in the long run the total revenue must be at least as large as total cost, when total cost includes all the implicit costs for factor services supplied by the owners of the business. Total revenue must be sufficient to pay for all inputs at their market value, or they will not continue to be available to the firm.

A corollary is that the long-run equilibrium output of the firm will not be smaller than the output at which LAC is minimized.

In the short run, however, the firm may continue to operate even if price is below average cost. The reason is that the firm may lose less money by continuing to operate than it would lose if it closed. In the short run, the firm has certain fixed costs which it cannot avoid even by closing. It probably owns capital goods which it has already paid for, and the interest and depreciation costs may exist even at zero output. Only variable costs are avoidable. If revenues exceed total variable cost, the firm will at least recover a part of fixed costs, rather than lose them all by closing. However, if price falls below minimum average variable cost, the firm would lose more by operating, even in the short run, than it would by closing. If the firm must pay out variable costs of $100 to produce 1 unit of output selling for less than $100, it is taking an out-of-pocket loss on every unit produced.

How long might a firm keep on operating at a price below minimum average cost? This depends on the condition of the firm's fixed assets. As durable capital items wear out, the firm will not replace them. A firm whose capital assets are old or short-lived may not continue to operate very long at $P < AC$. However, if the firm's capital assets are relatively new and durable, it may continue much longer at an unprofitable price. In the second case, however, the firm would consider the possibility of selling its capital assets. If they are assets of a very specific nature, which can only be used in the same industry, other firms are likely to be suffering from the same lack of profitability and will not be eager to buy capital assets. Much railway capital is of this sort. The tracks and roadbed represent very durable capital investment of a sort which is not of much value except to a railroad. In contrast, if the firm's capital could be used by other industries—if it consisted of items such as trucks and typewriters—then the firm would liquidate and close down much more rapidly in face of an unprofitable price. Thus the long-run adjustment is much slower, in the face of a low price, when the firm's capital is long-lived and specific to the industry.

It is still true, as in the case of output expansion, that the firm's willingness to make long-run adjustments reflects its conviction about the permanence of the change in price and demand conditions. A firm confronted with an unprofitable selling price which is expected to be short-lived may continue to produce, but use the output to build up its inventory, in the process keeping its work force available and in good working trim. It would be very unlikely to continue producing *and selling* at a price below minimum average variable cost, since revenues would not even meet the incremental or out-of-pocket costs, and the owners of the firm would lose less by shutting it down even if the physical assets have no resale value.

the firm's supply curves

We have now completed a major task. By showing that the firm in a purely competitive industry will adjust its output to keep $MC = P$, we have implicitly established that *the supply curve of the firm's output is its marginal cost curve*. The only qualification is that this relation holds only if the price is sufficiently high so that the firm continues to produce at all instead of shutting down, and is operating where MC is upward sloping.

In our diagram, the marginal cost curves have served precisely the function of supply curves—that is, each shows the output which the firm produces at each possible price. The short-run marginal cost curve corresponding to the firm's existing plant gives us the short-run supply curve of the firm for any price which exceeds the minimum level of average variable cost. The long-run marginal cost curve gives us the long-run supply curve of the firm for any price which is higher than the minimum level of average cost.

Bear in mind the assumptions we have made underlying the firm's cost functions. One assumption is that the firm is buying inputs in a purely competitive market, so the prices of the inputs are not affected by changes in the amounts the firm buys. And we assumed a given condition of the production function. Shifts in the firm's supply schedule of output would result from a change in prices of inputs, or in technology or organizational technique. For example, an increase in input prices would cause the cost curves to shift upward, reducing the output the firm would produce at any given price. An improvement in technology might lower the cost curves and increase the output which the firm would produce at any given price.

It would be nice if this were all there were to the analysis of supply. If the population of business firms could be taken as fixed, it would be nearly all. But in reality, important supply adjustments occur through changes in the number of firms in an industry, as well as through changes in output per firm. Also, changes in industry output tend to affect input prices. Thus we still have some steps to complete before we have developed an explanation of the supply behavior of an entire industry. Before taking those, let us examine the firm's behavior as a buyer of inputs.

the firm as buyer

Strictly speaking, we have already determined the firm's input decisions, as well as its output decision. Figure 10-3 shows how the specific input selection of the firm is determined by the steps we have already gone through. (We deal in this section with only long-run decisions.) First, the production function and the prices of the inputs were used to determine the output-expansion path, the least-cost input combinations. Each point on the output-expansion path is a point of tangency between a line representing output and a line representing cost. Combining the output and cost data yields a total cost function, and from that we derive average and marginal costs. The profit-maximizing output is located where marginal cost equals price. It only remains to locate that profit-maximizing output in the upper part of the diagram, along the output-expansion path, to identify the specific factor inputs consistent with maximum profits.

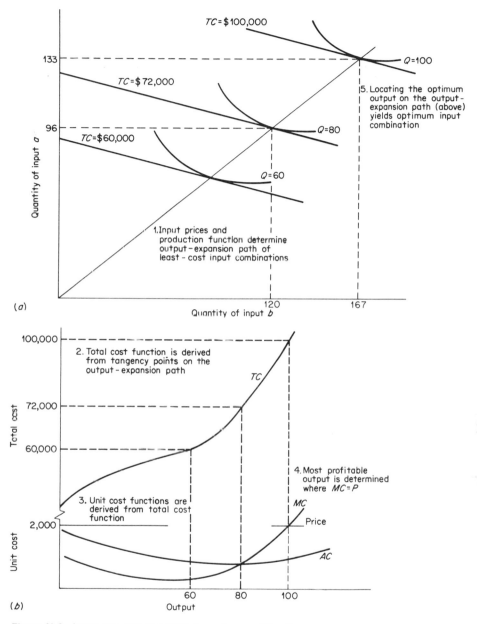

Figure 10-3 Input and output equilibrium of competitive firm.

A change in the price of the product would alter the firm's output, and consequently change its input purchases as well. For instance, a decline in the price of the product from $2,000 to $900 would, using the data in Figure 10-3, result in a reduction in output from 100 units to 80 units. In the upper part of the diagram, the firm would move back along the output-expansion path. Instead of employing 133 units of a and 167 units of b, it would employ only 96 units of a and 120 units of b.

change in input price

Assume now that there is a decline in the price of input b. Figure 10-4 shows how to trace the response. We begin in the upper section of the diagram. The decline in the price of input b shifts the entire output-expansion line to the right. In order to maintain equality between the marginal rate of input substitution and the ratio of input prices, the firm must alter its input mix so as to use more of b and less of a at each level of output. Speaking geometrically, we can observe that the isocost lines become flatter, and therefore the tangency point on each isoproduct curve is now further to the right. Here we have a substitution effect, represented in the diagram by the movement from x to y along the isoproduct curve representing 100 units of output.

The size of shift in the output-expansion path reflects the magnitude of the substitution effect, which in turn depends on the elasticity of substitution between the inputs. The larger that elasticity, the larger the shift in the input mix.

As a result of the reduction in the price of input b, it now costs the firm less to produce each level of output than before. The new isocost line tangent to the isoquant representing 100 units of output represents a total cost of $79,400, compared with a previous total cost of $100,000. Other costs shift in proportion. As a result, the firm's total cost function shifts downward, as shown in the middle part of the diagram. This also shifts the marginal cost function downward. The new marginal cost curve intersects the price of $2,000 at a larger output than did the old. Instead of an output of 100 units, the firm now finds that its most profitable output is 106.4 units. This increase reflects the *output effect* of a change in the price of an input.

The magnitude of the output effect depends partly on how much marginal cost shifts in response to the change in the price of input b. This shift will be larger, the larger the proportion of total costs going for input b. And the decline in costs will be greater, the larger the elasticity of substitution between the inputs, since the cheapened input is now used in place of the one which did not change in price.

The output effect also depends on the shape of the marginal cost curve in the equilibrium range. The steeper the MC curve, the smaller the horizontal shift associated with a given vertical change in MC. Finally, the output

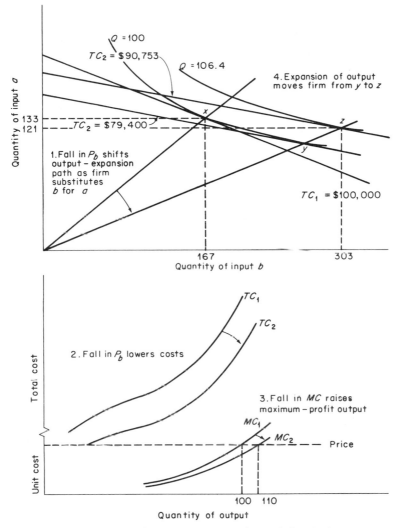

Figure 10-4 Adjustment of input and output to change in input price.

effect depends on the elasticity of demand for the product. We have assumed infinite elasticity of demand; thus the firm can expand its output without causing a decline in product price. If the firm confronted a downward-sloping demand curve for its product, increased output would lower the price, and the expansion of output would not go so far.

Our final step in analyzing the change in price of input b is to carry the new output back into the upper part of the figure. The firm's new input position is where the new output-expansion path intersects the isoproduct curve for 106.4 units of output, which is at the point z.

In all, the firm reacts to the halving of the price of b by increasing its employment of b from about 167 units to about 303 units, moving from point x to point z. It also reduces its input of a from about 133 units to about 121 units. This reduction in the employment of a reflects the predominance, in this particular case, of the substitution effect over the output effect.

Because of the need to consider both output effects and substitution effects, it is not easy to analyze the influence of input price changes using the analytical tools of this chapter. In Chapter 11, we shall develop an alternative way of organizing the same data, to facilitate the derivation of the firm's *demand schedule* for an input.

summary

To identify the profit-maximizing output of the firm, we employ the cost schedules derived from the production function and input prices, plus a set of revenue schedules. The average revenue schedule is the same as the demand curve, while marginal revenue measures the change in total revenue associated with a change in output. In pure competition, marginal revenue is equal to the price of the product; in imperfectly competitive markets, this equality does not hold.

The maximum-profit output of the firm is found where marginal cost and marginal revenue are equal. If the firm is producing at an output where marginal revenue exceeds marginal cost, it can increase its profits by expanding output. If the firm is operating at an output where marginal cost exceeds marginal revenue, it can increase its profits by curtailing output.

The short-run supply curve of the firm, showing how its output reacts to changes in price, is given by its short-run marginal cost curve, calculated on the basis of some existing endowment of fixed capital assets. However, the firm will not operate in the short run unless price exceeds minimum average variable cost.

The long-run supply curve of the firm is given by its long-run marginal cost curve, calculated on the basis of potential variation in the scale of plant. However, in the long run the firm will not operate unless price exceeds minimum average cost, including a normal return to the capital of the owners.

The cost and supply curves of the firm are calculated on the basis of a given production function and set of input prices. If the price of an input changed, output and substitution effects would follow. The firm would change its input mix to a new least-cost combination, using less of an input which had become more expensive. And since the firm's costs would be different after an input price change, its maximum-profit output would be altered. Both of these considerations are involved in deriving the firm's demand curve for an input, showing the dependence of its purchases of that input on the price of the input.

TERMS AND CONCEPTS

1. Total revenue schedule, curve
2. Average revenue schedule, curve
3. Marginal revenue schedule, curve
4. Output and substitution effects of change in price of an input

QUESTIONS AND PROBLEMS

1. Given a production function defined by the equation $Q = a^{1/3}b^{2/3}$, where Q represents the quantity of output and a and b represent the quantity of two inputs.

   (a) Draw the isoquants for outputs of 10 and 20.

   (b) Identify the scale elasticity of the function.

   (c) Assume that prices of Inputs are $P_a = \$4$ and $P_b = \$10$; then derive an expression for the output-expansion path of least-cost input combinations and diagram it.

   (d) Using the same input prices, derive expressions for the three cost schedules (total, average, and marginal), and diagram them.

   (e) Assume the price of the product is $464. Find the most profitable output and explain it in terms of marginal cost and marginal revenue. Identify the appropriate Input combination.

   (f) Starting from the input-output position which you determined for part e, treat input a as fixed in quantity in the short run, and derive an expression for the firm's short-run supply schedule. Compare its short-run and long-run reactions to an increase in the price of the product to $500.

   (g) Starting again from the equilibrium input-output position in part e, trace the short-run and long-run reactions of input and output to an increase in the price of input b to $12. Show the effects in a diagram. Identify the output effects and the substitution effects.

11

marginal productivity and demand for inputs

The analysis of demand for inputs which we employed in Chapter 10 is very explicit, but also very cumbersome. For many purposes the same ground can be covered somewhat more simply by the use of concepts relating to marginal productivity. Back in Chapter 6 we introduced the concept of the marginal physical product of an input. We defined *marginal physical product* as the change in output associated with a change in the quantity of one input when the quantity of the other inputs is given. In the simple one-commodity world of Chapter 7, the schedule of labor's marginal physical product formed the basis for the *demand schedule* for hired labor.

In a many-commodity world where transactions are measured in money terms, we can use concepts of the marginal product which are also expressed in monetary terms. For short-run purposes, we use the marginal revenue product. For long-run analysis, we employ the marginal net revenue product. Each provides a measure of the value of an input to the firm, and thus helps to analyze its demand for an input.

marginal revenue product

In the short run, we assume that the firm operates with a fixed amount of (at least) one input. Usually there are several variable inputs (labor, raw materials, electricity), but we will limit ourselves to only one variable input. There is a short-run production function which associates some quantity of output with each quantity of the variable input. This production function yields the (downward-sloping) schedule of marginal physical product of the variable input.

As a measure of the value of the variable input to the firm, we use the marginal revenue product, defined as the change in the total revenue of the firm associated with a change in the quantity of one input when the quantity of the other inputs is given. Marginal revenue product (MRP) can be derived from a total revenue function. It can also be derived by multiplying the marginal physical product (MPP) of the variable input times the marginal revenue of the product.

To illustrate, we assume the production function is $Q = a^{1/2}b^{1/2}$ and that the quantity of input b is fixed at 4 units, entailing a total fixed cost of $800. This yields a short-run production function $Q = 2a^{1/2}$. Let us leave the price of input a indefinite for the moment but assume that the price of the product is $350. Table 11-1 summarizes data on physical and revenue productivity for the integral values of the variable input a.

The marginal product concepts can be defined in either of two ways. We can measure each in terms of the finite changes involved in moving from one input position to another. For instance, increasing the quantity of input a from 2 units to 3 units raises total output by 0.63 units, which is the marginal physical product between those points. Increasing the quantity of input a from 3 units to 4 units raises total revenue by $188, which represents the marginal revenue product between those points. (Note that these arc measures are shown between the lines of the integral values of input a in Table 11-1.)

Marginal products can also be defined as derivatives at a point. Marginal physical product then becomes the derivative dQ/da of the short-run production function expressing output as a function of the input of a. Substituting a revenue measure in place of output yields a total revenue function, the derivative of which (dTR/da) is marginal revenue product. We are using a short-run production function $Q = 2a^{1/2}$. Assuming that the price of the product is $350, the total revenue function is $TR = 700a^{1/2}$. Taking the derivatives of these functions we find that $MPP_a = 1/a^{1/2}$, and $MRP_a = 350/a^{1/2}$.

To use MRP in analyzing the profit position of the firm, we need to compare it with some measure of expense. For this purpose, we introduce the concept of the *marginal outlay* for an input. Since the total outlay for an input is the total amount spent on it (equal to the quantity of the input times its price, which we have written as $a \cdot P_a$), the marginal outlay is simply the change in the firm's total outlay for an input associated with a change in the quantity of that input. When the firm is buying the input in a purely competitive market, the price of the input is not affected by the amount which the firm purchases. Under competitive conditions, therefore, the marginal outlay for an input is equal to the price of that input.

The MRP of an input measures the benefit to the firm from adding more of that input. The marginal outlay measures the burden to the firm from adding more

TABLE 11-1†

Units of Input a	Output	Total Revenue	Marginal Physical Product		Marginal Revenue Product		Marginal cost if $P_a = \$100$	Profit if $P_a = \$100$
			Difference	Derivative	Difference	Derivative	Derivative	
0	0	$ 0						
1	2.00	700	2.00	1.00	$700	$350	$100	$-200
2	2.83	990	0.83	0.71	290	248	142	-10
3	3.46	1,212	0.63	0.58	222	202	173	112
4	4.00	1,400	0.54	0.50	188	175	200	200
5	4.47	1,565	0.47	0.45	165	157	224	265
6	4.90	1,714	0.43	0.41	149	143	245	314
7	5.29	1,852	0.39	0.38	138	132	265	352
8	5.66	1,980	0.37	0.35	128	124	283	380
9	6.00	2,100	0.34	0.33	120	117	300	400
10	6.32	2,213	0.32	0.32	113	111	316	413
11	6.63	2,322	0.31	0.30	109	106	332	422
12	6.93	2,425	0.30	0.29	105	101	347	425
12.25	7.00	2,450	0.28	0.29	100	100	350	425
13	7.21	2,524	0.28	0.28	99	97	361	424
14	7.48	2,619	0.27	0.27	95	94	374	419

† All figures are rounded to the number of digits shown in the table. Marginal cost is derived as follows. Since total cost $= 800 + 100a$, and since $Q = 2a^{1/2}$, we derive $a = Q^2/4$, and therefore $TC = 800 + 25Q^2$. Marginal cost is the derivative of this last function; so $MC = dTC/dQ = 50Q$.

of that input. So long as the benefit exceeds the burden, the firm will gain by expanding the quantity of that input which it employs. Because of diminishing returns, the MRP of an input decreases as the firm uses a larger quantity of it, bringing MRP closer to the input price.

If the firm is employing a quantity of input a such that its MRP is less than the marginal outlay for it, the firm can increase profit by reducing its employment of a. This slides the firm up the MRP schedule, again bringing MRP closer to input price.

The most profitable position for the competitive firm is thus to employ a quantity of input a such that $MRP_a = MO_a = P_a$. To ensure that this is a true maximum, we must add a "second-order condition," namely that MRP_a be decreasing at this point (assuming that P_a is not affected by the quantity of a the firm purchases).

We showed in Table 11-1 the profit which would result to the firm at each input-output level, on the assumption that the price of input a is $100. So long as the $MRP_a > MO_a$, profit rises as input and output expand. The two become equal when the firm is using 12.25 units of a to produce 7 units of output, yielding a profit of $425.† The figures for marginal cost, shown at the right of the table, indicate that the maximum-profit output derived from $MO_a = MRP_a$ coincides with that derived from $MR = MC$. We shall discuss this correspondence later.

demand schedule for input

Under these conditions, the marginal revenue product schedule of an input is the demand schedule by the firm for that input in the short run. However, the MRP_a may not be in the form that we identify as a demand schedule; we do not usually write MRP schedules so that the input quantity is isolated on the left. To get an orthodox-looking demand schedule, we must rearrange the terms in the following fashion:

$$MRP_a = \frac{350}{a^{1/2}} = P_a$$

$$a^{1/2} = \frac{350}{P_a}$$

$$a = \frac{122,500}{P_a{}^2}$$

The last form gives us what we want, an equation for a normal downward-sloping

---

† Since MRP and MO are very close to each other in the whole neighborhood of inputs 12 and 13, it does not make much difference precisely where the firm operates in this neighborhood. Just for the record, however, we note that at input 12, the firm's output would be 692.82 units if we did not round the figures. This would yield total revenue of $2,424.87, for a profit of $424.87, compared with profit of $425 at input 12.25.

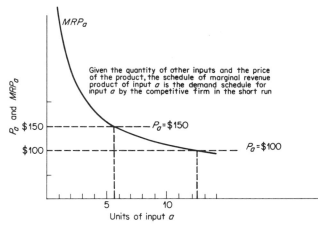

Given the quantity of other inputs and the price of the product, the schedule of marginal revenue product of input a is the demand schedule for input a by the competitive firm in the short run

Figure 11-1 Short-run input demand schedule of competitive firm.

demand curve. To maintain equality between MRP_a and P_a, the firm will tend to use more of input a if its price drops or less if its price rises.

One qualification must be added. The firm will not buy any of the variable input a if its price is greater than (the highest level of) its *average* revenue product, which in the short run is simply total revenue divided by the number of units of input a used. This is merely the input equivalent of the requirement that the selling price of the product must be greater than minimum average variable cost if the firm is to operate in the short run.

Figure 11-1 illustrates the relationship between the marginal revenue product schedule and the firm's (short-run) demand for input a. When the price of the input was assumed to be $100, the firm would maximize profits by purchasing 12.25 units of the input, the quantity at which $MRP_a = MO_a$. However, if the price of a were $150, the firm would use only about 5.5 units of it. The higher input price would mean a higher level for the marginal cost schedule. Thus the maximum-profit output of the firm would be smaller, and so would its employment of input a. Note that the emphasis in the short run is on the output effects of the change in input price.

equivalence of the two rules

As you have probably suspected, we have now said the same thing in two different ways. We have said that the firm maximizes profits by expanding *output* so long as marginal revenue exceeds marginal cost, stopping at the output where $MR = MC$. And we have said that the firm maximizes profits (in the short run) by adding units of the variable input a so long as MRP_a exceeds MO_a, stopping at an input position where $MRP_a = MO_a$. Since, in the short run, output is rigidly linked to the quantity of variable input employed, these two expressions must amount to the same thing.

Both approaches begin with a definition of profit (π) as equal to total revenue minus total cost. The output approach expresses profit, cost, and revenue as functions of output, and the input approach expresses them as functions of input. The output approach develops like this: $\pi = \pi(Q) = TR(Q) - TC(Q)$. To maximize $\pi(Q)$, find the output Q at which the derivatives of TR and TC are equal. The condition $dTR/dQ = dTC/dQ$ is simply a statement that marginal revenue equals marginal cost.

Using the input approach, we have $\pi = \pi(a) = TR(a) - TC(a)$. Setting the derivatives of the right hand side equal to each other, we obtain $dTR/da = dTC/da$, which is a statement that marginal revenue product equals marginal outlay.

In the short run, marginal cost at any input-output point is equal to the ratio MO_a/MPP_a. Let dTC/da represent marginal outlay and dQ/da the marginal physical product of a. Taking both functions at the same point, the ratio between them is $(dTC/da)/(dQ/da)$. This reduces to dTC/dQ, which is marginal cost.

We have already seen that there is a close relation between marginal revenue (which is measured per unit of output) and marginal revenue product (measured per unit of input). In derivative form, the relation is expressed as follows:

$$\frac{dTR}{da} = \frac{dTR}{dQ}\frac{dQ}{da}$$

Thus the marginal revenue product of the input equals the marginal physical product of the input multiplied by the marginal revenue of the product. Since $MRP_a = (MPP_a)(MR)$, it follows that $MR = MRP_a/MPP_a$.

Combining the foregoing, we can show that equality between MC and MR implies equality between MRP_a and MO_a. Note that

$$MC = \frac{MO_a}{MPP_a} = MR = \frac{MRP_a}{MPP_a}$$

The MPP_a terms cancel, leaving $MO_a = MRP_a$. This will work out neatly only if input a is the only variable input.

Under competitive conditions, the marginal outlay on the variable input is a constant—in our example, \$100. Because of diminishing returns, the marginal physical product of the variable input declines as its quantity increases. As a result, the ratio MO_a/MPP_a increases as the quantity of the variable input increases. Thus rising short-run marginal cost is simply a reflection of diminishing returns to the variable input.

The marginal cost schedule is used to determine the supply schedule of output of the firm, taking as given the prices of inputs and letting the product price vary. The marginal revenue product schedule is used to determine the short-run demand schedule of the firm for one variable input, taking as given the price of the product and the quantity of other inputs and letting the price of the variable input vary. In each case we take the production function as given.

determinants of MRP schedule

Our method of deriving the MRP schedule indicates that it is determined by the production function, the quantity of other input(s) used, and the marginal revenue schedule of the product. We shall consider each in turn.

1. The production function depends in part on the technology and organizational skill of the firm. However, it also depends on the quality of the inputs themselves. Production functions in agriculture depend on the climate and fertility of the land. Every production function depends upon the quality of the labor employed. We consider the qualitative aspects of factors of production more fully in subsequent chapters dealing with pricing of factors in the economy as a whole.

2. The quantity of other inputs on hand, in any short-run situation, reflects preceding long-run decisions by the firm. We consider these in subsequent sections of this chapter. Note that the MRP schedule of the variable input tends to be the higher, the larger the quantity of the fixed input.

3. The marginal revenue schedule of the product reflects the demand conditions confronting the firm. The purely competitive firm is faced with an infinitely elastic demand schedule, thus its $MR = P$. In imperfectly competitive markets, MR is typically less than P. We consider the latter situation at greater length in a later chapter.

Even in the short run, a firm is likely to use more than one variable input. Under those conditions, one would need to use a measure of marginal *net* revenue product for an input, which we shall discuss in the following sections.

input demand—long-run

Just as long-run supply schedules differ from short-run, so a firm's long-run demand schedule for an input differs from its short-run demand schedule. In the long run all inputs are variable. The firm has latitude to change its input mix. The firm can react in the long run to changes in input prices by movements along two margins, an output margin and a substitution margin. We have already analyzed this process; our problem here is to see whether there is not some long-run equivalent of the marginal revenue product concept which can be used as the basis for an input demand schedule.

Strictly speaking, both MPP and MRP are calculated for any one input on the assumption that for other inputs the *quantity used* is given. This assumption is clearly inappropriate for long-run analysis. We may consent to hold constant the prices of other inputs, but we want to leave the firm free to vary its quantities in order to make input substitutions. We deal with this difficulty by introducing a concept which takes account of changes along both margins of adjustment—the substitution margin as well as the output margin. We define the *total net revenue product* of an input a as the firm's total revenue at any given input-output position, minus its expenditures on all inputs other than a. From this can be derived a schedule showing total net revenue product $(TNRP)$ for each quantity of input a. From that schedule can be derived the marginal net revenue product $(MNRP)$ schedule.

In order to calculate these schedules of net revenue product, we must be able to associate with each level of input a a specific quantity of output and a specific quantity of the other inputs. Fortunately, our preceding analysis of short-run conditions provides us with the method for identifying such specific quantities of output and other inputs. In the short run the quantity of a is fixed, and the competitive firm adds units of the other inputs (let us deal with only one, namely b) up to the point where the MRP_b is equal to P_b. What we must now do is to repeat this operation for each possible level of a. At the point where $MRP_b = P_b$, there will be identified a quantity of output, a quantity of total revenue, a quantity of input b, a quantity of expenditure on input b, and therefore a quantity of total net revenue product to associate with that quantity of input a.

To illustrate, we derive the total net revenue product for 8 units of input a on the assumption that the production function is $Q_A = a^{1/3}b^{1/3}$, where the product price $P_A = \$10$, and $P_b = \$2$. The total revenue $(P_A Q_A)$ can be expressed by $20b^{1/3}$, and the marginal revenue product of b is the derivative of this total revenue expression. With 8 units of a, $MRP_b = 6.67/b^{2/3}$. When we set this equal to P_b and solve, we find the appropriate value for the quantity of b is 6.08 units. Inserting this into the production function yields an output of 3.65 units. Total revenue is therefore about $36.48 and expenditures on input b total $12.16. Thus the total net revenue product of 8 units of input a is about $24.32.

It is useful to obtain a general expression showing the appropriate amount of b to use with each quantity of a. At any specified quantity of a, the marginal revenue product of b can be obtained as the derivative of the total revenue schedule:

$$TR = 10a^{1/3}b^{1/3}$$

$$\frac{dTR}{db} = 3.33\,\frac{a^{1/3}}{b^{2/3}} = MRP_b$$

Setting this equal to P_b ($= \$2$), we obtain

$$3.33a^{1/3} = 2b^{2/3}$$
$$a = .216b^2 \qquad \text{or} \qquad b = 2.15a^{1/2}$$

These values define the optimum proportions between a and b, given the production function, the price of input b, and the price of the product.

Now that we know the appropriate quantity of b to use with each quantity of a, we can derive a general expression for the total net revenue product schedule of input a. First,

$$TNRP_a = P_A Q_A - b \cdot P_b = 10a^{1/3}b^{1/3} - 2b$$

($P_A Q_A$ represents total revenue.) Substituting in place of b, we obtain

$$TNRP_a = 10(2.15a^{3/2})^{1/3} - 4.3a^{1/2}$$
$$= 12.9a^{1/2} - 4.3a^{1/2}$$
$$= 8.6a^{1/2}$$

The final solution tells us that the total net revenue product associated with any given quantity of input a will be 8.6 times the square root of that quantity.

marginal net revenue product

Our analysis indicates the best way to use each quantity of input a, given the production function and prices of product and of input b. It remains to determine the optimal quantity of input a to employ, which depends on the price of input a. The concept of marginal net revenue product provides the instrument for solving this problem. We define the marginal net revenue product ($MNRP_a$) of input a as the change in the total net revenue product of input a associated with a change in the quantity of input a employed. The value of $MNRP_a$ may be calculated as a ratio of finite changes between two points or as the derivative of the total net revenue product schedule at any given point.

In Table 11-2 are shown the numerical values of total and marginal net revenue products of input a corresponding to the data used in the example above. In the table, $MNRP_a$ is calculated in two ways. The first is as the difference in $TNRP_a$ as we move from one integral value of input a to the next. The second is the derivative $dTNRP_a/da$. Since

$$TNRP_a = 8.6a^{1/2}$$

then
$$\frac{dTNRP_a}{da} = \frac{4.3}{a^{1/2}} = MNRP_a$$

Table 11-2 also shows average net revenue product, which is simply $TNRP_a$ divided by the quantity of input a. Thus

$$ANRP_a = \frac{8.6a^{1/2}}{a} = \frac{8.6}{a^{1/2}}$$

TABLE 11-2

| Quantity | | Output | Total Revenue | Cost of b $(b \cdot P_b)$ | Total Net Revenue Product of Input a | Marginal Net Revenue Product of Input a | | Average Net Revenue Product |
Input a	Input b					Difference	Derivative	
0	0	0	0	$ 0	$ 0			
1	2.15	1.290	$12.90	4.30	8.60	$8.60	$4.30	$8.60
2	3.04	1.824	18.24	6.08	12.16	3.56	3.04	6.08
3	3.72	2.232	22.32	7.44	14.88	2.72	2.48	4.96
4	4.30	2.580	25.80	8.60	17.20	2.32	2.15	4.30
5	4.81	2.886	28.86	9.61	19.24	2.04	1.92	3.85
6	5.27	3.162	31.62	10.54	21.08	1.84	1.76	3.51
7	5.69	3.414	34.14	11.38	22.76	1.68	1.63	3.25
8	6.08	3.648	36.48	12.16	24.32	1.56	1.52	3.04
9	6.45	3.870	38.70	12.90	25.80	1.48	1.43	2.87
10	6.80	4.080	40.80	13.60	27.20	1.40	1.36	2.72
20	9.61	5.766	57.66	19.22	38.44		0.96	1.92
30	11.78	7.068	70.68	23.56	47.12		0.79	1.57
40	13.60	8.160	81.60	27.20	54.40		0.68	1.34
50	15.20	9.120	91.20	30.40	60.80		0.61	1.21

Assumes $Q = a^{1/3} b^{1/3}$; price of product = \$10; price of b = \$2.

optimum input—final solution

The marginal net revenue product curve is shown in Figure 11-2. It is downward sloping because of two conditions. The first is that the marginal rate of input substitution is declining. Along the substitution margin, increases in the quantity of a displace smaller and smaller increments of b if output remains constant. The second condition is decreasing returns to scale. Along the output margin, increments of inputs in any given proportion yield increments of output in some smaller proportion.

The firm's input decision follows the logic of marginal analysis. So long as the marginal net revenue product of an input is greater than the marginal outlay required to obtain it, the firm will gain by adding more of the input. However, if marginal outlay exceeds marginal net revenue product at the existing rate of input utilization, the firm will gain by reducing its use of input a. Under competitive conditions the marginal outlay on an input is equal to its price. Thus the firm tends in the long run to employ a quantity of input a such that its marginal net revenue will be equal to its price. To obtain an expression for the demand schedule, set the

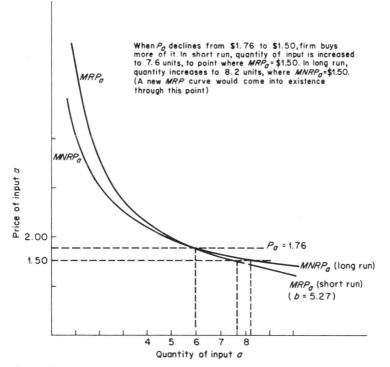

Figure 11-2   Long-run and short-run demand schedules for input by competitive firm.

$MNRP_a$ expression equal to P_a and solve for a, as follows:

$$MNRP_a = \frac{4.3}{a^{1/2}} = P_a$$

$$a^{1/2} = \frac{4.3}{P_a}$$

$$a = \frac{18.5}{P_a^2}$$

The firm moves toward this solution along both margins. So long as $MNRP_a >$ MO_a, this implies one or both of two conditions: either the marginal rate of substitution between inputs is not equal to the ratio of their prices, or marginal cost has not been equated with marginal revenue. The profit-maximizing input-output position of the firm is reached when equilibrium has been achieved along both margins simultaneously. And that same input-output position is the one at which $MNRP_a = MO_a$.

Suppose the price of $a = \$1.76$. Table 11-2 tells us that the best-profit point should be at the input of 6 units of a and an output of 3.162 units. It is possible to show that at that point the marginal rate of substitution between inputs a and b will be equal to the ratio of their prices. By taking output as given, we can convert the production function into an equation expressing a in terms of b. We arrive at this function: $a = 31.61/b$. The first derivative of this is the marginal rate of substitution, which is $31.61/b^2$ (ignoring the minus sign). Since $b = 5.27$ at the equilibrium point, the derivative reduces to 1.14. The ratio of input prices is $2/1.76 = 1.14$ also.

We can also show that marginal cost is equal to marginal revenue at the equilibrium output of 3.162. We know that marginal revenue is equal to the price of the product in this case, which is \$10. To determine marginal cost, we need an expression for total cost as a function of output. We know that total cost is the sum of the outlays for inputs a and b; thus, $TC = 1.76a + 2b$. Next, we find relationships between the two inputs and the output, by setting the marginal rates of input substitution equal to the ratios of input price. For input b, the calculation is as follows:

$$\frac{da}{db} = \frac{Q^3}{b^2} = \frac{P_b}{P_a} = \frac{2.00}{1.76}$$

$$b = 0.938Q^{3/2}$$

By setting the other derivative, db/da, equal to 1.76/2.00, we obtain $a = 1.066Q^{3/2}$. Now we substitute these values for a and b back into the total cost equation:

$$TC = (1.76)(1.066Q^{3/2}) + (2)(0.938Q^{3/2})$$
$$TC = 3.75Q^{3/2}$$

Taking the derivative of this total cost function, we obtain $MC = 5.625Q^{1/2}$. When Q is equal to 3.162, this marginal cost function has a value of 10, which equals the product price and marginal revenue.

The long-run equilibrium situation will also possess the properties which we identified in the short-run equilibrium. The marginal revenue product of each input will be equal to the price of that input. And the marginal revenue product of each input will be equal to its marginal physical product times the marginal revenue of the product.

In our illustration, the firm in equilibrium uses 6 units of a and 5.27 units of b, with a production function $Q = a^{1/3}b^{1/3}$. When the product price is $10, the total revenue function is $TR = 10a^{1/3}b^{1/3}$. Given the quantity of input b, the marginal revenue product of a is the derivative of the function $TR = 10(5.27a)^{1/3} = 17.4a^{1/3}$. The derivative of this is (ignoring the minus sign):

$$\frac{17.4}{3a^{2/3}} = \frac{5.8}{a^{2/3}}$$

When $a = 6$, the equation yields $5.8/3.3 = 1.76$ as the value of MRP_a, which was the price of a in the illustration. By a similar operation, we could show that the marginal revenue product of b is equal to its price of 2 in equilibrium. Try it for yourself.

reaction to change in price of input a

In the long run, the schedule of marginal net revenue product of an input is the firm's demand schedule for that input, given the production function, the price of the product, and the prices of other inputs. (However, if the price of an input exceeds the highest value of its average net revenue product, the firm will not buy any of it.) If the price of input a rises, the firm will reduce its use of that input, moving back along the $MNRP_a$ curve until equality is restored with MO_a. If the price of input a declines, the firm will increase its use of a, moving to the right along the $MNRP_a$ curve until equality is reached with the new value for marginal outlay.

The long-run adjustment to change in the price of input a involves both output effects and substitution effects. If P_a declines, the firm tends to increase its proportionate use of input a at any level of output; in addition, with lower marginal costs, the firm tends to increase output.

By contrast, the firm's short-run demand schedule for input a (which we assume is the variable input in the short run) is determined by the schedule of marginal revenue product, derived from the production function on the assumption that the quantity of other inputs is fixed. As an illustration let us start from the preceding equilibrium situation, where $P_a = \$1.76$ and $P_b = \$2.00$, with the firm employing 5.27

units of input b, which we assume to be fixed in the short run. With this quantity of b, the schedule of MRP_a is expressed by $5.8/a^{2/3}$. The short-run demand schedule is thus $a = 13.97/P_a^{3/2}$.

Figure 11-2 shows the curves for $MNRP_a$ and this particular MRP_a (bear in mind that there is another MRP_a schedule for each other value of the fixed input b). The $MNRP_a$ curve represents a long-run demand curve for input a, while the MRP_a represents a short-run demand curve for that input. The short-run curve is steeper; it rises to a higher level at low quantities of input a.

Suppose the price of a falls to $1.50. The initial response of the firm is to move along the short-run MRP_a curve to the point where it intersects the new price. The intersection point is approximately at 7.6 units of a. The adjustment in the short run is made entirely through changes in output. With lower costs, the most profitable output of the firm is larger than before.

If the firm expects the change to be of long duration, then a long-run adjustment will occur. The quantity of input b can be altered. Because the $MNRP_a$ curve is flatter, the firm expands its use of input a still further, to a level of about 8.2 units. In the process, it increases its use of input b. While the proportion of a is increased through the normal substitution effect, the output effect is large enough to cause a net increase in the use of input b.

Suppose the price of a were to rise from the initial equilibrium price of $1.76. Initially, the firm would adjust by reducing its input of a and curtailing output. In the long run, the quantity of a would be curtailed still further, as the quantity of input b would be reduced.

If one were considering the firm's demand for the fixed input b, the distinction between short run and long run would be even more pronounced. In the short run, the firm's employment of b is invariant with respect to the price of b. Thus its demand is completely price-inelastic. In the long run, however, the firm would have an $MNRP$ schedule for b and a corresponding demand curve, just as it has for a.

changes in data

When we constructed the long-run $MNRP_a$ schedule, we took as given the price of input b (representing all other inputs) and the price of the product. If either of these shifts, it would cause a shift in the entire $MNRP_a$ schedule. For instance, an increase in the price of b would tend to reduce the total revenue product of each input-output combination. For any given output, a larger proportion of a would be used (substitution effect). But with any given quantity of a, the optimum output would be somewhat lower (because of the output effect resulting from higher costs). The schedule of $MNRP_a$ would be reduced, on balance, by a rise in the price of input b.

Suppose the price of the product were to rise. This would raise the total and marginal net revenue product of any given quantity of input a; thus more of it would be used at any given price. However, the optimum proportion between inputs a and b would remain the same; the higher price of the product would produce output effects but not substitution effects.

A change in the physical input-output relationship, as measured by the production function, would also shift the schedule of $MNRP_a$. A technical improvement which caused the output from each input combination to rise by some fixed proportion would have the same effect on the $MNRP_a$ as a rise in the price of the product.

This is a good place to remind ourselves that the production function itself depends on the quality of the inputs employed. Thus the $MNRP_a$ of each input depends upon the quality of that input and the quality of the others working with it, as well as on technological and organizational skill.

average net revenue product

The average net revenue product of an input can be defined as the total net revenue product divided by the quantity of the input used. Average net revenue product ($ANRP$) behaves like the inverse of average cost. We assume that AC typically slopes down initially as output increases, then rises. The average net revenue product typically rises initially as the input increases, then declines. We know that marginal cost intersects average cost at the lowest point of AC. Marginal net revenue product intersects $ANRP$ at the highest level of $ANRP$.

In Figure 11-3 these revenue product relationships are illustrated on the assump-

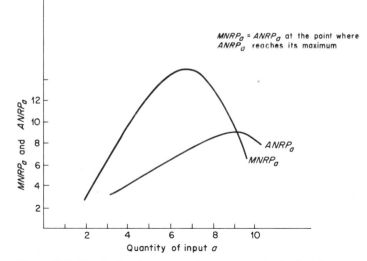

Figure 11-3 Marginal and average net revenue product schedules.

tion that the total net revenue product schedule for input a is equal to $0.33a^3 - 0.025a^4$, which yields $MNRP_a = a^2 - 0.1a^3$. The $MNRP_a$ curve rises initially, reaches a maximum between 6 and 7 units, then declines. It intersects the $ANRP_a$ schedule just short of 9 units of input. At that point both have the value of \$8.78. Test your understanding by deriving an expression for $ANRP_a$, demonstrating that average and marginal are equal when the quantity of input a is 8.89 units and that this represents the maximum value of $ANRP_a$.

Total or average net revenue product can be used as a guide to the profit position of the firm. The total net revenue product of some quantity of input a reflects the total revenue of the firm minus its expenditures on other inputs. If we subtract from $TNRP_a$ the expenditure on input a, we obtain a measure of total profit. Dividing both expressions by the quantity of a, we find that if average net revenue product is greater than the price of a, the firm is making more than a normal profit. If $P_a > ANRP_a$, the firm will be making less than a normal profit. If $P_a = ANRP_a$, the firm will just be making a normal profit. In the long run, the firm will not operate if $P_a > ANRP_a$.

summary

The firm's demand schedule for any single input can be determined on the basis of a given production function and set of prices for the product and for the other inputs. In the short run, the firm's demand schedule is given by the marginal revenue product schedule of the variable input. Marginal revenue product is simply the marginal physical product of the variable input multiplied by the marginal revenue of the product. For long-run analysis, we identify the total *net* revenue product schedule of an input as the total revenue at each input-output position minus the expenditures on other inputs at that same input-output position. From it we can derive the marginal net revenue product schedule, which measures the change in total net revenue product associated with a change in the quantity of the input employed.

The marginal outlay on the input measures the change in total expenditure on that input associated with a change in the quantity of the input purchased. For a firm purchasing under purely competitive conditions, the marginal outlay on an input is equal to its price. The firm maximizes profits by employing a quantity of each input such that its MRP (in the short run) or $MNRP$ (in the long run) is equal to the marginal outlay for it. Under competitive conditions, the schedule of MRP_a, constructed for a given endowment of fixed input, identifies a short-run demand schedule for input a. The schedule of $MNRP_a$ constitutes the long-run demand schedule for input a.

If the firm is operating where $M(N)RP_a$ exceeds P_a, the firm can increase profit by employing more of input a. Since the MRP_a and $MNRP_a$ schedules are downward sloping, this moves the firm toward a point where $M(N)RP_a = P_a$. If the firm is operating where P_a exceeds $M(N)RP_a$, it can improve its position by using less of input a.

In the short run, the firm adjusts to changes in the price of a variable input by changes in its output. In the long run, input-price changes set off both output effects and substitution effects. In either event, however, the firm's demand curve for any input is given by its marginal revenue product schedule in the short run (other inputs fixed), and by its marginal net revenue product schedule in the long run (all inputs variable.)

TERMS AND CONCEPTS

1. Marginal outlay schedule
2. Total net revenue product schedule
3. Marginal revenue product schedule
4. Marginal net revenue product schedule
5. Average net revenue product schedule

QUESTIONS AND PROBLEMS

1. Assume the production function $Q = 10a^{2/5}b^{1/2}$, where a and b represent the amounts of the two inputs. Assume the price of the product is $2, and the price of input b is $5. Derive an expression for the total net revenue product schedule of input a and graph it. Use the marginal net revenue product schedule of a to find the optimum input of a if $P_a = \$8$. Find the corresponding output and prove that at the optimum input both equilibrium conditions are satisfied: the marginal rate of input substitution equals the ratio of input prices, and marginal cost equals marginal revenue.

2. Using the same production function as in problem 1, assume that in the short run the quantity of input b is fixed at 9 units, costing $50 per unit. Calculate the schedule of marginal physical product for input a. If the price of the product is $5, what is the expression for the marginal revenue product schedule? If the price of input a is $7.50, what is the most profitable quantity of a for the firm to employ? Calculate the corresponding output, and show that marginal cost equals marginal revenue at that output.

product-market and factor-market adjustments in the competitive industry

In the preceding chapters we have concerned ourselves with the individual firm in a competitive industry. For the individual firm, prices of inputs and outputs are given: they are outside the control of the individual firm, which is too small to affect them. On the basis of prices and its own production function, the firm determines the *quantities* of inputs to acquire and the *quantities* of outputs to produce and sell.

When we come to consider all the firms in one industry, viewed collectively, it is no longer proper to regard prices as fixed, given magnitudes. Prices themselves become things to be determined by the behavior of all the firms in the industry. We have already confronted a more elementary version of this problem in Chapter 5, where we discussed the interaction of supply and demand. Our task at this point is to show how the analysis of the individual firm, which we have covered in Chapters 8 through 11, helps to explain the supply and demand conditions for an entire industry.

assumptions

In analyzing the behavior of the industry as a whole, we need to specify certain magnitudes which are taken as given. They are as follows:

1. Production function. We assume that each firm has a production function expressing real output as a function of real inputs and based upon a given condition of technology and organizational skill. We assume each firm does as well as it knows how, but this does not imply that all firms use the same methods of production. However, we shall see that the pressure of competition has some tendency to force firms toward similarity in production methods.

2. Demand for product. We assume that there exists a demand schedule for the product as a whole, which is negatively sloped (so that quantity purchased varies inversely with price charged). We also assume that there exists one uniform price for the product, to which each firm adjusts the quantity of its inputs and outputs. For the individual competitive firm, of course, the demand curve appears as a perfectly horizontal line at the level of the existing market price.

3. Supply of inputs. We assume that there exist supply schedules of the inputs which the industry uses. It is possible, if the industry is very small, and if the inputs it uses are widely used in other sectors of the economy, that those inputs may have supply schedules of virtually infinite elasticity with respect to the industry in question. If input supply has infinite elasticity, the industry can vary its purchases of inputs (within a normal range) without altering their prices. It is more probable, however, that the supply curves of inputs to the industry will be upward sloping; that is, if the industry attempts to increase its employment of an input, the price of that input will rise.

We assume, further, that inputs are supplied under conditions of pure competition and that there exists one uniform market price for each input. Of course, to the firm, the supply curve of each input is a horizontal line at the level of the existing market price.

equilibrium conditions

In the short run the firms already existing in the industry adjust their employment of variable inputs, in combination with their existing quantity of fixed-capital assets, to achieve an output such that marginal cost equals marginal revenue (i.e., equals price of the product, under competitive conditions). However, any firm which finds the price below the minimum level of average variable cost will produce no output at all.

In the long run, each firm adjusts the scale of its plant to achieve a size of operation at which its long-run marginal cost is equal to marginal revenue (is equal to price of the product). Even more important, however, is a dimension of variation we have not considered—variation in the *number* of firms in the industry. Such variation takes place through the *entry* of firms into the industry when it is very profitable, and through the *exit*, or departure, of firms when the industry is unprofitable.

We assume that it is possible for new firms to enter the competitive industry and to function without being at a substantial disadvantage relative to those already there. An industry characterized by a large number of small firms is likely to be relatively easy to enter, since it is likely to be an industry where large amounts of capital are not necessary for efficient operation and where the technology is not highly complex. Entry may occur through the establishment of new firms, but it also commonly occurs through shifts in the activities of existing firms already producing in other industries. The existing firm which enters a new field through diversification may already have developed managerial and technical expertise so that it is not at a disadvantage compared with firms already in the new field.

When will additional firms wish to enter the industry? This will depend on the rate of profit which is being earned by the firms already there. We have already assumed that there exists for the economy as a whole some average normal rate of profit (expressed as a percentage of capital invested). We now use that concept to make a further assumption: we assume that additional firms will enter a given competitive industry whenever the rate of profit in that industry is higher than the normal return on capital in the economy as a whole. We also assume that firms will tend to depart from an industry if the rate of profit earned by capital is less than the normal return prevailing in the economy.

This assumption fits in closely with our analysis of the costs of the individual firm. We have defined costs to include a normal rate of return on the capital employed by the firm, whether obtained by borrowing or from the owners. It follows that the average cost provides a kind of break-even point in judging incentives for entry or departure. We have already established that, in the long-run, if the product price falls below the lowest average cost at which the firm can produce, the firm will go out of business—that is, it will exit from the industry. We now add the counterpart assumption that if the price is above the lowest average cost at which typical firms can produce the product, additional firms will enter the industry.

Variation in the number of firms becomes a powerful element in the process by which an industry approaches long-run equilibrium. So long as price is above average cost, additional firms tend to enter the industry. But this entry itself tends to bring price and average cost closer together. Additional output from the additional firms adds to supply and pushes down price. Additional demand for inputs from the additional firms adds to demand and may push up input prices, raising costs.

A similar process may operate if the price is below average cost. Individual firms drop out of the industry at a rate of speed which depends on the durability, age, and specificity of their fixed-capital assets. Their departure reduces output and brings the price up, while also reducing demand for inputs and perhaps leading to reduction in input prices and costs for the remaining firms.

It follows that the industry is in (long-run) equilibrium when the price of the product is equal to the lowest (long-run) average cost at which it can be produced by the typical firm.

costs in equilibrium

The equilibrium condition we have just stated may not mean very much if some firms in an industry have cost curves which are much higher or lower than those of other firms. Such differences may arise because firms do not all have the same production function, or because some are not using the most appropriate input combination. Some firms may fail to achieve the lowest possible costs because of ignorance: they may simply not have sufficient knowledge of production techniques to use the best ones. However, it is also possible that some firms do not minimize costs because the motivations of the management do not correspond with the usual assumption that firms desire to maximize profits. In a large corporation, the management may be a group separate from the owners. Management officials may be chiefly concerned with their own salaries, with security of employment, and perhaps with maintaining a congenial climate of interpersonal relations. Cost minimization may place a strain on interpersonal relations, requiring that each person be judged chiefly on his efficiency and productivity. Large differences in managerial efficiency may arise because firms differ in the tone and style of interpersonal relations.

Profit maximization may also be an inaccurate description of the motivations of a family business. For personal reasons, the firm may be eager to employ family members to the point of paying them more than the value of their marginal product, and will be reluctant to hire outsiders even if they could be employed for less than the value of their marginal product.

Case studies of actual industries indicate that the effectiveness of cost minimization may depend on the intensity of competition, and the likelihood that a firm may be forced to close if it does not reduce costs. In competitive industries, there are several forces which cause firms to tend toward relative equality of average cost schedules. One such force is the Darwinian process of survival of the fittest. Firms whose costs are substantially above the industry average may simply find themselves sustaining losses and be driven out of business. Uniformity is approached because the nonconformists have left the industry. However, this process may not work very rapidly in an industry where family firms predominate and where large proportions of costs are implicit costs which do not require cash outlays.

Where money prices and market forces work more strongly, costs may move toward uniformity by means of changes in the prices and costs associated with certain inputs of the deviant firms. Suppose that one firm earns superior profits because it has a superior location and that location rests on land which is leased by the firm. Other firms will find it to their advantage to bid for the advantageous tract of land, and the owner of the land, when existing leases expire, can increase the rent sufficiently to appropriate for himself the extra profits which are attributable to location.

Downward adjustments in the values of previously produced capital goods may help bring about uniformity of costs. Consider a coal mine which is unable to earn a normal profit on the capital sum originally spent to construct it. If the original owners sell the mine, its price will be lower than the original cost of constructing it, for no investor will buy it unless he can earn a normal return on his investment. For such a new investor, burdened with a much smaller investment, the average cost of producing coal will be much lower because of the revaluation of the fixed capital. (As long as the capital asset can be reproduced at a cost similar to its original cost, its market value will not rise much above its original cost. Can you see why?)

Other, more complex reasons may be involved in cost differences between firms. But the general principle remains valid: if the superior or inferior profitability of the firm can be attributed to any specific element of input—a tract of land, a capital asset, a particular executive or other employee—in the long run the costs associated with that input will tend to adjust in such a manner as to eliminate the profit superiority or inferiority. Even if such specific attribution is not possible, variations in profitability will tend to be eliminated when the ownership of entire firms is transferred, for the valuation placed upon the firm as a whole will tend to be such as to yield the new owners only a normal return on their investment.

the firm in industry equilibrium

We will assume that the firms in an industry tend toward a situation of uniform lowest average cost, so there is no serious ambiguity in stating the equilibrium condition in terms of the relation between the price and the average cost. Let us now see what the industry equilibrium position implies for the individual firm.

We have stated that in the pursuit of maximum profits, the individual firm in a purely competitive industry will always wish to produce an output at which marginal cost equals marginal revenue (equals price). In addition, the industry as a whole is in equilibrium when the price of the product is equal to the average cost of producing it. These two conditions can exist simultaneously only if price is equal to both marginal and average cost at the same time. That can only occur when individual firms are operating at an output where marginal cost equals average cost. And that, we have already established, is true only at the output for which average cost reaches its minimum level on the firm's cost curve.

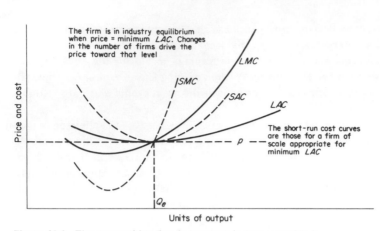

The firm is in industry equilibrium
when price = minimum *LAC*. Changes
in the number of firms drive the
price toward that level

LMC

SMC

SAC

LAC

The short-run cost curves
are those for a firm of
scale appropriate for
minimum *LAC*

p

Q_e

Price and cost

Units of output

Figure 12-1 The competitive firm in long-run industry equilibrium.

Figure 12-1 illustrates the significance for the individual firm of the industry equilibrium conditions. Assuming cost similarity, with price P_e and output Q_e, price equals long- and short-run average and marginal costs. The firm is just covering average costs, and earning a normal return on its capital. New firms would have no incentive to enter the industry, and existing firms have no incentive to leave it.

However, if a higher price prevailed, disequilibrium would be created for the industry as a whole. With price above average cost, the return to capital would be above normal, and entry of additional firms would be encouraged. Nor would a price lower than P_e be consistent with industry equilibrium, for some existing firms would drop out of the industry.

the industry supply schedule—short run

How will the output of the competitive industry respond to a shift in the demand schedule? We assume that the industry is initially in a long-run equilibrium position. Each firm is in a position like that shown in Figure 12-1, producing at an output of lowest LAC; at that same output LMC, SAC, and SMC are all equal to the price. Existing firms have no incentive to change their output, and there is no reason for the population of firms to change.

Suppose now that the demand schedule for the product shifts upward, causing the price to increase. Individual firms would expand output initially by increasing their use of variable inputs; they would move up their short-run marginal cost curves to an output where SMC would be equal to the new price. If input prices were not affected by this increase, the industry's short-run supply curve would be a summation of the SMC curves of the existing firms. However, the supply curve of variable input for the industry as a whole may be upward sloping (even though for

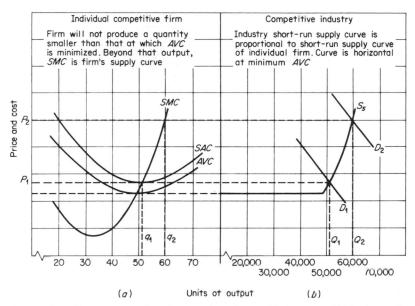

Figure 12-2 Short-run reaction of competitive firm and industry to shift in demand: infinite elasticity of supply of variable input.

the individual firm in isolation input supply has infinite elasticity). If the industry as a whole expands output, the prices of variable inputs tend to rise. Such an increase would cause the SMC curves of the firms to shift upward. The new equilibrium would still be reached at a point where price would equal SMC, but the SMC curve itself would have shifted. The industry's short-run supply curve depends, in this case, on the extent to which SMC shifts as well as on the elasticity of existing SMC. And the shift in SMC is larger, the lower the elasticity of supply of the variable input(s).

Figure 12-2 describes the relation of the firm and the industry to an increase in demand for the product when the supply of variable input is infinitely elastic. Starting from P_1, a shift in demand from D_1 to D_2 causes output and price to adjust along the short-run supply curve S_s. Relative changes in price and quantity reflect the elasticity of the short-run marginal cost schedules, reflecting the extent to which firms encounter diminishing returns to the variable input as they expand production with a given stock of fixed-capital assets. The S_s curve reflects the shape of the firms' SMC curves, with the added proviso that a firm will produce zero output at a price below minimum average variable cost.

By contrast, Figure 12-3 shows the relation of firm and industry supply when the price of the variable input responds positively to changes in the industry's demand for it. Because of the upward shift in SMC, the increase in output by each firm is less than in the previous case. The industry short-run supply curve has a lower

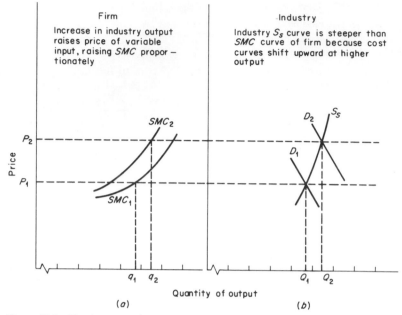

Figure 12-3 Short-run reaction of competitive firm and industry to shift in demand: finite elasticity of input supply.

elasticity than the SMC curve of the typical firm, the difference being greater, the lower the elasticity of supply of the variable input to the industry.

Finally, consider the other limiting case in which the variable input has a totally inelastic supply to the industry as a whole. In such a case, efforts by the industry to expand output will be unavailing. The only results will be that the price of the variable input will rise and that the SMC curves of firms will rise enough so that the old output will still be produced at a price and SMC determined by the point where the new demand curve crosses the old output. Moreover, the industry S_s curve would be vertical. This situation is not drawn for you. Test your understanding by drawing a pair of diagrams similar to Figure 12-3 to describe the case of totally inelastic input supply.

the industry supply schedule—long run

In the long run, the output of the industry may involve two additional dimensions of variation. Existing firms may alter the scale of their plant, and the number of firms may change. In either event, long-run changes in industry output involve commensurate variations in inputs. All inputs are variable.

A shift in demand tends to create a gap between price and average cost, which in turn tends to change the number of firms in the industry. Output will change sufficiently to restore equality between price and average cost. We can identify the industry's long-run supply schedule by determining how much change in output is required to bring price and cost back to equality. If the firms' LAC curves are unaffected by changes in industry output, output must change sufficiently to bring price back to its original level. The industry will have an infinitely elastic long-run supply schedule. More commonly, however, firms' costs will be altered by changes in industry supply. Thus adjustments will occur in both costs and price.

The firm's cost schedules might be affected by changes in industry output in two ways. First, the production function of the firm might be affected by changes in the size of the industry. For simplicity, we will assume that this does not occur. Second, the firm's costs will be affected by changes in input prices resulting from changes in the output of the industry. The lower the elasticity of supply of inputs to the industry, the greater the rise in firm's LAC curves as industry output expands, and the smaller the increase in output which will result from a given increase in demand.

Figure 12-4 considers the long-run adjustment of firm and industry to increased demand when input prices are not affected by industry output. Firms are assumed to be initially in long-run equilibrium at price P_1. The increase in demand raises the price to P_2, and existing firms expand output along their short-run marginal cost

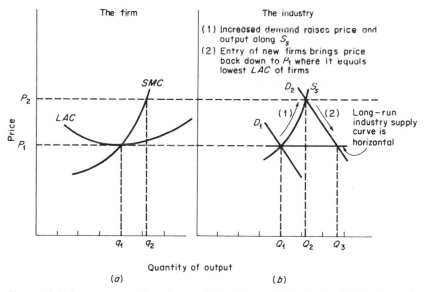

Figure 12-4 Long-run reaction of competitive firm and industry to shift in demand: infinite elasticity of input supply.

curves from q_1 to q_2. Industry output moves from Q_1 to Q_2. However, the new higher price P_2 is well above average cost. Thus firms are earning more than a normal return on their capital. Consequently new firms will be attracted to enter the industry. Since the supply of inputs is perfectly elastic, the cost curves of existing firms are not raised. As the newcomers add to the output of the industry, output increases beyond Q_2, and the price comes back down again. It continues to fall until it reaches a level at which no further entry takes place—a level only reached when the price returns to its original level. Since average costs are unchanged, the long-run equilibrium price must be the same as it was originally.

By implication, then, we have derived the long-run supply curve for the industry. It is simply a horizontal line at a level corresponding to the lowest point on the long-run average cost curve of the typical firm. We can conclude that if the inputs used in the industry have infinite elasticity of supply, the industry's output will also have infinite elasticity of supply.

Note the interesting implications for the firm which was already in existence. Initially that firm expands output to q_2. But as pressure from entry of additional firms drives the price back down, the optimum output position of the firm is at q_1 again. Thus the long-run change in industry output has occurred entirely through the change in the *number* of firms, without any change in the scale of operation of individual firms.

long-run industry supply—finite elasticity of input supply

More typically, we would expect to find that the supply curves of the industry's inputs would be upward sloping. Consequently, an increase in the industry's output causes the prices of inputs to rise, and as a result, each firm's average cost curve shifts upward. Figure 12-5 illustrates the adjustment pattern of firm and industry under this condition. As before, the increase in demand from D_1 to D_2 causes price initially to rise to P_2, along the industry short-run supply curve, and individual firms expand output to points corresponding to Q_2. Again, the excess of price over average cost attracts entry and the price recedes from P_2. However, demand pressure by firms in the industry tends to raise the prices of inputs, a tendency reflected in an upward shift in the average-cost curves of all firms in the industry. As a result, the industry equilibrium condition, $P = LAC$, is reached at a higher price than in the preceding case. We show it at P_3. The industry's long-run supply curve, traced out in the movement from Q_1 to Q_3, is upward sloping, and the elasticity of supply of the industry's output derives directly from the elasticity of supply of the inputs.

The shape of the industry's long-run supply curve thus depends on how much the average cost schedules of the firms shift when industry output changes. Since the production function of the individual firm is not likely to be affected by the level of industry output, the only force making for shifts in average costs is change in input prices. Individual firms, buying under competitive conditions, are confronted

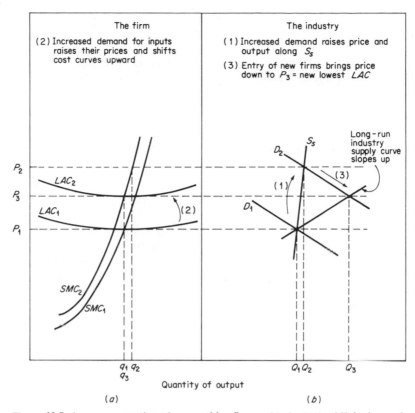

Figure 12-5 Long-run reaction of competitive firm and industry to shift in demand: finite elasticity of input supply.

by a perfectly elastic supply schedule for each input. But to the industry as a whole, the supply curve of inputs is likely to be upward sloping. The less elastic the supply of inputs is, the greater the tendency for average cost curves to shift upward when industry output increases. Thus low elasticity of input supply tends to create low elasticity of product supply.

It is entirely possible that the input shifts may take place within individual firms producing more than one product. Geographic and occupational mobility of resources may be less necessary under such circumstances. In any event, the shift of inputs represents a kind of substitution by producers. Diversified firms may be substituting one output for another; factors of production may be substituting one occupation or location for another. The more readily such substitutions come about, the higher the elasticity of supply of the products involved tends to be.

It is likely that the various inputs will not have the same elasticity of supply. In that case, the increase in output by the industry will tend to raise the prices of some inputs more than others. This in turn will lead to shifts in the input mix as firms substitute against the input(s) which rise most in price (have the lowest elasticity of supply). In such a case, the influence of input-price changes on the costs of individual firms will depend on the ease with which input substitutions can be made. Costs will rise somewhat less if substitution is easy (high elasticity of substitution) than if it is difficult.

a numerical example

We can illustrate the derivation of an industry supply schedule if we assume that there is a definite production function *for the industry as a whole*. Such a concept is a useful one for many purposes and we will use it on several subsequent occasions. In order for competitive equilibrium to be determinate, the production function of the firm must yield an LAC function with a minimum point, a point which separates a range of increasing returns from a range of decreasing returns to scale. Such functions are algebraically complex; however, under certain conditions they can be aggregated into much simpler industry production functions. In an appendix to this chapter, we shall demonstrate that if each firm has a production function represented by

$$a^{1/2}b^{1/2} = Q_A^{1/3} - 0.2Q_A^{1/2} + 0.01Q_A^2$$

(a function which yields a U-shaped LAC), the corresponding industry production function takes the familiar form $Q_A = 4a^{1/2}b^{1/2}$. (Subscript A refers to product, while a and b are inputs.)

For the present purposes, let us assume that that is the industry production function and that the supply conditions of the two inputs are identified as follows: $a = 16P_a$ (supply of input a has unitary elasticity), and $P_b = \$8$ (supply of input b has infinite elasticity). The least-cost proportions of the inputs are identified in the customary manner by setting the marginal rate of substitution (da/db in the industry production function) equal to the inverse ratio of input prices:

$$MRS = \frac{da}{db} = \frac{Q_A^2}{16b^2} = \frac{a}{b}$$

We substitute into this the input supply functions to obtain $a/b = 16P_a/b$. Equating this with the inverse price ratio yields $16P_a/b = 8/P_a$ so that, $b = 2P_a^2$. We can now substitute for a and b in the production function expressions involving P_a. In place of a we use $16P_a$, and in place of b we use $2P_a^2$, The result is as follows:

$$Q_A = 4\sqrt{ab} = 4\sqrt{16P_a \cdot 2P_a^2} = \sqrt{512P_a^3}$$

which can be squared to obtain

$$Q_A^2 = 512P_a^3 \quad \text{so that} \quad P_a = \frac{Q_A^{2/3}}{8}$$

The industry is in equilibrium when price is equal to average cost, which means that total revenue equals total cost at the equilibrium output. Thus we have $Q_A P_A = a \cdot P_a + b \cdot P_b$. Again we substitute to convert the right-hand side into an expression in P_a as follows:

$$Q_A P_A = (16 P_a)(P_a) + (2 P_a^2)(8) = 32 P_a^2 \quad \text{and} \quad P_a^2 = \frac{Q_A P_A}{32}$$

We now have two expressions involving P_a and we can eliminate this term by setting the two equal to one another. We square the first to obtain $P_a^2 = Q_A^{4/3}/64$ and set it equal to $Q_A P_A/32$, which yields

$$P_A = \frac{Q_A^{1/3}}{2} \quad \text{so that} \quad Q_A = 8 P_A^3$$

This last equation is the industry supply schedule expressing output as a function of price. Table 12-1 shows the input-output combinations which would result at a few integral values of P_A. (Because of the way we have derived the industry production function, this supply function is not accurate for small quantities of output.)

When product price and output are low, the price of input a is also low, and firms use relatively much of it compared with input b. Higher levels of product price and output bring higher prices for input a, and firms shift their input mix away from it. When product price is $4, the prices of the two inputs are equal and firms use equal amounts of the two. At higher product prices and output, input a becomes increasingly costly and is used more sparingly.

The elasticity of supply of the product reflects the elasticity of supply of the inputs and the elasticity of substitution between them in production. This particular product-supply schedule has an elasticity of 3 throughout. (Can you prove that?) That elasticity value lies between the elasticity values for the two inputs, which are unity and infinity. The higher the elasticity of supply of the product, the more easily the firm can substitute against the input which is rising in price. If the

TABLE 12-1

Price of Product A	Output of Product A ($8 P_A^3$)	Total Revenue	Price of Input b	Quantity of Input b	Price of Input a	Quantity of Input a	ab ($Q_A^2/16$)
3	216	$ 648	$8	40.5	$ 4.50	72	2,916
4	512	2,048	8	128.0	8.00	128	16,384
5	1,000	5,000	8	312.5	12.50	200	62,500
6	1,728	10,368	8	648.0	18.00	288	186,624

elasticity of input substitution were lower (it is unity in our example), costs would rise more for a given increase in the price of input a, and output would not expand as much in response to a rise in product price.

In sum, the long-run supply schedule for the competitive industry is determined by the response of average cost schedules to changes in the output of the industry. Increased output typically brings an upward shift in cost schedules, because of the need to pay higher prices for larger quantities of the inputs. The industry supply schedule assumes that the industry production function is given, as well as the supply schedules of the inputs. Changes in the production function or in input supply conditions would shift the entire supply schedule for the product.

An industry's short-run supply schedule of output is typically less elastic than its long-run supply schedule, because a condition of diminishing returns causes short-run cost schedules to rise more sharply than long-run. Now we can add a second reason: in the short run, the supply schedules of inputs to the industry are likely to have a lower elasticity than they do in the long run. It takes time to bid resources away from other employments in the economy. A firm trying to expand its labor input may find itself forced to offer a higher wage, if it wants to add workers rapidly. Thus its unit cost schedule is likely to be the more steeply rising, the more rapidly it wants to expand output.

industry demand for inputs

To analyze the industry's demand schedule for any specific input, we take as given the demand schedule for the product of the industry, and the supply schedules of other inputs. Assume once again that we begin with the industry in a position of long-run equilibrium. Each input is used in such quantity that its price equals its average and marginal net revenue product. Then there occurs a shift in the supply schedule of one of the inputs. By examining the industry's response to such a supply shift, we can obtain an idea of the industry's demand schedule for that input.

Assume that the supply schedule of input a increases. Its price will fall, and existing firms will increase their purchases by moving along their short-run marginal revenue product curves to the new intersection point. Since we assume the quantity of other inputs cannot be increased in the short run, the firms' reaction is concentrated on the output effect. The lower price of a is reflected in a reduction of average and marginal cost schedules of the existing firms. As all firms expand output, however, the price of the product declines. If elasticity of demand for the industry's product is high, only a small change in product price will occur. If the elasticity of demand for the product is low, however, product price will fall sharply, and the increase in output may be very small.

The decline in the price of the product would lead in turn to a downward shift in the firms' MRP schedules relating to input a. Remember that the competitive firm's schedule for MRP_a equals product price multiplied times MPP_a. The lower the elasticity of demand for the product, the greater the downward shift and the smaller the increase in the quantity of a employed by the industry.

In the long run, the range of repercussions is greatly extended. Since the lower price of a has lowered costs, existing firms make profits above normal, and there will be a tendency for new firms to enter the industry. As they do so, output will expand, the price of the product will be forced down, and input prices will be forced up, until a new equilibrium position is reached. This position will be one in which there is equality between product price and long-run average cost on one side, and the price of each input and its long-run average net revenue product on the other side.

The long-run response of the industry to an increase in the supply of input a depends on three categories of elasticities. Their influence is as follows:

1. **Elasticity of demand for the product.** If this is high, then the market can absorb a lot more output before price is pushed down to the level of the new long-run average cost minimum. Thus the output effect will be large, and the industry will tend to add a large amount of input a in response to the reduction in its price. Consequently, elasticity of demand for input a tends to be higher, the higher the elasticity of demand for the product.

2. **Elasticity of substitution between input a and other inputs.** If this is high, reduction in the price of a will cause a substantial shift in the input mix, as firms use more of input a and less of other inputs to produce any given output. This itself will tend to produce a high elasticity of demand for input a.

3. **Elasticity of supply of other Inputs.** The preceding output and substitution effects of the lower price of a are likely to cause changes in demand for other inputs. There is a useful rule to observe in analyzing this situation. If the elasticity of demand for the product is higher than the elasticity of input substitution, then a decrease in P_a will cause output to expand sufficiently to increase the demand for input b.† If the supply of b has a low elasticity, its price will be forced up sharply. This will raise costs and reduce the tendency toward an increase in output. Of course, the higher price of b will tend to augment the substitution of a for b. But output is more sensitive to the price of b than the input mix is. On balance, therefore, low elasticity of supply of b reduces the tendency for firms to employ more of a as its price falls.

Suppose, however, that the elasticity of demand for the product is less than the elasticity of substitution between inputs. Then a fall in the price of input a will, on balance, reduce the demand for input b. If the supply of b is inelastic, its price will fall substantially. This will reduce the tendency for firms to employ more of a by substitution. Of course, the lower price of b will also reduce costs and augment the

---

† For proof and illustration, see Joan Robinson, *Economics of Imperfect Competition*, Macmillan, 1933, pp. 258–262. The proposition holds only under conditions of constant returns to scale, which is a reasonable assumption for the production function of an entire industry.

output expansion. But output is less sensitive to a change in the price of b than the input mix is. On balance, then, low elasticity of supply of b will reduce the tendency for firms to employ more of input a when its price falls.

Thus the increased supply of input a may cause either an increase or a decrease in the demand for input b. But in either case, low elasticity of supply of b cuts down the degree to which firms employ more a in response to a fall in the price of a. The industry's demand for a is more elastic, therefore, the higher the elasticity of supply of b. A numerical illustration is given in the appendix to this chapter.

supply of inputs to the industry

The terms on which any input is available to one industry are largely a reflection of conditions elsewhere in the economy. Consider an input as versatile and mobile as labor, which is used in every industry. One industry considered by itself will typically employ only a small proportion of the total labor supply in the economy. To obtain labor, an industry A must offer wages as high as or higher than workers can earn elsewhere. The wages they can earn elsewhere tend to equal the value of their marginal product, viewed in any of several ways. We know that the value of the marginal product tends to be the lower in any industry the more labor there is employed (given the state of technology, product demand, and supply of other factors). If industry A bids workers away from the rest of the economy, the marginal product of the workers remaining in the rest of the economy will be higher. Consequently their wage will tend to be higher, and if industry A wants more workers, it will have to offer a higher wage for them. In short, the supply curve of labor to industry A tends to be upward sloping, because labor is subject to diminishing marginal productivity in the rest of the economy.

However, the elasticity of supply of labor to one industry will tend to be high, because that industry typically accounts for only a small proportion of total labor employment. If industry A is already employing 1 percent of the total labor supply, it can double its labor input and still reduce the labor available to the rest of the economy by only about 1 percent.

There are some inputs which are not used extensively throughout the economy, but are heavily specialized in individual industries. This is often true of natural resources, such as mineral ores. To take a limiting case, suppose a resource is used only in one industry at customary market prices. Then its elasticity of supply to the industry is the same as its elasticity of supply in general.

input prices in equilibrium

The interaction of the industry's demand for any input, and the supply schedule of that input to the industry, will tend to produce an equilibrium price which the industry pays for the input, and also an equilibrium quantity of the input employed in the industry. If the input is widely used elsewhere, and has a high elasticity of supply to industry A, it is relatively trivial to analyze the input's equilibrium price in terms of industry A alone. The reason is that the input will tend to have the same price throughout the economy, which will reflect the conditions of supply and demand everywhere. Analysis in terms of industry A alone will primarily tell us how much of the input is employed by that industry. This will depend on all the things which condition the revenue productivity schedule of that input in industry A. In particular, the industry's employment of any input will tend to be the greater, the stronger the demand for the product of industry A.

If the input in question is relatively specific to industry A, and has a relatively inelastic supply, then its equilibrium price will depend much more heavily on the special conditions in industry A. Prices or rents of oil-bearing lands will tend to be strongly influenced by the demand for petroleum products, for example.

In long-run competitive equilibrium, each firm individually will employ any given input up to the point where its marginal net revenue product is equal to the input price. Through entry and exit, the number of firms will be such that each firm is forced to operate at the point where the average net revenue product of the input is at its maximum. These conditions are the input counterparts of the conditions previously noted on the output side—namely, that each firm operates where product price equals average and marginal costs. The industry's demand curve for inputs is based on the points of highest $ANRP$, just as its supply curve for output reflects the points of minimum LAC.

summary

The short-run supply schedule for an industry's output reflects the way in which the existing firms change output in response to a change in demand and price. If input prices remain constant, the industry short-run supply curve is simply the summation of the SMC curves of the existing firms, since each firm will adjust output to the level at which SMC equals product price. However, input prices may vary positively with industry output. In that case, the industry short-run supply schedule is less elastic than the firms' SMC curves, depending on the supply elasticity of the variable inputs.

The long-run supply schedule for an industry's output reflects the response of output to changes in demand when the number of firms can change. We assume that firms will enter an industry as long as the profit rate in the industry is above the normal profit rate generally prevailing in the economy and leave the industry when its profit rate is below normal. The number of firms in a competitive industry can only be in equilibrium, therefore, when product price equals the lowest average cost at which firms can produce. For the individual firm in industry equilibrium, long-run and short-run average and marginal costs are all equal to product price.

If demand for the product shifts, industry output will shift to whatever extent is necessary to restore equality between product price and average cost. If input prices are not affected by changes in industry output, the industry's long-run equilibrium price remains constant in face of shifts in demand, and quantity produced adjusts to the level where the demand curve intersects that constant price. It is likely, however, that input prices are positively affected by industry output. In that case, increased output forces input prices up, shifting firms' cost schedules upward. This condition generates an upward-sloping long-run industry supply curve, the elasticity of which reflects the elasticity of supply of the inputs. If input supplies are inelastic, a small increase in industry output will be sufficient to raise costs to the point where price equals average cost. If input supplies are highly elastic, however, the industry can carry out a larger increase in output before reaching an equilibrium position. Thus the elasticity of supply of the product varies directly with the elasticity of supply of the inputs which go into it.

The industry's demand schedule for an input reflects its potential response to a change in the supply schedule of that input. An increase in the supply schedule of input a would tend to lower its price. This in turn would cause the industry to expand output, and to substitute input a for other inputs. The output effect would be greater, the greater the elasticity of demand for the product. The substitution effect would be the greater, the higher the elasticity of input substitution. However, low elasticity of supply of other inputs would tend to reduce the net effect of these two.

QUESTIONS AND PROBLEMS

1. How is it possible that the production function for an industry can display constant returns to scale, while the production function for the individual firm displays decreasing returns to scale?

2. In the analysis of an industry's long-run supply behavior, it is average cost rather than marginal cost which is of central importance. Explain why this is so. Why does price tend toward minimum long-run average cost?

3. In the text, we asserted that the industry supply function $Q_A = P_A^3$ has a constant elasticity equal to 3. Prove this.

4. A decrease in the supply schedule of one input a to an industry might either increase or decrease the industry's demand for another input b in the long run. Explain the conditions under which the demand for another input would increase and the conditions under which it would decrease.

5. A competitive industry is only in equilibrium, in purchasing an input a, when it is using a quantity of a such that the average net revenue product of a is equal to P_a. Using the definition of average net revenue product, prove this condition is equivalent to equality between product price and average cost.

ppendix

deriving an industry production function

In order for competitive equilibrium to be determinate, the production function of the individual firm must be such as to yield a long-run average-cost curve which has a minimum point at some positive output. A function which has this property is this one: $a^{1/2}b^{1/2} = Q_A{}^{1/3} - 0.2Q_A{}^{1/2} + 0.01Q_A{}^2$. The left-hand side of the function retains the characteristic that the individual isoquants are symmetrical rectangular hyperbolas, but the right-hand side provides that isoquants representing equal increments of output are not equally spaced. In fact, this production function yields a least-cost output of 10.7 units regardless of the prices of the inputs. And at that output, the inputs are used in such a manner that $ab = 7.26$. If we assume that the industry as a whole expands output by adding more firms of optimum size, the industry production function can be derived as follows. Let F represent the number of firms in the industry, and a_i and b_i represent the amounts of the two inputs used by the typical firm. For the entire industry, the amount of input a used is a_iF, and the amount of input b is b_iF. Thus $a_i = a/F$ and $b_i = b/F$. Substituting these values in the firms' production function, we obtain:

$$a_i b_i = 7.26 = \frac{a}{F} \cdot \frac{b}{F} = \frac{ab}{F^2}$$

Thus
$$ab = 7.26F^2 \quad \text{and} \quad F = \sqrt{\frac{ab}{7.26}}$$

Since each firm produces 10.7 units of output, the output Q_A of the entire industry is 10.7F, and $F = Q_A/10.7$. Set these two expressions for F equal to each other, and obtain $F = \sqrt{ab/7.26} = Q_A/10.7$, so that $Q_A = 3.971 \sqrt{ab}$, which rounds off to $4 \sqrt{ab}$. Since the industry expands by adding firms of (constant) optimum size, the industry production function displays constant returns to scale, even though the production function for the individual firm does not.

deriving the industry demand schedule for an input

The industry's demand schedule for one input can be determined for given values of the demand schedule for the industry's product, the production function, and the supply conditions of the other input(s). Unfortunately, the simplest illustrations involve unitary elasticities and do not yield very interesting results. We offer a slightly more complicated illustration which is constructed to dovetail with the data underlying Table 12-1. We assume that the demand schedule for the product has the following form: $Q_A = 6,000/(P_A + 1)$. Thus the total revenue schedule is $TR = 6,000 - Q_A$. At a price of $5 this demand schedule yields a quantity of 1,000 units, which corresponds to the quantity supplied at that price under the supply conditions used to determine the data in Table 12-1. We retain the industry production function $Q_A = 4 \sqrt{ab}$; thus we can rewrite the industry's total revenue function in this form: $TR = 6,000 - 4 \sqrt{ab}$.

In our industry supply schedule example above, we assumed that the supply schedule of input a displayed unitary elasticity, and that for input b, infinite elasticity. We now assume that the supply schedule of one input is given the same form as before, and solve our equation system for a demand schedule for the other input, in which its quantity demanded is expressed as a function of its price.

First, we assume that input b is, as before, available in infinitely elastic supply at a price of $8. Equating the marginal rate of input substitution to the inverse price ratio, we obtain

$$\frac{da}{db} = \frac{a}{b} = \frac{8}{P_a}$$

$$b = \frac{a \cdot P_a}{8}$$

Our industry is in equilibrium when total revenue equals total cost; therefore:

$$6{,}000 - 4\sqrt{ab} = a \cdot P_a + b \cdot P_b = 2a \cdot P_a$$

$$2a \cdot P_a = 6{,}000 - \sqrt{16ab}$$

Substituting into the last term to eliminate b we obtain:

$$2a \cdot P_a = 6{,}000 - \sqrt{\frac{16a^2 P_a}{8}} = 6{,}000 - a\sqrt{2P_a}$$

$$a = \frac{6{,}000}{2P_a + \sqrt{2P_a}}$$

The last expression gives us the demand schedule for a as a function of its price. We can test its consistency with Table 12-1 by solving it for a price of $12.50, and find that the quantity demanded is indeed 200 units as Table 12-1 would imply.

The elasticity of this demand schedule for input a lies between the elasticity of demand for the product and the elasticity of input substitution. At an output of 1,000 the demand schedule for the product has a point elasticity of 0.83. Our demand schedule for input a does not lend itself to easy determination of point elasticity, but it is not hard to approximate it by finding the arc elasticity between prices of $12 (quantity 207.6) and $13 (quantity 192.9). The arc elasticity proves to be about 0.92 here, approximately the average of the elasticity of demand for the product and the (unitary) elasticity of input substitution. This tidy result comes on the assumption that the supply of input b is infinitely elastic.

If we now take the supply schedule of input a as given ($a = 16P_a$) and solve for b, we can see what difference arises from a less-than-infinite supply elasticity for the other input. This time our marginal rate of substitution analysis produces the following results:

$$\frac{da}{db} = \frac{a}{b} = \frac{P_b}{a/16} \quad \text{thus} \quad a^2 = 16b \cdot P_b$$

Our total revenue condition gives us this equation, as before:

$$6{,}000 - 4\sqrt{ab} = a \cdot P_a + b \cdot P_b = 2b \cdot P_b$$

Unfortunately, when we substitute to eliminate a from the left-hand side of this equation, we end up with a messy expression involving b. The final solution can be written in this form:

$$b \cdot P_b + 4b^{3/4} P_b^{1/4} = 3{,}000$$

No further simplification is feasible.

We can test the consistency of this demand schedule with Table 12-1 by letting $P_b = \$8$, which does in fact yield a quantity of 312.5 for input b. At a price of $7, the industry will buy 352.89 units of input b. Between these prices the arc elasticity is about 0.91, which is somewhat lower than the value we determined for input a. This lower elasticity of demand for b reflects the lower elasticity of supply of input a. The difference is slight, because the elasticity of input substitution does not differ much from the elasticity of demand for the product.

factor markets in the competitive economy: labor

The traditional political economy developed in Great Britain more than a century ago established the custom of thinking in terms of three basic categories of factors of production, namely land, labor, and capital. This classification has been attacked on many grounds. At an early stage, the French economist J. B. Say argued for the inclusion of enterprise, or entrepreneurship, as a separate factor. The importance of entrepreneurship to a market economy is very great. But to identify entrepreneurship as a separate factor of production has not proved very satisfactory. In the sort of static equilibrium analysis used in economic theory, the entrepreneur function reduces to the provision of certain types of labor services plus capital. And in any environment, entrepreneurship does not lend itself to the sort of quantification which is applied to other factors.

Even if one does not add to the traditional trio of production factors, the dividing line separating one from the other may be difficult to identify. We understand the category *land* to refer broadly to elements of the natural environment and particularly those elements which are capable of appropriation and ownership by individuals. By *capital* we mean capital goods, things produced by human effort and destined to contribute to further production. To the extent that human effort is bestowed on improving the land, however, it may be difficult to sustain a distinction. Where land is leveled, or drained, or cleared of obstructing trees and rocks, it is hard to distinguish the land from the capital.

For all the ambiguities, there seems to be no factor classification superior to the traditional trio, particularly in view of the dual purpose for which we study factors of production. On the one hand we are interested in their role in production; on the other, we study their function as the basis for the distribution of incomes among households in a market economy. Our analysis will proceed as if there were three categories of productive factors named land, labor, and capital.

labor

By *labor* we mean human effort of all kinds directed toward productive activity. Labor includes the activities of the business executive, the self-employed profes-sional, the farmer, and the storekeeper, as well as hired employees.

A law enacted in the United States half a century ago stated that "the labor of a human being is not a commodity or an article of commerce." Strictly speaking, the statement is nonsense. There is a market for labor services, and the services of individual workers bear specific prices or wage rates. It is possible to speak of the supply of a particular type of labor, and of the demand for a particular type of labor. To ignore the ways in which labor *is* an article of commerce is to lose sight of important causes of labor conditions.

Yet at the same time, one must be aware of ways in which labor differs from inanimate commodities. Labor services cannot be separated from the people who render them. To many of these people the labor relationship contains many ele-ments of great importance to their lives. To be sure, the wage received for labor services constitutes a source of income to the household. But in addition, the worker is concerned with many other aspects of his work situation. A person's employment is closely linked with his place of residence. His job tends to occupy a major part of his time and activity. It is an important aspect of his relationships with other people, a determinant of social class, prestige, and power. People are likely to have strong preferences about these aspects of their lives, and their psychological well-being may be strongly affected by these various non-wage aspects of a job.

Another important consideration is that a person's employment is not a single transaction which can be casually concluded, but is potentially a long-term associa-tion. Many of the aspects of a job which are important to people can be learned only gradually. The same is true of some of the narrowly economic dimensions as well. Workers are concerned with whether they can hope for periodic wage increases, whether they are in danger of being laid off, whether they can expect promotions, and whether the specifications of their jobs will be changed to their disadvantage. These are all matters which become known only gradually.

Similar considerations can be cited for the employer as well. The qualifications of an individual worker to function efficiently in a specific job can be determined only as he performs the job. Most employment requires that the worker acquire knowledge on the job, thus relating not merely to its technical features but also to the people with whom he must work and the specific practices and procedures of his firm.

When a satisfactory working relationship has developed, both sides may become relatively insensitive, in the short run, to purely wage-oriented conditions. The worker may be reluctant to leave merely because he can obtain a higher current wage elsewhere, because of uncertainties about so many of the things he cares about. The employer may be reluctant to dismiss a long-time employee merely because there is available at a lower wage some other worker whose qualifications are less well known. And the employer may refrain from trying to reduce the wage of the long-time employee, fearing he may leave or become disgruntled and disruptive to efficiency.

These considerations have much to do with the way in which labor markets function and with the significance of labor conditions for the welfare and happiness of individuals. They do not change the fact that fundamental forces of supply and demand are at work in the determination of wages, as with other prices. In studying demand and supply in the labor market, we shall be concerned with their operation in relation to labor as a whole, and also with respect to particular occupations.

labor productivity and demand for labor

We have already studied the demand schedule for labor at two levels, the individual firm and the individual industry, under conditions of pure competition. For the individual firm, the long-run demand schedule for an input is based on the schedule of marginal net revenue productivity of that input to the firm. Such a schedule can be derived from the production function, the prices of other inputs, and the price of the product, all of which are taken as given by the individual firm. The firm employs a quantity of each input sufficient to bring its $MNRP$ into equality with the price of that input.

For the competitive industry, the prices of the inputs and of the product are typically not constant, but depend on the amount the industry buys or sells. In analyzing the (long-run) industry demand for input a, we take as given the production function of the industry (assuming each firm operates at its least-cost output), the demand schedule for the product, and the supply schedules of the other inputs. The industry adjusts its purchases of input a until the average net revenue product of a is equal to its price. If $ANRP_a$ exceeds P_a, firms will be making more than a normal profit, and additional firms will enter the industry. If P_a exceeds $ANRP_a$, firms are suffering losses, and some will leave the industry in the long run. In equilibrium, each individual firm will be employing enough of the input so as to be at the highest point on its $ANRP$ schedule, where the average and marginal net revenue products are equal. The equilibrium solution for the industry yields values for the prices of inputs and output as well as their quantities, provided input-supply and product-demand schedules slope. The equilibrium price and quantity of input a will depend on the elasticity of its supply schedule to the industry, which depends on the proportion of it used in other sectors of the economy and the shape of its marginal product functions in those other sectors.

In both cases, the long-run demand schedule for an input depends on two classes of influences. One class relates to the physical productivity of that input itself, while the other relates to the supply conditions of other inputs and the demand conditions for the product.

What are the determinants of the physical productivity of an input such as labor? Formally, physical productivity depends on the production function, but we want to examine more basic determinants.

The physical productivity of labor depends, first of all, on the quality of the labor itself—that is, all the attributes of labor which enable it to turn out a large quantity of output. Physical strength, skill, and coordination, intelligence, education, and experience in problem-solving, initiative, responsibility, and facility in working with other people—all of these can be important dimensions of labor quality.

Second, the physical productivity of labor depends on the condition of technology and organization in the various firms and industries. Improved technology and efficient organization can obtain high productivity even from a labor force of only mediocre quality. Third, the greater the supply of capital goods and natural resources, the higher the schedule of labor's marginal physical productivity will be.

Finally, the specific value which the average and marginal products of labor will have in equilibrium depends on the supply of labor. The larger the size of the labor supply, the lower the equilibrium level of the marginal and average physical products will be. But this is getting ahead of proper topic sequence.

When we analyzed the demand for input by one industry, an important determinant was the strength of demand for the product of the industry. If we are trying to explain wage rates for specialized occupations, we may still want to consider relative strength of product demand. Demand for the services of movie stars depends on the public's demand for motion picture entertainment. However, there are many occupations which are not specific to particular products or industries. In a study of the wages of secretaries or truck drivers, for instance, the strength of consumer demand for particular products may be of little importance.

demand for labor by entire economy

We believe that it is meaningful to think of the average wage level in a given country and to compare it with average levels in other countries, or in the same country in times past. Such an average is particularly meaningful if the dispersion has some stability over time, so that changes in the average wage level reflect similar changes in most individual wage categories. To explain movements in the average wage level, we need an analysis which deals with the supply of and demand for labor in general.

In some ways, analysis of demand for labor in the entire economy reverts to the simplicity of Chapter 7. We need not concern ourselves with the demand for individual products and services. Further, we will assume that the members of the society have unlimited *desires* for output in general, so that there is no problem of general overproduction. One could go further and argue that willingness to perform labor services is itself evidence of unfulfilled desires for output. Such a claim is really a form of Say's law. Modern economics recognizes that it is not necessarily true—but it is not likely to be far wrong.

Further, for most of our analysis of the entire economy, we will assume that the supply of land and capital goods is completely inelastic. This is not literally true for capital, but its supply elasticity Is certainly quite low, and we will not seriously distort things by our assumption.

As in Chapter 7, we are concerned with the real wage rate, and wlth the real productivity of labor. By real wage, we mean the quantity of goods and services which can be purchased with the money wage. In Chapter 7 we had only one product and could express the real wage in units of that product. Now we need some kind of unit to measure real wages in terms of "goods-in-general" when there are many products in the economy. There is no unambiguous measure for this. However, we will follow the custom used in interpreting national-income data. We adopt as our unit of real wages the amount of goods which could be purchased for one dollar during some base period of time. We use the prices which prevailed during the base period for valuing the output produced in other periods (even though prices themselves may change). Thus our measure of real wage is in units of national product valued at constant prices.

the economy's production function

When we analyzed demand for labor in the early chapters, we found that it was based on the production function. We need some counterpart for our present analysis. In the preceding chapter, we constructed a long-run production function for an individual industry, on the assumption that individual firms operated at the most efficient scale of output, which was independent of input and output prices. Now we go one step further and assume we can construct a production function for the economy as a whole. We assume that all industries are purely competitive and all firms operate at equilibrium input-output positions. We measure national output as gross national product in constant prices of some base period and assume there are no major shifts in the composition of output or in relative prices of individual products. Earlier we noted that the typical industry production function is likely to display constant returns to scale. Thus a production function for the entire economy might display constant returns also.

Such a production function is in common use. It is the so-called *Cobb-Douglas function*, originally developed to explain the behavior of wages in the United States. A general form of the Cobb-Douglas function is

$$Q = ka^x b^{1-x}$$

where Q represents the quantity of real output, k is a constant, and x lies between 0 and 1. Functions in this form display constant returns to scale: proportional increases in the inputs will result in an equal proportional increase in output. Such functions also display diminishing returns to one factor.

There are many problems in trying to express national production in such a simplified function. One serious difficulty is that, strictly speaking, the production function is only meaningful if each input is homogeneous. One unit of labor must be qualitatively the same as another, and one unit of capital the same as another, or the function loses its determinacy. In fact, inputs in such broad classes as used here are notoriously lacking in homogeneity. To evade this difficulty, we assume that, although units of each input differ from one another in quality, the *average* quality of the input category remains constant. Thus construed, our analysis yields conclusions about an average marginal product and an average wage. Later we consider the problem of differentials within the average.

Let us assume that the national production function takes the form $Q = 10a^{\frac{1}{2}}b^{\frac{1}{2}}$. We take as given the quantity of factor b, which can be assumed to represent land. Let its quantity be 10,000 units. The production function then can be reduced to the form $Q = 1,000a^{\frac{1}{2}}$. (There is nothing particularly "short-run" about the latter function, if the fixity of land quantity is a relatively permanent condition.) A schedule of MPP for labor can be obtained by taking the familiar derivative of the production function; thus $MPP_a = dQ/da = 500/a^{\frac{1}{2}}$.

In earlier sections, when we used a production function, output was measured in physical units of some specific product. Here, however, in order to cope with a heterogeneous output, we must use the "dollar's worth" as our unit of measurement. The Q term will be a money value, but one which uses prices from one unchanging base period.

From our preceding sections we know that each firm and industry will be employing labor in such quantity that the money wage is equal to the MRP of labor. And since each firm is operating under conditions of pure competition, the wage will also equal the value of the marginal product (VMP), which may be defined as the marginal physical product of labor multiplied by the product price. If we express W, MRP, and VMP in real terms, dividing each term through by a price index expressing the ratio of current to base-period prices, the equality will still hold. Such an adjustment would express the real value in constant prices of labor's VMP, which would be equivalent to the derivative dQ/da of the aggregate production function, in which Q is measured in dollars of base-period purchasing power.

We conclude that, properly interpreted, the schedule of labor's MPP derived from the economy's production function is a demand schedule for labor under competitive conditions. This conclusion follows from the assumptions that individual firms and industries have achieved positions of competitive equilibrium, and that the production function for the economy is a simple aggregate of those for individual industries. If each firm operates at an input-output position at which marginal and average net revenue product of labor are equal to the (real) wage, and if the wage is uniform for all firms, the equilibrium real wage will equal the marginal product of labor as derived from the aggregate production function. The demand schedule is downward sloping. More man-hours will be demanded at a lower real wage, given the condition of technology, the supply conditions of other factors, and the willingness of the public to purchase as much output as they can obtain. If nonlabor inputs are fixed in quantity, then demand for labor slopes down because of diminishing returns. If the nonlabor inputs have some finite elasticity of supply, then substitution effects come into the picture also.

The demand schedule is obtained by setting the wage equal to the expression for labor's MPP obtained above:

$$W = \frac{500}{a^{\frac{1}{2}}}$$

$$a^{\frac{1}{2}} = \frac{500}{W}$$

$$a = \frac{250,000}{W^2}$$

This could be interpreted to be a demand for man-hours as a function of the hourly real wage rate. With a real wage equivalent to $2.00 per hour, for example, the economy would demand 62,500 man-hours of labor.

supply of labor

The equilibrium wage rate will settle at the level which equates the demand schedule for labor with its supply schedule. The supply of labor for the entire economy depends on the size and composition of the population and on the psychological preferences and attitudes of potential workers. One can envision a supply schedule in which the number of man-hours offered is a function of the real wage available. Efforts to identify the shape of such a schedule have been rather inconclusive.

In Chapter 3, we analyzed the supply of labor by a given population in terms of the income and substitution effects. Potential workers choose between work and leisure in the allotment of their limited available time. The "price" one must pay for leisure is the wage rate foregone by not working. At any given wage rate, there is some optimum balance between work and leisure. But how will this optimum be shifted if the wage rises? The higher wage rate will have a substitution effect. It makes leisure more costly, and people will tend to substitute work for leisure. But the higher wage also has an income effect. With a higher income, people may choose to spend more of their time not working; leisure and the consumption of goods tend to be complementary. Such an income effect can neutralize the substitution effect or even exceed it.

The conclusion of the theory is that a higher wage rate may induce the amount of labor offered to increase, to stay the same, or to decrease, depending on the balance between income and substitution effects. Over the past century in the United States the great increase in real wages has been associated with a substantial decline in the number of hours worked by each person per year and with a decrease in the labor of young people, who have instead been staying in school longer. Since the 1930s, however, hours worked have not declined very much, and the decreased participation of young people has been about offset by increased participation of older women. For conditions of the 1960s, the supply of labor offered appears to be relatively unaffected, on balance, by the trend of real wages.[1]

For simplicity, we assume initially that the supply of labor is completely inelastic to real wage rates, but that it tends to shift over time as the population changes.

equilibrium wage levels

On the usual assumptions, the equilibrium average wage for the economy as a whole is the (real) wage which equates the demand for labor with the supply. This will tend to equal the marginal physical product of the labor force as a whole, assuming the supply schedule of labor to be completely inelastic with respect to the real wage level. Under such assumptions, it is the demand of labor—based on the degree of labor quality, the quantity and quality of other resources, and the state of technology and organization—which acts upon a given supply to produce the equilibrium wage. In our example above, the MPP schedule for labor was $500/a^{1/2}$ Given the supply of labor, the equilibrium wage is obtained directly by evaluating this expression. Suppose the labor force provides 40,000 man-hours. The marginal physical product of this labor input would be $500/200 = \$2.50$ per man-hour. If the actual wage were below this equilibrium level, firms would attempt to hire more workers than the available amount; their efforts would force the wage rate up until

---

[1] This is not to deny a short-run business-cycle response, in which increases in job opportunities attract more people into the labor force. Such a phenomenon reflects market imperfections rather than a response of supply to real wage under equilibrium assumptions.

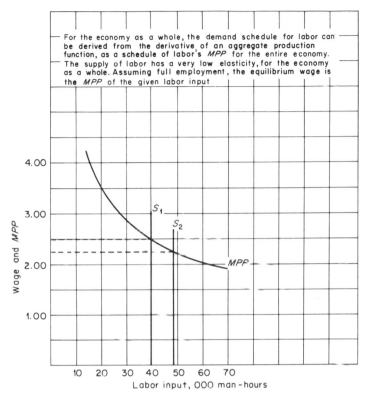

For the economy as a whole, the demand schedule for labor can be derived from the derivative of an aggregate production function, as a schedule of labor's *MPP* for the entire economy. The supply of labor has a very low elasticity, for the economy as a whole. Assuming full employment, the equilibrium wage is the *MPP* of the given labor input

Figure 13-1 Economy's demand schedule for labor.

job openings would just absorb the available workers. If the wage were above the equilibrium level, firms would not be willing to provide enough jobs for all who want to work. The wage would tend to fall. Thus efforts of firms to hire more or fewer workers tend to push the wage rate toward the equilibrium level. The equilibrium wage is shown in Figure 13-1.

shifts in labor supply

Over time, the size of the labor force has tended to increase as population has grown. Such shifts in labor supply tend to reduce the equilibrium level of the average real wage, given supplies of other factors and the state of technology.

Figure 13-1 shows the impact of an increase in the supply of labor, using the previous assumptions. The curve of MPP slopes downward. The original labor supply (40,000) intersects the MPP curve at a real wage of \$2.50. If we increase the labor input to 48,400, the marginal product of labor falls to $500/220 = \$2.27$, and so does the equilibrium wage.

This conclusion is predicated on the assumption that full-employment conditions prevail. The fact that people are willing to work is itself evidence that their desire for real income has not been satiated; thus there is a desire to consume the additional output which additional labor can produce. However, the elasticity of demand for individual products will determine where the added labor is employed. We do assume that the market mechanism works smoothly enough to channel labor into the area where it is most wanted.

factor shares

If each factor of production receives a real reward per unit equal to the marginal physical product of that unit, we can identify the way the total output is divided up between the factors. It is a general property of the Cobb-Douglas production function that each factor receives a share in the total output equal to the exponent which it bears in the production function.

Consider a production function in general form $Q = a^m b^n$. Setting the (real) price of each factor equal to its MPP we obtain

$$P_a = \frac{dQ}{da} = ma^{m-1}b^n$$

$$P_b = \frac{dQ}{db} = na^m b^{n-1}$$

Multiplying the price of each factor times its quantity yields its total real income, which is

$$a \cdot P_a = ma^m b^n = mQ$$
$$b \cdot P_b = na^m b^n = nQ$$

In our example above, with $Q = 10a^{1/2}b^{1/2}$, a labor input of 40,000 man-hours, and a land input of 10,000 units, we would obtain a total output worth $200,000 in base-year prices. The equilibrium wage is $2.50, and the total income for labor would be (40,000)($2.50) = $100,000. With this quantity of labor, the MPP schedule for land would be $1,000/b^{1/2}$, which has a value of $10 when $b = 10,000$. Each unit of land thus earns $10 for its owners. The total income of landowners would be

$$(10,000)(\$10) = \$100,000$$

The total income is precisely sufficient to pay the factors, with labor receiving one-half and land one-half. The sum of factor shares will equal the total income when the sum of the factor exponents in the production function is equal to 1 (that is,

$mQ + nQ = Q$). If the aggregate production function displays increasing returns so that the factor exponents sum to more than 1, there will not be enough total income to pay the factors the value of their marginal products ($mQ + nQ > Q$). And if the aggregate production function contains factor exponents which sum to less than 1, total income would exceed the sum of the implied factor shares ($mQ + nQ < Q$).

If individual firms and industries meet the characteristics of pure competition, the aggregate production function will tend to display constant returns to scale, for the same reason that the industry production function in Chapter 12 showed this tendency. If the aggregate production function does not show constant returns, this suggests that pure competition is not everywhere present, or that some firms are not in equilibrium, or that the marginal products on which private decisions are based are not the same as those implied by the aggregate production function.

shifts in the demand schedule

A change in the quantity of the other input would change the marginal product schedule of labor and alter the equilibrium wage rate for a given labor supply. Suppose the supply of land decreased, because of a flood or other natural disaster, to 9,000 units. The production function would then be $Q = 948.7a^{1/2}$. From this we can take the derivative dQ/da, which would be $474.4/a^{1/2}$. With 40,000 units of labor, the equilibrium wage rate would be $2.37 (compared to $2.50 with 10,000 units of land). This illustrates a very important proposition. The productivity of a given labor force, and therefore its equilibrium real wage, tends to vary directly with the amount of other resources which labor has to work with. This is very evident in international comparisons of wage levels. The highest wages tend to be in those countries which have the most capital per worker. In preindustrial times, wages tended to be highest in areas with the greatest amount of good land per worker.

positive elasticities of factor supplies

For simplicity, we have limited our attention to a situation in which elasticities of factor supply were zero. However, the existence of non-zero supply elasticities would not substantially alter our conclusions concerning the determinants of real wages. The equilibrium real wage would now have to be determined at the level at which demand and supply would be equal, in the markets for labor and for other factors. Existence of upward-sloping supply schedules would complicate the calculations.

If we assume a positive elasticity of supply for capital (as the factor cooperating with labor), its supply elasticity becomes one of the determinants of the elasticity of demand for labor. Conversely, the elasticity of supply of labor becomes a determinant of the elasticity of demand for capital.

To derive a demand schedule for labor at the aggregate level, assuming an upward-sloping supply schedule for other factors, one cannot use the schedule of marginal physical product but must revert to analysis in terms of marginal net revenue product. Assume that factor b is supplied in accordance with the expression

$$b = 100 P_b^{2/3}$$

so that $\qquad P_b = \dfrac{b^{3/2}}{1,000} \qquad$ and $\qquad b \cdot P_b = \dfrac{b^{5/2}}{1,000}$

This demand schedule is inelastic, but quantity supplied is a positive function of price.

The total net revenue product schedule for factor a associates with each quantity of that factor a quantity of total revenue minus a quantity of expenditure on factor b. In the aggregate production function, Q represents the value of output in constant prices of some base period. Thus Q is itself a measure of total revenue and there is no need for separate consideration of product prices. We need to identify the output and quantity of b which will be associated with any given quantity of factor a. For each quantity of a, the optimum quantity of b is that for which $MRP_b = P_b$. With a production function $Q = 10a^{1/2}b^{1/2}$, the marginal revenue product of factor b is $dQ/db = 5a^{1/2}/b^{1/2}$. Thus optimum factor proportions are achieved when

$$P_b = \frac{5a^{1/2}}{b^{1/2}} \qquad \text{and} \qquad b = \frac{25a}{P_b^2}$$

By definition, the $TNRP_a$ schedule can be expressed as

$$TNRP_a = Q - b \cdot P_b$$
$$= 10a^{1/2}b^{1/2} - \frac{25a}{P_b}$$
$$= \frac{25a}{P_b}$$

Taking the derivative of $TNRP_a$, we obtain

$$MNRP_a = d\frac{TNRP_a}{da} = \frac{25}{P_b}$$

To deal with P_b, we now bring in the supply schedule of factor b, as follows:

$$b = 100P_b^{2/3} = \frac{25a}{P_b^2}$$
$$P_b^{8/3} = 0.25a$$
$$P_b = 0.5945a^{3/8}$$

Substitute this value in the $MNRP_a$ expression:

$$MNRP_a = \frac{25}{P_b} = \frac{25}{(0.5945a^{3\!/\!8})} = \frac{42.05}{a^{3\!/\!8}}$$

Set this equal to P_a and rearrange to obtain a demand schedule for a:

$$P_a = \frac{42.05}{a^{3\!/\!8}}$$

$$a = \frac{21,410}{P_a{}^{8\!/\!3}}$$

This is the demand schedule for factor a under the conditions specified. Previously, when we took the quantity of factor b as given (completely inelastic supply) we obtained a demand schedule in the form $250,000/P_a^2$, which has an elasticity of 2. Now with input b having positive supply elasticity, our demand schedule has a higher elasticity, namely $8\!/\!3$. Thus it appears that a higher elasticity of supply for factor b tends to yield a higher elasticity of demand for factor a. Since we have implicitly assumed an infinitely elastic demand for output, the potential output effects of factor-price change tend to exceed the substitution effects. Suppose the supply of factor a increases. This tends to increase output. The potential rise in output is greater when the quantity of factor b responds positively to an increase in the demand for it.

Given a demand schedule for labor identified by its $MNRP$ schedule, the equilibrium wage would be at the level equating supply and demand. If labor supply has zero elasticity, one would merely substitute the quantity of labor into the $MNRP$ function and solve for the equilibrium wage. If the supply of labor is functionally dependent on the real wage, one must set the supply schedule equal to the demand schedule and solve.

If the factors have positive elasticity of supply, output will be more responsive to a shift in the supply schedule of either factor. An increase in the supply schedule of one factor will tend to raise the reward and the quantity of the other factor as well.

The elasticity of supply of the capital stock tends to be low because customary annual production is only a small proportion of total capital stock. If annual output of capital goods averages only 10 percent of the existing capital stock, a doubling of current output makes an additional 10 percent increase in the total stock.

There is no certainty that the supply of labor will be upward sloping. Higher real wages will call forth greater labor supply if the substitution effects of wage changes predominate. However, if income effects predominate, a higher real wage may reduce the quantity of labor offered. Such a backward-sloping supply schedule would tend to reduce the elasticity of demand for capital. An increase in the supply schedule of capital would increase the reward for labor, causing the quantity of labor offered to decrease. Total output would thus increase less, and the return to capital decline more, than if the labor quantity were constant or increasing with a higher wage.

shifts in the production function

The effect of technical change on factor prices and the distribution of income is a subject rich in controversy and ambiguity. However, if we assume that the production function follows the Cobb-Douglas form, we can clarify a few confusing points. Recall that the typical function has the form $Q = ka^x b^{1-x}$. At this point, we will assume that a and b represent the quantities of labor and capital respectively. We can assume that if a technical change is put into effect at all, it will have the effect of raising the output which the economy can obtain from the resources in use at the time of the innovation. The innovating industry itself may be content to produce the same output at a lower cost, but the lowering of cost represents a release of resources which become available to increase output elsewhere in the economy. Innovations which increase productivity may simply increase the value of the constant term k. Such innovations are relatively neutral; they leave unchanged the division of income between labor and capital, since the exponents of the production function have not changed.

However, technical change is often "labor-saving" or "capital-saving." As often used, these are very confusing terms. However, we can argue that an innovation is labor-saving when it leads to a reduction in the amount of labor used per unit of output at any given set of factor prices. Geometrically, such an innovation would change the shape of the production isoquants, such that the marginal rate of substitution at any given input point would be altered.

In terms of the Cobb-Douglas function, a labor-saving innovation would involve a decrease in the value of x (the exponent for labor in the production function) and a corresponding increase in the exponent $1 - x$ of the capital term. (Probably k would increase also.) Reducing the size of x means that the proportional share of the national income going to labor declines. However, if the rise in k is substantial, the actual real wage may remain unchanged or even increase.

Ideally, we should deal with an aggregate production function containing three or more factor terms. Using three terms would remind us that income and output depend on land as well. Because the quantity of land is fixed, output cannot be expected to rise in proportion to a given proportional rise in labor and capital alone—a condition of diminishing returns occurs. Historically, however, the tendency for diminishing returns to labor-plus-capital has probably been counteracted by land-saving innovations, which have lowered the exponent of the land term in the equation and raised those of labor and capital.

limitations of analysis

To discuss an equilibrium wage rate for the entire economy it is necessary to make two assumptions. One is that average wages tend toward equality (or at least that each classification of labor comes to have a uniform wage rate). The second is that wage rates rise or fall in such a way as to equate supply with demand. Assumptions like these were not unrealistic in discussing product markets. In the labor market, they are not nearly so realistic. Individual workers are reluctant to change jobs solely on the basis of small wage differentials. In addition, arbitrage, which helps equalize product prices, is not feasible in the labor market. There tends to be one price for grain in a given market area because sharp-eyed traders take advantage of price differentials, buying cheap and selling dear, until the differentials are minimized. The labor relationship does not lend itself to such arbitrage.

Even in equilibrium, wage-rate uniformity may not be achieved because workers choose jobs on the basis of other considerations in addition to the wage. Other things being equal, a job which has pleasant nonwage dimensions, such as good location, enjoyable social relationships, and interesting activity, can sustain a wage rate lower than a less pleasant employment would need to pay for labor of a given quality. Under such conditions the value of labor's marginal product would not be equated in all uses; rather, the "marginal net advantages" of employment—both wage and nonwage—would tend to be equated in all activities.

As for the degree to which wages move to equate supply and demand, we note an apparent lack of symmetry. The historical record indicates that the existence of excess demand for labor has usually pulled wage rates up. However, the existence of an excess supply of labor, as manifested in a high rate of unemployment, has not had an equal tendency to force wage rates down. Employers, particularly in larger firms, may be reluctant to dismiss the "inside" workers, with their experience, to take on untried strangers. In addition, the long-run productivity and goodwill of the workforce may be lowered by a wage reduction. In industrial economies, flexibility of real wages has not been sufficient to eliminate unemployment.

In spite of these analytical deficiencies, the supply-demand marginal-productivity theory of wages provides satisfactory explanations to some major questions relating to wage behavior. Differences in wage levels between different countries do depend upon differences in the marginal productivity of labor, arising from differences in labor quality, in technology, and in the quantity and quality of other resources, such as land and capital. The ratio expressing the amount of capital goods per worker is highly correlated with real wages, as the theory would predict.

Marginal productivity theory also provides an explanation for the upward trend in real wage rates which has been characteristic of western industrial countries over the past century or more. Of particular note is the period between 1850 and 1914, when real wages tended strongly upward, despite a rapid increase in population and labor supply, in an environment characterized by very little labor union development or government social legislation and by a lack of what we would now regard as "enlightened" or "humanitarian" attitudes on the part of businessmen as employers. The period was one of rapid technological progress, capital formation, and development of natural resources. All of these would tend to raise the marginal productivity of labor. The spread of education probably raised labor quality somewhat, although this was probably not a major element in the rise of productivity as it has become in the twentieth century.

occupational wage differentials

Many individual segments of labor markets are not characterized by conditions of pure competition. Nevertheless, differentials in labor reward can usually be interpreted in terms of supply and demand. Often the existence of occupational wage rates well above or below the average is a sign of disequilibrium. A decline in demand may cause a drop in the labor income of a particular occupational group, such as the hand-loom weavers in England during the early nineteenth century. But sooner or later there comes a decline in the number of workers in such an occupation. If nothing else, young people do not enter it, and the death, retirement, and other exodus of the incumbents steadily reduce the total. If a substandard wage persists, it may reflect the fact that workers, because of unwillingness to move geographically, or lack of qualifications, are not willing or able to obtain better paying jobs elsewhere.

An increase in the demand for a particular occupational speciality may raise its labor income above the average, but this differential also will tend to be eliminated by the entry of more workers. If nothing else, young people entering the labor force tend to flock into the well-paying areas. However, labor incomes above average may persist if there are obstacles to entry into a certain occupation, or if people dislike its other features and have to be paid extra to be willing to engage in it. Persistent positive differentials of labor income occur where only a few people can qualify because of innate characteristics, training, or education.

Productivity is contagious. It is relatively pointless to try to explain labor-income conditions in particular occupations without some reference to the total environment. One reason is that each person's labor productivity depends in large degree on conditions extrinsic to himself—on the amounts and quality of capital goods and natural resources per worker, and on the state of technology—which tend to affect most people in a given society in a same manner. The business executive who earns $100,000 a year in the United States might earn far less in an Asian country which could not link up his organizational talents with the appropriate capital, technology, and labor skills. The medical specialist who earns $50,000 a year on New York's Park Avenue might be just as effective in healing the illnesses of Egyptian peasants, but he would find that their low productivity would make it impossible for them to pay him his accustomed fees. His high value productivity is a result not merely of personal skill and accumulated medical technology but also of a society which is productive enough all around to be able to place a high valuation on his services.

To put these matters another way, both the supply schedule of workers available for a given occupational specialty and the demand for the output of that specialty will depend, among other things, on the general productivity of labor in the economy. In a high-wage, high-labor-productivity economy, workers will be available to a particular occupation only if it pays them high wages reasonably comparable to those obtainable elsewhere. The demand for any product or factor service, on the other hand, is limited by the total real income of the population. In a high-productivity society, the abundant output of goods and services in general provides a basis for strong real demand for individual products and services. This is a true element in the much maligned principle of Say's law, which reminds us that the supply of products is the ultimate basis for the demand for products.

It is also worth remembering that the marginal productivity of workers depends on how many of them there are. Given the state of demand for labor, an increase in the labor supply tends to lower labor's real reward. In many less developed countries, high birthrates and rising population tend to offset hard-won increases in capital and improvements in technology and represent a major obstacle to the increase of real incomes obtainable from work.

summary

The average real wage rate in a competitive economy is determined by the interaction of supply and demand. The supply of labor is largely determined by size and attitudes of the population and is relatively inelastic with respect to real wages. If the supply schedules of other factors are completely inelastic, the demand schedule for labor consists of the schedule of labor's marginal physical product, measured in units of national product at constant prices. The productivity schedule of labor is determined by the quality of the labor force, by the quality and quantity of other resources available for labor to work with, and by technology and organization. The equilibrium real wage will tend to equal the real value of the marginal physical product of the number of workers employed. Increases in the size of the labor force tend to lower the equilibrium real wage, while increases in the supply of other resources, or improvements in technology, may tend to raise the equilibrium real wage.

In cases where nonlabor factors have positively inclined supply schedules, we must derive the demand schedule for labor from a marginal net (revenue) product schedule. However, land and labor typically have relatively low elasticities of supply and the analysis will not be seriously distorted if zero elasticities are assumed.

Occupational wage differentials reflect the degree to which supply responds to demand. Demands for workers in particular occupations are constantly changing, but if supply responds promptly and fully, wage differentials are soon eliminated. A wage above the average will persist only if there are limits on the willingness or ability of people to work in that occupation, perhaps because of high requirements of skill, education, or physical qualifications. Likewise wages below average will tend to persist only if the low-paid occupations continue to attract a substantial number of workers.

TERMS AND CONCEPTS

1. Entrepreneurship
2. Factor shares
3. Say's law

QUESTIONS AND PROBLEMS

1. Increases in wage rates may call forth either more labor or less. Show how the result depends on the relative importance of the income effect and substitution effect of a wage change.

2. The income of a physician is likely to be higher than the national average wage, and the income of an unskilled worker is likely to be less than the average wage. Explain why. It is possible that the wage paid in an unpleasant but unskilled job might be below average at one time and above average at another time. Explain why this would be possible.

3. Assume that the production function for the economy is $Q = 10 \, a^{2/3} b^{1/3}$ and that the input of b is 8,000. Determine the algebraic expression for the marginal physical product schedule of a. If a represents labor, find the equilibrium real wage on the assumption that the labor input is 27,000. Calculate the total output at that level, and note how it is divided between the two factors. What would be the marginal product of b at the equilibrium?

4. What is the (point) elasticity of demand for labor in the equilibrium position determined for question 3?

5. In *The Wealth of Nations*, published in 1776, Adam Smith observed that wages in colonial North America, which was then only thinly settled, were higher than in Europe. How could one use marginal productivity analysis to explain that fact?

6. If the government enacts a law forbidding payment of wages below some specified level, and if that level is higher than the equilibrium wage, what will the results be, under conditions of pure competition? Explain.

7. Barbers in Bangkok are better than barbers in the United States. They work faster and do a better job. Their shops are just as pleasant as those in the United States. Yet barbers in Bangkok earn no more than one-fourth as much as barbers in the United States. How can you reconcile this fact with the theory that labor income depends on labor productivity?

factor markets in the competitive economy: capital and land

capital

No concept has caused more trouble in economic discussion than that of capital. The concept is riddled with ambiguity, and similar ambiguity attaches to the iden- tification of the price of capital. Capital means different things in accounting, in ordinary speech, and in technical economics. Accountants use the term "capital" to refer to the ownership claim against the property of a business, and in ordinary speech we may refer to a person's capital when we mean his wealth or assets.

The chief concern of technical economic analysis is with *capital goods*. We have defined capital goods to mean things which have been produced by human effort and which are in turn destined to contribute further to productive activity, rather than to yield satisfaction directly to consumers.

Traditionally, a distinction has been made between fixed capital and circulating capital. Circulating capital consists chiefly of stocks, or inventories, of goods. Some of these stocks may consist of raw materials, or fuel, which will be physically altered in the production process. Others consist of goods actually in the process of production, and still others are goods which have been produced and are working their way through the hands of transport agencies, wholesalers, and retailers on their way to the final consumer.

Fixed capital, by contrast, consists of productive assets such as machinery or buildings, the destruction or exhaustion of which is not essential to their productive use. Indeed, if machinery and buildings could be made indestructible, this would be advantageous, whereas if coal, fuel oil, iron ore, and other raw materials and fuels were indestructible they would be useless!

We use the term *investment* to refer to the production or purchase of capital goods. For the economy as a whole, investment refers to additions to the stock of capital goods, and results from an excess of production over current consumption.

Production of capital goods represents one use for the pre-existing scarce resources of the economy. The use of some resources for capital production imposes an implicit sacrifice of the consumption goods which might have been produced during the same period with those resources. People are willing to accept this sacrifice of current consumption because the use of capital goods may permit the future output of the economy to rise by more than the reduction of current consumption. The existing supply of labor and other resources may yield a greater total output if some part of them goes into indirect or roundabout production, through capital formation, rather than being devoted directly to consumption. Production of capital goods typically involves a transmutation of one batch of input services, used to *make* the capital goods, into another batch of input services rendered *by* the capital goods themselves in further production. Initial inputs produce a stock of physical capital assets, which in turn yield a flow of their own services over time. This necessarily imposes a delay on the community, which must wait longer for the services of the capital assets.

There is nothing inherently productive about capital formation per se. Merely converting labor and other current inputs into physical assets does not guarantee that those physical assets will be more productive than the inputs required to make them. But given appropriate conditions of technology and organization, devoting some resources to capital goods may permit other transmutations of input services which do increase productivity. Capital goods permit the productive process to achieve extremes of temperature, pressure, precision, uniformity, continuity, and many other dimensions which could not be achieved by other means. There are qualitative differences between the services which a capital good can yield and the services available from the labor and other inputs used in making it. The fact that factor services are "embodied" in the form of a physical asset can be a necessary condition for increased productivity, but is not in itself a sufficient condition. It is through a market process involving supply, demand, and profit maximization that the economic system tends to identify capital investments which will have a positive net productivity—which will add more to future output than the sacrifice they impose on current consumption.

For the community as a whole, the sacrifice of current consumption is the *opportunity cost* of capital formation. The sacrifice may be voluntarily accepted by individual households deciding to save a part of their incomes, or the sacrifice may be imposed involuntarily through government taxation or forced labor. In this chapter we limit our attention to a competitive market economy and ignore the use of government coercion as a method for directing resources away from consumption. Private saving is probably subject to "increasing reluctance"—the more people are already saving, the less willing they will be to reduce current consumption further. Decreasing marginal utility of current consumption would provide a plausible reason for this.

The analysis of capital goods pricing and the interest rate is an effort to show how market forces of supply and demand respond to underlying relationships involving the potential productivity of capital goods, on one hand, and people's willingness and ability to devote resources to capital formation, on the other.

demand for capital goods by the firm

The individual firm's demand for capital goods arises from a demand for their services. The flow of services will be available, however, only if an appropriate stock of capital goods exists. And such a stock is produced only if someone is willing to pay for it.

In a market economy without slavery, labor services are paid for at approximately the same time they are performed. The firm pays its wage costs, in effect, out of the proceeds of the output which the labor has produced. The same is true for purchased inputs of electricity and water, raw materials, transport, and other services. But the essential element of capital goods is that they must be paid for by someone *before* they are used.

However, the firm wishing to obtain the services of capital goods may have the opportunity to do so without buying the capital goods themselves. Buildings and motor vehicles, for example, can commonly be leased or purchased, and leasing was long customary for shoe machinery and computers. If opportunities for short-term leasing or some counterpart are available to the competitive firm, its demand for services of capital goods can be analyzed in terms similar to those for any input. On the basis of its production function, the price of its product, and the prices of other inputs, a schedule of marginal net revenue product can be derived for services of any specific form of capital assets. The schedule will tend to be downward sloping because of the decreasing marginal rate of input substitution and because of diseconomies of scale (which must exist beyond some output in order for competitive equilibrium to be feasible). The firm maximizes profits by employing a quantity of each capital service up to the point where its $MNRP$ is just equal to the lease charge for the appropriate time period.

The analytical problems posed by capital are not avoided by allowing leasing, however; they are merely pushed off on another firm. We will simplify their treatment if we now assume that users of capital goods purchase them. Decisions to purchase a stock of assets now in order to obtain a flow of services extending into the future create problems of financing and valuation.

Since the initial purchase of capital goods cannot literally be paid for out of the revenues from their use which have not yet been received, such purchase is typically financed either out of the saving of the owners of the firm or by use of borrowed funds.

If capital goods are financed by borrowing, the borrowers will customarily have to pay interest on the borrowed funds. This interest charge will be part of the calculation of whether a specific capital investment is worth making or not. Even if capital goods are financed out of the owners' saving, interest represents an implicit (opportunity) cost of the funds, since they could have been used to acquire interest-bearing financial claims.

The fact that interest is involved in the financing of capital expenditures underlies the tendency to treat the interest rate as the price of capital or the return on it. However, strictly speaking, interest is simply a charge for loans of money. Such loans may arise to finance consumption, government expenditures, or transfers of existing land and other wealth, as well as for new capital formation. Not all capital gives rise to explicit interest payments; the return on the owners' investment may be regarded as profit in the accounting sense. However, we shall see that the interplay of market forces tends to produce definite equilibrium relations between the rate of return on capital, however financed, and the rate of interest on loans, whatever their purpose.

The valuation problem arises when the firm attempts to compare the net revenue from capital goods, which will come as an income stream extending into the future, with the purchase price which must be paid immediately. The problem is further complicated by the risk and uncertainty attached to the expected stream of net revenue.

present value

The revenue yielded by a capital good is spread out over time. A given sum of revenue represents different amounts of *present value* to the firm, depending on when it is received. The further in the future it is expected to come, the smaller its present value. This tendency to value future revenue less highly than present may have a purely subjective basis. Economists have traditionally believed that most people have a *time preference* for present income and consumption as compared to future. However, in an economy where an interest rate exists, discounting the future also has an objective basis. Present revenue can be used to acquire interest-bearing assets which will yield a larger future sum. And interest must be paid if borrowed money is used to finance the acquisition of income-bearing assets.

In evaluating the potential advantage of acquiring a capital asset, the firm can estimate the additions to its expected receipts which will result from adding the asset. These additional revenues come at various dates in the future. To form such estimates, the firm must consider the increase in output which the new asset makes possible, the revenue to be expected from this increased output, and the increased costs of variable inputs necessary to produce the added output. The kind of data involved would follow the logic of Table 14-1.

The firm can convert such a revenue stream into the present value of the asset by a process of *capitalization*. Each element in the stream of expected revenue is divided by a factor containing the rate of interest. This factor is weighted more heavily the further into the future the revenue is expected. The process of scaling down expected future revenues into present value is also called *discounting*. The more remote an expected revenue increment is, the more heavily it is discounted in determining present value.

If we let Y_1, Y_2, . . . , Y_n represent the net revenue expected during each future time period t_1, t_2, . . . , t_n, and assume that the interest rate is r, the present value of any capital good can be determined by this formula:

$$V = \frac{Y_1}{1+r} + \frac{Y_2}{(1+r)^2} + \frac{Y_3}{(1+r)^3} + \cdots + \frac{Y_n}{(1+r)^n}$$

Strictly speaking, this formula is appropriate only when revenue is received in discontinuous chunks, as with the income on a bond. A more complex formula, but embodying the same concept, would be required where part of the income comes every day. Other modifications would be required if the interest rate is expected to change. The simple case is complicated enough, and we will not attempt to explore these variants.

To illustrate the calculation of present value, Table 14-1 presents a set of hypothetical expectations relating to investment in a machine which is expected to last for five years. The terms in the right-hand column of Table 14-1 correspond

TABLE 14-1 DERIVATION OF EXPECTED NET REVENUE FROM A CAPITAL ASSET (Hypothetical Data)

Year	Added Units of Output	(×)	Price of Output	(=)	Added Total Revenue	(−)	Added Expenditures on Other Inputs	(=)	Added Net Revenue
1	1,100		$1.20		$1,320		$220		$1,100
2	2,327		1.25		2,909		489		2,420
3	3,697		1.30		4,806		813		3,993
4	3,079		1.30		4,003		709		3,294
5	2,659		1.30		3,457		638		2,819

to Y_1, Y_2, etc. Suppose the rate of interest is 10 percent. To determine the present value of this machine, the firm must solve the following:

$$V = \frac{\$1,100}{1.10} + \frac{\$2,420}{1.21} + \frac{\$3,993}{1.331} + \frac{\$3,294}{1.464} + \frac{\$2,819}{1.611} = \$10,000$$

Thus, discounting the expected revenues back to the present, we find that the present value of the machine is $10,000. The logic of present-value calculations can be demonstrated by working in the opposite direction. If one had a capital sum of $10,000 and invested it for five years at 10 percent compound interest, at the end of that time it would be worth approximately $16,105. And if one were to take the net income from the capital good, invest it as received at 10 percent interest, after five years that also would total up to $16,105. The present value of the capital asset is therefore that sum of money which, invested at compound interest, would have the same value at the end of the useful life of the capital asset as would the asset's income stream, similarly invested. Table 14-2 shows how the asset's net revenue would be cumulated forward for this sort of comparison.

A present value can be estimated in this manner for each individual capital good—each truck, for example. For each category of capital goods, such as trucks, there will be a schedule of present values, showing the (discounted) $MNRP$ of trucks as a function of the number of trucks employed. The sort of calculation shown in Table 14-1 might be appropriate for evaluating the addition of one truck. Repeating the calculation to consider a second truck would tend to show a slightly smaller present value. The tendency for present value to decrease as quantity of asset increases reflects diminishing returns, decreasing marginal rate of input substitution, and decreasing returns to scale. If we extended calculations like those in Table 14-1 to add more and more trucks, we would find that the added output per truck would tend to decline, and perhaps the amount of variable inputs required would tend to become larger. Between these influences, the net revenue stream

TABLE 14-2

Net revenue of 1st year, compounded forward 4 years at 10%	$1,100 × 1.464 =	$1,610
Net revenue of 2d year, compounded forward 3 years at 10%	2,420 × 1.331 =	$3,221
Net revenue of 3d year, compounded forward 2 years at 10%	3,993 × 1.21 =	$4,832
Net revenue of 4th year, compounded forward 1 year at 10%	3,294 × 1.10 =	$3,623
Net revenue of 5th year	2,819 × 1.00 =	$2,819
Total, end of 5th year		$16,105

and its present value would tend to become the smaller, the larger the quantity of the capital asset employed.

A schedule relating discounted $MNRP$ (present value) to quantity of capital would constitute a demand schedule for the capital asset for the firm. The firm would maximize profits by using a number of trucks such that the discounted $MNRP$ (present value of the marginal truck) would be equal to the price of trucks. If a firm determines that the present value of a new truck is $10,000, and if it can purchase one for $8,000, the purchase will be advantageous. Strictly speaking, the difference between present value and asset price represents a potential increase in the net worth, or present value, of the firm itself. The actual profit the firm makes will be spread out over the lifetime of the asset.

At any rate, the firm will tend to add additional units of capital as long as their price is below their present value. Adding more units decreases present value at the margin, however, until eventually the firm reaches a profit-maximizing position where it has brought discounted $MNRP$ of each type of capital asset into equality with the price of that type of asset. The schedule of discounted $MNRP$ for each asset would be a downward-sloping function of its quantity. That $MNRP$ schedule would identify the demand schedule for that capital asset, expressing quantity demanded as a function of asset price.

From Table 14-1 we can see that the $MNRP$ of an asset would depend partly on its physical productivity (reflecting its intrinsic quality, the supply of cooperating inputs, and the production function), on the expected selling price of the product, and on the expected quantities and prices of variable inputs to be used with it. In addition, the demand schedule for a capital asset would depend on the interest rate. An increase in the interest rate would reduce the present value of any given expected future income stream. A rise in the interest rate from 10 percent to 12 percent would reduce the present value of the asset in Table 14-1 from $10,000 to $9,446. Thus a rise in the interest rate would tend to shift downward the firm's entire discounted $MNRP$ schedule for capital goods, other things being equal. A decrease in the rate of interest would tend to raise the demand schedule for capital goods.

Using the present value of expected revenue product as the basis for the firm's demand schedule for capital is valid if the firm can in fact obtain the funds to carry out its purchase desires. This condition is fulfilled if the firm can borrow as much as it wants at the going rate of interest. The assumption is not a realistic one and we will examine it subsequently.

the firm's demand schedule—alternative approach

The present-value approach to capital-goods demand has the advantage of being congruent with the general marginal-productivity approach to factor demand and factor pricing. However, it may be misleading if the firm cannot borrow all it wants, or if the firm must pay a higher interest rate to borrow larger quantities. Also, the present-value approach does not lend itself very well to certain types of aggregation. An alternative analysis stresses the calculation of the rate of return of each capital good. Rate of return calculation appears to conform to the investment criteria employed by many firms. It combines familiar elements in a somewhat different manner and yields some results not obtained by other approaches.

We define the internal rate of return of a capital asset as that rate of discount (d) which makes the present value (V) of the asset equal to the price (P_c) at which the asset can be purchased from its producers. The previous discount formula can be used in calculating the internal rate of return, as follows:

$$V = \frac{Y_1}{1 + d} + \frac{Y_2}{(1 + d)^2} \cdots \frac{Y_n}{(1 + d)^n} = P_c$$

We are now assuming that the price of the capital asset is known, as well as the expected income stream. We solve the equation for the discount factor d to make $V = P_c$.

If a capital asset yields an internal rate of return of 10 percent, its net income stream will, on the average, be as large as one could get by investing the purchase price of the asset in a 10-percent compound interest bearing asset. Using the information in Table 14-1, if the price of the capital asset were $10,000, its internal rate of return would be 10 percent. If its price were $9,500, its rate of return would be about 12 percent. Given the expected income stream in dollars, the internal return varies inversely with the price. Given the price, the rate of return tends to be higher, the higher the expected dollar income stream itself.

TABLE 14-3

Project	Cost	Rate of Return, %	Cumulative Sum of Investment Out- lays Yielding That or Higher Return
A	$ 10,000	45	$ 10,000
B	3,000	33	13,000
C	6,000	29	19,000
D	35,000	24	54,000
E	5,000	21	59,000
.	.	.	.
.	.	.	.
.	.	.	.
Z	285,000	6	2,519,000
.	.	.	.
.	.	.	.
.	.	.	.

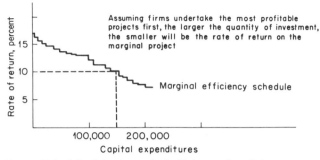

Figure 14-1 Schedule of marginal efficiency of capital.

We can imagine that each firm estimates the prospective internal rate of return on various capital investment projects open to it, as well as the capital expenditure required for each project. The various projects could be arranged in tabular form, starting with the project with the highest return and listing the others in descending order. Table 14-3 illustrates a hypothetical tabulation of this sort.

Such a tabulation represents the firm's schedule of the *marginal efficiency of capital*. Assuming that the highest-yielding projects will be most likely to be undertaken, the schedule can be interpreted in two ways. First, if we know the amount the firm has to spend on capital goods, we can find the marginal efficiency—that is, the rate of return on the marginal project. With $10,000 to spend, marginal efficiency would be 45 percent. With $54,000 it would be 24 percent. Conversely, if some minimum rate of return is specified, the schedule indicates the quantity of investment which would yield that minimum or more.

The marginal efficiency schedule can be illustrated graphically, as in Figure 14-1. For a small firm, the ME schedule would tend to descend by steps, because of the size of individual projects and gaps between rates of return. The ME schedule is downward sloping simply because some projects yield more than others. There are more projects yielding 10 percent or more than there are yielding 20 percent or more.

The ME schedule can guide the choice of investment projects. If the firm can borrow all the money it wants at the going rate of interest, it will maximize profits by making all the investments which yield a rate of return higher than the rate of interest. It will carry its total investment spending up to the point where the marginal efficiency of capital is equal to the rate of interest. In this situation, the rate of interest represents a form of marginal cost and the marginal efficiency (internal rate of return) is a measure of marginal revenue. (Even if the owner's funds are used, the interest rate is an implicit cost; it represents a foregone alternative to investment in capital goods.) In Figure 14-1, when the interest rate is 10 percent, the firm invests $150,000 in purchasing capital goods.

A fall in the rate of interest would tend to increase the firm's investment expenditures. Some projects not profitable at an interest rate of 10 percent would be profitable if the interest rate were 8 percent. And the higher the interest rate, given the ME schedule, the lower would be the firm's investment spending.

If a firm finances its capital expenditures entirely by borrowing, the marginal efficiency schedule also becomes a demand schedule for loan funds by the firm. At any interest rate, the amount of funds the firm will seek to borrow will be the amount appropriate to make ME equal to that interest rate.

If the firm finances part of its investment from owners' saving, its demand schedule for loan funds will still look like the ME schedule, but lie below it graphically. Normally, the firm will tend to borrow more at lower interest rates. Should the marginal efficiency schedule shift, through a change in profit expectations or a change in the price of capital goods, the firm's demand schedule for loan funds would tend to shift in the same direction.

We have now developed two ways of looking at the firm's investment decision. Utilizing the first, we conclude that the firm tends to purchase a quantity of each specific capital good such that its discounted $MNRP$ (the present value of the marginal asset) is equal to its price. Utilizing the second, we conclude that the firm's total purchases of capital goods will be carried to the level which equates the marginal efficiency of capital (the internal rate of return on the marginal project) with the rate of interest.

The two methods differ in emphasis, but they share many implications in common. Both imply that the amount of capital goods demanded varies inversely with their price. This is explicit when we use discounted $MNRP$, from which we derive a conventional downward-sloping demand curve. It is implicit in the marginal efficiency analysis, where an increase in the price of capital goods, other things being equal, reduces the internal rate of return on them. Both methods imply that the demand schedule for capital goods will shift in the same direction as shifts in the expected flow of net revenue. And both methods imply that the quantity of capital goods demanded will vary inversely with the rate of interest. This is explicit in the use of marginal efficiency analysis, which yields the equivalent of a downward-sloping demand curve for capital goods as a function of the interest rate. And it is implicit in the use of discounted $MNRP$, where a rise in the rate of interest reduces the present value of any asset, given its expected income. Finally, both methods imply that the firm's demand for loan funds will tend to vary inversely with the rate of interest and with the price of capital goods, and directly with the expected stream of net revenue from capital assets.

risks, uncertainty, and limited funds

In the real world, investment analysis is heavily colored by the fact that the future income stream from a capital asset is uncertain. This in turn makes investment risky; the firm may fail to earn the expected rate of return or may indeed earn nothing at all. This situation gives rise to several analytical problems. One is the managerial problem of how to form reliable estimates of what future net revenues will be. Firms experiment with various forecasting techniques in an effort to form such estimates. A second problem is to convert a set of uncertain estimates into a single-valued "certainty equivalent." One method of looking at this is to assume that the firm can estimate a probability distribution of possible net revenue for each future time period. Each revenue expectation can be weighted by its probability to yield a determinate "mathematical expectation" for that period. The method has a mathematical appeal, but does not seem to conform to business practice. Probabilities themselves are often unknown to the firm.

More significant are the modifications required because of risk. Every investment project has some chance, however small and uncertain, that it will inflict losses on the firm. For a small firm, such losses may drive the firm out of business. One of the simplest methods a firm might allow for risk is simply to require a safety margin between the expected return on an asset and the rate of interest. With an interest rate of 8 percent, for example, the firm might require at least a 10 percent return on a project before undertaking it. Another method is to hedge in favor of projects with shorter lifetimes. Perhaps a firm might avoid any project which entails more than some nominal probability of bankrupting the firm.

The main point is that the mere desire to maximize profits in the usual sense of the term does not identify one particular "correct" method for handling risky investment decisions. A firm enjoying complete information has no reason not to employ a factor service up to the point where its marginal net revenue product equals the marginal outlay for it. But a firm with uncertain knowledge cannot be regarded as irrational for failing to buy capital goods, however large the expected return, if such purchase entails some risk of loss and business failure.

One way out is to introduce into the analysis an additional variable, some sort of preference function of the entrepreneurs. For example, one might depict a sort of indifference map comparing risk (if it can be quantified) and expected rate of return. A firm might be indifferent between one project with low risk and low expected return and another project with high risk and high expected return. Such an approach may formalize our ignorance but does not dispel it.

Because of uncertainty and risk in capital investment, firms typically cannot borrow all the money they want at the going rate of interest. Lenders protect themselves against risk by limiting the amount they will lend to a particular borrower. Often the limit is related to the amount of ownership capital invested in the borrowing firm. If a firm is subject to some maximum limit on the amount it can borrow, it cannot purchase all the assets for which $MNRP$ exceeds price or internal rate of return exceeds rate of interest. It might still move along its marginal efficiency schedule, using its limited funds for those projects with highest internal rate of return. However, such a firm may have a bias in favor of quick returns on investment, because revenues are themselves a potential source of investment funds for subsequent periods. By reinvesting quick profits the firm may enlarge its borrowing capacity, total capital, and total profit for the long run. In subsequent sections, we ignore the complications arising from uncertainty, risk, and limited borrowing capacity.

capital goods: supply and demand

Since capital goods are formally similar to other commodities, their supply conditions can be analyzed in similar fashion. The supply of currently produced locomotives, tractors, or steel rails will depend on the costs of producing such items, which will depend on the technology and organization of production, and on supply conditions of inputs used in producing capital goods. Since capital goods are often close substitutes on the production side for other manufactured goods (trucks and automobiles are a good example), supply elasticity for particular capital goods is likely to be high. For capital goods as a group, an additional consideration deserves comment. Capital goods compete with current consumption goods for the scarce productive resources of the society. The larger the proportion of income which the members of the society devote to current consumption, the less plentiful will be the resources for the production of capital goods. The more workers are drawn into auto production, the fewer remain to produce trucks. One of the functions of saving is to lessen the competing pressure for resources and make it easier to divert them into production of capital goods.

In considering the supply of capital goods, we must also consider the stock of existing assets, which may be bought and sold in second-hand transactions. Their quantity may be assumed to be fixed. Since the existing stock of assets tends to be much larger than current production, the elasticity of the total stock is much less than the elasticity of current production.

For each type of capital good, there exists a downward-sloping demand schedule. It reflects the quality of the capital good itself (durability, mechanical efficiency), the production function of users of the capital good, the supply conditions of other inputs, demand conditions in markets for final products, and the level of interest rates. The demand schedule slopes down because of diminishing returns, decreasing marginal rate of substitution among inputs, and downward-sloping demand schedules for individual final products.

equilibrium in capital market

As each firm individually attempts to adjust its employment of each type of capital asset to reach the input position at which the discounted $MNRP$ of the asset equals its price, market conditions change along several fronts. First, of course, the output and prices of currently produced capital goods adjust to the pressure of demand on the basis of factor-supply elasticities. In addition, the prices of the existing stock of capital goods may rise or fall with demand pressures. And third, the interest rate itself may be forced higher or lower, depending on the pressure which capital financing develops in the market for loanable funds. Bear in mind that both the supply side and the demand side in the market for a capital good will consist of business firms. Competitive sellers will be in equilibrium when the price of the capital good is equal to its marginal cost and, in the long run, to its average cost of production. Competitive buyers will be in equilibrium when the price equals the (discounted) marginal net revenue product of the capital good, and, in the long run, the average net revenue product as well.

Thus the average and marginal cost of a machine, as incurred by the producers, must be equal to the average and marginal net revenue product of that machine for the firms which use it. Figure 14-2 shows this relationship for one typical firm on the selling side and another on the buying side of the market in the case of a specific type of machine (m). Note that the quantity axis on the left refers to quantity of machines produced in the current time period, while the right-hand side refers to the stock of machines used. The latter may include machines produced in previous time periods, as well as those currently produced.

Of course there are additional conditions required for equilibrium. The quantity supplied by producers of the machine must be equal to the current purchases of the machine by the users. The total quantity of machines demanded by the users must be equal to the total stock in existence, including both those newly produced and those previously in existence.

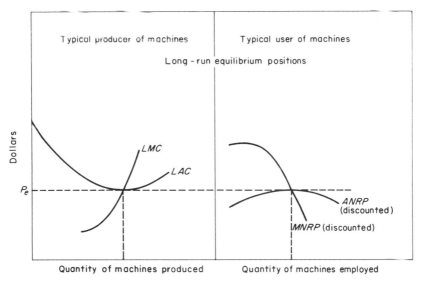

Figure 14-2 Capital goods equilibrium: production and use.

To illustrate adjustment to a change in data, let us assume that a technological innovation raises the expected productivity of a particular type of capital good, such as trucks. The discounted $MNRP$ and $ANRP$ schedules shift upward. This causes quantity demanded to exceed quantity supplied at the initial price. The price of trucks tends to rise, at least in the short run, and sellers tend to expand output. The long-run response of price and output of trucks depends on the elasticity of supply of trucks and the inputs required to make them. On the other side of the market, the increase in the expected profitability of investment stimulates greater demand for loan funds and this tends to raise the interest rate. In the new long-run equilibrium, the output and (relative) price of trucks will tend to be higher than initially, and so will the interest rate.

In the economy as a whole, investment in all forms of capital goods will be carried to a level where the marginal efficiency of capital equals the rate of interest. An increase in investment incentives would shift the marginal efficiency schedule upward, leading to some combination of higher output of capital goods, higher prices for them, and a higher rate of interest.

The price effects which are relevant to investment decisions are changes in relative prices. It is usually assumed that present-value or marginal-efficiency schedules are specified in real terms. A doubling of all prices would presumably leave the real investment function unchanged while doubling the value of an investment function specified in money terms. The investment incentive is dampened by an increase in the relative purchase price of capital goods—relative to prices of goods in general.

investment, saving, and the rate of interest in the economic system

If we attempt to raise the level of our analysis to the economic system as a whole, to correspond with the previous chapter, we encounter serious difficulties. The phenomena of investment, saving, and interest rates are in the real world heavily influenced by matters relating to money and to the financial system. Further, analysis of such matters runs strongly in terms of disequilibrium conditions in an economy in which full employment (factor-market equilibrium) may be absent. The analysis in this book is largely confined to equilibrium conditions; roughly speaking, we deal only with an environment in which full employment of resources is achieved. Resources may be temporarily displaced when an initial equilibrium is disturbed, but we assume they have been absorbed again when a final equilibrium is reached (unless they have voluntarily withdrawn from the market).

In full-employment equilibrium, the amount saved must be equal to the amount invested in currently produced capital goods. Indeed, the terms are alternate definitions of the same thing. Saving is measured by the amount of income (output) not devoted to current consumption. And products not consumed are, broadly speaking, capital goods. More important, in order for equilibrium to exist, there must be equality between the amount people want to save and the amount people want to invest. Otherwise conditions will not remain at rest.

When we exclude the monetary complications of a disequilibrium world, the equilibrating process which brings desired saving and desired investment into equality works through product and factor prices and through the interest rate. To explore this process we need to explore the influence of prices and interest rates on saving and investment.

We have observed that investment tends to vary inversely with interest rates, other things being equal. What about saving? Traditionally, saving was treated as a typical supply variable, and was assumed to be a rising function of its "price," the rate of interest. However, we have already seen in examining labor supply that factors of production, viewed as national aggregates, do not necessarily follow this pattern. And there is much similarity in the case of saving. As with labor supply, the relation of saving to the interest rate depends on income and wealth effects and on substitution effects, which may be working in opposite directions. Each household may be viewed as having a preference function comparing current consumption with saving, or increase in net worth, or future consumption. Just as the wage rate is an (implicit) price of leisure, so the interest rate is an (implicit) price of current consumption. A higher interest rate increases the cost of current consumption, the relative attractiveness of wealth, and the amount of future income and consumption one may enjoy by consuming a bit less at present. Substitution effects would lead one to expect higher saving (out of a given income) at a higher interest rate.

However, changes in the interest rate will also have income effects and wealth effects. One sort of income effect occurs because a rise in the interest rate increases the amount of future consumption one can obtain with an additional dollar of current saving. If people decide to take some of this potential for increased consumption in the current time period, they may reduce saving somewhat.

Interest-rate changes will cause inverse changes in the prices of income-bearing property, real or financial, if the expected money income from such property remains unchanged. Thus the market value of wealth tends to be reduced by an increase in the interest rate. Indeed, such changes in asset values are the principal means by which interest rates change. Quite possibly some families' saving and consumption behavior will be affected by changes in wealth value, although it is not easy to identify the probable direction of influence.

Observation of saving behavior in the United States suggests that the net interest-rate effects are relatively neutral—a conclusion similar to the one we reached for labor. Saving as a proportion of income does not appear substantially raised or lowered by variations in interest rates, within the range of experience.

There may be relative-price effects on saving, as we have observed with investment. But the complexities of dealing with these at an aggregate level defeat any attempt at generalizations. We will merely cite a few possibilities ad hoc in the following.

Suppose again that we begin from an equilibrium position and assume an increase in the marginal efficiency schedule. Increased profit expectations lead to increased demand for loans and tend to raise interest rates. Demand for specific capital goods increases, producers bid for more inputs, and input prices rise. Consumption goods using the same inputs may experience rising costs and charge higher prices. If consumers are willing, in face of higher commodity prices and higher interest rates, to consume less and save more, the potential rise in real investment becomes effective. If consumers continue to consume the same quantities as before, no additional resources become available to produce capital goods, and prices and interest rates must rise to the point where real investment is no larger than before. In such a sequence, *relative* prices may end up where they started. But the interest rate ends up higher than before.

Returning to the initial equilibrium assumption, assume now that there is an increase in consumers' desire to save. This will tend to increase the supply of loan funds, lowering the interest rate. Decreased consumption would tend to lower prices of productive resources, making capital goods cheaper. Both of these would tend to increase real investment. But the drop in consumption might have an adverse effect on profit expectations. If investment is not increased, on balance, then equilibrium can only be restored when price decreases and lower interest rates bring real consumption back to its original level. Relative prices may emerge unchanged, but the interest rate will be lower than initially.

Thus in equilibrium, desired saving and desired investment must be equal, and the interest rate must be equal to the marginal efficiency of capital. However, our understanding of the adjustment process is clouded by the fact that there are so many margins along which adjustment can proceed.

capital in a production function

It is well to remember that capital represents the use of labor and natural resources in indirect or roundabout methods of production. The equilibrium rate of interest and marginal efficiency represent the superiority, at the margin, of using labor and natural resources in indirect forms. An equilibrium interest rate of 10 percent would indicate that a given quantity of resources would deliver 10 percent more output if used in roundabout ways which would deliver the final output a year hence, as compared with ways which would deliver the final output now.

In the previous chapter, we analyzed the productivity and reward of labor by relating the supply of labor to an aggregate production function for the economic system. It is tempting to do the same for capital. There are measurement difficulties in deciding how to represent the size of the physical stock of capital, but these arise in any case where we attempt to use an aggregate production function. The most common solution is to use a money measure of the value of the capital stock, adjusted by a price index to some common base period.

In analyzing the labor market for the entire economy, we concluded that the marginal product of labor could be identified as the derivative dQ/dL of an aggregate production function, so long as quantities of other factors were constant. However, the corresponding derivative dQ/dK relating to capital goods is not necessarily equal to the discounted marginal product of capital goods as we have analyzed it in investment decisions. The derivative dQ/dK is termed the *marginal output-capital ratio* (MOC), a concept widely used in analysis of economic growth. Two capital goods having the same discounted marginal productivity may have different MOC ratios because they differ in durability or in the time-shape of their yield.

Compare two capital assets, each lasting three years. One yields $6,000 a year for each of the three years. The other yields $8,480 the first year, $6,000 the second, and $3,000 the third. At an interest rate of 10 percent they both have a present value (discounted $MNRP$) of about $14,921 (or, if their prices were both $14,921, both would yield an internal rate of return of 10 percent). But their impact on first-year output is not the same.

The problem is essentially one of homogeneity, and it arises in all analysis at a highly aggregated level. In analysis of capital, it may be useful to assume that although individual capital assets differ in durability and time-shape of payoff, the average composition of capital in the economy as a whole does not change. By this means, one can bring the MOC ratio into identity with the discounted marginal product of capital. For example, one might define one's measurement of capital in such a way that investment represents a permanent addition to the capital stock which will yield the same contribution of productive services each year. Under such simplifying assumptions, if the marginal efficiency of capital were 10 percent, this would imply that a small permanent addition (say $1,000) to capital would raise output by 10 percent as much ($100) in each subsequent year. Suppose the aggregate production function took the familiar form $Q = K^{1/2}L^{1/2}$, with output (Q) and capital (K) both expressed in dollar values calculated at prices of some base period. Suppose there are 10,000 units of labor input and $250,000 worth of capital, yielding an output of $50,000. The marginal product schedule of capital, with a fixed labor input, would be $dQ/dK = L^{1/2}/2K^{1/2} = 100/1,000 = 0.10$. The solution tells us that adding one dollar's worth of capital would increase output by ten cents worth. Thus the marginal output-capital ratio, the marginal efficiency of capital, and the equilibrium interest rate would all tend to be 10 percent.

If each unit of capital receives a reward of 10 percent, the total income of owners of capital would be $25,000, leaving $25,000 for labor. This is consistent with the income-distribution results we achieved in the preceding chapter. Each factor category receives total income equal to its marginal product multiplied by the number of factor units. With a production function displaying constant returns to scale, the resulting factor incomes add up to the total output of the system.

Our analysis has assumed that technology does not change and that the labor force is constant. Under such assumptions, increases in the quantity of capital would be subject to diminishing returns. Such increases would cause the equilibrium rate of interest to decline, which might erode the incentive for further saving and investment. In the real world, technological progress has more than offset this tendency toward static diminishing returns. Increases in the efficiency with which capital goods can be produced, and in their productivity once produced, have constantly tended to shift the marginal efficiency schedule upward. As fast as investment uses up one set of good projects, another set appears on the horizon. Further, technological progress generally requires embodiment in capital goods before it raises productivity.

Our analysis implies that increase in the quantity of capital tends to raise the marginal product (and equilibrium real wage) of the labor force. Historically, this tendency has been operative on the average, though it need not work for every category of labor.

Saving and investment are thus important sources of increased output and also of increased per capita labor income. Saving may be carried out by private persons, by business firms (particularly corporations), and by government. In most countries, the flow of saving has varied directly with total income, both for individual saving units and for the economy as a whole. Societies with high total income tend to save more, in absolute magnitude, and thus can add substantially to their existing capital. Countries with low income find it more difficult to save and to expand capital.

Within a private-enterprise economy, a high proportion of income tends to be saved by persons who are owners of business. In industrial countries, a large proportion of total saving is performed by business corporations. Owners of unincorporated businesses and farms have also been high savers in some relatively developed countries. It is probable that a higher proportion of profit income is saved than of other incomes.

In most underdeveloped societies, per capita income is so low that most families must spend all their income merely for the physical necessities of life. Yet such societies urgently need more saving as one means of increasing their capital goods and output. In western countries, inequality in the distribution of incomes enabled a few families to receive high incomes and to save and invest, despite the poverty of the masses. However, rich people in underdeveloped countries are sometimes not willing to save and invest. Further, public opinion may not wish to tolerate extreme inequality in present incomes, even if inequality does promote future growth. Under such conditions, underdeveloped countries will be able to add to their capital only if they receive aid and investment from foreign sources, or if their governments are able to aid in the saving and investment process. Government may be able to reduce private consumption by taxation, and enlarge the quantity of capital either by making productive investments itself or by financial support to private investment, through loans or subsidies.

the form of capital goods

Decisions by the individual firm concerning the input mix and technique of production include a concern for the specific form which capital assets should take. The optimum form of capital is related to the optimum mix between capital and other resources. For example, if land is very cheap and the optimum mix involves a lot of land per unit of capital, the firm might well prefer a low building spread out over a large area. But if land is scarce and expensive, the proper form for the building may be a very tall one occupying a much smaller ground space. Similarly, the form of capital goods needs to be adjusted to the number of men who will be working with a certain money-value of capital goods.

At any given time, the existing stock of capital goods is "frozen" into one particular pattern of forms. Alterations of form for the economy as a whole can come only in that proportion of capital goods which is currently produced. Efforts by individual firms to alter the form of their capital will tend to lead to changes in the relative prices of existing assets until someone is willing to use them.

It is important for the efficiency of the economy as a whole that the form of capital be appropriate to the other inputs which are to be used with it. Failure to achieve such adaptation may mean that the productivity of the total supply of scarce capital is less than it might be.

One consequence of the uncertainty which exists in the real world is that firms may prefer to embody their capital in forms which possess great flexibility and adaptability to changes which may occur in final demand, factor prices, and technology.

scarcity and the rate of interest

There is no single unambiguous measure of the cost or price of capital. Each capital good has two elements of cost. One is the price which must be paid to purchase the capital good, reflecting the value and quantity of scarce resources which go into production of the capital good. The other is the interest rate, reflecting the scarcity of loanable funds. However, both of these costs can be traced to the same origin. The cost of producing capital goods is higher, the stronger the demand for resources to produce consumer goods instead. And the scarcity of loanable funds can be traced ultimately to scarcity of saving, which is simply a willingness to refrain from consuming a portion of present real income.

Both elements of the cost of capital help to ration it among possible uses. If the market mechanism is working well, capital goods will flow into those uses which have the highest marginal productivity. These are the uses which will ultimately yield the greatest increase in the value of the output of the economy.

In the real world, investment activities and the functions of financial markets are riddled with rigidities and uncertainties. As a consequence, much of the rationing of loanable funds is made on a non-price basis. Lenders may impose ceilings on the amount they will lend to an individual borrower, based on his income, wealth, or some other criterion. Thus the market for loans is not one in which borrowers can obtain all the funds they want at some going market price.

Even so, the interest rate still acts to limit demands for funds by creditworthy borrowers and encourages individual business firms to select those investment projects with the highest expected payoff.

Our analysis of capital in this chapter has not dealt fully with the kinds of incomes which arise from capital. Where capital goods have been financed by ownership capital, the income they yield may be identified as profit. Where they are financed by borrowing, a part of their income may go in the form of interest. Such questions are further considered in Chapter 15.

We have touched only briefly on the relationship among capital, economic growth, and income distribution. These matters are further explored in Chapter 17.

land rents and prices

We have already noted (Chapter 5) that the distinguishing feature of the market for land lies in the inelasticity of its total supply. The demand for land involves a combination of familiar elements. Some land is desired for the direct enjoyment of consumers, for living space. Land is desired by business firms (including farms) on the basis of its productivity. Land productivity may stem from the fertility of the soil, or some other rich endowment, such as minerals. However, differences in the desirability of different tracts of land also arise from considerations of *location*. An entire branch of economic theory has arisen to explain why firms locate where they do, and such "location theory" could be used in evaluating the productivity of different land tracts. The attractiveness of a location arises from some combination of lower costs or superior revenues. Locating close to customers helps the firm to realize a larger net revenue from each unit of sales. Locating close to sources of inputs keep costs down. Depending on the technology of the firm and the transport costs of various products, some balancing between revenue and cost considerations is made.

Contractual renting of land is widespread. In addition, we have pointed out that when land is used by its owner it can still be said to have an implicit rental value. Business firms can determine the most profitable quantity of land to employ by comparing the rental required to obtain it with the $MNRP$ of its services during the rental period. If annual rental is less than $MNRP$, firms will bid for existing land tracts and their rentals will rise. If $MNRP$ is less than rental, firms will refrain from such bidding, and rentals will fall. Through this process, annual rental value tends to equal the $MNRP$ of land services during the year.

Decisions about purchasing land reflect the logic of discounting and present value. A firm has an incentive to buy a tract of land if the discounted value of expected revenues on it exceeds the purchase price. The expected revenues may arise from actual use, but also from resale of the land. As with capital goods, adjustments by buyers and sellers tend to bring selling price and present value into equality.

Since supply is fixed, variations in demand lead only to variations in price. This condition led many observers to regard land rent as a functionless sort of income. Nineteenth-century social reformers, influenced by Henry George, urged heavy taxation of land rents as a way of raising government revenues without any adverse effects on economic incentives, and with beneficial effect on the fairness of income distribution.

However, the market levels of land rental do serve the function of allocating land among various competing uses. Tax burdens which lowered the rental value of land would encourage firms to try to use too much of it. In the aggregate, of course, they would not be able to use more land than there is. But in the process very likely land allocation would fail to meet the condition of equalization of marginal product, which assures maximum output. And individual firms, using too much or too little land, would be operating with inappropriate factor combinations and quite possibly inappropriate forms of capital.

On the other hand, one should not become too romantic over the efficiency with which the price mechanism allocates land. Because each tract of land is unique, conditions of pure competition cannot really exist in respect to location. Lack of homogeneity also aggravates problems of uncertainty, which are further accentuated by the prevalence of long-term leases which may impede transfer of land use.

stock and flow elasticities

There are many raw materials derived from natural resources of which the total physical stock is fixed. Coal, iron ore, and petroleum are important illustrations. While the stocks of such items are completely inelastic, the actual flows of output are not. The reason is that the flow requires the use of cooperating inputs which have alternative uses elsewhere in the economy. Increased demand for petroleum products would tend to increase production, since the higher price would encourage the use of added labor and capital for drilling and other extraction and distribution costs. Similar considerations apply to land itself. Land use commonly requires cooperating factors. If demand for final products is not sufficiently strong, or if supply of cooperating factors is too small, land may remain out of use. Its stock elasticity is zero, but the elasticity of the flow of its services is positive. The amount of cultivated land in the United States did not reach a maximum until the twentieth century. In some less-developed regions (such as southeast Asia) cultivated area is still increasing steadily.

In the short run, however, most of the inputs involved in land use or mineral extraction may be fixed. In that case, the short-run flow elasticity may be very low also. Once an oil well is successfully drilled, the short-run variable costs of removing the oil are very low. The same is true for a coal mine. Even farming displays some of this tendency.

summary

The competitive firm's demand schedule for capital goods derives from the schedule of the marginal net revenue product of capital goods. However, since capital goods yield their services over time, the expected flow of net revenue must be discounted by the rate of interest to obtain the present value of the capital good. The firm would maximize profit by using a sufficient quantity of each kind of capital good to make its discounted $MNRP$ equal to its price. Given the expected income stream, the discounted $MNRP$ varies inversely with the rate of interest. The expected return on a capital good can also be expressed as its internal rate of return, calculating a discount factor which equates expected income with the price of the capital good. The marginal efficiency schedule is an ordered aggregation of the internal rates of return of possible projects. If the firm can borrow all the funds it wishes at the going rate of interest, it will maximize profits by making all the investment outlays with a rate of return higher than the interest rate. A demand schedule for loan funds emerges from the marginal efficiency schedule.

As all firms undertake to maximize profits, output and prices of capital goods adjust; the price of each capital good tends to be equal to its average and marginal costs of production, on the producing side, and to its average and marginal net revenue product, on the using side. Efforts of firms to use borrowed funds may affect interest rates. In equilibrium, the interest rate tends to equal the marginal efficiency of capital for the economy. If the composition of capital is relatively stable, the equilibrium interest rate tends to be equal to the marginal output-capital ratio yielded by an aggregate production function of the Cobb-Douglas type.

Both the availability of real resources to produce capital goods, and the availability of loan funds to finance their purchase depend on the willingness of the society to save—that is, to refrain from devoting all of current real income to current consumption. The equilibrium interest rate and expected rate of return on capital tend to vary directly with the productivity of capital (and the efficiency of capital-goods production), but they tend to vary inversely with the willingness to save, other things being equal. The equilibrium interest rate rations scarce capital among competing uses, ideally directing it into the most productive uses and forms. And the equilibrium interest rate reflects the gain, at the margin, of using resources in a roundabout manner, to increase future production, instead of employing them directly for current consumption.

Because the stock of land is completely inelastic, its current rental value varies with changes in demand. Demand arises from the utility of land to consumers and from its marginal productivity in business uses. In equilibrium, the market price of a tract of land adjusts so that the expected rental income yields the market rate of interest on the price.

In the real world, markets for both land and capital diverge considerably from long-run competitive equilibrium. Calculations of marginal net revenue product of capital are subject to a large degree of uncertainty and risk. Financial markets rely heavily on nonprice rationing devices, and individual tracts of land are not homogeneous. Nevertheless, marginal productivity analysis is essential in understanding the pricing and allocation of these resources. In particular, it is useful to remember that the price of each factor of production tends to vary inversely with its own supply, and directly with the supply of the other factors.

TERMS AND CONCEPTS

1. Present value
2. Saving
3. Investment
4. Marginal output-capital ratio
5. Internal rate of return
6. Schedule of marginal efficiency of capital

QUESTIONS AND PROBLEMS

1. A capital good which costs $2,000 is expected to yield net revenue of $1,000 a year for each of the next three years. Calculate the internal rate of return of this investment.

2. Calculate the present value of the capital good in question 1 on the assumption that the market rate of interest is 5 percent.

3. "Without technological change, the economy's incentive to add to its capital would soon wither away." Explain.

4. Compare the concept of the marginal efficiency of capital with the concept of the discounted marginal net revenue product of capital. How are they related? Show that the long-run competitive equilibrium conditions stated in terms of ME are equivalent to those stated in terms of discounted $MNRP$.

5. Karl Marx argued that in a private-enterprise market economy too small a proportion of total output was devoted to capital investment and that ideally the community should enlarge its stock of capital goods until the rate of interest (and the marginal efficiency of capital) would be reduced to zero. Do you think this would be a good idea? What limits the amount of capital in a market economy?

income distribution in the competitive economy

In a market economy, households "earn" their incomes through the sale of productive services of labor and property to business firms. The income of each household is determined by the quantity of services which it sells, and by the price which it receives for each service. In this chapter we consider the distribution of factor incomes in an economy characterized by pure competition. But first, we must consider what there is to distribute.

Households receive their income in the form of money payments. But their chief concern, and ours as well, is with their *real income*—that is, the purchasing power of their money income, the amount of goods and services which they can obtain for it. For the entire economic system, the amount of real income is essentially equal to the amount of output produced by the system. Modern national-income accounting provides systems of definitions and measurement procedures within which total output and total income are identical. In terms of money flow, as long as government is ignored, all of the revenues received by producers from the sale of output are eventually paid as incomes to factors of production. This results because there is one income share, that of profits, which is a residual. Profits are "what's left";

they adjust to whatever level is required to keep total income equal to total output. This does not mean that profit income is arbitrary, or can be ascertained *only* as a residual.

Some definitions of income would not produce identity between total income and total output. For instance, if capital gains arising through increased prices of assets are counted as income, total measured income may appear larger than total output. If gifts and donations are counted as income to the receiver without being deducted from the income of the giver, a similar result would occur. For some purposes, it may be appropriate to include capital gains and transfer receipts as income. For our purposes, however, it seems preferable to retain a definition of income which keeps it equal to output. This identity reminds us of the important fact that it is production which determines the amount of goods and services which people will actually be able to consume, use, and enjoy.

The pattern of income distribution is the outcome of two sets of conditions. One set includes the elements dealt with in the last two chapters—supplies of factors of production, their real productivity, and the amount of each owned by each household. The other set involves a pattern of financial relationships which overlies the "real" resource-productivity pattern. The financial relationships are chiefly those of debtor and creditor, lessor and lessee, and possibly those of stockholder and manager. We need to consider the formal ownership of real wealth—land and capital goods—but also the ownership of financial assets which may involve claims against the income arising from real wealth.

labor income

In a modern industrial economy, most income is earned from the sale of labor services. Labor income may be in the form of wages, based on a wage rate per hour or per piece of work. It may be in the form of salary paid weekly or for longer periods. Labor income may also be an element in the income of the self-employed business man. For a doctor or lawyer, labor income will come in the form of fees. For a shopkeeper, labor income will be a part of the net income he earns from the business. It may not be easy to identify the share of labor income in his total, but one can estimate it by estimating what he could earn if he hired out to work for someone else.

In long-run competitive equilibrium, the wage rate tends to equal the value of the marginal product of labor. Differences in marginal net revenue product provide a major explanation for differences in the labor income of specific workers in a nation's economy. But we must remember all the different things which may cause differences in marginal net revenue productivity. There are of course differences in the qualities and attributes which individual workers possess—strength, skill, experience, education, responsibility, ability to work with other people, and many others. Different jobs place emphasis on different qualities. Workers may differ in productivity because one has found a job which suits his personal qualifications, while another, with those same qualifications, has found a job for which yet other qualifications are more important.

The income available in different occupations depends on the strength of consumer demand for specific products. And the productivity of workers in specific employments depends on the technological conditions of production in those employments. The availability of natural resources and capital goods influences the general level of productivity throughout an economic system.

In addition to these influences on the demand side, labor income depends on the supply of labor. The larger the total supply of labor, relative to the supply of capital goods and natural resources, the lower will be the average level of labor income, other things equal. Likewise, the labor income from any specific occupation will tend to be lower, the larger the number of people practicing it, given the conditions of demand. (We refer to labor income per worker.)

In the real world, of course, things are not in a state of long-run competitive equilibrium. There are elements of monopoly in many product and factor markets. Access to well-paying jobs may be closed off by union restrictions or by employer discrimination. We shall consider the influence of imperfect competition on factor markets in a subsequent chapter.

Even in competitive markets, equilibrium conditions may not have been reached. In particular, employers may not be employing an appropriate number of workers so as to bring marginal net revenue product into equality with factor price—in other words, they are not maximizing profits. Often firms do not know their demand and cost conditions sufficiently well to locate the maximum-profit position, but must go through a trial-and-error process of experimentation to seek it. And workers do not always identify and choose the highest-paying employments.

The labor income of any household depends not only on the prevailing rates of wages but on the number of members of the household who are working. In a high-wage economy like that of the United States, a family with two or three wage earners may easily rank in the top fifth of the income scale.

interest income

Interest income is earned from ownership of certain types of financial claims. These are customarily *debt* claims against business firms, government units, or individual persons. Much of the interest income earned by households comes from specialized savings assets such as savings deposits with banks or bonds issued by the government.

In the real world, different financial claims bear different rates of interest because of differences in risk and in maturities. However, it makes some sense to speak of *the* interest rate, since the various rates tend to rise or fall together in response to forces of supply and demand.

In long-run competitive equilibrium, the rate of interest will tend to equal the marginal efficiency of capital or the rate of return on the marginal investment. Assuming constant composition of the capital stock, this will also equal the marginal output-capital ratio dQ/dK of an aggregate production function. The equilibrium rate of interest, multiplied by the quantity of capital, will equal the income accruing to capital. However, this information will not tell us how much of that income will accrue in the form of interest and how much of it will appear under the name of profit.

The amount of income classed as interest depends upon the economy's structure of financial assets and liabilities, as well as its real factor supplies and production function. Where capital goods have been paid for out of the personal funds of the owners, no explicit interest income arises. The income of the owners is classed as profit by accountants. But in competitive equilibrium each firm earns on its capital only the market rate of interest. What appears as accounting profit is, therefore, implicit interest.

Where capital goods have been purchased on borrowed money, the income they yield takes chiefly the form of explicit interest. Income from interest need not arise solely from the services of capital goods, however. If land ownership is financed by borrowing, a portion of interest payments will reflect the productivity of services of land. Even ignoring government debt for the moment, we must take account of borrowing for consumption. Consumer borrowing and dis-saving reduce the net saving of the household sector considered as a unit. And a flow of interest payments may arise from consumer debt, from the "impatient" consumers who are willing to pay a premium in order to consume now, to the patient ones who are willing to wait when they can receive a premium for doing so.

In the real world, much of the borrowing by households is associated with the purchase of durable assets such as houses, automobiles, furniture, and appliances. Broadly speaking, these could be classed as capital assets, and the interest flow on such borrowing could be related to their productivity. The capital concept can be extended further to cover debt-financed expenditures on medical care and education, which are forms of "investment in human capital." Interest on such loans may reflect the resulting increased productivity of the labor force.

After allowing for these, there will still ordinarily be a portion of the flow of interest income which reflects pure consumption borrowing. Such a flow does not appear to reflect a payment for the services of a factor of production in the same sense that we have analyzed them. In particular, pure consumption loans do not have the same "self-financing" tendencies as loans for financing capital goods which will increase productivity and incomes. It might be necessary to classify interest payments on pure consumption loans as transfer payments in order to keep total income consistent with total output and total factor inputs as customarily defined.

Thus we conclude that not all payments for the services of capital goods take the explicit form of interest and that not all explicit interest income arises from payments for the services of capital goods. All interest income has in common an origin in some form of fixed-term debt contract. Existence of such contracts, particularly those of long duration, gives rise to some important relationships between interest rates and interest income, and between the position of the owner of a productive asset and a creditor.

interest-bearing assets

In a modern industrial economy, households receive interest income in reflection of their ownership of various interest-bearing debt claims. In a large portion of the cases, these are claims against specialized savings institutions. The most familiar and clear-cut example is a savings deposit. Such a claim is typically payable on demand (in fact if not in law) on the basis of a fixed dollar value. The price of a savings deposit is always equal to its redemption value. Ownership of such savings assets is typically not transferable. However, the interest rate paid on a savings deposit can be changed unilaterally by the savings institution. And the interest income changes in the same proportion.

The other source of interest income consists of debt claims which are not payable on demand at the request of the creditor, but which have some fixed date for redemption. These are generally claims against nonfinancial businesses, households, or the government, and constitute the bulk of the assets held by savings institutions; from these they obtain the income to pay interest to their own creditors. Such debt claims typically can be transferred, and they are widely bought and sold at market prices which may differ substantially from the redemption value. The interest income from such assets is typically fixed by the original contract and does not change once the asset has come into existence. Changes in the prevailing level of interest rates will be reflected, however, in *inverse* changes in the market *prices* of such assets.

Where the income and redemption terms of an interest-bearing financial asset are specified, the present value of the asset can be determined by the formula we used in Chapter 14. Given the income flow $Y_1, Y_2, \ldots, Y_n$ (where Y_n may include the redemption payment) and the interest rate r, the present value V is expressed as follows:

$$V = \frac{Y_1}{1+r} + \frac{Y_2}{(1+r)^2} + \cdots + \frac{Y_n}{(1+r)^n}$$

The market price of the asset tends to equal its present value.

Suppose the interest rate is 6 percent and a bond is available which yields $100 interest each year and will be redeemed two years hence for $1,000. What will be its present value? We obtain (rounding to whole dollars):

$$V = \frac{100}{1.06} + \frac{1,100}{(1.06)^2} = 94 + 979 = 1,073$$

The present value would be about $1,073. The income and redemption payment of the bond will yield an investor the equivalent of 6 percent if he buys the bond at $1,073.

If the price of the bond does not equal its present value, market transactions will occur which will tend to make the two equal. If the bond is selling below $1,073, it will offer a prospective purchaser more than 6 percent interest, and investors will bid for this bond in preference to other 6 percent assets. The price of this bond will tend to be bid up. If it is selling at more than $1,073, anyone who owns the bond will benefit by selling it and reinvesting his money in a 6 percent asset. Its price will tend to fall.

Given the expected income, the price of such an interest-bearing asset will tend to vary inversely with the prevailing rate of interest. A rise in the interest rate to 10 percent would reduce the price of the bond in our example to $1,000. The longer the time to redemption, the wider tends to be the change in price in response to a given change in interest rates.

The effect of a change in interest rates on interest incomes will depend on the relative importance of long-term versus short-term debt claims in the economy. If all debt claims (interest-bearing assets) were of short maturity, interest incomes would change in a manner very similar to interest rates. Debtors would be refinancing their entire liabilities continually and would have to pay the going rate on all of them without much delay. The larger the proportion of long-term debt claims, however, the larger the potential disparity between interest rates and interest incomes. If all existing debts were in long-term form, borrowers would have to match interest-rate changes only on their new borrowings. They would continue to pay the old interest incomes on their previously existing liabilities. Changes in interest income would tend to be much smaller than changes in interest rates.

Indeed, in a world where long-term marketable debt claims predominate, increases in interest rates would tend to make existing creditors appear worse off, because the current money prices of their assets would tend to decrease. If they hold the claims to maturity, they need suffer no direct loss, but some creditors are likely to want their money sooner and will be injured. Holders of savings deposits and similar assets need not suffer a loss of capital value, but the savings institutions themselves may. And interest income on savings assets will change as sluggishly as does the interest income received by the savings institutions.

The relative use of long-term and short-term debt claims is itself the outcome of the individual decisions of borrowers and lenders, reflecting a balancing of complex considerations of various uncertain expectations. For instance, the buyer of a long-term interest-bearing security accepts a greater price risk but a smaller income risk than the buyer of a short-term claim. A large structure of analysis has developed to explain such matters as they relate to the term structure of interest rates.

The existence of relatively long-term debt contracts introduces a difference between the position of the creditor and that of the debtor-owner of real capital assets. Unforeseen changes in the income yielded by the capital asset will be borne largely by the owner. His obligation to pay interest is not, under ordinary debt contracts, altered by such changes. However, the creditor does not escape all risks. Variations in market interest rates will affect the price of his asset, as noted. In addition, extreme adversity may make the debtor unable to pay his obligations.

We concluded earlier that, ignoring problems of risk and market imperfections, the percentage rate of return earned on ownership capital would tend to be equal to the market rate of interest. However, under conditions of risk, two circumstances may combine to upset this conclusion. One is the tendency for owners of capital to allow a safety margin between the expected rate of return on new investment and the rate of interest. The second is the use of nonprice rationing by lenders as one method of restricting loans to any individual borrower. The first condition may make entrepreneurs unwilling to carry investment to the level which equates the interest rate with MEC; the second condition may make them unable to do so, whatever their desires.

money, financial claims, and the interest rate

Our contention that the equilibrium rate of interest emerges from the interaction of the incentive to invest in capital goods and the willingness to save out of current income is a useful conclusion, but one of limited relevance to the real world. In the real world, the behavior of interest rates reflects the behavior of monetary variables as well as the real forces underlying saving and investment.

Changes in the interest rate reflect shifts in the supply of, or demand for, loanable funds. Saving is one source of loan funds, although not all saving flows into this channel. Investment is one element in demand for funds, although not all investment is financed by borrowing. The other important source of loan funds comes through money newly created by the commercial banking system. Whenever the banks hold excess reserves, they are able to increase their loans by creating more deposits. Such additions to the supply of loanable funds tend to lower the interest rate, at least temporarily. A corresponding element on the demand side of the market arises from the demand schedule for cash balances. The amount of currency and demand deposits people want to hold (and are willing and able to pay for by giving up something else of value) tends to vary directly with the level of money income and inversely with the rate of interest.

A state of monetary equilibrium exists only if the quantity of money demanded at existing income and interest levels is equal to the quantity which the monetary system brings into existence at those levels. If supply is greater than demand, the excess cash will tend to be spent for current output (raising money income) or used to acquire interest-bearing assets (lowering interest rates). Excess demand for money would tend to lower income and raise interest rates. In the real world, such movements in money income can cause variations in production and employment. In a hypothetical world of full-employment equilibrium, they would cause changes in the price level.

The flow of money income can be in equilibrium only if desired saving is equal to desired investment at existing income and interest levels. The rate of interest can only be in equilibrium, therefore, if this condition is achieved *and* if the quantity of money demanded is equal to the supply. Our saving-investment criterion is still valid, but it is no longer a sufficient condition to identify an equilibrium interest rate. The equilibration process works through changes in money income as well as through changes in the interest rate itself.

The interest rate is also an element in the supply-demand equilibration for other financial assets besides money. Just as the economy contains a large existing stock of real capital assets, so does it also contain a large stock of financial assets, most of them representing interest-bearing debt claims. Movements in the rate of interest help to equate the quantity of such assets demanded with the quantity in existence. Suppose the interest rate on 20-year bonds were 5 percent, and there occurred an increase in the demand for such assets. Their market prices would tend to rise, lowering their yields and reducing the quantity demanded. The increased prices and lowered yields will also encourage prospective borrowers to issue such debt claims in larger amount. Adjustments in asset prices, quantities, and yields would all be involved in the equilibration process.

Adequate analysis of the relationships among money, other financial assets, and the interest rate lies far beyond the scope of this study. Such analysis is heavily conditioned by the influence of risk and uncertainty and by deviations of the real economic system from pure competition and from full employment.

income from rent

Household income from rent depends on the quantity of property rented out, and on the rental value of each unit. Economists have used the term *rent* chiefly in reference to land. But of course any kind of property may be subject to rental arrangements. Land is unique in being fixed in supply; thus its rental value tends to vary in response to demand conditions. Rental values for assets which can be replaced out of current production, however, tend to yield the market rate of interest on their current selling price, which in turn tends to equal the cost of production. In the case of land, the capitalization process tends to make the price of a tract of land equal to its rental discounted by the market rate of interest.

In nineteenth-century England, much of the land was owned by a small number of wealthy landlords, and explicit rent was a large element in the national income. That is one reason why the English economists gave it so much attention. However, in the United States the majority of the people own the land on which they live. They do not receive or pay explicit rent. Instead, an implicit rent is involved, either as a part of farm income, or as a direct component of consumer utility outside of measured money income. The implicit rent of a piece of land can be estimated on the basis of what it could be rented for in the market, which would reflect its marginal productivity.

profits

Income from the ownership of business is generally lumped together under the heading of profit. However, from an economic standpoint much of the income earned by owners of business is better classified as implicit wages, interest, or rent. If the owner of the business provides labor services, then part of his income is an imputed wage, estimated on the basis of what he could earn working for someone else. Similar imputations can be made for the income from his capital and land. We are interested in profits not as usually measured, but in the economic sense—a residual after the deduction of the imputed returns to specific factor services.

In long-run competitive equilibrium, there are no profits. Owners of businesses receive the market value of their labor and property services (equal to their marginal product), but no more. Thus the analysis of profit must take us outside of the condition of long-run competitive equilibrium. The existence of profit may indicate that the market is not purely competitive, or that it is not in long-run equilibrium.

It is useful to remember the simple truism that profit represents an excess of revenue over cost (including in cost implicit as well as explicit expenses). Profit may occur in pure competition as a result of a change in conditions, a departure from equilibrium. A firm which introduces a cost-reducing innovation in its method of production will find itself making profits. An increase in demand for the product, or an increase in the supply of an input, may create profits for all of the existing firms in an industry.

The lure of profits encourages industry adjustments under competitive conditions, which tend to eliminate the profits. With abundant knowledge and easy entry, the profitable innovation will be adopted by other firms. New firms will enter the profitable industry, until product price has fallen and input prices have risen enough to eliminate the profits. Such adjustments improve methods of production and allocation of resources. They can only occur, however, if entry and imitation are relatively easy. Imperfect knowledge and restrictions on entry may thus preserve profits against the eroding force of entry and imitation. It is not true that imperfections of knowledge and barriers to entry always lead to profits. They do permit an initially profitable cost-revenue situation to remain profitable.

The temporary profits which arise in a competitive disequilibrium may be merely a matter of luck. But the prospect of earning profit, even temporarily, may provide an incentive to anticipate shifts in demand and supply conditions so as to be in a position to benefit from them. The profit incentive also encourages each firm to pursue efficiency, and to seek to improve its technology and organization.

Even if other firms ultimately imitate the innovator, he still may reap handsome gains in the short run.

It is sometimes argued that profit is a reward for assuming risks under conditions of uncertainty. Formally, there is truth in this. If there were no uncertainty about changes in demand, firms would all adjust to them without delay, and profits would tend to be eliminated almost instantaneously. If firms knew what innovations in technology were to be discovered, they would all introduce them immediately. Thus an element of uncertainty, and attendant risk, is probably a necessary condition for the kind of disequilibrium profit we have been discussing.

However, it is misleading to speak as if risk taking itself were inherently a profitable action or profit in itself a reward for risk taking. There are many risky activities which are not intrinsically profitable or productive. It is risky to drive an automobile blindfolded, or to draw to an inside straight, or to go over Niagara Falls in a barrel, or to play Russian roulette. But these are not activities recommended for the seeker of profit. If profit is to be regarded as a reward for anything, it should simply be termed a reward for carrying on activities which meet the dictates of the market economy, for helping to create and resolve disequilibrium in an efficient direction.

John Maynard Keynes expressed this aspect of profit very succinctly: "Profit accrues . . . to the individual who, whether by skill or good fortune, is found with his productive resources in the right place at the right time. A system which allows the skillful or fortunate individual to reap the whole fruits of this conjuncture evidently offers an immense incentive to the practice of the art of being in the right place at the right time."[1]

Similar considerations apply to the assertion that profit is a reward for innovation. Not all innovations are profitable. Under competitive conditions, profitable innovations are essentially those which reduce costs or which increase revenues by novelties in regard to the product. Again, the reward of profit arises from those changes which tend to make the system work better. Cost-reducing innovations reduce the quantity of scarce resources required to produce a given output and thus increase the total output available from the existing supply of resources. Profitable product innovations are those which bring the composition of output more in line with consumer desires.

Profit may arise in connection with departures from pure competition. Even here, however, there must be a favorable potential relation between the demand schedule and the average cost schedule. Not all monopolies are profitable. Given a favorable cost-price situation, however, the ability of a monopolist to earn profits in excess of a normal return on capital depends on his ability to remain a monopolist. His position may be protected by economic circumstances, such as economies of scale, which make it difficult for newcomers to compete with him. Or there may be

---

[1] John Maynard Keynes, *Laissez-Faire and Communism*, New York New Republic, 1926, pp. 39–43.

obstacles to entry imposed by government, in the form of a franchise, patent, or license. Perhaps the monopolist uses physical force to exclude competitors, or spreads misleading reports about their products. There must be some obstacle to entry, or his profits will soon evaporate.

In a well-functioning market economy, firms earn profit by doing things which are generally beneficial—producing those products which are especially in demand, using more efficient methods of production, making constructive innovations. One of the essentials of wise public policy is to see to it that a close correspondence exists between those activities which are profitable to business and those which are beneficial to the public.

income from profit

Much of the income from the ownership of business accrues to the same persons who manage the business. Most business firms in the world are small firms—farms, stores, workshops, service establishments. Most of their income is not really profit, and such profit as they do earn may be more a matter of luck than anything else. But it is certainly true that the ownership of a business offers the *chance* to earn profit.

In large business firms, there typically exists a separation between the owners and the managers. The large American corporation may be owned in the legal sense by thousands of stockholders, while the management is carried on by salaried professional administrators who do not necessarily own much stock in the firm. In law, the profits of such a firm are earned by the firm itself, as an entity. They belong to the stockholders, but in practice it is largely up to the administrators what to do with them. In particular, the management may have considerable discretion about reinvesting profits in the business, as opposed to paying them out to the stockholders.

In economic analysis, it may be very hard to identify the profits or their recipients. Certainly a part of the reward paid to the stockholders represents imputed interest on their investment. Conversely, the compensation of the management may contain a substantial element of profit. This may be explicit if there is a bonus system or stock-option plan, or it may simply arise out of the fact that the executives of a large, profitable firm have the power to pay themselves well. Formally, the stockholders can act as a group to change policies or executives which they disapprove of. However, the area of discretion for management is typically broad.

It remains true, however, that variations in the economic profits of a firm usually show up in variations in reported profits as well. And these in turn are reflected in the market price of the stock of the firm. Of course, the price of a stock depends on the profits which investors expect the firm to earn in the future, but such expectations are always colored by what is currently happening.

For many companies, stock prices are heavily influenced by the rate of growth of reported profits. A progressive and expanding company may find that its stock sells at twenty or thirty times current profits, because people expect the profits to grow at a rapid rate in the future. Should the rate of increase of profits slow down, the stock may fall in price.

If stock prices are sensitive to changes in current profits, the individual stockholder may be in a position to reap windfall gains. However, he may suffer heavy losses if profits fail to match expectations. Thus some households may sustain substantial changes in their wealth as a result of changes in stock prices. Even in wealthy industrial countries, however, only a small proportion of the population receives any large amount of income from profits, dividends, and capital gains.

wealth and income

In the early stages of economic development, an economic system is likely to have an abundance of labor, perhaps of relatively low quality, and a relative scarcity of land and capital. Under such conditions, a large part of income may arise from the ownership of property, and much of the difference between rich and poor may be traced to the distribution of wealth. Karl Marx was only one of many economists who identified the problem of poverty with the problem of wealth ownership.

In modern industrial economies, wealth ownership has receded from the center of attention. Labor productivity has risen sufficiently that some families can achieve very high incomes for labor services alone. And the distribution of wealth has become somewhat more dispersed, with most families owning financial assets, houses and residential land, if not business capital goods themselves.

The sort of analysis we have used in this book does not really explain the distribution of wealth itself, which is the reflection of historical evolution in any society. At any given time, a large part of existing ownership of wealth probably reflects acquisition through inheritance or gift from previous generations. Economic analysis does provide some explanations for changes in wealth ownership over time. A family's wealth tends to increase as it saves part of its income. It may also increase through capital gains, through increases in the prices of assets. However, an important element in the evolution of wealth distribution occurs through the sequence of generations, as individual persons pass from childhood to maturity, retire, and eventually die. Wealth transfers in this process reflect the society's laws and customs respecting the family itself and specific practices of bequest and gift.

The distribution of wealth in modern industrial societies is also bound up closely with the institution of the business corporation. Much real wealth—land and capital goods—is owned directly by corporations, not by natural persons. Control over the use of such real assets, including much power in disposing of the income they yield, rests with the management of a corporation, who are not always large stockholders in the firm. The stockholders own the corporation, but this is not at all identical with owning its real assets.

Institutional considerations of this sort will affect the amount of real capital goods in existence, because corporate structure and other institutional conditions affect the facility with which saving and investment take place. They affect the efficiency with which capital is used and the detailed flow of income from property into such specified forms as interest, dividends, rents, undistributed corporate profits, and income of unincorporated business.

evaluation of competitive income distribution

The fairness or justice of income distribution has concerned mankind throughout recorded history. In the nineteenth century, the market economy came under particularly heavy attack from Karl Marx and from other social critics who claimed that capitalism resulted in an unjust and immoral distribution of income. Defenders of the market economy fought back, however, and by the end of the century were using the marginal productivity theory of factor pricing as a justification for the way in which a market economy divides incomes. The American economist John Bates Clark made a particularly strong defense. In essence, he argued that each person is rewarded in proportion to his contribution to production. Each household earns an income equal to the value of the marginal product of its factor services. The marginal product reflects the net addition of the household's services to total output. Thus there is perfect balance between contribution and reward.

The marginal productivity theory did show up the cruder fallacies of Marx's labor theory of value. But it did not provide a *proof* that the market economy distributes incomes fairly, nor is such a proof possible. For fairness and justice are, ultimately, value judgments, rather than matters which can be established by evidence or logic alone.

One might argue, for instance, that each person in the economy should be rewarded in proportion to his moral worth. The saintly man would thus be rewarded most abundantly, and the wicked would receive little. But who is to identify the saintly man, and by what tests? One method would be to use the standards of some widely accepted religious creed, such as Christianity, or Buddhism. However, religious texts are often very ambiguous, and do not furnish clear-cut standards. Also, there are usually many specific attributes which we associate with virtue or vice, and few people are clearly superior or inferior in all.

However difficult it would be to reward people in accordance with their virtue, there is certainly no tendency for a market economy to use virtue in any customary sense as a criterion of reward. The market economy rewards actions and results, not the intentions and attitudes which are stressed in much religious and philosophical teaching.

Suppose we try another possibility. Can we not argue that the market economy rewards people on the basis of their efforts? This is also an ambiguous standard. Do we mean effort in terms of physical exertion? Clearly the unskilled manual laborers who expend the most physical energy are not the most prosperous people in the economy. Do we mean effort in terms of the willingness to do things one dislikes? Many well-paid people enjoy their work. Nor is time devoted to the job a satisfactory guide to earnings. In truth there is no satisfactory single measure of effort which one could associate with the income distribution in a market economy.

We are still left with Clark's claim that the competitive economy is fair and just because it rewards each person in proportion to the contribution which he makes to production. However, this contention has several deficiencies. It does not deal very satisfactorily with dependents. The family system of a society is an important determinant of the income and consumption status of individuals. Some family members, particularly children, depend for their economic status on the incomes of other family members. In societies where the "extended family" prevails, older adults, their children, and their grandchildren may all live together or at least share substantially their incomes and consumption. By contrast, the "nuclear family" prevails in the United States, consisting merely of husband, wife, and their children. The more extensive the sharing of real income among family members, the less the correspondence between the real income of any individual and his productivity.

Clark's standard does not seem to apply adequately when income from property is involved, either. Labor income may indeed be proportional to a *person's* productivity, but income from property ownership is based on the productivity of things, not of people. Admittedly, if a person uses his own savings to acquire income-bearing property, we might extend some justification to it. But when property has been acquired by inheritance or gift, the income from it hardly reflects any productive contribution by the owners.

Even income from labor may be subject to all sorts of injustice. In some countries there is discrimination against racial or ethnic groups or castes, who therefore receive less income than their productivity might warrant. Even worse, the discrimination may affect their education, and even their personalities, in such a manner as to make them less productive, thus apparently justifying and perhaps perpetuating the discrimination. Many differences in labor quality and earning power are beyond the control of the individual. A person born in Thailand has a much lower expectation of earnings during his lifetime than a person of the same innate ability living in the United States. The reason is that labor productivity is higher in the United States, where there is more capital and better productive technology and organization—thus wages tend to be higher in the United States even for persons of the same innate quality. The market economy has no mercy for persons who are unproductive—the sick, the crippled, the very young, and the very old.

The more deterministic one feels about earning power, the less he attaches moral significance to it. If each individual is shaped by his biological inheritance and by his environment, then one can hardly attribute moral worth to his actions.

By most conventional value judgments, there is little inherent moral justification for the pattern of income distribution in a market economy. Its defense and justi-fication rest instead on *functional* grounds. Whatever its morality, the competitive market does reward people who act to promote the efficient functioning of the economic system. Thus modern defenders of the market economy stress the incentive aspects of income distribution. We do believe that individuals have some free will, and can choose between alternatives. The quest for incomes guides them in their choices. The prospect of higher incomes encourages people to improve themselves by education and training. The prospect of higher incomes draws people into occupations with a high priority in meeting strong consumer needs and desires.

Economists have recognized that it is not possible to make scientifically objective evaluations of the fairness of income distribution. However, many problems of public policy influence income distribution, and the economists do not wish it to be ignored. Suppose one is trying to decide on the desirability of a government policy action, such as the imposition of an import tariff. The tariff will affect output; production of some products will increase, and that of others will decrease. Is it possible to set a standard by which to judge whether the situation is better with the tariff or without it?

Three possible standards have been suggested. First (and least questionable), it has been argued that a policy change should be regarded as beneficial if it raises some people's real incomes without lowering anyone's real income. How-ever, not many policy changes have this effect. The second standard is designed to deal with a situation in which the change makes some people better off and some people worse off. According to the second standard, the change is beneficial if the gains to those who gain are large enough so that the gainers can compensate the losers for their loss and still end up better off than before. (Such considerations could be used for the questions raised at the end of Chapter 7.) If the gainers can compensate the losers, this suggests either that total output has increased or that the composition of output has altered in a manner which some people approve of. The third standard is a variant of this compensation principle, and links it with the first standard. The third standard specifies that a policy change is desir-able if the gainers can *and do* compensate the losers. If this condition is met, presumably no one is made worse off by the change.

Even choice among such standards can only be made on the basis of value judgments, and there is no agreement among economists on their use. A strong advocate of equality might even object to the first standard in a case where a policy change might make rich people richer and leave the condition of the poor unchanged.

A very different set of value judgments may be applied to the problem of income distribution if one argues that the major concern is with economic growth. The extreme inequality of incomes in nineteenth-century England and America has been defended on grounds that it promoted saving, investment, and economic growth. In more recent times, a similar defense might be made for the low incomes permitted to farmers under the agricultural policies of Soviet Russia. Decisions in an underdeveloped country to impose heavy taxation in order to finance investment do raise questions of fairness and justice. In particular, they may involve a transfer of income from persons currently living to those who will be living a generation or two hence.

government and income distribution

Even in countries with a strong devotion to free markets and competition, government is likely to influence income distribution in several ways. First, some people will work for the government, and receive their incomes from it. Second, there are likely to be programs of transfer payments, for which no current services are rendered. Third, taxation will alter directly the disposable incomes which remain for people to spend. Fourth, government may intervene in the functioning of the market mechanism in order to change the pattern of private incomes.

A century ago, governments in the developing industrial countries such as England and the United States employed only a tiny fraction of the labor force. In the modern world, however, governments typically employ an important proportion of the nonagricultural labor force, both in advanced and in underdeveloped countries. We consider in later chapters matters relating to the magnitude and scope of government operations. Government employment raises some difficult issues relating to proper compensation. If government employees are not paid sufficiently, the quality of government services will suffer. On the other hand, since government tax revenues are collected with an element of coercion, the public may not be able to protect itself against the danger that government officials will be overpaid—particularly those who are highly placed and can influence basic revenue and expenditure policy. There are also problems in determining the appropriate number of employees to perform any given services and in designing a system of evaluation and reward which will promote efficient performance of duties. In many underdeveloped countries, government employment is regarded as a pleasant and prestigious way of earning a comfortable income without working very hard. This may cause the quality of government service to suffer; in addition, it may drain off talented people who might be more productive in private activity.

Clearly in government employment there is no automatic force at work tending to bring labor's remuneration into equality with the value of labor's marginal product.

In most free-market economies, programs of government transfer payments have been established to fill many of the gaps left by the market system—poor relief, old-age pensions, unemployment compensation, workmen's compensation for sickness and accidental injuries. Transfer programs may be undertaken purely for humane and charitable motives. However, many of them can also be defended as aids to development of human resources. Low-income families have many children, and increases in their incomes may help improve the psychological and physiological development of future members of the labor force.

There are also important government services which may help reduce income inequality in the long run. Public education gives each child some opportunity to develop earning power, and public health programs help to conserve this potential. Experience with such programs has indicated that much can be done to improve the equality and humanity of free-market income distribution without impairing its incentive functions.

However, government actions to change income distribution have sometimes taken other forms less favorable to incentives. Governments have attempted to alter factor prices from their equilibrium values, usually in an effort to raise wages and to lower interest rates. By statute or degree, governments have prohibited paying wages below some specified level, and in other regulations have attempted to prohibit interest rates *above* some specified level. If minimum-wage laws and usury laws are effective, they can prevent equilibrium from being achieved in factor markets. If labor's marginal product is worth less than the minimum wage, job opportunities will be curtailed and some prospective workers will not find jobs. If interest rates are effectively held down, nonprice rationing will be required to reduce demand to the available supply of loanable funds. There will not be enough funds to finance all the projects yielding more than the legal maximum interest rate. Some higher yield projects may be screened out (especially if they are risky) in favor of others with lower payoff. Keeping wage rates above, and interest rates below their equilibrium levels will also give firms an incentive toward using an inappropriate input mix. Methods of production will tend to economize unduly on labor and to use capital to excess. Capital may be embodied in excessively labor-saving forms. Structural unemployment may afflict part of the labor force, and those resources which are employed may be less productive than their potential.

Governments have also intervened in product markets for reasons of income distribution. Protective tariffs and import restrictions, farm-price supports, export controls, special industry taxes or subsidies, restrictions on entry, compulsory cartels—all have been used in efforts to benefit (or protect from adverse change) specific income recipients. Insofar as such policies push the economy away from competitive equilibrium, they may reduce the value of total output. Even if some persons gain increased incomes, others lose, and the losses are likely to exceed the gains for most policies which restrict competitive freedom.

summary

Households earn their incomes by the sale of productive services. Each household's income depends, therefore, on the quantity of services which it sells and the price it receives for each. The price of productive services have been explained in terms of supply and demand. Demand for the services of any factor arises from its expected marginal productivity. The schedule of marginal productivity of labor, for instance, depends on the quality of the labor force itself, on the amount of capital and natural resources available for labor to work with, and on the condition of technology and organization. However, the marginal product of labor tends to vary inversely with the quantity of labor, along a given marginal productivity schedule.

The rental value of a piece of land tends to equal its marginal productivity, and the interest rate tends to be equal to the marginal efficiency of capital goods. However, not all land yields explicit rent, and not all capital goods yield explicit interest. The name given to the income reflects details of the legal-institutional structure of society, the pattern of ownership and financial claims.

Profit in the narrow sense arises from departures from long-run competitive equilibrium. However, the word "profit" is used in accounting to cover incomes which are implicitly interest, rent, or labor income, arising where the owners of business contribute the services of their own capital, land, or labor.

Whether one approves ethically of the pattern of income distribution which arises in a market economy is a matter of value judgments, on which rational men may differ. It is clear, however, that the competitive market economy does not reward people on the basis of either their virtue or their effort. It does, however, reward them for actions which promote the efficient functioning of the economic system.

QUESTIONS AND PROBLEMS

1. Distinguish between implicit and explicit rent, interest, and labor income. What is the relation between implicit factor incomes and the proper economic definition of profit?

2. What do you believe to be the attributes of a virtuous person? Which of these attributes would tend to give a virtuous person good earning power in a market economy? Which would give him low earning power?

3. "Without labor there would be no production, no real income. Therefore labor is the only truly productive resource, and should receive all of the output of the society." Analyze this statement.

4. Most economists would probably prefer to see government attempt to improve income distribution by enlarging public education in preference to setting a high statutory minimum wage. Explain this preference.

5. Suppose there were a socialist state in which all land and capital goods were owned by the government. Explain why the government might promote economic efficiency by charging rent for the land and interest for the use of capital instead of offering them for use without charge.

resource allocation in the competitive economy

The preceding chapters have analyzed some of the conditions which would prevail in a competitive economy in long-run equilibrium. In this chapter we consider the equilibrium conditions relating to the composition of output and the allocation of resources. We shall consider the determination of output of different products and the manner in which productive resources are utilized in producing one product or another.

ultimate determinants

The underlying influences which shape resource allocation in the competitive economy can be divided into three major categories, as follows:

1. **Productive resources.** We take as given an existing stock of capital goods, land and natural resources, and an existing population. We also assume an

existing distribution into family units of the potential workers and consumers as well as a distribution of the ownership of nonhuman productive resources.

2. Tastes and preferences. We assume that there exists among the population generally some given set of attitudes and preferences relating to the various aspects of economic life. These include consumer preferences toward various items of consumption. They also include attitudes toward saving versus current consumption and the uses to which saving may be put. They include the preferences of potential workers as among work, income, and leisure. And they include the attitudes of owners of nonhuman resources concerning the uses to which those resources might be put.

3. Production functions. We take as given the real production functions of the firms and industries of the economy, resting on some existing condition of technology and organizational methods. These enable us to specify one particular quantity of any given commodity which could be produced with each combination of inputs.

From these three sets of data, it is possible directly to derive supply functions for some factors of production. The existing endowment of land is combined with the psychological preferences of its owners to yield a supply schedule for land to the economy as a whole. The size of the existing population is combined with the psychological attitudes of potential workers to yield a supply schedule for labor. We do not have quite enough information to determine the supply schedule of capital. In addition to the existing data on the stock and ownership of existing capital goods and owner attitudes, we need data on the level and distribution of current income; this, in combination with preferences concerning saving, yields a supply schedule for capital.

We wish to determine the quantity of each product which will be produced and the way in which the available productive resources will be used. We will also want to find out how the available output is divided up among the households of the economy. In determining these matters, we will also be interested in the way in which prices of final products and factors of production are shaped for the economy as a whole.

In carrying out the analysis, we will make a number of additional assumptions. One is that all markets in the economy are characterized by pure competition. The number of buyers and sellers is so large that no one can influence the price of things he buys or sells. We also assume that each product or factor has one uniform price and that buyers and sellers know what this price is. We assume the existence of a monetary unit, a price system, and a market economy. However, it should be noted that our analysis really concerns *relative* prices. In particular, we assume that the supply of labor to the economy is a function of the *real* wage—that is, the money wage deflated by the price level of consumer goods—and that the supply of saving is a function of the real income of households.

equilibrium conditions

The competitive economy is in equilibrium when all its members are in equilibrium positions, as we have identified them in previous chapters, and when supply-and-demand balance exists in every market. Let us work our way around the circular flow and summarize these conditions.

1. Consumers. Consumers allocate their incomes among individual consumption goods and savings outlets on the basis of their tastes and preferences. The quantities of individual items purchased are adjusted so that the (subjective) marginal rate of substitution between any pair of products is equal to the (inverse) ratio of their prices. Since each product has a single uniform price, the equilibrium value of MRS for any pair of products must be uniform for all consumers.

2. Business firms. Each firm produces an output such that marginal cost equals the price of the product. In buying inputs, each firm minimizes costs by achieving an input position where the marginal rate of substitution between any pair of inputs used is equal to the (inverse) ratio of their prices. As a result, the ratio between the marginal physical product of each input and its price is uniform for all inputs, and the firm will be employing each input in a quantity such that its marginal net revenue product is equal to its price. Looking at these conditions in combination, we find that the equilibrium value of marginal cost is equal to the cost of acquiring the quantity of inputs required for the marginal unit of output. Since each input has a single uniform price, its marginal net revenue product will have the same equilibrium value in all areas where it is used at all.

The number of firms in each industry adjusts so that the price of the product just equals long-run average cost and so that the average net revenue product of each input is equal to the price of the input.

3. Workers and owners of productive property. Each resource owner applies his labor or property in such a way as to maximize the net advantages, balancing consideration of income and of psychological preferences relating to work. Workers adapt the amount of their work so that the subjective marginal rate of substitution between leisure, on the one hand, and work plus income on the other, is equal to the real wage rate. Owners of property, if they are indifferent to considerations other than income, allocate their property where it yields the highest income.

implications

When we put together the various equilibrium conditions, we find that they contain a number of interesting implications, many of which suggest that competitive equilibrium is a position in which the economy is functioning efficiently. Some important implications are as follows:

1. Each owner of a factor of production receives an income which is equal to its marginal net revenue product.

2. Each firm produces at that level of output at which its long-run average costs are minimized. This result follows from the pressure of entry or exit.

3. Since long-run equilibrium price equals average cost, firms do not earn any profits above a normal return on their capital and enterprise—that is, a sum sufficient to keep them operating.

4. In long-run competitive equilibrium, each factor is allocated in such a manner that its marginal net revenue product is the same in all uses. By similar reasoning, it can be shown that the marginal revenue product of each factor is equalized in all uses and that the value of the marginal product is equalized in all uses.

The consequence of this equalization of marginal products, applied to all factors, is to maximize the value of the output of the economy. This proposition is a variant of the simpler one which we stated in Chapter 7. There we showed that in a simple one-commodity economy, the maximum quantity of output is achieved when the marginal physical product of the variable factor is equalized among all individual producers.

The principle of marginal-product equalization for a two-commodity world can be simply illustrated in terms of marginal revenue product. We assume that the MRP schedules for labor are given for industries A and B. This implies that we take as given the production function of each industry, the demand schedules for products A and B, and the prices and quantities of other inputs used in industries A and B. We assume that total revenue product schedules in the two industries take the following forms:

Industry A	$TRP_A = 500L_1 - L_1{}^2$	(L_1 is labor input to industry A)
Industry B	$TRP_B = 1,000L_2 - 2L_2{}^2$	(L_2 is labor input to industry B)

Corresponding to these functions are the linear MRP schedules shown in Figure 16-1:

Industry A	$MRP_A = 500 - 2L_1$
Industry B	$MRP_B = 1,000 - 4L_2$

Assuming that total labor input is 200 units, the marginal revenue product will be equalized between the two industries if industry A employs 50 and industry B 150 units. To see how this maximizes the value of output, imagine a transfer of 10 units of labor out of B into A. The value of output of B will decrease by the shaded area under the MRP curve in Figure 16-1. This consists of the rectangle k, which has an area of 10 × 400, plus the small triangle g. The value of product A will increase by the shaded area under its MRP curve; this can be measured as the rectangle k minus the small triangle h. By construction, the net effect must be a

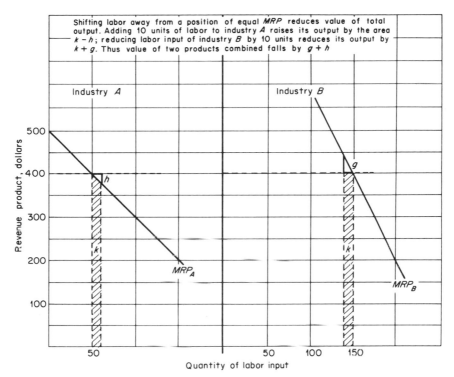

Figure 16-1   Equalization of marginal products.

decrease in the combined value of the two products by the sum of the areas g and h.

The total revenue product schedules (just a cumbersome name for total revenue schedules expressed as a function of an input) show the comparative totals. The initial equilibrium position is as follows:

Industry A	Industry B
Labor input = 50 units	Labor input = 150 units
Total revenue = $22,500	Total revenue = $105,000
$MRP = \$400$	$MRP = \$400$

After shifting 10 man-years from B to A, the following situation results:

Industry A	Industry B
Labor input = 60 units	Labor input = 140 units
Total revenue = $26,400	Total revenue = $100,800
$MRP = \$380$	$MRP = \$440$

The net effect has been to increase total revenue of industry A by $3,900, but to reduce the total revenue of industry B by $4,200; thus the combined revenue falls by $300. Since total revenue is equal to the value of output, a departure from the position of equal marginal product reduces the total value of output.

The same data can be used to show the adverse effect of raising the labor input of industry B above 150 units and reducing A below 50.

We have used straight-line MRP curves for simplicity, but the result follows from the downward slope of the MRP curves regardless of their precise slope or elasticity. The MRP curves slope down for two reasons. First, as labor is added to a given endowment of other inputs, diminishing returns operate. A departure from equal MRP means that the two industries are not using the most efficient input mix. Second, a transfer of excess labor into industry A causes the price of product A to decline, while the price of B rises in response to a decrease in its output. Evaluation of the meaning of these price changes really requires us to consider the relative strength of consumer demand for them, which we do more fully in a subsequent section.

Marginal revenue product is, of course, only a short-run concept. The assumption that industries continue to use the same quantities of other inputs is very restrictive. Assume instead that, starting from a position of equal marginal products, we shift out of industry B a bundle of all inputs, chosen to keep B operating with an efficient input mix. There will still be a tendency for the value of total output to decline; but no tidy illustration of this is possible. For one thing, changes in the product prices will still operate; the price of A will tend down and that of B up—yet we will not be distorting the input mix in industry B. It is unlikely, however, that the input mix which is efficient in industry B is also the ideal one for industry A. Questions of this sort are more appropriately approached from a different viewpoint, as in a later part of this chapter.

To return to our main point: competitive equilibrium, with a uniform price for each input, tends to allocate factors of production in such a way that their marginal products (defined in any of three ways) are equalized in all uses. This tends to draw a larger quantity of a factor into the sectors where it is most productive. This pattern is illustrated by Figure 16-1. A much larger quantity of labor is drawn into industry B than industry A, reflecting its usefulness there. In this way available supplies of scarce resources are rationed among alternative uses in an efficient manner.

A corollary is that firms adjust their methods of production in such a way as to make use of the factors of production actually available. A factor in abundant supply will be relatively cheap, and firms will have an incentive to employ a lot of it. A relatively scarce factor will be more expensive, and firms will tend to use it more sparingly. A further implication is that the form of capital goods will tend to be relatively appropriate for the quantity of land and labor which is available relative to the quantity of capital.

the composition of output

We turn next to a set of important propositions about the composition of output in competitive equilibrium. Before stating these, however, it will be useful to discuss the construction of an analytical device which we described very early in the book, namely the production-possibilities curve. Geometrically, this curve shows all the combinations of two products which might be produced given the resources, technology, and organization of the economy. Larger numbers of products can be included if one uses a mathematical production-possibilities function rather than a two-dimensional curve. However, we will limit ourselves to two products, although intending them to represent a wider array of possibilities.

If we know the production functions for the two products, and the total available supply of productive factors, we can derive a production-possibilities curve (or function). We assume that each industry displays constant returns to scale. Consider first a simple special case in which the production functions for the two products contain the same factor exponents, as in the following:

$$Q_A = 5a_1^{2/3}b_1^{1/3}$$
$$Q_B = 10a_2^{2/3}b_2^{1/3}$$

Assuming each factor has a uniform price, both industries will use the factors in the same proportion. Whatever the actual proportion chosen, it will always be possible to increase the output of product A by 2 units with the factors used in producing 1 unit of product B. The factor prices will adjust so that both industries use the factors in the proportion of the available supply. Suppose there were 1,000 units of each factor available. Since the marginal rate of substitution da/db is $a/2b$, the price of a must be double that of b to induce firms to use the factors in equal quantities.

The production-possibilities curve for these data is shown in Figure 16-2. If all the factors were used in production of A, there would be 5,000 units of A and none of B. If all were used for B, there would be 10,000 units of B and none of A. And most important, the intervening combinations would all lie on a straight line, reflecting the fact that an additional unit of A would always require the reduction of B by two units. The slope of the line would be one-half, reflecting the ratio of coefficients in the production function.

If the factor exponents are not the same in the two industries, the production-possibilities curve will not be a straight line. Let our two industry production functions be as follows:

$$Q_A = 5a_1^{2/3}b_1^{1/3}$$
$$Q_B = 10a_2^{2/3}b_2^{1/4}$$

With differing exponents, the expressions for marginal rates of substitution will not have identical forms in the two industries, and the two industries will not

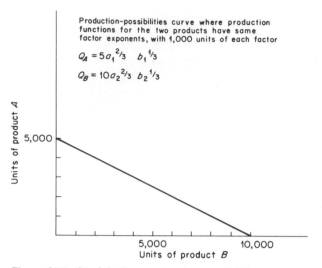

Production-possibilities curve where production functions for the two products have same factor exponents, with 1,000 units of each factor

$$Q_A = 5a_1^{2/3} \; b_1^{1/3}$$

$$Q_B = 10a_2^{2/3} \; b_2^{1/3}$$

Figure 16-2 Straight-line production-possibilities curve.

use the factors in the same proportion. The marginal rate of substitution (da/db) in industry A is still expressed by $a_1/2b_1$, but in industry B it is now equal to $2a_2/b_2$.

If there are 1,000 units of each factor, the end points of the production-possibilities curve will be the same as those in Figure 16-2. But the intermediate points will not lie on a straight line. They will bulge out from the origin, as shown in Figure 16-4. Locating the intervening points is a bit tricky. We can specify the output of one industry and try to determine the corresponding output of the second. However, specifying the output of one industry does not identify a unique batch of factors. Rather, it identifies one isoquant. We must locate on that isoquant the factor combination which will meet our equilibrium conditions, so that each industry equates the marginal rate of substitution with the inverse ratio of the factors' prices.

Since the quantity of the two factors is given, we can show the logic of the solution by a "box" diagram, as in Figure 16-3. The size of the box is measured by the supplies of factors a and b. Industry A's employment of factors is measured from the conventional origin at the lower left, and some of its isoquants are drawn. Industry B's factor use is measured from the upper right, and its isoquants correspondingly appear upside down. A uniform price will rule for each factor, and each industry will equate the marginal rate of factor substitution to that price ratio. Thus the marginal rate of factor substitution must be the same for both industries. Situations of equal MRS are identified in the diagram by points of tangency between the isoquants of the two industries. Each point of tangency represents a determinate allocation of the available factor supply between the

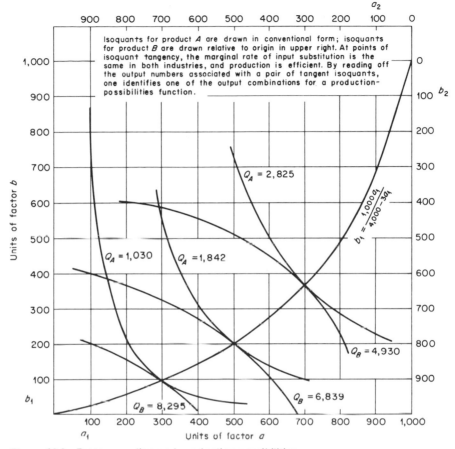

Figure 16-3 Factor supplies and production possibilities.

two industries, and the outputs of the industries are identified by the two tangent isoquants. Each point of tangency represents a point on a production-possibilities curve. A line connecting all the tangency points can be called a production-possibilities line, provided we remember that this diagram measures quantities of factors and that we need to transform it into an output diagram to obtain the conventional production-possibilities curve.

It is not difficult to find an algebraic expression for this production-possibilities line in the factor-space diagram, Figure 16-3. Let the factors used in industry A be a_1 and b_1 and those used in industry B a_2 and b_2. Each isoquant in industry A takes the form $a_1^2 b_1 = (Q_A/5)^3$, and each isoquant in industry B has the form $a_2 b_2^2 = (Q_B/10)^3$. Since the marginal rate of substitution must be the same for both, we obtain the respective expressions for da/db and set them equal, as follows:

$$\frac{a_1}{2b_1} = \frac{2a_2}{b_2}$$

We also know that $a_2 = 1{,}000 - a_1$ and $b_2 = 1{,}000 - b_1$. Substituting this information in the preceding equation, we obtain

$$\frac{a_1}{2b_1} = \frac{2(1{,}000 - a_1)}{1{,}000 - b_1}$$

which can be solved for b_1 to yield

$$b_1 = \frac{1{,}000a_1}{4{,}000 - 3a_1}$$

This expression describes the combinations of factors which fulfill the equilibrium conditions for efficient production in the two industries. Each point on this line represents a tangency point between isoquants of the two industries, provided one is drawn upside down. Some of these isoquants are illustrated. If we take a_1 as 500, the equilibrium value of b_1 is 200. Substituting these quantities into the production function tells us we will obtain approximately 1,842 units of product A. Substituting this into the production function converts it into the expression $1{,}842 = 5a^{2/3}b^{1/3}$, which can be simplified to yield $a^2b = 50{,}000{,}000$.

This is the expression for the isoquant for product A passing through the selected input point. By subtraction, we find that a_2 is 500 and b_2 is 800, from which we can estimate the output of product B as 6,839 units and determine an expression for its isoquant through the same point.

At a given point on the production-possibilities line, the marginal rate of factor substitution is equal in the two industries. With a_1 of 500 and b_1 of 200, the MRS in industry A (da_1/db_1) expressed by $a_1/2b_1$, will have the value 5 to 4. The MRS in industry B (da_2/db_2) expressed by $2a_2/b_2$, will also have the value 5 to 4. In competitive equilibrium, this common ratio will also be the ratio of the relative prices of the two factors, written inversely. Thus $da/db = P_b/P_a = 5/4$.

A change in the composition of output, represented by a move to a different point on the production-possibilities line, would represent a different equilibrium price ratio for the two factors. Where a_1 is 300, b_1 is 97, and output of A is about 1,030 units, the common MRS (da/db) in the two industries will be about 1.55 and P_b will be $1.55P_a$. This comparison reflects the general tendency for P_b/P_a to be greater, the larger the proportion of output represented by product B, in which factor b has the higher exponent.

In Figure 16-4 we show the conventional production-possibilities curve identified by units of output. Each point on it can be determined from the input equilibrium

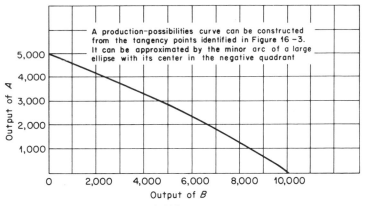

Figure 16-4 Production-possibilities curve.

conditions above. There is no simple method for deriving the algebraic expression for the production-possibilities curve in terms of output units. However, the curve can be approximated by the arc of an ellipse. Analytic geometry provides a formula for an ellipse, and we can fit one to individual points which lie on this curve. The ellipse we obtain is expressed as follows:

$$4Q_A{}^2 + 151,212Q_A + Q_B{}^2 + 75,606Q_B = 856,015,707$$

An expression in this form cannot easily be expressed in a manner which isolates one variable, so our simple rule for the derivative cannot be used to obtain the marginal rate of substitution. However, more advanced calculus tells us that the derivative dQ_A/dQ_B of such a function can be derived by finding the derivatives of the entire production-possibilities equation with respect to Q_A and Q_B and putting them in ratio form. The result is as follows:

$$\frac{dQ_A}{dQ_B} = \frac{2Q_B + 75,606}{8Q_A + 151,212} - \frac{Q_B + 37,803}{4Q_A + 75,606} \qquad \text{(minus sign omitted)}$$

In Figure 16-4, the curvature is so gentle that we might take the curve for a straight line. However, this algebraic expression makes it clear that we will encounter an increasing marginal rate of substitution. As we move to the right, increasing Q_B and decreasing Q_A, the curve becomes steeper and the absolute value of dQ_A/dQ_B becomes larger.

This rising marginal rate of substitution represents the tendency toward increasing marginal opportunity cost. As production of product A is increased, the amount of product B which must be sacrificed for an additional unit of A tends to increase. This tendency toward increasing cost arises from the fact that the two production functions differ in respect to factor exponents. Each factor differs in effectiveness depending on whether it is used for product A or product B. And the optimum factor proportions differ between the two products.

When all factors are used for product A, the quantity of factor b is employed to a point where it has a relatively low marginal product. The price of factor b is only one-half that of factor a, in order to induce industry A to employ 1,000 units of each factor. At that level of factor prices, however, the optimum factor proportions in industry B will use 4 units of b for each unit of a. Production of B can be expanded, therefore, mainly by shifting factor b—a shift which does not require much sacrifice of product A but permits a relatively large increase in product B. As more and more factors are transferred, however, this kind of disparity in factor proportions tends to disappear; indeed, after a point the disparity shifts to factor a. When most factors have been shifted to product B, further increases in B occur chiefly by shifting factor a out of its more productive area and into its less productive area.

We can now use the production-possibilities function to illustrate some more important general equilibrium relationships, adding them to the numbered sequence of implications begun on page 276.

5. In long-run competitive equilibrium, the price of each product tends to equal both the cost of the resources used in producing the marginal unit and also the value of other products which could have been produced with the same quantity of resources. We know that the price of each product tends to equal its marginal cost. Remember also that each input must be paid an amount equal to the value of its marginal net revenue product in the rest of the economy. Combining these ideas yields the idea that the marginal cost of one product measures the value of other products one could have obtained with the same resources.

These propositions can be stated in a slightly different way appropriate to the production-possibilities function. In long-run competitive equilibrium the prices of each pair of products will tend to be in the same ratio as their marginal costs, and that ratio will be equal to the marginal rate of substitution between the two products along the production-possibilities curve.

These propositions can be illustrated at the point on the curve where production consists of 1,842 units of A and 6,839 units of B. We have seen that industry A will employ 500 units of factor a and 200 of factor b, while industry B employs 500 units of a and 800 of b. The marginal rate of substitution (transformation) along the production-possibilities curve is given as follows:

$$\frac{dQ_A}{dQ_B} = \frac{Q_B + 37,803}{4Q_A + 75,606} = \frac{6,839 + 37,803}{4(1,842) + 75,606} = 0.54$$

This result implies that we can increase the output of A by 0.54 units by transferring into industry A the factors required to produce 1 unit of product B. To confirm this, suppose we transfer out of industry B 5 units of factor a and 8 units of factor

b and use these to increase output of A. Resolving our production equations, we find that output of B falls to 6,771, a decrease of 68 units, while output of A increases to 1,879, a rise of 37 units. Comparing the two changes, we have

$$\frac{\Delta A}{\Delta B} = \frac{37}{68} = 0.54$$

Since all our equilibrium price conditions are in relative terms, we can choose one price as "numeraire" and set it equal to 1. Let the price of product A be equal to unity; then we can obtain equilibrium values for other prices, costs, and revenue productivities. We can quickly obtain equilibrium values for the prices of the two factors by determining their marginal revenue productivities in industry A. Since $P_A = 1$, the MRP schedule for each factor is the same as its marginal physical product schedule, which we can obtain from the derivatives of the production function of industry A.

$$Q_A = 5a_1^{2/3}b_1^{1/3}$$

$$MRP_{a1} = MPP_{a1} = \frac{dQ_A}{da_1} = \frac{10}{3}\left(\frac{b_1}{a_1}\right)^{1/3} = \frac{10}{3}\left(\frac{200}{500}\right)^{1/3} = 2.456 = P_a$$

$$MRP_{b1} = MPP_{b1} = \frac{dQ_A}{db_1} = \frac{5}{3}\left(\frac{a_1}{b_1}\right)^{2/3} = \frac{5}{3}\left(\frac{500}{200}\right)^{2/3} = 3.070 = P_b$$

As a check, we confirm that $3.070/2.456 = 5/4$, which we have earlier shown to be the marginal rate of substitution between the factors in this input-output situation.

We have now obtained equilibrium values for the prices of the two factors. From these we can identify the equilibrium marginal costs of products A and B. From our equilibrium factor conditions, we know that $a_1 = 2.5b_1$ and $b_1 = 0.4a_1$. Let us substitute the former of these into the production function, as follows:

$$Q_A = 5a_1^{2/3}b_1^{1/3} = 5(2.5b_1)^{2/3}b_1^{1/3} = 5(2.5)^{2/3}b_1 = 9.21b_1$$

Therefore $b_1 = 0.1086\,Q_A$ in equilibrium. By using the other substitution, we would obtain $Q_A = 3.684a_1$; so $a_1 = 0.2714Q_A$.

These equivalences can now be used to solve a total cost function, as follows:

$$\begin{aligned}
TC_A &= a_1 \cdot P_a + b_1 \cdot P_b = 2.456a_1 + 3.070b_1 \\
&= (2.456)(0.2714Q_A) + (3.070)(0.1086Q_A) \\
&= 0.667Q_A + 0.333Q_A = Q_A
\end{aligned}$$

Therefore $MC_A = 1$.

Our cost calculations indicate a total cost equal to Q_A, with corresponding marginal cost of 1, which is consistent with our assumption that the price of A is unity.

In industry B, optimum factor proportions are $a_2 = 0.625b_2$ and $b_2 = 1.6a_2$. Substituting those through the production function we obtain these equivalences:

$$a_2 = 0.073Q_B \qquad \text{and} \qquad b_2 = 0.117Q_B$$

These can then be used to derive a total cost function, as follows:

$$\begin{aligned} TC_B &= a_2 \cdot P_a + b_2 \cdot P_b \\ &= (2.456)(0.073Q_B) + (3.07)(0.117Q_B) = 0.54Q_B \end{aligned}$$

From this in turn we derive $MC_B = 0.54$, which is the same as the marginal rate of substitution between the two products on the production-possibilities curve. This will also be the equilibrium price of product B.

Observe that our cost functions have been calculated from an industry production; thus they are not the cost functions of individual firms. However, each individual firm will be producing an output such that its marginal cost will be equal to 0.54 in industry B and 1 in industry A.

Since equilibrium product price equals marginal cost in each industry, the ratio of product prices must be equal to the marginal rate of substitution between products along the production-possibilities curve. This means that a tangent to the curve at the equilibrium output point will have the same slope as the ratio of product prices. Figure 16-5 illustrates this condition.

We have still not yet determined where the system will operate along the curve, or how the equilibrium product-price ratio is itself determined. These results are part of the next consideration.

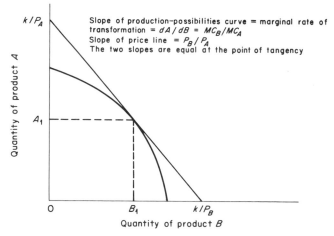

Figure 16-5 Equilibrium of relative prices and composition of output.

6. In long-run competitive equilibrium, the marginal rate of transformation between any pair of products (along a production-possibilities function) is equal to the (subjective) marginal rate of substitution between those products in the minds of consumers. This result comes about through adjustments by producers and consumers to prices, and through adjustments in prices themselves to the pulling and hauling of supply and demand. We know that in equilibrium each consumer is buying products in such a combination as to equalize his MRS with their (inverse) price ratio. We have just seen in item 6 that the marginal rate of output transformation is also equated to that inverse price ratio. It follows that the two marginal rates of substitution are equal to each other.

If we carry our analysis of consumer indifference curves a step beyond Chapter 3, we can use this proposition of equalization of marginal rates of substitution to demonstrate that the competitive equilibrium is a good thing. That is, we show that the composition of output is the best possible in terms of meeting consumer desires.

To do this requires some aggregate indicator of consumer tastes. For this we introduce the device of community indifference curves. In a diagram, a community indifference map looks just like one we might draw for an individual consumer. However, to construct a set of community indifference curves, there must be some method of weighting the importance of each household. If we are to use community indifference curves to illustrate the workings of a market economy, we must weight each household by its income. In order to use the indifference map to explain the determination of prices and output, however, we must assume that income distribution is independent of the final composition of output. This is a bit embarrassing, since we have just shown that factor prices tend to be affected by the composition of output. However, if each household owned equal amounts of both factors a and b, then the household distribution of income would still be unaffected by shifts in factor prices. We could also salvage the community indifference curve if all households had sufficiently similar tastes and preferences, so that income shifts would not substantially alter the actual composition of demand in the aggregate. These are both rather restrictive assumptions—too much so for many economists, who have regarded the community indifference curve as an illegitimate device. However, there is nothing else which can be used to show the relative strength of demand for the products, so we retain it, conceding that it has deficiencies.

The community indifference map is an indication of how the members of the community evaluate different combinations of goods. Along a given indifference curve are connected different combinations of goods which are equally desirable. All combinations outside ("northeast" of) a given indifference curve are preferred to those on the curve and to those inside it.

The production-possibilities curve represents the output combinations which are possible given the scarce resources of the economy and its level of technology and organizational skill. Which output combination will be chosen depends on the strength of demand, and it is here that consumer preferences, and the indifference map, enter the picture. In Figure 16-6, we combine a set of community indifference

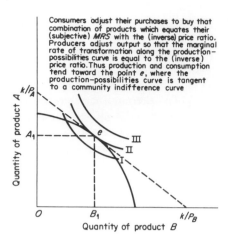

Consumers adjust their purchases to buy that combination of products which equates their (subjective) *MRS* with the (inverse) price ratio. Producers adjust output so that the marginal rate of transformation along the production-possibilities curve is equal to the (inverse) price ratio. Thus production and consumption tend toward the point e, where the production-possibilities curve is tangent to a community indifference curve

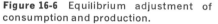

Figure 16-6 Equilibrium adjustment of consumption and production.

curves with a production-possibilities curve. Of course in a diagram we can show only two commodities; these must be understood to represent a much larger number. By assuming full-employment equilibrium, we assume the economy will operate *on* its production-possibilities curve, not inside it. In long-run competitive equilibrium, the output must be such that the marginal rate of transformation along the production-possibilities curve equals the marginal rate of substitution along the community indifference curve. There is only one point on the production-possibilities curve which meets this condition. That is point e, where the production-possibilities curve is just tangent to an indifference curve. And there is only one equilibrium price ratio equal to the (inverse) slope of the two curves at the point of tangency.

If the price ratio were different, supply and demand would not be equal. If the relative price of A were below the equilibrium level, consumers would attempt to buy more than the quantity OA_1, but producers would produce less. Producers would produce more of B than the quantity of OB_1, but consumers would take less. Only at the point e would prices and quantities be mutually consistent. By similar reasoning, one can show that any output away from point e would not be an equilibrium output. If prices were equal to marginal or average costs at some other output, consumers would not buy the indicated output. And if prices were not equal to unit costs, the one industry would expand output and the other contract.

It is easy to see that the output combination represented by e is the best use of the community's resources. It enables the community to reach a higher indifference curve than could be attained with any other feasible output combination. However, the result is ideal only for a given distribution of income. And the validity of the result depends on whether the whole community indifference map is a legitimate device.

Viewed in these terms, the long-run equilibrium position of the competitive economy appears to constitute a Pareto optimum, in that no opportunity remains to improve one person's situation without worsening that of someone else. If competitive equilibrium does not exist, on the other hand, there typically are opportunities to make some people better off without making others worse off. If, for instance, factors are misallocated and marginal products are not equalized, improved allocation will permit a higher total output, which could benefit some without harming others. If the composition of output does not equate the marginal rate of output transformation along the production-possibilities curve with consumers' subjective marginal rate of substitution, then a change in the composition of output can move consumers to a higher indifference curve. However, both the realism and desirability of the competitive equilibrium need to be examined critically, an exercise which is undertaken in Chapter 19.

reaction to change in consumer demand

The basic data of the competitive economy are factor supply conditions, production functions, and tastes and preferences. A change may originate in any one of these and set off changes in the output and price pattern of the economy. We will consider several types of such changes. We consider first a shift in the preference pattern of consumers, such that with any given real income they desire a larger quantity of product A and a correspondingly smaller amount of product B.

The immediate reactions are easy to chart. With a decreased demand for B, its price will fall, and less of it will be produced. Producers of B will reduce their demand for inputs correspondingly, and *their* prices will fall. At the same time, the price of A will rise, and production of it will increase. Producers of A will increase their demand for inputs, tending to pull their prices up.

The interesting and complex problems arise in the impacts which the demand shift has on markets for factors of production. We can distinguish several cases, from which you will get the general idea. Suppose, at one extreme, that both A and B are produced with the same resources used in the same proportion. A shift in demand from cups to saucers, or from forks to spoons, might illustrate this kind of situation. The price of each productive resource might remain unchanged. Demand by industry B would be less, but demand by industry A would be greater and the two changes would just cancel out. Of course, more of each factor would now be employed by industry A. Since the prices of inputs remain unchanged, so do the long-run average costs of the two products. As a result, the long-run equilibrium prices of A and B return to their original levels. (However, their prices may diverge temporarily pending the achievement of long-run equilibrium.)

At the other extreme, let us suppose that industry A uses only factors of production which are not used at all elsewhere in the economy—something as specific as iron ore or some other mineral resource. And we make the same assumption about industry B. (This is not a very realistic assumption, but we will make a better one later.) We assume further that the resources used by A and B are completely inelastic in total supply. Now the decreased demand for product B causes the price of its specific inputs to drop, and since their only use is in production of B, their prices must fall far enough to restore their full employment, which must occur when the output of B is restored to its original level. With lower factor prices, the costs of B fall; consequently, firms can produce the old output even at the new, lower price. Similarly, efforts to raise the production of A force up the prices of its specific inputs. Since the supply of inputs is inelastic, it is impossible to increase the output of A, and only its price changes. Its price rises to the point where the old quantity intersects the new demand curve.

Now consider a third, intermediate case. We assume that each industry uses one factor which is specific to it, but that its other inputs are used throughout the economy. This means there is a difference in the elasticities of resource supply confronting the industries. Industry A uses some specific factor a, the supply of which has a low elasticity, while other inputs have a high elasticity of supply to industry A because they can be bid away from other sectors of the economy.

A decrease in the demand for product B will lead its producers to reduce their demand for inputs. This will affect different input prices differently. Factor b, the specific input to industry B, has a totally inelastic supply, so its price falls substantially. The other factors, such as labor, have a high elasticity of supply, and their prices fall very little. As a result, producers of product B have an incentive to change their input mix—to substitute factor b for other inputs. So do other producers, if they can do so. This helps cushion the fall in the price of factor b, but it falls anyway. As a result, the average cost of product B falls below its initial level, helping to keep the long-run normal price lower than it was originally. However, costs do not fall sufficiently far to keep the output of B where it was originally. Product B ends up with a lower price and a lower output.

Producers of product A increase their demand for inputs. This causes the price of the specific factor a, with inelastic supply, to rise substantially, whereas other factors, such as labor, with higher supply elasticities, do not increase very much. Firms producing product A therefore have an incentive to substitute against factor a, and use more of the nonspecific factors. This prevents the price of a from rising so much, but it rises nevertheless. Thus the cost of product A rises, and so does its long-run equilibrium price. However, the price rise is not sufficient to restore output to its old, lower level. Instead, both price and output remain higher than they were initially.

In the case of the nonspecific resources, such as labor, this case is much like the first one. Resources are transferred from product B to product A, and the net effect on factor prices may be slight. With the specific factors, the effect is like the second case. Factor prices change, rather than factor allocation. Because prices of different factors change to different degree, factor substitutions occur, and product prices are permanently changed. The product-price change will, of course, set off demand repercussions, extending to the substitutes and complements of A and B. And the factor-price changes will alter the distribution of incomes and probably the composition of consumer expenditures.

Finally, we consider a case in which both A and B use resources which are widely used elsewhere in the economy and thus have high elasticities of supply to one industry; but we assume that the production functions of industries A and B are very different in shape. Industry A uses relatively more of factor a at any given set of factor prices, while industry B uses relatively more of factor b. The demand shift from B to A leads, on balance, to decreased demand for factor b and increased demand for factor a. Factor b therefore tends to fall in price relative to a. This encourages factor substitution throughout the economy, firms tending to use more of b and less of a than before. And this in turn tends to affect the relative costs of different products. Some firms can readily substitute the cheaper factor; consequently their costs and prices fall and their output expands. In the end, however, it is still likely that factor a will remain more expensive and factor b cheaper and that the price of product A will be permanently raised as that of B is permanently lowered—with all the consumer repercussions entailed.

Our general conclusion is that the impact of changes in consumer tastes depends greatly on the conditions in the markets for factors of production. The more extensively factors are used throughout the economy, and the higher the ease of substitution by producers and consumers, the smaller will be the price effects of demand shifts and the greater the changes in composition of output. In other words, high elasticities of supply and demand keep down price changes. Factor mobility, factor substitutability, and product substitutability are all elements contributing positively to high elasticities of supply and demand for factors and products. If elasticities are low because of factor immobility or low substitutability by producers and consumers, then demand shifts are likely to cause greater changes in prices and smaller changes in the composition of output.

changes in factor supply

Starting from a position of general competitive equilibrium, let us assume there occurs an increase in the supply of one productive resource, factor a. We continue to assume that each factor has a very low price-elasticity of supply but that factor-supply schedules tend to shift.

The increase in the supply of factor a tends to lower its price. Firms expand output and also tend to use more of factor a per unit of output. The movement down its marginal product schedule lowers the real price of a, measured in units of output. Other inputs sustain an increase in their marginal product schedules, and their real prices rise.

Some products sustain a larger increase in output than others. If the decline in price of factor a causes a big drop in the costs of a product, and if demand for it has a high elasticity, then its output would expand a great deal. Output would not expand much for commodities the costs of which are relatively unaffected by the price of a, or for which consumer demand is relatively inelastic.

It is appropriate to note again that the price mechanism provides an incentive for producers to adjust their methods of production in order to use the resources which are actually available in the economy. An increase in supply of factor a leads, through a fall in its price, to an incentive by firms to use more of factor a per unit of output. In this process, changes in the specific form of capital goods may play an important role in the long run. The kind of capital goods which might be optimal for an economy with only $1,000 of capital per worker would not be the same as the kind which would be optimal for a developed economy with $100,000 per worker.

shifts in production functions

Changes in the production functions of firms may occur through changes in technology or organizational methods. Generally such changes have been brought about deliberately as ways of reducing costs and increasing productivity. They generally mean that more output becomes available per unit of input. Let us consider first an innovation which raises proportionately the amount of output available from any given input combination without changing the relative input mix. Such an innovation would tend to reduce costs and consequently to produce an increase in output. The magnitude of this increase would, however, depend on the elasticity of demand for the product to which the innovation applied. With low elasticity of demand, the output increase might be small. It could be so small that the industry could reduce its demand for inputs, so that their prices would fall. However, consumers would then have more money to spend on other products (why do we know this?), and increased demand for factors would occur in those areas.

If the technical innovation occurs in a product with a high elasticity of demand, then the output effect may be substantial enough to raise the demand for factors by that industry. This will imply that consumers spend less on other products, however, which will release factors into the expanding industry if the factor mix is similar.

Technical innovation often changes the optimum input mix. For instance, innovations in machinery might cause the shape of the production isoquants to shift in such a way that the firm would use more capital and less labor than before to produce any given output at any given set of factor prices. In such cases, even if product demand has high elasticity, the output increase may not be sufficient to prevent a decline in demand for some factors of production. The innovating industry might tend to use more capital than before, pushing up its price, but less labor than before, lowering its price. Shifts in relative factor prices would lead to factor substitutions, shifts in costs of other products, and so on.

the price system as an information system

A competitive free-market economy in which prices keep relatively close to their equilibrium values serves up a remarkable amount of information about matters which would otherwise be difficult to ascertain. And because the material well-being of people is affected by their economic behavior, they have strong motivations to pay attention to the information which the price system furnishes to them. Prices furnish a guide to conduct, and the motivation of material well-being provides an incentive to follow the guide. In the process of following the guide, the behavior of individuals brings about a particular pattern of economic activity. This pattern produces a solution to the basic economic problems: What is to be produced, in what quantities, by what methods? Who is going to do what? How shall the products be divided up among the members of the society? Our contention is that the guidance is toward an efficient solution to these problems.

Consider the manner in which each participant in the economic system is guided by the prices which confront him. Buyers are attracted by low price and repelled by high price, other things being equal. We have seen that the prices of products reflect their costs, which in turn reflect the amount of resources required for their production—which are in turn valued by what else they could have produced. High-priced products make a relatively large drain on the scarce resources of the economy. Economic efficiency is served if consumers can fulfill a given desire with a low-priced product rather than a high-priced one.

Among productive resources, price tends to reflect productivity. If a resource bears a high price, this indicates it is scarce relative to the productive uses to which it can be put. The cost of a resource to one firm reflects the value of what it could produce elsewhere. Each firm buys only so much of a given resource as will yield at least as much as that resource could produce elsewhere. In the process, firms economize on those resources which are highly productive elsewhere, and each resource tends to find employment in those areas where it is most productive.

Sellers are attracted by high prices and repelled by low prices. The business firm is encouraged to produce more of products for which the selling price exceeds the unit cost. But the unit cost of one product reflects the value of other products which must be foregone; it is thus a measure of the value which consumers place on resources used elsewhere in the economy. By following the guidance of price and profit, the firm also adapts production more closely to the relative strength of consumers' preferences.

To workers and owners of productive property, price furnishes a guide to where their services are most in demand. If an occupation carries a high remuneration, this indicates that there is a shortage of people to perform it. And of course the prospect of higher incomes provides an incentive to increase one's own productivity by working harder, obtaining further education, etc.

Thus the guideposts offered by a competitive economy help to direct the actions of producers and consumers toward an efficient pattern for the use of scarce resources. Those products are produced which are most strongly preferred by consumers. Methods of production will be used which are adapted to the particular resources available in the economy. Individual resources will be drawn into employments which meet strong demands and for which they are particularly well suited. And products will be distributed so as to reward households whose resources furnish the largest contributions to productivity.

Observe how prices help to transmit information which would not otherwise be easy to obtain. Prices help to register the strength of consumers' preferences among thousands of different goods and services. The price of a product also provides a quick indicator of the drain which it imposes on the resources of the community. The price of each resource tells each firm at a glance how productive that resource is in a vast number of other uses.

This is an inspiring spectacle. Does it correspond to anything in the real world? It is easy to find flaws in this as description. In the real world competition is imperfect, and disequilibrium is more common than equilibrium. The participants in the economic system possess very imperfect knowledge about its details and are influenced by their attitudes toward risk and uncertainty. We will explore these limitations of the competitive theory in a subsequent chapter. Here it is sufficient to state that the entire conception of this book is based on the conviction that the competitive model, though unrealistic in detail, has considerable relevance to the understanding of actions in the real world. In particular, the analysis of competition is useful for dealing with problems of international economic relations and with the proper role of government. These form the subject matter of several of the chapters which follow.

the matrix of production—input-output analysis

Our exposition has stressed the output of products sold to final consumers. In reality, however, a large portion of the transactions in an economic system consists of sales of products from one firm to another. Most of the inputs used by firms are the output of other firms in the economy—so-called intermediate products. In many cases, the same product is sold partly to final consumers and partly to business users. Gasoline is used both in consumer autos and in business vehicles. Some corn is sold directly to consumers as food; some is fed to livestock to aid in production of meat or eggs.

The existence of a complex web of intermediate-product relationships greatly complicates the pattern of general equilibrium, of balancing supply and demand in all the markets of the economy. The final output of the economy must achieve a consistency between the input decisions of the users of each intermediate product and its producers.

Description and analysis of such a network has been carried on with the aid of input-output analysis. The basic instrument is a sort of "sources-and-uses" table for each industry in the economy. On one hand, the table shows the quantities of various inputs (both factors of production and intermediate products) used by the industry during a given period. On the other hand, it shows the disposition of the industry's output in the same period—that is, the quantity sold to each other industry in the economy as well as to final consumers. Accurately constructed for all industries, an input-output table would provide a picture of the resource and product flows through the economy. Consistency would be achieved in that the total output of each industry would have to be consistent with the inputs of its industrial users plus final consumer sales.

Further, the input-output table can be used analytically if one assumes that there is a fixed, linear relation between input and output in each industry. That is, one assumes that the quantity of each input per unit of output is fixed and that the marginal quantity of any input required is equal to the average. On that assumption, one can feed into the table any pattern of final output—that is, output available for purchase by consumers, government, and export markets—and find out the entire input-output pattern required to obtain it. By the use of matrix analysis, mathematicians can determine the total output of each intermediate product and the total input of each factor of production required to yield a specified "bill of goods" for final users. We illustrate the nature of the input-output matrix with a simple numerical example in Table 16-1. We assume there are only two products in the economy, corn and pork, and two factors, land and labor. The economy produces 600 tons of corn, which output requires 400 units of labor and 1,600 units of land. However, only half the corn output is purchased by consumers; the other 300 tons is used to feed the pigs from which the pork is obtained. The pork output of 100 tons is all sold to final consumers; it requires direct labor of 600 units and 400 units of land.

We assume fixed input requirements per unit of output. On the right, we show the net amount of each factor required to provide consumers with a unit of the product. Half the land and labor used in corn production produce the 300 tons which consumers get; thus the gross ratios are 200 to 300 for labor and 800 to 300 for land. For pork production, we must add together the factors which produce the

TABLE 16-1

| | | Quantity Used by Sector | | | Factor Requirements per Unit of Consumption | |
| | | | | | | |
Source	Quantity Supplied	Corn	Pork	Consumption	Labor	Land
Corn	600 tons	0	300	300	$\frac{2}{3}$	$\frac{8}{3}$
Pork	100 tons	0	0	100	8	12
Labor	1,000 man-years	400	600	0		
Land	2,000 acre-years	1,600	400	0		

corn used to feed the pigs, plus the factors directly used in raising the pigs. The gross ratios are 800 to 100 for labor and 1,200 to 100 for land.

The input-output analysis does not use the kind of information which would help us understand how prices influence the final choice of outputs. However, it could be used to analyze the relation of changes at one end to changes at the other. For instance, we could use the data to analyze what increases in factors would be required to expand final output to consumers to 450 corn and 200 pork. Our factor requirements coefficients tell us we shall require 1,900 units of labor and 3,600 of land. These will be allocated to produce total output of 1,050 units of corn, of which 600 are required to feed the pigs.

The input-output model is a special type of production function. Its linear form enables it to be applied to situations where both inputs and outputs are numerous. As customarily applied, it plays down the role of ultimate productive factors such as labor and stresses the interplay among intermediate product sectors of the economy. Given its assumptions, it could be used to generate a production-possibilities function, identifying all the feasible combinations of output, or to test whether any given output combination would be feasible with existing resources and technique. Analytically, the input-output approach is complementary to more orthodox continuous-substitution production functions; each can do or illustrate things that the other cannot.

Input-output analysis is an extremely useful technique for purposes relating to economic planning. It enables decisions relating to one sector of the economy to be made consistent with those for another. Its application to underdeveloped countries is hampered, however, by shortages of the kind of data required. A more serious limitation, perhaps, is the assumption of fixed coefficients of production. This eliminates many considerations of choice and maximization in the production process. Substitutions among inputs or processes are left out of the picture; so are possible departures from constant returns to industry scale.

As a practical matter, input-output analysis has not been widely used in government economic planning. Although Russian economists helped develop the technique, communist countries have only recently begun to experiment with it as a practical instrument of planning. Its use by the United States government has been hampered by ideological hostility to substantial government planning and control of economic life. Input-output analysis has played a role in the so-called indicative planning system employed in France. Investment targets for individual firms and industries were determined by input-output analysis applied to a government-endorsed target for the expansion of final output.

summary

If all markets in the economy were characterized by pure competition, and if a state of equilibrium were achieved throughout the economy, a number of significant results would occur. The price of each product would equal the average and marginal cost of that product at the optimum scale of production for individual firms. In consequence, the ratio of any pair of product prices would equal the marginal rate of transformation between those products along a production-possibilities curve. This would also be equated to the subjective marginal rate of substitution between those products in the minds of consumers. Thus the output of the community would be ideally adapted to the pattern of consumer preferences.

It would also be true that each factor of production would bear a price equal to the value of its marginal product, which would be the same in all uses. As a result, each factor would be allocated among alternative uses in a manner which would maximize the value of the output of the society as a whole.

For these principal reasons, the guidance given to production and consumption in a competitive free-market economy may be regarded as efficient—that is, it helps to direct scarce resources into a pattern of use which achieves the maximum possible in meeting consumer preferences.

A competitive equilibrium exists only on the assumption of a given state of technology and organizational technique, of factor supplies, and of consumer preferences. However, the competitive market also provides a means by which prices and production adapt to changes in any of these underlying data.

Description of the complexity resulting when one industry's output is another industry's input can be made with an input-output table. This can also be used to analyze the implications of changes in input or output, but only by using very restrictive assumptions.

TERMS AND CONCEPTS

Input-output table

QUESTIONS AND PROBLEMS

1. "The real cost of any product is the other products which must be sacrificed in order to get it." Explain this relationship in a state of general competitive equilibrium.

2. It is a common situation that farmers earn less income than people who work in commerce or industry even in countries where governments support farm prices above equilibrium levels. What remedy is suggested by the analysis of marginal product equalization? Prove that the remedy would raise the value of the nation's output.

3. Assume an economic system in general competitive equilibrium. (Assume it is self-sufficient; ignore international trade.) Now there occurs a discovery of an extensive deposit of iron ore, and many firms spring up to mine and process it into final products of iron and steel. (Remember that steel-making uses a lot of coal.) Construct a plausible explanation of how these actions would affect each of the following:
   (a) The general level of real wages
   (b) The output and price of automobiles
   (c) The output and price of petroleum
   (d) The rate of interest

4. Suppose the economy produces two products, A and B, according to the following production functions:

$$Q_A = a_1{}^{\frac{1}{4}} b_1{}^{\frac{3}{4}}$$
$$Q_B = a_2{}^{\frac{3}{4}} b_2{}^{\frac{1}{4}}$$

The economy contains 1,000 units of factor a and 1,000 units of factor b.

Construct a box diagram showing the different combinations of efficient factor allocation between the two products, illustrating with isoquants for two separate nonzero output combinations. Derive a mathematical expression for the production-possibility line measured in factor space (as in Figure 16-3). Using the two end points and your two intermediate combinations, draw an approximation to the production-possibilities curve. Ask your professor to derive the algebraic expression for it.

17

aggregate production functions and economic growth

We originally introduced the production function with reference to the input-output relationship within the individual firm. In Chapter 12, we were able to move to a higher level and develop a production function for a competitive industry. This could be done on the assumption that the allocation of output among firms was determinate (a result we obtained by assuming that the optimum scale of each firm was constant and that each firm would operate at that scale in the long run). The industry production function would also be determinate if the division of output among firms were unimportant, as it would be if all firms operated subject to constant returns to scale but did not grow rapidly enough to undermine the condition of pure competition.

From industry production functions it is possible to aggregate still further. In Chapters 13 and 14 we used an aggregate production function for the economy as a whole to analyze factor pricing and total factor incomes. To make this determinate, we had to assume that the proportional composition of output remained constant. In Chapter 16, however, we made a different sort of aggregation, using industry production functions as the basis for a production possibilities curve to analyze the composition of output itself. In this chapter, we examine the use of aggregate production functions for the analysis of economic growth and its relation to factor supplies and income distribution.

The Cobb-Douglas function, which we have used so extensively, has long been applied to the analysis of growth and distribution. The economic model of classical economics, which was the basis for our Chapter 7, can be derived from a Cobb-Douglas function with the supply of land held constant. A simpler model widely used for growth analysis is the *Harrod-Domar model*, in which only the capital input is explicitly treated. The input-output analysis developed by Wassily Leontief can also be used as the basis for a growth analysis.

neoclassical growth models

Paul Douglas originally developed the Cobb-Douglas function as a contribution to the theory of income distribution; it was a way of applying the marginal productivity theory to the national economy. In the 1950s, a number of economists perceived the possibilities of using the Cobb-Douglas function to analyze economic growth. Resulting models have generally been termed *neoclassical* because of their properties of continuous substitution possibilities among factors and their compatibility with the marginal productivity theory of distribution. The Cobb-Douglas function has another attractive property. A function

$$Q = a^x b^{1-x} \qquad (1 > x > 0)$$

has the property that

$$\log Q = x(\log a) + (1 - x) \log b$$

meaning that the logarithm of output is a linear function of the logarithms of the inputs. The logarithmic form of the function lends itself to the analysis of empirical data through least-squares regression analysis.

The strict Cobb-Douglas function may be required to have exponents equal to 1, which results in constant returns to scale. There is no assurance that economic growth proceeds along a path of constant returns to scale, but the assumption is not strongly contradicted by the evidence, and it simplifies the analysis a great deal. Such an assumption produces one condition of particular interest, which we have already commented upon: the proportional share of each factor in total income is equal to its exponent in the production function. This makes it possible to estimate, for example, labor's exponent in the production function from estimates of labor's share in the national income.

If the production function itself is taken as given (meaning that technology, organizational skill, and the quality of the factors of production do not change), economic growth occurs when the supplies of the factors increase. If both factors grow at the same rate over time, output will grow at that same rate. More interesting results occur when the factors do not grow at the same rate.

Suppose, for instance, that the labor force grows at an annual rate of 1 percent while the stock of capital grows at 5 percent per year—rates approximately true for the United States in the twentieth century. The growth rate of output is, as one would expect, between the growth rates of the two factors. We can illustrate this using the aggregate production function $Q = L^{3⁄4}K^{1⁄4}$, the exponents of which have some rough correspondence to historical experience. (L represents labor, K capital.) By putting the data into logarithmic form, we can easily determine that output will grow at a constant rate of 2 percent. Thus $\log Q_1 = \tfrac{3}{4} \log L_1 + \tfrac{1}{4} \log K_1$, letting the subscript indicate the time period. In the second period, $\log L$ will have increased by about 0.00432 ($= \log 1.01$), and $\log K$ will have increased by about 0.02119 ($= \log 1.05$). Thus we would have

$$\log Q_2 = \tfrac{3}{4}(\log L_1 + 0.00432) + \tfrac{1}{4}(\log K_1 + 0.02119)$$

Subtracting the two, we have

$$\log Q_2 - \log Q_1 = \tfrac{3}{4}(0.00432) + \tfrac{1}{4}(0.02119) = 0.008539$$

The logarithm of output in the second period will always be greater than the logarithm of output of the first period by a constant; therefore the percentage growth rate of output will be a constant. Taking the antilog of 0.008539, we find the growth rate of output to be 2 percent.[1] If we multiply the growth rate of each factor by its exponent in the production function and add the resulting numbers, the sum represents the growth rate of output. In our example, we have the following:

Factor L	Growth rate $1\% \times$ exponent $\tfrac{3}{4} = 0.75\%$
Factor K	Growth rate $5\% \times$ exponent $\tfrac{1}{4} = \underline{1.25\%}$
	Output growth rate $= 2.00\%$

saving-investment feedback

The preceding analysis implies that the growth rate of capital is, like that of labor, autonomously determined. But the growth of capital comes about through saving and investment. A portion of current output is preserved from consumption and added to the capital stock. Since the economy is assumed to produce at full employ-

---

[1] The logarithmic calculation shown is not precisely accurate, but the slippage is insignificant for growth rates on the order used in the example. The antilog of 0.008539 is 1.99, rather than 2.00.

ment, there is no problem of a discrepancy between saving and investment. We must also assume that investment is drawn by price-profit considerations into the most profitable remaining outlets. The analysis can be made more interesting and realistic if we assume that saving and investment are related to the level of output. Suppose, for example, that the desire to save is such that 10 percent of total output is saved and invested. (We refer to net investment, that which is beyond what is needed to replace capital items wearing out.) The growth of capital under this assumption will no longer be an autonomous constant.

To illustrate the effects of such feedback, we assume that saving and investment are part of a sequential process. The output of one time period is determined by the stock of labor and capital available at the beginning of that period. Saving and investment out of the output for that period add to the capital stock in place at the beginning of the next period. To simplify the arithmetic, we assume that the initial stocks of labor and capital are represented by 100 units and that capital stock and output are measured in the same units. We continue to assume that the labor force grows at a constant rate of 1 percent and that the aggregate production function is $Q = L^{3/4}K^{1/4}$. The behavior of the system under these assumptions for five time periods is shown in Table 17-1. As a result of the output in period 1, saving and investment add 10 units to capital for use in period 2. But since the labor force grows by only 1 percent, output growth is 3.25 percent in period 2. The amount added to capital rises slightly in absolute terms, but is a smaller percentage increase. Consequently output growth in period 3 is slightly less than 3.25 percent. As output growth slows, so does the growth of capital. Each acts as a brake on the other. By period 5, output is growing by only 2.8 percent. The output and capital growth rates must continue to decline as long as they exceed the growth rate of the labor force. The system thus tends toward an equilibrium growth rate of 1 percent, which it will approach as a limit.

As long as the capital stock is growing at a higher rate than the labor force, output will be growing at a slower rate than capital. But the growth rate of *investment* is equal to the growth rate of output. With investment growing by only about 3 percent per year, the growth rate of total capital cannot be maintained at any higher level. An equilibrium growth rate can only exist when capital stock and investment are

TABLE 17-1

Period	Labor	Capital	Output	Saving and Investment
1	100.0	100.0	100.0	10
2	101.0	110.0	103.25	10.33
3	102.01	120.33	106.51	10.65
4	103.03	130.98	109.41	10.94
5	104.06	141.92	112.47	11.25

growing by the same proportion. This can only occur when capital and output are growing at the same rate, which they can do only when they grow at the rate of increase of the labor force.

The feedback mechanism can be made even more intricate by bringing in the influence of the rate of profit on investment. Suppose that desired saving is not simply a function of total output but a positive function of the profit rate, so that a larger proportion of income is saved at a higher rate of profit.

Our model yields an implicit value for the rate of profit. We know that the shares of income going to the factors of production will be proportional to the exponents they have in the production function. Thus capital will receive one-fourth of the output. If we express this as a proportion of the capital stock, the ratio is a possible measure of the profit rate. In period 1 when there are 100 units of labor and 100 units of capital, the income going to capital is 25 and the profit rate is 25 percent.

Suppose that the proportion of income people want to save is equal to two-fifths of the rate of profit. This will produce the same amount of saving and investment in period 1 as shown in Table 17-1. In period 2, however, profit income rises to 25.8, while the amount of capital has risen to 110. Thus the rate of profit falls to 23.5 percent. Consequently, saving and investment are only 9.4 percent of output, or 9.71. Thus investment actually falls, and the growth rates of capital and output decline more rapidly than in Table 17-1. The new pattern is shown in Table 17-2. Not only does the proportion of output saved decline, but the amount of saving and investment declines. This reflects the decrease in the profit rate, which itself results from the fact that profit income does not grow as fast as the capital stock. Profit income grows only as fast as total income, while capital is growing more rapidly. The decrease in the profit rate reflects a kind of diminishing return; as the capital stock increases more rapidly than the labor force, the marginal productivity of capital decreases, and with it, the income per unit of capital.

The system described in Table 17-2 will approach the same equilibrium growth rate as before: the 1 percent growth rate of the labor force. In order to maintain a constant growth rate, profit income must grow at the same rate as the capital stock, the profit rate must remain constant, and capital and output must grow at the same rate. Only at a 1 percent growth rate can these all be achieved.

TABLE 17-2

Period	Labor Force	Capital	Output	Profit Income	Profit Rate, %	Saving Rate, %	Saving and Investment
1	100	100	100	25	25	10	10
2	101	110	103.25	25.81	23.5	9.4	9.71
3	102.01	119.71	106.17	26.54	22.17	8.87	9.42
4	103.03	129.13	109.01	27.25	21.10	8.44	9.20
5	104.06	138.33	111.74	27.94	20.19	8.08	9.03

Another variant is to assume that saving is performed only by the "capitalists" who receive profit income. In our particular model, this does not add anything interesting to the process shown in Table 17-2, since the share of income going to capitalists is constant. However, if the elasticity of factor substitution were not equal to unity, shifts in income distribution could occur over time and add another element to the adjustment process. A disproportionately rapid growth of capital might reduce the share of income going to capitalists, adding another reason why the growth of capital might slow down.

a classical model

We can easily use a Cobb-Douglas function to illustrate the growth model implicit in classical British political economy, derived from the ideas of Malthus, Ricardo, and John Stuart Mill. (We have already dealt with this model in a simpler way in Chapter 7.) We must now assume there are three factors of production, land, labor, and capital, and that the quantity of land is fixed. Assume the production function is $Q = L^{6\%0}K^{15\%00}Ld^{25\%00}$, with Ld representing land.

An important feature of the classical model was its assumption that the supply of labor was functionally dependent on the real wage. With wages above some level of subsistence, population and labor force would increase. With wages at the subsistence level, population and labor force would remain constant. And if wages fell below the subsistence level, population and labor force would decrease. We identify the subsistence wage as 0.50 units of output per worker per time period and assume the labor force grows in the next period by a percentage equal to one-fifth of the excess of actual wage over subsistence wage.

Saving and investment are positive functions of profit rate and profit income. We assume that capitalists save and invest a proportion of profit income equal to four times the profit rate.

As before, we assume an initial position in which the quantity of each input is 100 units, output is also 100 units, and capital is measured in the same units as output. Each factor receives a share of output proportional to its exponent in the production function; thus initially wage income is 60, profit income 15, and rent 25. The wage rate is thus 0.60, which is above the subsistence level by 0.10; therefore population in period 2 will reflect growth of 2 percent. The profit rate is 15 percent; thus capitalists will save and invest 60 percent of their incomes, so capital in period 2 will rise to 109 units. Table 17-3 shows the growth pattern which follows.

In the early periods, the rate of saving and investment is sufficiently high to cause output to grow faster than the labor force. As a result, the wage rate increases. This produces a Malthusian effect of a more rapid rise in the labor force. The high rate of capital growth cannot be maintained, however; for the very reason that capital is growing faster than output or the other inputs, the profit rate falls, and with it the rate of saving and the level of investment. This in turn slows output

TABLE 17-3†

Period	Land	Labor	Capital	Output	Wage Income	Wage Rate	Profit Income	Profit Rate	Rent Income	Saving Rate	Investment
1	100	100.0	100.0	100.0	60.0	0.500	15.0	15.0	25.0	0.600	9.0
2	100	102.0	109.0	102.5	61.5	0.603	15.4	14.1	25.6	0.564	8.7
3	100	104.1	117.7	105.0	63.0	0.605	15.8	13.4	26.2	0.536	8.4
4	100	106.3	126.1	107.4	64.5	0.606	16.1	12.8	26.9	0.511	8.2
5	100	108.6	134.4	109.8	65.9	0.607	16.5	12.3	27.5	0.490	8.1
6	100	110.9	143.4	112.3	67.4	0.608	15.9	11.7	28.1	0.470	7.9
7	100	113.3	151.4	114.7	68.8	0.607	17.2	11.4	28.7	0.455	7.8
8	100	115.7	159.2	117.1	70.2	0.607	17.6	11.0	29.3	0.441	7.7
9	100	118.2	166.9	119.4	71.6	0.606	17.9	10.7	29.9	0.429	7.7
10	100	120.7	174.6	121.7	73.0	0.605	18.3	10.5	30.4	0.418	7.6
11	100	123.3	182.2	124.0	74.4	0.604	18.6	10.2	31.0	0.408	7.6

† Land and labor are in physical units; capital, output, and investment are in units of output, valued at constant prices, and so are wage, profit, and rent incomes. Figures are rounded and will not add up precisely. Calculations were performed to one additional figure.

growth, and in period 6 the wage rate reaches its maximum. From period 7 on, output is growing less rapidly than the labor force, and the wage rate declines. From here on, the system will continue to follow the course indicated by the last few periods. Both wage rate and profit rate will continue to decline. Therefore both labor force and capital growth rates will continue to fall. As long as the land input is fixed, the system cannot find an equilibrium growth path at any positive rate of growth. As a limit, the system will approach a "stationary state," in which labor force and capital stock cease to grow. Since the profit rate cannot literally fall to zero in our model, the stationary state is never reached. The system slows down perpetually, but never stops entirely.

Because of the special form of our production function, the share of total output going to landowners does not change. However, their reward per unit of land tends to increase as the other inputs grow, while the reward per unit of the other inputs tends (at least after some point) to decrease.

Economists of the early nineteenth century were almost obsessed with the importance of diminishing returns resulting from the fixed supply of land. In the actual experience of Western industrial countries, however, technological progress and growth of capital have relegated the problem to relatively minor status. Indeed, most neoclassical growth models neglect the land input entirely.

The special results in the classical case can be regarded as illustrations of some principles inherent in the Cobb-Douglas function generally. These may be summarized as follows:

1. If some factors of production grow at rates which are positively related to the rewards per unit received by those factors, and other "autonomous" factors grow at rates which are constant, the equilibrium growth rate of the system can only be achieved at the growth rate of the autonomous factor. Modern neoclassical models tend to treat the labor force as growing autonomously, yielding results similar to Tables 17-1 and 17-2. In the classical model, land is the autonomous factor, and its zero growth rate would be the only rate which could be sustained.

2. Since in the Cobb-Douglas function the share of each factor class in total income is constant, the factor's reward per unit can be constant only if total output grows at the same rate as the stock of that factor. This can only occur if all factors grow at the same rate.

limitations and modifications of Cobb-Douglas growth analysis

We have noted that the Cobb-Douglas function has proved attractive for statistical investigations of economic growth, since the logarithm of output is a linear function of the logarithms of the inputs. Least-squares regression analysis can be carried out by conventional statistical techniques on the logarithms of the data.

Strictly speaking, however, such measurement operations, and models such as we have presented in this chapter, all rest on the assumption that the production function itself remains constant over time. More specifically, this means that the technological conditions of production do not change, and the quality of the factors of production remains constant. These assumptions may be reasonable for static equilibrium analysis, but they are very unacceptable for growth analysis. In industrial countries, a large part of the process of economic growth has arisen from technological change and from improvement in the quality of the labor force and the stock of capital. Unfortunately, it is very difficult to give quantitative measures to either technical progress or upgrading of factor quality. Resourceful investigators have devised various possible methods for approximating such measurements, but the results remain highly controversial.

Using the Cobb-Douglas function for growth theorizing imposes one limitation on the results which may be undesirable. This is the property that factor shares remain unchanged in face of change in factor quantities. The constancy of factor shares arises from the fact that the elasticity of substitution among inputs is always unity in the Cobb-Douglas function. In order to analyze cases where factor shares are not constant, but may depend on relative factor supplies, economists have developed a more complex form of aggregate production function, called the *constant-elasticity-of-substitution function (CES)*. Such a function is linear and homogeneous, and displays diminishing returns to any single input. However, the elasticity of factor substitution need not be equal to unity, and factor shares are therefore not necessarily constant. Since the Cobb-Douglas function does display constant elasticity of substitution, it becomes a special case of the CES function.

The CES function takes the following form:

$$Q = a[gK^{-x} + (1 - g)L^{-x}]^{-1/x}$$

where a, g, and x are constants, and typically $1 > g > 0$ and $x > 1$. As an illustration, if a is equal to 1, g is 0.25, and x is 2, $Q = [0.25K^{-2} + 0.75L^{-2}]^{-1/2}$, which could also be written as follows:

$$Q = \frac{1}{\sqrt{0.25/K^2 + 0.75/L^2}}$$

The mathematical intricacies of the CES function are far beyond the scope of this discussion.

the Harrod-Domar model

A far simpler model of economic growth is the Harrod-Domar model. Harrod's original use of the model was in relation to a Keynesian analysis of growth and fluctuations, but since the 1940s the model has become popular for analysis and planning in underdeveloped countries. In its simplest form, the model postulates that there is a constant proportion between the stock of capital goods and output. Thus on its face the model assumes a one-factor production function. The growth of output results from the growth of capital. Capital growth stems from investment, which is related to existing output by a propensity to save. If some constant proportion of income is saved, the growth rate of the economy can be expressed in terms of the capital-output ratio and the saving fraction. If the capital-output ratio is designated by k and the saving fraction as s, the growth rate of the economy will be equal to s/k.

For example, suppose the capital-output ratio is 2, and 10 percent of output is saved and added to capital each year. The growth pattern can be observed in Table 17-4.

We do not need to go further to observe that the system grows at a rate of 5 percent per year. We could have determined this directly by solving $s/k = 0.1/2 = 0.05$. The growth rate is higher, the higher the proportion of income saved and the lower the capital-output ratio.

In application, the model can be improved by using a marginal capital-output ratio, which need not be the same as the average. A least-squares regression equation relating capital stock (CS) to output would typically take the form $CS = a + kQ$, where k would be the marginal capital-output ratio. The growth rate of output would still be equal to s/k and would not be affected by the value of a. Similarly, the model could use a *marginal* propensity to save which need not equal the average propensity.

In its simplest form, the Harrod-Domar model appears to deny the existence of diminishing returns. However, there is nothing to prevent one from using a capital-output equation which is nonlinear, if the gain in realism seems worth the loss in mathematical simplicity.

Analytically, the assumptions underlying the simple forms of Harrod-Domar model seem to have little to recommend them. In practice, models in this form have had a number of advantages, particularly for persons involved in economic planning for growth in underdeveloped countries. Typically the planning process has emphasized capital as a variable amenable to policy influence. And economic plans and related documents have involved measuring the past and future productivity of capital. A major policy focus for an underdeveloped country tends to be on

TABLE 17-4

Period	Capital	Output	Saving and Investment
1	200	100	10
2	210	105	10.5
3	220.5	110.25	11.025

foreign loans and foreign aid, and these are associated with emphasis on capital formation. These considerations alone would not warrant using an oversimplified model if it were not for another very important consideration: in practice, the Harrod-Domar model has been a pretty good descriptive approximation of the growth pattern in many countries, viewed retrospectively.

By comparison with a more sophisticated model, we can see that the Harrod-Domar model appears to ignore such matters as changes in the supply and quality of the labor force and changes in technology, as well as diminishing returns to capital. Descriptively, however, these omissions are to a large extent mutually offsetting. If the labor force is increasing in quantity and improving in quality, and if technology is improving, these influences will help offset the tendency toward diminishing returns which would result if only capital were growing. Thus one should not regard the Harrod-Domar model as a picture of what would happen if capital grew while other things remained unchanged; it is better viewed as showing what is likely to happen when capital grows *and* some "normal" rate of growth or improvement is taking place in labor force and technology. There remains the danger, of course, that planners may overlook the importance of the labor-force and technology changes, and particularly fail to make policy decisions such as support for research and education which would increase the rate of qualitative improvement.

the Leontief input-output model

The input-output analysis associated with Wassily Leontief involves a very different sort of aggregate production function. The models we have considered so far are highly aggregated; they relate total output to total quantity of one or more factors of production without any explicit concern for the composition of output. The input-output model, by contrast, permits explicit identification of many separate products and services. Cobb-Douglas and other CES production functions admit of continuous substitutions among productive factors. The input-output model assumes that no such substitutions are possible. Each product in the input-output model has its own production function, but this function is a purely linear relationship. The model can handle production functions with a large number of different inputs, but only by assuming that each unit of output requires some constant amount of each of the inputs. The marginal product of one input changed in isolation is zero; output only expands if all inputs increase in proportion.[2]

An input-output model cannot be identified simply by an equation of the sort we have used for other aggregate production functions. Instead it is described

---

[2] However, some input substitution can be introduced without destroying the linear quality of the system. For any given product, there may exist several available processes, each requiring fixed input-output coefficients; however, those coefficients will differ from one process to another. A least-cost combination of processes can be identified by linear programming, given criteria for cost minimization.

by a matrix, a table of numbers. One might list horizontally all the suppliers in the economy. This could include labor, products supplied to other industries, and products supplied to final consumers. Vertically one could list all the buyers in the economy, including business firms buying intermediate products from other firms. It is one of the descriptive virtues of the input-output model that it deals so extensively with inter-industry relationships.

Below each of the horizontal categories of sellers would appear a column of numbers representing the value of sales by that sector to all of the purchasing sectors. Next to each vertical buyer category would be a row of numbers representing the dollar purchases of that sector from all of the selling sectors. A column for labor would represent the total wage and salary bill of the economy, broken down by sectors. A row for households would represent their total expenditures for current production, broken down by industries from which they bought.

Under the usual classifications, capital goods do not appear separately in the tabulation. Instead, industries appear under such classes as steel and construction (both of which produce a lot of capital goods, but a lot of other things also).

The input-output model permits estimation of the indirect inputs required to produce any item. The automobile industry's direct purchases can easily be identified, but one may wish to know, for instance, how much coal is needed to make the steel which is needed for $10,000 worth of automobiles. By mathematical manipulations too complex to be described here, the data in an input-output table can be used to estimate all the indirect inputs.

Going one step further, one could use a detailed input-output model to estimate all of the input and production implications of a given increase in total output. The growth pattern might be some simple, across-the-board formula, such as 5 percent growth of "everything," but such uniformity is not required. One could just as well investigate the requirements if all consumer durables increased 5 percent, all nondurables 4 percent, and all consumer services 6 percent—or a more detailed breakdown. The input-output model yields one unique solution to such a problem. It does not yield unique solutions if one starts from the other side, assumes a given increase of resources and asks what will happen to output.

A detailed input-output matrix is a tour de force of descriptive data. There exist estimates of the input-output pattern in the United States for specific past years which include hundreds of separate products and services. As usual, one gains in detail at the sacrifice of ease of manipulation. As description, an input-output model is very simple. To use it requires techniques of matrix algebra which are far beyond the scope of this discussion.

summary

Aggregate production functions can be used to analyze the process of economic growth. More precisely, they are useful in analyzing growth in the supplies of factors and the resulting interplay of output and income distribution. They do not provide any easy way for analyzing changes in technology or in the quality of the inputs, nor for change in the composition of output.

If the production function approximates the Cobb-Douglas form (with factor exponents summing to unity and the state of technology given), the growth rate of output will be equal to an average of the growth rates of the inputs, each weighted by its exponent in the production function. If the growth of capital is proportional to the (previous) growth of output, while the growth of the labor force is exogenously determined, the growth rate of output will tend toward the rate of labor-force growth. A similar result is likely if capital growth is proportional to the rate of profit earned on existing capital, or to the level of profit income. A Ricardian growth model can be derived by including a land-input term in the function, and holding the supply of land constant. If labor-force growth is determined by the relation of actual wage to subsistence wage, and if capital growth is positively related to the profit rate, the system tends perpetually to slow down, though it may never actually cease to grow.

Since the Cobb-Douglas function implies unitary elasticity of factor substitution, the proportional share of each factor remains constant, and equal to its exponent in the production function. Variations in distributive shares can be analyzed by using a more complex CES (constant elasticity of substitution) form of the production function.

The Harrod-Domar model is a production function expressed in terms of only one input, capital, and based on the assumption that the marginal relationship between capital stock and output is constant. The input-output model of production stresses the extent to which the output of one industry becomes the input of another. By assuming fixed input proportions, the input-output model can be used to trace through all the impacts on supplier industries which result from a change in the production of some final end product.

TERMS AND CONCEPTS

1. Harrod-Domar model
2. Input-output model

QUESTIONS AND PROBLEMS

1. A Harrod-Domar production function might be written in the form $Q = a + bK$ where a and b are constants, Q is total output, and K is total capital stock. Identify the marginal output-capital ratio (which is also the implied marginal product of capital). Why is it claimed that the Harrod-Domar model neglects diminishing returns?

2. If the true production function approximates the Cobb-Douglas form (using labor and capital as the inputs), prove that a Harrod-Domar model will be descriptively accurate as long as capital and labor grow at the same rate.

3. Assume an aggregate production function takes the form $Q = K^{3/10}L^{7/10}$. What will be the shares of labor and capital in the total output? Illustrate (by choosing specific values for capital and labor) that the proportional factor shares are not altered by changes in factor supplies or factor prices (provided equilibrium conditions are maintained), and explain how this constancy comes about.

4. "Using aggregate production functions to analyze economic growth tends to leave aside the most important elements contributing to the growth process." Why could this accusation be made?

international trade between
competitive economies

The concepts and techniques we have developed are extensively used in the theory of international economic activities. This chapter is designed to illustrate how this is done, with particular reference to the use of production-possibilities and indifference curves.

Our analysis follows somewhat the same pattern as that of Chapter 7. There we began with a community of self-sufficient farmers, then introduced the possibility of a market economy. The result was the emergence of a more efficient pattern of economic organization. Now we assume that there exist two countries, each of which is initially self-sufficient and cut off from international trade. Then we introduce the possibility of trade and see what happens.

We assume conditions of pure competition in product and factor markets, with large numbers of buyers and sellers, homogeneous products in each industry, and free entry into each industry and occupation within each country. Each country has its own monetary unit. There is no mobility of productive factors from one country to another. We limit our analysis to cases involving only two countries and two commodities.

In order for international trade to take place, it must be profitable for individuals to acquire goods in one country and dispose of them in the other. Such profitable opportunities arise when the relative prices of the commodities differ between countries by an amount sufficient to cover the costs of transporting them. For simplicity, we will assume transfer costs are insignificant.

Suppose our two countries are Thailand and Japan, the respective monetary units are the baht and the yen, and the two commodities are rice and cloth. If the initial price ratio in Japan differs from that in Thailand, the possibility of profitable trade exists. Suppose under initial conditions of national self-sufficiency the money prices are as follows:

	Thailand	Japan
Rice, bu	30 baht	10 yen
Cloth, sq yd	20 baht	3 yen
Ratio (P_R/P_C)	1.50	3.33

Since the two countries initially have no international economic relations, their national monetary units have no foreign-exchange rate. We do not know how many baht it costs to buy one yen. So long as individual traders are prepared to deal in both commodities, however, no foreign-exchange market or rate is necessary to permit advantageous trade.

We have already noted that the real cost of one product is the amount of other products one has to sacrifice in order to get it. In competitive equilibrium, the price of any product measures that sacrifice, and the ratio of any pair of prices measures the marginal rate of transformation between those products. In our example, the real cost of rice can be expressed in terms of units of cloth. The real cost of a unit of rice in Thailand is $1\frac{1}{2}$ units of cloth, while in Japan it is $3\frac{1}{3}$ units of cloth. Conversely, the real cost of a unit of cloth in Thailand is $\frac{2}{3}$ of a unit of rice, while in Japan it is $\frac{3}{10}$ of a unit of rice.

Whichever measure of real cost one uses, it is clear that the real cost of rice is lower in Thailand than in Japan and that the real cost of cloth is lower in Japan than in Thailand. From this condition it follows that traders would find it advantageous to acquire cloth in Japan and exchange it for rice in Thailand, then bring the rice to Japan for sale.

Suppose a trader begins with 9,000 yen in Japan. He can acquire 3,000 square yards of cloth, which he can sell for 60,000 baht in Thailand. With this money he can buy 2,000 bushels of Thai rice, ship it to Japan, and sell it for 20,000 yen. Not a bad deal—11,000 net profit beyond his initial investment of 9,000 yen.

Similar opportunities confront the trader who begins in Thailand. A trader with 18,000 baht can buy 600 bushels of rice in Thailand. This can be sold in Japan for

6,000 yen. With that sum, the trader can buy 2,000 units of cloth, which can be sold in Thailand for 40,000 baht. Note that the ultimate revenues of the sellers bear the same proportion to their initial outlays, for 20,000 to 9,000 equals 40,000 to 18,000.

principle of comparative advantage

It is not the absolute money price of one commodity which determines whether it can advantageously be imported or exported. Without a foreign-exchange rate we cannot determine whether the money cost of rice is higher in Japan or in Thailand. Rather, one must compare the price *ratio* of two commodities in one country with the price *ratio* in the other. Such a comparison gives rise to the principle of *comparative advantage*. The country with the lower opportunity cost for a product (measured in units of the other product which must be sacrificed to obtain it) tends to have a comparative advantage in that product. Thailand has a comparative advantage in rice, since the real cost of rice in Thailand is only $1\frac{1}{2}$ units of cloth, compared to $3\frac{1}{3}$ units in Japan. Japan has a comparative advantage in the production of cloth, which has a real cost in Japan of only $\frac{3}{10}$ of a bushel of rice, compared to $\frac{2}{3}$ of a bushel in Thailand.

In the real world, there are many countries and many commodities. Thus it is not so simple to express the real cost of any one commodity merely by comparing it to one other commodity. In the real world, international trade is undertaken by traders on the basis of the money costs of individual commodities, adjusted by the appropriate foreign-exchange rates. However, the money price of any commodity in competitive equilibrium remains a measure of its real cost. And the actions of traders will still tend to follow the pattern illustrated by our oversimplified example.

price and quantity adjustments

Once trade is undertaken, it will tend to have an effect on the prices of commodities within each country. Traders are buying cloth in Japan and selling it in Thailand. This action will tend to raise the price of cloth in Japan and lower it in Thailand. Similarly, traders are buying rice in Thailand and selling it in Japan. This will tend to raise the price of rice in Thailand and lower it in Japan.

The probable result is that when the volume of trade has reached a certain level, the difference in relative prices and costs which made trade profitable will be virtually eliminated (except for a small gap which permits the traders to cover expenses and earn a normal profit on their investment).

There will probably be additional repercussions. The added demand for cloth in Japan will tend to encourage greater production of cloth there, while in Thailand the inflow of imported cloth will tend to cause a lowering of cloth production. On the other hand, Thailand will tend to produce more rice than before, while Japan will produce less rice than before. Factors of production tend to shift accordingly. In Japan, resources tend to move from rice production into cloth production, while in Thailand the shift moves in the opposite direction.

How far will production change, as compared to the initial situation of self-sufficiency? What will be the equilibrium ratio of prices, toward which both countries tend? What quantities of the two products will be imported and exported, when the new equilibrium is reached? And how will prices of factors of production be affected? All of these are questions with which the theory of international trade has been concerned. To deal with them, we resort to our favorite analytical principles, supply and demand.

indifference-curve analysis

The conditions relating to product supply in each country can be represented by the production-possibilities curve (for two commodities) or by some corresponding mathematical function (for any number of commodities). And the conditions of demand can be represented by a set of community-indifference curves (recognizing the limitations of this device). As usual, we assume one given condition of technology and organizational skill, factor supplies, and tastes and preferences.

Figure 18-1 shows a hypothetical initial equilibrium situation for Thailand. Output and consumption of the two commodities are originally equal at the point e, where there is tangency between the production-possibilities curve and an indifference curve. At that point, the price ratio is equal to the slope of both curves, such that $P_C/P_R = \frac{2}{3}$.

Suppose now that Thailand has the opportunity to trade with Japan, and that the Japanese price ratio of 10 to 3 would continue to prevail no matter how much rice Thailand sold nor how much cloth Thailand bought. We can show this possibility by drawing a new price line tangent to Thailand's production-possibilities curve but with a slope of 3 to 10.

If this price ratio is available to producers, they will move to point p, producing more rice and reducing the output of cloth. As long as Thai rice can be traded for Japanese cloth at this price ratio, consumers in Thailand can consume at any point along that new price line tangent to p. The price line represents a sort of "consumption-possibilities curve." Given the initial combination of goods identified at point p, consumers can obtain 10 more units of cloth for each 3 units of rice they are willing to give up—if the price ratio does remain unchanged. Consumers will move along the price line to the highest possible indifference curve—to the point of tangency identified as c. Thai consumers now consume more cloth than before, but less rice. Rice production in Thailand now exceeds Thailand's rice

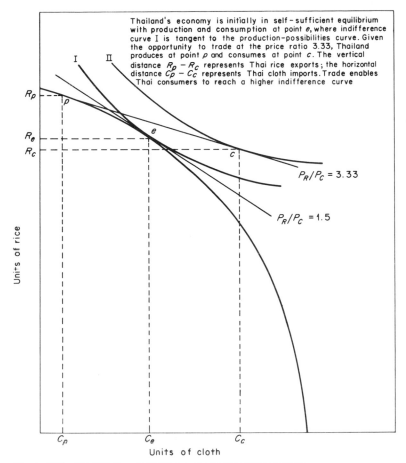

Figure 18-1 Thailand's production and consumption pattern.

consumption; the difference is exported to Japan. Thai cloth consumption now exceeds Thai cloth production; the difference is imported from Japan. And the happy Thai consumers are able to reach a higher indifference curve.

However, we know that the price ratio of 10 to 3 will not be sustained. Instead, the price ratio will tend to settle somewhere between the two initial ratios. Is there any way to find the equilibrium price ratio? It is the price ratio which equates supply and demand. This means that production and consumption decisions in the two countries must be mutually consistent. The quantity of rice produced in Thailand must equal Thai consumption plus exports, and Thai exports must equal Japanese imports, which equal the excess of Japanese consumption over Japanese rice production. There are similar relations for cloth production, consumption, imports, and exports.

TABLE 18-1

		Rice				
	THAILAND			JAPAN		
P_R/P_C	Output	Con-sumption	Export	Output	Con-sumption	Import
3.33	760	639	121	566	566	0
2.40	738	643	95	538	581	43
2.10	722	646	76	522	591	69
2.06	720	647	73	520	593	73
2.00	715	648	67	515	598	83
1.50	665	665	00	466	629	163

		Cloth				
	THAILAND			JAPAN		
P_R/P_C	Output	Con-sumption	Import	Output	Con-sumption	Export
3.33	49	449	400	231	231	0
2.40	108	336	228	309	204	105
2.10	144	303	159	345	200	145
2.06	148	298	150	349	199	150
2.00	158	292	134	359	192	167
1.50	244	244	0	443	200	243

If we know the quantities which each country will produce and consume, we can draw up a numerical table showing the potential imports and exports which would be forthcoming at each price ratio. This would in turn serve as a double-barreled supply-demand schedule, from which we locate the equilibrium position. Table 18-1 shows a hypothetical example of such a table.

The output data are derived from a set of production-possibilities functions.[1] For each price ratio, one can identify the output combination on the production-possibilities curve at which the marginal rate of transformation is equal to (the inverse of) that price ratio. To obtain consumption figures, construct a tangent

---

[1] Specifically, the functions used are

$$\text{Thailand:} \quad R^2 + 400C + C^2 = 600{,}000$$
$$\text{Japan:} \quad R^2 + 400R + C^2 = 600{,}000$$

to the point of production and extend it until it is tangent to an indifference curve. The latter point of tangency identifies the consumption quantities.[2]

In our example, equilibrium is reached when the price of rice is 2.06 times the price of cloth. At that ratio, the amount of rice export which Thailand supplies is equal to the amount which Japan demands for import. The amount of cloth export offered by Japan is equal to the amount demanded by Thailand for import. And for each bushel of rice moving in one direction 2.06 square yards of cloth move in the other direction.

The outcome for the two countries is shown in Figure 18-2. Each country was originally at point E, where the production-possibilities curve is tangent to a domestic indifference curve. At the new price ratio, each shifts its production to the point P on the production-possibilities curve. Japan produces less rice and more cloth; Thailand produces more rice and less cloth. Consumption in each country shifts to point C, where the new price line, drawn tangent to point P, is tangent to an indifference curve. In each case, consumers are able to reach a higher indifference curve.

reciprocal demand curves

Because international trade involves at least two commodities being exchanged for each other, ordinary demand and supply schedules cannot easily be used. Instead, economists employ a device developed by Francis Edgeworth and Alfred Marshall, called the *reciprocal demand curve*. Each point on a country's reciprocal demand curve indicates its desired imports and desired exports at one particular price ratio. Thus when $P_R/P_C = 2.4$, we find Thailand's desired rice exports to be 95 and desired cloth imports to be 228. Connecting all such points yields Thailand's reciprocal-demand curve. Note that a straight line drawn from the origin through a point on the curve has a slope equal to the price ratio represented by that point. Curves for both countries are shown in Figure 18-3. Each country's desired imports and exports are derived from the sort of information contained in Table 18-1.

The original price ratios in the separate countries act as limits. Japan will not export cloth if P_R/P_C exceeds 3.33, and Thailand will not export rice if the ratio falls below 1.5. The two countries' desired imports and exports are mutually consistent only at the equilibrium price ratio of 2.06, as shown by the intersection of the two reciprocal demand curves. The equilibrium price ratio itself is indicated by the slope of the line from the origin through the point of intersection, and the quantities traded are identified by the dimensions of that point.

In the real world, we would not expect complete equalization of price ratios between the countries. They would continue to differ from each other, in long-

---

[2] Thai indifference curves are assumed to take the form $(R - 502)C = k$; Japan's are $(R - 496)C = k$.

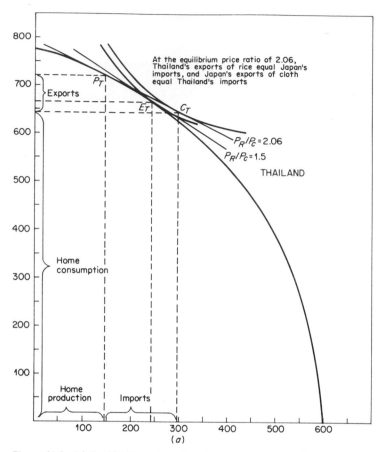

Figure 18-2 (a) Equilibrium international exchange: Thailand.

run competitive equilibrium, by the amount of transportation costs and import or export taxes levied by the trading countries. The higher such expenses, the smaller would be the volume of trade corresponding to any given set of production and demand conditions in the individual countries.

bases for trade

We have seen that the basis for profitable trade exists if the price ratio in one country differs sufficiently from the price ratio in the other. There are three principal conditions which might cause such a difference in the price ratios, as follows:

1. Difference in the production function between the two countries. The countries may employ different technology or organization. However, in the long

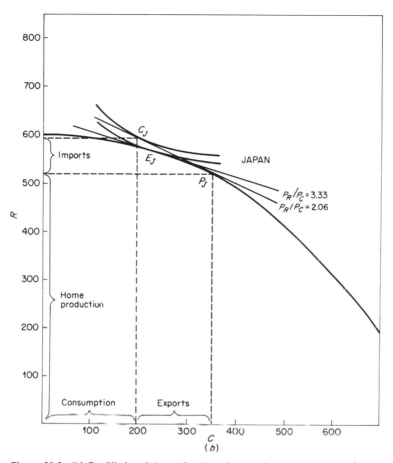

Figure 18-2 (b) Equilibrium international exchange: Japan.

run each country would tend to adopt the superior methods of production as knowledge of them spreads.

2. Difference in supplies of productive resources. Even if two countries have the same technological development, their production-possibilities curves will differ if factor supplies are different in the two countries. Some factors of production are better adapted for producing rice, others for producing cloth. Thailand and Japan may differ in climate and soil conditions, and in the relative amount of labor compared to the amount of land. Historically, much international trade has involved products of agriculture or mining. Such trade often arises because of differences in climate and natural resources.

3. Differences in consumer preferences. Even if two countries had identical production-possibilities curves, initial price ratios could differ if there were differences in consumer preferences between countries.

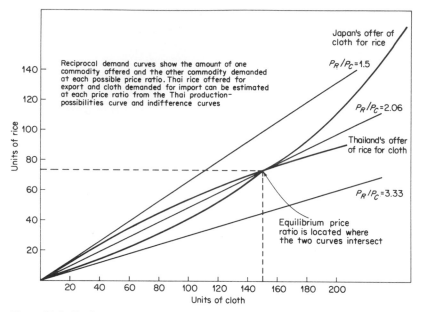

Figure 18-3 Reciprocal demand curves and international equilibrium.

gains from trade

Figure 18-2 indicates that specialization and trade between Japan and Thailand enable both countries to reach a higher consumer indifference curve. If we examine the figures in Table 18-1, we find that the total output of both commodities is increased by specialization and trade. Output of rice increases from 1,231 units before trade to 1,240 after, and output of cloth increases from 475 units to 497. This increase comes about as the result of specialization, through which each country employs its resources in producing more of the commodity in which it has a comparative advantage.

The extent to which the trading countries share in the benefits of greater efficiency depends on the relative prices of the commodities, on the "terms of trade." The higher the equilibrium price of rice, the greater the relative gain for Thailand and the smaller the gain for Japan.

However, not all persons in the trading countries necessarily benefit from specialization and trade. Trade may alter the distribution of income, through its influence on the relative prices of factors of production.

trade and factor prices

Let us assume that production-possibilities curves differ between Japan and Thailand because Japan has a larger quantity of labor relative to the quantity of land. This gives Japan a comparative advantage in cloth, which requires somewhat more labor, and Thailand a comparative advantage in rice, where the land input is more important.

Such a set of conditions in factor markets will be reflected in the relative height of wages and land rents in the two countries. In Japan, wage rates will tend to be somewhat lower, relative to land rents, than in Thailand. When trade is initiated, each country tends to specialize in that product which uses the more abundant resource. This tends to raise the demand for that resource, relative to the less abundant one. Japan, with more abundant labor, tends to specialize in cloth. Greater cloth production increases the demand for labor, while the curtailment of rice production in Japan lowers demand for land. Thus wages rise relative to land rents. In Thailand, land is abundant, and initially rents are low relative to wages. Trade encourages Thailand to specialize in rice, which uses more land. Greater rice production tends to raise demand for land, while curtailment of cloth production lowers demand for labor. Thus wages in Thailand fall, relative to land rents.

Under these conditions, the benefit from trade goes primarily to the factor of production which was initially in most abundant supply. And the scarcer factor may find that its reward is actually reduced by trade. Import restrictions are sometimes imposed at the urging of people who might sustain loss of income because of competition from imports.

many countries, many commodities

In reality, trade takes place between many countries and involves thousands of commodities. However, the same principles of comparative advantage operate to determine the imports and exports of each country and the prices at which they will be traded.

Trade among countries tends to be *multilateral*. We need not expect to find that Thailand's imports from Japan are precisely equal to her exports to Japan. More likely, a country will have an export surplus with some countries, and an import surplus with others. The country which is Thailand's best customer for rice may not be the best source of supply for the commodities which Thailand wants to import.

However, if multilateral trade is to occur freely and efficiently, there must be some sort of money to serve as a medium of payment. Thailand must be able to sell exports in one area and obtain some generally acceptable medium of payment which can be used to buy machinery somewhere else. Traditionally, gold fulfilled this role. In more recent times, American dollars or British pounds have served as international money, usually in the form of checking deposits of banks. However, any nation's monetary unit can enter into international exchange, through the operations of a foreign-exchange market.

foreign-exchange rates and practices

Import and export operations may give rise to transactions in which one national monetary unit is exchanged for another. If a Thai firm specializes in exporting goods to Japan, the firm will receive its revenues in yen, but it needs to obtain baht to pay its expenses in Thailand. Another Thai firm specializing in imports into Thailand receives baht for its sales, but needs yen to purchase goods in Japan. In the foreign-exchange market, the exporting firm can sell yen and purchase baht, while the importing firm can sell baht and purchase yen. In the absence of government intervention, such buying and selling would tend to produce an equilibrium rate of exchange between baht and yen.

If all foreign-exchange transactions arose from current import and export transactions, the rate of exchange would tend toward the level at which there would exist *purchasing power parity* between Japan and Thailand, in those commodities traded internationally. We have seen that in equilibrium the relative prices of rice and cloth must be the same in both countries. We now add that the equilibrium foreign-exchange rate must be such that the absolute money price of any traded commodity is the same in each country (abstracting from transfer costs). In our example above, we found that the equilibrium price ratio between rice and cloth was 2.06 to 1. Suppose that in Japan rice sells for 20.6 yen per bushel, while cloth sells for 10 yen per square yard. And suppose that in Thailand rice sells for 103 baht per bushel, while cloth is 50 baht per square yard. The ratio between the Thai price and the Japanese price will be equal to the equilibrium exchange rate—in this case, a rate of 1 yen to 5 baht.

This is the equilibrium rate because if the money prices are not equal, the pattern of imports and exports will shift. Only if the money price of each commodity is the same in the various countries (or differs by no more than the costs of transfer) can the existing import-export pattern remain stable.

However, foreign-exchange transactions arise from financial transactions as well as trade. In particular, a country's currency may be purchased by people who want to make investments in that country. Within that country, people may be purchasing foreign money in order to pay interest or dividends on existing investments.

The various sources and uses of foreign exchange are brought together in tabular form under the name of a country's *balance-of-payments statement.* Each source of foreign exchange (chiefly exports and inflow of foreign capital) constitutes a supply element in the foreign-exchange market. Against this can be set the country's demand for foreign exchange, to buy imports, repay foreign debts, pay interest on loans, etc.

If the foreign-exchange rate is free to fluctuate, the equilibrium exchange rate would simply be the rate which would equate total supply of foreign exchange with total demand. However, most countries do not permit the foreign-exchange value of their monetary unit to fluctuate freely. Most countries subscribe to the Articles of Agreement of the International Monetary Fund, under which they agree to keep a stable rate of exchange between their currency unit and gold or the American dollar.

Such a fixed rate may not be an equilibrium rate. If it is not, a country will find itself with a disequilibrium in its international payments. This will cause changes in the country's national money income and in its monetary and financial situation. However, such matters lie outside the scope of this book.

summary

International exchange arises in response to differences in relative prices and real costs between countries. Such price and cost differences may reflect differences in the production functions of the individual countries, either because they do not operate at the same level of technology and organizational skill or because they have different relative supplies of factors of production. International price differences may also reflect differences in the strength of consumer demand for the respective commodities.

Each country tends to export the commodities in which it enjoys a comparative advantage—that is, those commodities which it can produce at a lower real cost (measured by the sacrifice of other products) than can other countries. As in the domestic economy, the profit-seeking activities of individual buyers and sellers will tend to push the input and output pattern of each country in the direction of such a position. In the process, the total quantity of world output and real income can be increased.

Given the production-possibilities functions of the individual countries, and the pattern of consumer demand, it is possible to analyze a country's desired production and consumption, imports and exports, at each possible price ratio. Production will tend to occur at the point on the production-possibilities curve where the marginal rate of transformation is equal to the (inverse) price ratio. Quantities consumed can be identified by constructing a tangent to the production-possibilities curve at the point of production and extending it to the point where it is tangent to a community-indifference curve. Desired imports and exports are then identified by the difference between consumption and production of each product. If we plot the combinations of desired imports and exports at each price ratio, we can construct a reciprocal demand curve for each country. Equilibrium in a two-country, two-commodity case occurs where the reciprocal-demand curves intersect.

International trade affects prices of factors of production. If each country tends to export products which utilize its relatively abundant factor, that factor will enjoy a higher relative price than would be true in the absence of trade.

TERMS AND CONCEPTS

1. Principle of comparative advantage
2. Principle of purchasing power parity in foreign-exchange rates
3. Reciprocal demand curve

QUESTIONS AND PROBLEMS

1. Assume that, in the absence of international trade, the price of rice in Thailand is 20 baht per unit and the price of cloth is 10 baht per unit. In Japan the price of rice is 30 yen per unit and the price of cloth is 10 yen per unit. There are no substantial costs or barriers to trade. Prove that a basis for profitable trade exists, and show which commodity each country would tend to export. What would trade do to the prices of cloth and rice?

2. Explain how the imposition of an import tax would tend to reduce a country's total real output (income), assuming it was initially in free-trade full-employment equilibrium. Explain how some people in the country might gain an increase in income as a result of the import tax.

3. It is sometimes asserted that the movement of commodities is a substitute for movement of factors of production. In other words, commodity trade tends to produce effects similar to those which would occur if factors of production were highly mobile between countries. Evaluate this assertion.

4. In Chapter 3 we used a box diagram to show how two individuals might both benefit by exchanging existing stocks of commodities. A similar construction can be used to show that total production can be increased if two countries shift from self-sufficiency to trade. Using the assumptions underlying Table 18-1, construct such a diagram, comparing the position of the two countries before and after trade, using their production-possibilities curves.

5. Sketch the combination of equations or equilibrium conditions involved in deriving a set of reciprocal demand curves from production-possibilities functions and community indifference functions.

limitations of the competitive model as welfare ideal and as description

We have limited our exposition to conditions of pure competition, assuming markets with large numbers of buyers and sellers and easy entry. These are not realistic assumptions, but they have two major advantages. One is that by such simplification we can obtain a level of generality, viewing the economy as a whole, which would be difficult to achieve by other means. Further, the competitive model helps us to identify conditions of economic efficiency in the allocation of resources. In particular, a purely competitive economy in general equilibrium could represent a situation qualifying as a Pareto optimum. This would mean that no opportunities remained which would permit making some people better off without making others worse off. Productive resources would be efficiently used, so that the quantity of output would be the largest possible with existing technology and managerial skill. The composition of output would be adjusted to the strength of consumer demand. These conclusions result from the fact that the price of each product is equal to average and marginal cost (and is the same to all buyers) and that the price of each input is equal to the value of its marginal product. Further, the marginal product of each input is the same in all uses, and the marginal rate of substitution between inputs is equal to the (inverse) ratio of their prices. However, even if a condition of Pareto optimality were achieved, one might still find fault with it. Further, there are reasons why a purely competitive equilibrium might fail of being a Pareto optimum. Finally, it is doubtful that conditions of competitive equilibrium would prove feasible in the real world. This chapter explores these last three considerations.

consumer sovereignty

It is sometimes claimed that a purely competitive economic system would be good because it would provide for *consumer sovereignty*, in the sense that the composition of output would be optimally adjusted to the strength of consumer preferences and consumer demand. However, this claim can be criticized on several grounds.

It can be argued that consumer preferences, as revealed in consumer-purchase decisions, are not a good guide to the proper composition of output. Social critics note that consumers may be heavily influenced by advertising, by fads, desires for conspicuous consumption, and other irrational influences. At best, consumers' knowledge about products is incomplete; at worst, they may be misled by deliberate falsehood in advertising. For such reasons, critics argue that consumer spending does not reflect what consumers really want.

It may be very desirable for government to punish untruth in advertising. The fact that consumer choices even then might be volatile and perhaps irrational is not sufficient to prove that some alternative standard would produce a better pattern of resource allocation. A competitive market economy may be a good environment for a learning process. Given the opportunity to shop around, to exercise repetitive choices, consumers have the opportunity to learn from their mistakes and avoid repeating them.

Of course, the phrase "consumer sovereignty" is misleading, since it implies that consumers possess the initiative in getting what they want. In fact, they must choose from the alternatives offered by business firms. At any given time, it is doubtful that business firms will have thought of and experimented with all the things consumers might be willing to buy; but at least the competitive market gives firms an incentive to try.

consumption and income distribution

Much criticism of the market economy has been based on the claim that it produces the wrong things because it produces for the wrong people. What a wicked system, say the critics, to lavish resources on luxuries for rich people while at the same time poor people lack the necessities of life.

This is at root a criticism of the distribution of money income. Each consumer's desires and preferences are weighted in the market economy by the amount of money which he can spend. Rich people can spend more; thus their preferences will carry more weight per person in decisions concerning how much to produce of one product versus another.

Whether one pattern of income distribution is good or bad is a matter of one's value judgments; there is no scientific criterion of social justice. The criteria of Pareto optimality stop short at this point; they concern the possibility of making some people better off without making others worse off. Some economists have attempted to extend the criterion by using some form of the *compensation principle*. They argue that a change is advantageous if those who gain by it can compensate the losers and still have something left. This is not a useless amendment, but it does not help much in deciding issues such as the appropriate way of raising additional revenue from the income tax.

It is quite possible that some criteria concerning income distribution are very widely accepted in the society, and that voluntary private action might bring about desirable results. Those persons who feel that everyone should have enough to eat may be willing to back this up with philanthropic effort. However, it may be necessary, or more appropriate, to use government action as a method of making effective the consensus on income distribution. The trouble is that such consensus may not exist; if each person is convinced he should receive a larger share of the national income than the average, this is hardly the basis for any workable government program.

Some economists have tried to work around the problem by postulating the existence of a *social welfare function*, which is simply an ordering or ranking of different social conditions as better or worse. Such a function is not restricted to income distribution. The question remains, however, whether such a function can be derived from the preferences and desires of the public, or whether it must be conjured up out of thin air.

At the opposite extreme, many take the view that the only objective way to evaluate income distribution is in terms of its contribution to the other objectives of the system. This tends to focus on the incentive aspect of income distribution. If the system promotes growth, productivity, and efficiency, perhaps one need not worry much about whether it is just and fair as well.

products desired but not profitable

Another problem in adjusting private production to consumer desires concerns services which consumers desire but from which no private firm can earn a profit. Each potential consumer might be willing to pay a price sufficient to cover costs, rather than go without. The problem may arise because it is impossible (or undesirable) to restrict the benefit of the service to those who have paid for it. If "free-loaders" can benefit without paying, each customer may be unwilling to pay except on condition that others who benefit also pay.

Consider the case of a lighthouse placed to guide shipping. Each ship stands to benefit from the operation of the lighthouse, whether its owners have paid a share of its costs or not. Of course, in the short run the potential benefit might be great enough to induce one shipping company to construct and operate the lighthouse, even if others might benefit from it. However, this would give an advantage to nonpaying firms, whose number might increase until revenues were merely sufficient to cover costs exclusive of the lighthouse, and the firm operating the lighthouse would suffer losses correspondingly.

Even if it were possible to exclude nonpaying beneficiaries, it would be economically wasteful to do so. There is no need to ration the services of an operating lighthouse, because their use by one beneficiary does not reduce the amount available for others. The marginal cost of flashing the light on an additional ship is zero.

Radio and television broadcasts are the modern counterpart of the lighthouse. In a given locality, one family's decision to turn on the set does not reduce the signal strength available for the neighbors. And indeed, the tradition of American broadcasting has been that anyone owning a receiving set is entitled to receive the broadcasts, without paying the broadcasters. Advertisers have taken over the role of paying the bills, with the result that the quantity and quality of broadcasting services have no clear relationship to consumer preference. Yet it is not easy to demonstrate that any feasible alternative yields superior results.

Many of the most fundamental functions of government have this sort of collective quality. If an economic system is to function efficiently, there must be a system for maintaining law and order. Individuals must be protected against physical assault from others. There must be a set of rules respecting such fundamentals as property rights and the obligations of contract. The benefits to members of the economic system from law and order are potentially very great. Yet it is difficult to limit the benefits of law and order to persons who have paid for them through market transactions, and socially inefficient to limit the benefits in such fashion even if it were possible.

One of the most important activities in this category consists of the search for new knowledge through research. In the twentieth century, economic growth and progress have come to depend increasingly on advances in science and engineering. New discoveries in pure science have brought forth improvements in such fields as chemistry, drugs, and electronics. Yet once new knowledge has been developed, the maximum social benefit may result from having it made available without cost to all who seek it. No rationing problem arises: my learning about polymerization does not reduce the amount of knowledge of it left for you.

But if new knowledge is made open to everyone, what reward accrues to the discoverer? What incentive exists to see that an appropriate amount of effort is devoted to research? In a free market, the amount of resources devoted to pure research is likely to be less than the socially optimal amount. Governments have attempted to deal with this problem by granting patents to inventors, giving the inventor a limited monopoly over his invention. This adds to the incentive to perform research, but it is not an ideal solution, since it restricts the use of new knowledge. Anyway, the most fundamental advances in pure science do not result directly in patentable inventions.

social versus private costs and benefits

The cases we have just considered illustrate that the allocation of resources in a free-market economy can be ideal only if there is close correspondence between the *private* costs and benefits, as perceived by producers and consumers, and the *social* costs and benefits applicable to the society as a whole. It is the private costs and benefits upon which producers and consumers act in market behavior. These are not always identical with the social costs and benefits.

It is possible that a product or service imposes costs on the society which need not be borne by the producers. Pollution of air and water by industrial firms is a good example. Another would be the erosion and potential flood damage to adjoining land which can result from improper conservation practices in farming or forestry. Such divergence between social and private cost may mean that producers are not using the technique of production which is optimal from a social standpoint. It may also mean that the product which gives rise to the added social cost is being produced in an excessive amount. If consumers had to pay a price for it which covered all costs, they would not buy so much of it.

On the other hand, there may also be divergence between the private benefits from a product or service and the total benefit to the society. Such divergence often involves so-called neighborhood or third-person effects, in which transactions affect people who are not directly parties to them. The pleasantness and beauty of the physical environment in which we live are greatly affected by what our neighbors do. My enjoyment is increased if my neighbors have attractive homes, well cared for. My enjoyment may be greatly reduced if someone decides to use the lot next door for a garbage dump or a smelly factory. The use of zoning, through which government restrictions are imposed on urban land use, results directly from perception of such neighborhood effects.

Divergence between social and private benefits is often present in situations involving health and education. Each person's health can be affected by the health of the persons with whom he associates. Likewise, each of us stands to benefit as other members of the society become better educated. They will also tend to become more productive, and since productivity tends to be contagious, each of us may find his own marginal productivity increased. Research activity, previously mentioned, is likely to yield social benefits far greater than the private benefits which individual research workers can expect in a market economy.

Products or services which give rise to social benefits to persons not directly involved in the transaction will tend to be underproduced. If individuals must purchase all their health and education services at market price, for example, the total amount of resources devoted to those functions will probably be less than the socially optimum amount.

The phrase *external economies* is sometimes used in discussing deviations between private and social costs and benefits. One might speak of external economies of consumption in a case where one person's consumption confers added benefits on others. External economies often occur in production when one firm performs activities which benefit other firms but for which it cannot collect from them. An important example is the training of employees. A firm with a good training program may find itself losing workers to a rival which hires only experienced people and perhaps can afford to pay them more because it does not incur the cost of training them.

Certain products, such as alcohol and narcotics, may give rise to external diseconomies of consumption, reflecting the harm the drunk or addict may inflict through automobile accidents, crime, or neglect of family responsibilities.

dependency

A large number of persons in any society are dependent children. Their long-run welfare is influenced by actions taken by their parents, affecting their physical health and nutrition, their education, their moral and psychological development. Dependency places several gaps between action and reward. Costs of feeding, educating, and loving the children must be borne now by the parents. Benefits may come chiefly in the future, chiefly to the children. And the amount of benefit to be expected from any given effort or expense is highly uncertain. There is no reason to expect optimum attention to child welfare in a free-market economy.

consumption, saving, and investment

One of the most important resource-allocation problems concerns the division of output between present consumption and capital goods. It is hard to identify an optimum level for saving and investment, since the outcome affects the distribution of benefits as between persons currently living and those who will be living at various times in the future. Even without this consideration, it seems likely that when they look back on their lives, many people find they have saved less than they would like to have saved. The risks and uncertainties attending investment probably aggravate the tendency to save and invest too little. Certainly, no automatic tendency exists in a free market to give adequate attention to the welfare of persons yet unborn. Some countries—nineteenth-century Western

Europe and the United States—bequeathed a very rich economic legacy to their posterity. The high per capita incomes of present inhabitants of those areas are in large degree a result of the capital formation and technical progress carried out by preceding generations. But elsewhere, and notably in China, India, and the Near East, those who lived in the nineteenth century left little except a large posterity to divide a meager output.

potential role of government

The foregoing identifies situations in which a competitive equilibrium would fail to be ideal from the standpoint of economic welfare. Such situations offer guidance to activities which might beneficially be carried on by government even in a world of competitive equilibrium. Government might appropriately act to change the distribution of income, assuming that there exists some criterion of what is a good pattern of distribution. Also, government might appropriately act to insure that private advertising does not falsify information; it might go further and make tests and evaluations of products to aid consumers in their choices. Government might undertake functions which people want but for which it would be impossible or undesirable to charge a price. Government could (either by direct production or by taxes and subsidies) encourage greater output of things for which social benefits exceed private benefits and smaller output of things for which social costs exceed private costs.

This is not to assume that anything government chooses to do in these areas will necessarily be good. We consider this problem at greater length in Chapter 24. Before we reach that point, however, it is necessary to turn to another criticism of the competitive model—its departures from realism.

the prevalence of disequilibrium

Our welfare judgments relating to the competitive economy were all based on the assumption that equilibrium conditions existed. Yet there is good reason to believe that even if an economic system were characterized by pure competition, it would be in a condition of disequilibrium most of the time. Static equilibrium analysis does not tell us anything about how long it takes to reach equilibrium; it merely establishes the conditions of equilibrium and identifies the situation which would meet those conditions.

Two types of possible disequilibrium warrant particular attention. The first is structural disequilibrium, which involves relative imbalance between one sector of the economy and another. Because of shifts in supply and demand conditions, perhaps because of technological change, it often occurs that one sector of the economy contains a relative excess of resources, while another sector is deficient.

Individual factors of production may have differing marginal products in different sectors. In developed economies, agriculture is often the sector which contains an excessive amount of resources. Deficiency may exist in heavy industry, or in services such as medical care and education.

In theory, such misallocations tend to correct themselves. Firms in the overextended sector incur losses and drop out of the industry, while new firms flock into the deficient sector. Factor incomes are below average in the overextended sector and above average in the deficient sector. But in reality, resource transfer may be very slow. Fixed capital investments may take a long time to wear out. The individual workers in the overextended sector may lack the knowledge or the willingness to move themselves occupationally or geographically. Small firms employing chiefly family labor may be particularly slow to leave an overcrowded industry. Most of their costs may be implicit costs of nonwage family labor and of owners' own land and capital. Failure to earn revenues which cover these implicit costs does not drive the firm out of business.

Structural disequilibrium between one productive sector and another may impose painful burdens on producers in the overextended sector. Situations of this sort tend to give rise to petitions for government assistance to protect or support the injured producers. Governments may undertake measures which soften the blow, but these sometimes impede the movement towards a new equilibrium. Protective tariffs and agricultural price supports have sometimes had this tendency. From a welfare standpoint, the petitions for assistance may be quite meritorious. They often come from producers whose suffering arises from events entirely beyond their own control. It is a challenge to develop public policies which might protect from loss former producers in an overextended area such as agriculture, while at the same time promoting a better adjustment of resource allocation. Government subsidies to aid in moving workers geographically and in training them for different employments might perform both functions.

Structural disequilibrium may also arise because factors of production are not combined in an appropriate manner. In particular, the form of capital goods may be inappropriate to the number of workers. One might find an underdeveloped country in which highly mechanized construction equipment provides jobs for only a few people, while in rural areas farm production is hampered by lack of simple hand implements.

The resolution of structural disequilibrium may be impeded by intrinsic imperfections in the markets for factors of production. Factor supplies lack homogeneity, and are strongly affected by a long-run orientation in which risk and uncertainty are large. In product markets the process of equilibration is greatly helped by the existence of arbitrage, but this is absent from the labor market. Equilibration is also helped when people can shop around, exercise repetitive choices, and learn by trial and error. Factor-market decisions may offer little scope for such actions. In the market for loan funds particularly, the degree of risk and uncertainty is so great that nonprice rationing methods are extensively employed.

The result is that the projects with the highest potential yield do not always receive the needed financing. Projects involving less risk or uncertainty may be preferred, even if they have lower actual payoff.

Even if funds are available, entrepreneurs may be deterred from investing by unwillingness to take risks. A large firm with many projects can afford to play the percentages; the fact that some projects end up as losses is compensated by the gains from others. But a small firm may be wiped out by a single loss; consequently it may avoid investments where the risk of large loss is present even if the mathematical expectation of gain is high.

In discussions of underdeveloped countries, attention has been given to problems of structural disequilibrium viewed in terms of a problem of *dual economy*. Many underdeveloped countries display sharply contrasting sectors. There is often a relatively advanced economic sector, urbanized, using relatively large amounts of capital per worker, where worker and management skills and motivations correspond relatively well to those of developed countries. By contrast, there may also be a relatively backward sector, probably rural, agricultural, marked by stress on noneconomic attitudes and motivations, pursuing subsistence living in a traditional manner. Dualism may be based partly on lack of social integration— differences in language, religion, social caste or class, skin color may impede efforts of workers to move from the backward sector to the advanced. Dualism might also reflect merely lack of knowledge or of desire by workers to make such changes.

In any case, dualism of this sort reflects disequilibrium in factor allocation. Marginal products are not equalized between sectors. The marginal product of labor is likely to be much higher in the advanced sector, with insufficient flow out of the backward sector to achieve equalization. The marginal product of capital, on the other hand, may well be much higher in the backward sector. However, lack of knowledge, and perhaps lack of a good financial system, prevent the transfer of capital into agriculture. With this is likely to go disequilibrium in the form of capital goods. Each dollar's worth of capital may thus employ far fewer workers than it might in another form. Such disequilibrium keeps total output lower than it might be and also creates wide disparities in income distribution which may seem unjust.

Many of these possible departures from equilibrium reflect either a failure to maximize (in the narrow sense) or imperfect knowledge leading to uncertainty and risk. Formal economic analysis has long been criticized for lack of realism in its maximization postulates. At best, these postulates should be regarded as a statement of central tendency. For such a conception to be valid, the central tendency must describe behavior practiced by some of the people some of the time, departures from which are essentially randomly distributed and thus relatively self-canceling. Economic analysis is also largely limited to a world of pseudo-certainty. Strictly speaking, all economic analysis is based on expected utility, expected prices and profits, expected productivity, etc. For determinate analysis, there must be some identifiable link between what people have actually experienced recently and what they expect. Much interesting current research in economics is directed to linking experience with behavior via expectations.

disequilibrium in aggregate demand

Free-market economies have been plagued also with problems arising when the flow of aggregate expenditures for current output has not matched up well with the supply of output available at existing price levels. At times aggregate expenditures have been too great, causing inflation of prices, with resulting distortions in the distribution of incomes and wealth. At other times, aggregate expenditures have been too small, and the result has been unemployment among workers and bankruptcy among business firms and others with fixed-value debts.

Some economists believe that the flow of aggregate expenditures depends largely upon the quantity of money and are convinced that appropriate variation in the quantity of money can keep the flow of aggregate spending at a level appropriate to full employment and stable prices. Others hold the less optimistic view that the instability is inherent in business investment spending in a free-market economy, a kind of spending which in their opinion is not sensitive to monetary conditions. They stress fiscal policy as the more promising remedy.

Traditional economics dismissed the problem, largely on the ground that flexibility of prices would enable the economy to operate at full production and employment regardless of the state of aggregate demand. However, there is no certainty that a free-market economy would tend in the long run toward such an equilibrium. Even if it did, a vast amount of pain and suffering might still be inflicted before the equilibrium was reached. Therefore it seems much more desirable to keep the flow of total spending from getting out of order, if possible, rather than to suffer the pain which may result from prolonged disequilibrium.

The problem of aggregate expenditure has come to occupy a central position in modern economics in developed, industrial countries. In less-developed countries, which are primarily agricultural, the volume of output and employment may be relatively insensitive to the flow of expenditure. A decrease in aggregate spending need not mean a loss of output and employment. Even in such a situation, however, wide variations in total spending may produce instability of the price level with adverse effects on income distribution. Price instability may breed social unrest, especially in an economy where many people owe debts which are fixed in money terms. Fluctuations in the expenditure flow may also upset the balance of international payments. Thus concern for the flow of aggregate expenditures may be proper even in an underdeveloped country.

Most economists regard control of the volume of total expenditures as an important responsibility for government. Some prefer placing the emphasis on fiscal policy, others prefer monetary policy. Either approach can be carried out without involving the government in the details of resource allocation and income distribution.

departures from pure competition

In the real world, it is often the case that the number of buyers and sellers in a market is simply not large enough to fulfill the conditions of pure competition. Two economic elements contribute to this result. The first is economies of large-scale operation. The output at which the firm's average cost is lowest may be relatively large, compared with the output of the industry as a whole. The second element is differentiation. Often the product of one firm is not identical with those of its competitors—or at least consumers do not regard them as perfect substitutes. Individual firms often attempt to create differentiation, either in the product itself or in incidentals such as packaging and service to the customer.

When the individual firm is large, relative to the industry, or when the firm's product is differentiated, the demand curve confronting the firm is likely to be downward sloping. The firm does have some influence over the price it charges. Such conditions require amendments to the analysis we employed in dealing with pure competition. In the next three chapters, we shall explore more fully the analysis of imperfect competition in product and factor markets.

summary

A purely competitive economy, if feasible, would not necessarily produce economically optimum results. The scope of consumer choice would be limited by the degree of entrepreneurial initiative in offering goods for sale. Income distribution in the competitive economy would not necessarily correspond to anyone's ideal standard; yet the composition of output would be influenced by the amounts which various individual families were able to spend. Some products strongly desired might not be produced by private enterprise, because there would be no feasible method of collecting a price from the beneficiaries. Products and services for which private benefit differs from social benefit, or private cost differs from social cost, would not necessarily be produced in optimal amounts.

Even if market conditions of pure competition existed, there is no certainty that the economy would be in equilibrium. If mobility of productive factors is low, resource allocation may be slow to adapt to changes in technology or shifts in demand. The path to optimum allocation may involve heavy interim losses of welfare to persons whose factors services were in the unlucky sectors.

Another type of disequilibrium involves the so-called business cycle. The flow of money expenditures does not automatically achieve a level appropriate for full employment and stable prices if left to purely private determination.

In the real world, many markets are not purely competitive. Imperfection may arise because firms are very large and markets small, or because firms differentiate their products.

TERMS AND CONCEPTS

1. Consumer sovereignty
2. Collective services
3. Social costs, benefits
4. Structural disequilibrium

QUESTIONS AND PROBLEMS

1. Explain why markets for factors of production may be expected to work less well than markets for products.

2. "If firms are subject to extensive economies of scale, pure competition may be impossible." Explain.

3. It is argued that private competitive firms in agriculture or forestry will not necessarily employ the sort of conservation practices which would, if followed by all, be most beneficial to all. Explain why one firm, acting independently, might have little incentive to follow good conservation practices.

4. Explain why the quantity of medical services produced in a society is likely to be below the optimum amount if each consumer has to pay the full market price for the services. Do you think medical services should be available to all without charge? What problems would arise if this were done?

imperfect competition in
product markets: monopoly

Our analysis of pure competition was based on the assumptions that the number of buyers and sellers in each market was so large that no individual buyer or seller could affect the price at which he bought or sold, that each seller's product was identical with that of his competitors, and that entry and departure of firms were relatively easy. When these conditions are not fulfilled, the situation is characterized by imperfect competition. In particular, imperfect competition in product markets refers to situations where the individual firm has some influence over its selling price, either because it is large relative to total market demand for the product or because of differentiation between its product and that of its closest competitors.

Matters such as the number and relative size of firms, the degree of product differentiation, and the ease of entry are all aspects of the *market structure* of a particular industry. We are interested in the ways in which different conditions of market structure may be reflected in different patterns of *behavior* by the firms: for example, their pricing policies, their use of nonprice competition, their possible tendency toward collusion or cutthroat tactics. Finally, having observed how they behave, one may pass judgment on how *well* they behave, with reference to various aspects of *performance:* whether the composition of output reflects the relative strength of consumer desires, whether output is produced efficiently, etc.

Since such variables as number and relative size of firms can take an infinite variety of magnitudes, there is no limit to the potential number of market structures one might consider. As a beginning, however, three prototypes of imperfect product markets are identified. These are monopoly, monopolistic competition, and oligopoly.

monopoly

In formal economic analysis, the term *monopoly* is applied to a situation where there is only one seller of a product and no close substitute for the product. The definition of the product is of considerable importance in this context, and situations of monopoly shade off into situations of monopolistic competition as we examine cases of increasingly close substitution. General Motors is the only producer of Chevrolets, but we consider other makes of car to be close substitutes. A local bus company may be the only one operating in a given territory, but private cars and taxicabs may in fact offer close substitution opportunities. It may be rather arbitrary whether we consider the bus company a monopoly or not.

Although one tends to associate the idea of monopoly with industrial firms employing thousands of workers and operating subject to economies of scale, the monopoly may be a relatively small firm in terms of output and employment. A local physician, lawyer, insurance agent, or barber may possess considerable monopoly power in relation to his main clientele, even while operating on a very small scale in terms of number of persons employed.

Situations of genuine monopoly are relatively infrequent in the modern economy, particularly as transport facilities improve and more people live in cities or suburbs. It could happen, of course, that an individual firm's production function was subject to increasing returns to scale over a very large range of output and that its costs would be lower than those of potential (and smaller) competitors. Even so, its ability to exploit a monopoly position would be limited by the possibility of entry. Situations where one firm of efficient size may be sufficient to supply an entire market have sometimes given rise to the special case of the regulated public utility, which we will analyze subsequently. Complete private monopoly might arise from ownership of the entire source of some critical raw material, such as a mineral ore. And it might result from the use of collusion or cutthroat competitive practices. Where collusion and cutthroat tactics are outlawed, as in the United States, genuine monopoly is infrequent except in situations where government helps the firm to maintain its single-seller status. Patents or franchises may protect a single seller in its position; so may special consideration in the awarding of contracts to sell to the government.

The category of pure monopoly is thus not a category of extensive descriptive relevance any more than the category of pure competition is. However, the logical analysis of the monopoly firm, even if only a theoretical construct, is a further stepping stone toward the analysis of real-firm behavior.

If there is only one seller of a product, the demand schedule confronting that firm is the same as the market demand schedule for that product. The demand curve will be downward sloping. Thus the monopolist can control the price at which he sells. However, the quantity he can sell at any price will depend on the demand schedule. The higher the price he charges, the smaller the quantity of the product buyers will be willing to purchase. The larger the quantity he places on the market, the lower the price he will receive for it.

The fact that a firm enjoys a monopoly position in its product market need not mean that it is a monopoly buyer of inputs. For simplicity we will assume initially that the monopoly firm is buying inputs in competitive conditions. Thus its purchases have no effect on input prices, and it assumes it can purchase any desired quantities at the existing market prices. Under such assumptions, the cost functions of the monopoly are derived in the same manner that we have already analyzed, using the production function and identifying the least-cost input combination for each output level. Later we shall consider the situation where the prices of inputs are affected by the purchases of the firm.

It is possible that the monopolist will charge different prices to different buyers. We shall consider the possibility of price discrimination subsequently. First, we shall assume the monopolist charges the same price to everyone. We want to identify the price which will be most profitable for the monopolist and the quantity which would be associated with it.

marginal revenue

When we analyzed the firm in a purely competitive industry, we concluded that the most profitable output for the firm would be the one at which marginal cost and marginal revenue were equal. The same conclusion is valid for the monopolist. The difference lies in the calculation of marginal revenue. Under pure competition, the individual firm can sell as much as it wishes at the going price. Thus the marginal revenue is equal to the price. For the monopolist, however, the demand curve is downward sloping. To sell a larger output, he must accept a lower price. His marginal revenue depends on the relation between price and quantity along the demand schedule.

Remember that marginal revenue is defined as the change in the firm's total revenue associated with a unit change in output. If the demand schedule confronting the monopolist is given, one can determine the total revenue associated with each level of output. Marginal revenue can be calculated as a finite difference between two points on the total revenue schedule. Or it can be calculated at a

TABLE 20-1

Price	Quantity Demanded	Total Revenue	Marginal Revenue	
			Finite Difference	Derivative
$10	1	$10		$9
			$8	
9	2	18		7
			6	
8	3	24		5
			4	
7	4	28		3
			2	
6	5	30		1
			0	
5	6	30		−1
			−2	
4	7	28		−3
			−4	
3	8	24		−5
			−6	
2	9	18		−7
			−8	
1	10	10		−9

single point by taking the derivative of total revenue with respect to output, assuming that the function is continuous.

Suppose our monopolist is confronted by a demand schedule expressed by the equation $Q = 11 - P$. Table 20-1 illustrates how we can derive the total and marginal revenue schedules from the price-quantity points on the demand schedule.

By multiplying price times quantity, we obtain total revenue. The change in total revenue as we change output gives us one measure of marginal revenue. The increase in output from 2 to 3 units, for instance, increases total revenue from $18 to $24.

To calculate marginal revenue by the derivative method, it is necessary to express total revenue as a function of the quantity of output. Since $TR = P \cdot Q$, we can substitute to obtain $TR = (11 - Q)Q = 11Q - Q^2$. To obtain marginal revenue, we find the first derivative of this:

$$MR = \frac{dTR}{dQ} = 11 - 2Q$$

Marginal revenue is closely related to price-elasticity of demand. If elasticity of demand is high, then the percentage decrease in price will be small for any given percentage increase in quantity. Consequently total revenue will increase sub-stantially, and marginal revenue will be large. But marginal revenue is always less than the price. If elasticity of demand has a coefficient of 1, total revenue is unchanged when output changes; thus marginal revenue is 0. If elasticity of demand is less than 1, a given proportional increase in output causes a larger proportional decrease in price. Total revenue declines, and marginal revenue is negative. If we let e represent the coefficient of price-elasticity of demand (omitting the minus sign), the relationship to marginal revenue can be expressed as follows:

$$MR = P\left(1 - \frac{1}{e}\right)$$

This can be illustrated with the demand schedule $Q = 11 - P$ (which is equivalent to $P = 11 - Q$). The elasticity of the demand schedule is $e = (dQ/dP)(P/Q)$, and since dQ/dP is equal to (minus) 1, the elasticity reduces to

$$e = \frac{P}{Q} = \frac{11 - Q}{Q}$$

Therefore

$$1 - \frac{1}{e} = 1 - \frac{Q}{11 - Q} = \frac{11 - 2Q}{11 - Q}$$

We have already established that $MR = 11 - 2Q$, and our demand schedule itself tells us that $P = 11 - Q$. Therefore,

$$1 - \frac{1}{e} = \frac{MR}{P} \qquad \text{and} \qquad MR = P\left(1 - \frac{1}{e}\right)$$

As e becomes larger, we approach the situation of pure competition, and marginal revenue becomes closer and closer to the price. Test your understanding by select-ing a point in the table and seeing whether the marginal revenue and elasticity are related as the formula indicates.

Geometrically, we can draw a marginal revenue curve corresponding to any given demand curve and lying below it in the diagram. If the demand curve is a straight line, the construction is easy. The marginal revenue curve is also a straight line and is always half the horizontal distance to the demand curve. This situation is shown in Figure 20-1.

This geometric result can be illustrated also by the demand schedule $Q = 11 - P$. We have seen that $P = 11 - Q$, while $MR = 11 - 2Q$. Thus the quantity associated with a price of $5 would be 6 units, while the quantity associated with a marginal revenue of $5 would be 3 units.

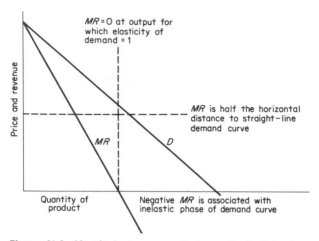

Figure 20-1 Marginal revenue and demand schedules for monopolist.

maximum-profit price and output

If the monopolist is operating at a price-quantity position where marginal revenue is greater than marginal cost, he can increase his profits by increasing output, even if this requires that he lower the price. Increased output will be advantageous only when the demand has sufficiently high price elasticity so that the increase in quantity sold is sufficient to offset both the decrease in price and the increase in total cost associated with the quantity increase. As output is expanded, marginal revenue will tend to fall, and eventually a point will be reached where $MR = MC$. The maximum profit output is found where marginal revenue equals marginal cost, providing MC is rising, or is constant, or is declining less rapidly than MR.

The most profitable solution is shown in Figure 20-2. The most profitable output is found at Q, where $MC = MR$. The most profitable price is found by moving vertically at Q until the demand curve is reached. This locates the price at which the market will purchase the profit-maximizing quantity of output. This price will be higher than marginal cost by a factor related to the elasticity of demand; since $MR = P(1 - 1/e)$, with $MR = MC$ we will have $P/MC = e/(e - 1)$. Since marginal cost will be positive, the maximum-profit output will be one at which marginal revenue is positive also. And this can only be true if the elasticity of demand is greater than unity at that output.

Total cost is measured by the area of the rectangle marked off by the equilibrium output and the average cost. Total revenue is measured by the area of the rectangle marked off by output and price. Thus profit is the area of the rectangle bounded by average cost, price, and output.

There is, of course, no guarantee that the monopolist will make a profit at all. There are many products which cannot be produced cheaply enough to be sold at a

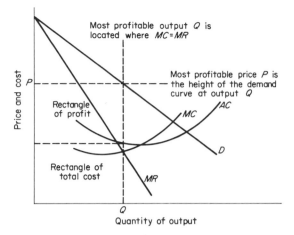

Figure 20-2 Profit-maximizing output and price for monopolist.

profit. The monopolist's average cost curve must lie below the demand curve some-where, or he will not earn a profit at any level of output. Figure 20-3 illustrates the entirely possible situation of the unprofitable monopolist.

The monopolist will conform to the same shut-down conditions we identified for the competitive firm. In the short run, he will only operate if he can charge a price which exceeds average variable cost. Thus he will shut down if the average variable cost curve does not lie below the demand curve at any output. In the long run he will close if he cannot obtain a price which exceeds average cost. The firm in Figure 20-3 would close in the long run, rather than replace its capital assets.

If the monopolist is protected against entry, then there is no tendency for him to produce at the output which minimizes average cost. (We assume that he pro-duces his chosen output using the least-cost input mix.) The monopolist's chosen

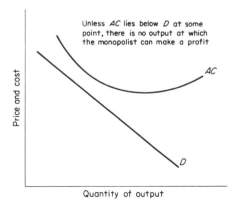

Figure 20-3 The unprofitable monopolist.

output may be greater than, or less than the output which minimizes LAC. Since he lacks the pressure of entry, there is no reason for him to deviate from the preferred output, where $MC = MR$. And his "excess" profits can also be sustained indefinitely.

In the real world, virtually every product has substitutes. Even if a firm has a guaranteed monopoly position (for instance, through a public utility franchise), if demand and cost conditions yield it a profit other firms will have an incentive to come as close as they can to it. Large customers may find it feasible to produce for their own needs a monopolized service such as electric power production; they can own or lease their own trucks if common-carrier transport firms exercise monopoly power.

Under these circumstances, the prudent monopolist may find it more profitable not to exploit his monopoly position to the fullest possible degree. He may look for a price which is just below the level at which new competitors could feasibly enter and survive. His price-output policy would not be a simple function of current costs and current demand but would take account of the long-run entry and demand possibilities.

These observations have important implications for a firm which might enjoy a monopoly position either because it was the first producer of a given product or because it has lower costs than potential competitors. Its ability to remain a monopolist might be contingent on not acting like one. Of course, being first in a field or enjoying superior efficiency may permit a large firm to obtain an unfair advantage through superior opportunity to employ discriminatory or predatory tactics, or by gaining political favoritism. We consider these matters further in the next chapters.

monopoly response to changing demand

In analyzing the competitive industry, we used the concept of a supply schedule to identify the response of industry output and price to shifts in demand. There is not a similar, determinate supply schedule for the monopolist. In terms of behavior, we cannot treat his output as a function of the price, since he may determine price. And the firm's output is not a function merely of the level of the demand schedule but also of its elasticity.

Still, the monopolist's response to a shift in demand will resemble the response of a competitive industry, in that the relative response of price and quantity will depend on the monopolist's marginal cost schedule.

Consider first a demand shift with no change in demand elasticity. Assume the demand schedule confronting the monopolist has the general form $Q = k/P^2$, with k representing some constant. Such a demand schedule has a price elasticity of 2 at all points. By changing the value of k one can shift the demand schedule without changing its elasticity. The monopolist's response to such a demand shift

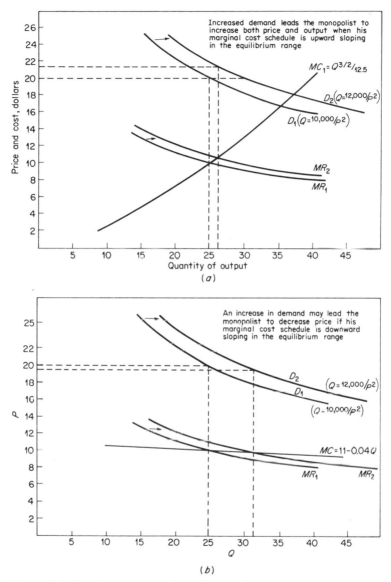

Figure 20-4 Reaction by monopolist to increase in demand.

will depend on the shape of his marginal cost schedule in the neighborhood of equilibrium.

Figure 20-4 illustrates possible response to an increase in demand under two different conditions of marginal cost. In each case we assume the initial demand schedule is given by $Q = 10,000/P^2$ (which can also be written $P = 100/\sqrt{Q}$). The total revenue schedule can be expressed as $TR = 100\sqrt{Q}$ and marginal revenue as $MR = 50/\sqrt{Q}$. Marginal cost equals marginal revenue where both have a value of $10. The firm maximizes profit by producing 25 units of output and charges a price of $20.

Now we assume that the demand schedule increases to $Q' = 12,000/P^2$. Figure 20-4a illustrates the response when the marginal cost is upward sloping beyond the original equilibrium output, using a marginal cost function $MC_1 = Q^{3/2}/12.5$. With the new demand schedule, total revenue is $109.5\sqrt{Q'}$ and marginal revenue is approximately $54.8/\sqrt{Q'}$. We find the new equilibrium output by setting marginal revenue equal to marginal cost, as follows:

$$\frac{Q'^{3/2}}{12.5} = \frac{54.8}{\sqrt{Q'}}$$
$$Q'^2 = (12.5)(54.8) = 685$$
$$Q' = 26.2$$

With this output, the price is obtained by substituting into the demand schedule, yielding $P' = \$21.40$. The increase in demand has raised both price and output. Allowing for rounding, the monopolist's response has an arc elasticity of about $\frac{2}{3}$ which would be the elasticity of supply implied by a marginal cost curve in the form we have chosen.

By contrast, consider what happens in Figure 20-4b, where we have assumed the marginal cost is decreasing at the equilibrium level. When we were analyzing pure competition, we concluded that marginal cost had to be rising at the point of maximum profit. (Why?) In the monopoly case, however, MC can be decreasing at the profit-maximizing output. We assume the marginal cost schedule is given by the expression $MC_2 = 11 - 0.04Q$. The same increase in the demand schedule occurs. The new maximum-profit output will be approximately 31.7 units, where marginal cost and marginal revenue are both approximately $9.73.

When we calculate the new price, we are in for a surprise, for the new price is *lower* than the initial one; price falls to approximately $19.45. Upon reflection, we can see that this result must occur, given the conditions that $MC = MR$, that MC is declining and that $MR = P(1 - 1/e)$. With an elasticity of 2, price will be double marginal revenue and thus also double marginal cost at the profit-maximum output.

Of course our assumption of a constant-elasticity demand schedule is a very restrictive one. The demand schedule might be one with differing elasticities at different phases (as in a straight-line demand curve). Further, the demand shift might alter the elasticity pattern of the demand schedule itself. Our assumption enables us to isolate the influence of demand shift. Now consider the effect of a change in elasticity by itself.

Suppose the demand schedule changed in such a way that it had a different elasticity in the neighborhood of the original equilibrium but continued to pass through the point of original price and quantity. Suppose the demand schedule shifted from our original value, in which $Q = 10{,}000/P^2$, to $Q = 200{,}000/P^3$. The new schedule passes through the original equilibrium output of 25 units at a price of \$20. But it has an elasticity of 3. Consequently, the equilibrium ratio between price and marginal cost is lowered; it is now $\frac{3}{2}$ instead of 2. Therefore the firm will tend to lower the price and sell a larger quantity. Contrariwise, a decrease in the demand elasticity would tend to lead to a higher price and reduced output. This indicates why a monopolist might attempt by advertising or other sales promotion measures to reduce the elasticity of demand for his product.

Combinations of demand shift and elasticity change would require us to consider both of the tendencies we have identified. An increase in demand would have a greater tendency to raise price if demand elasticity fell in the process, but a greater tendency to increase output if demand elasticity increased in the process.

response to a change in cost

The monopolist's response to a shift in his cost schedules is less equivocal than his response to a change in demand. We obtained equivocal results in the preceding section partly because marginal cost may be either increasing or decreasing at the maximum-profit output. There is no such choice about marginal revenue; it is always downward sloping at the point where it intersects marginal cost. Consequently an increase in costs always tends to reduce output and increase price, while a decrease in costs tends to increase output and reduce price. (We restrict our attention to across-the-board changes in the total cost schedule and do not attempt to analyze complex changes in the shape of marginal and average costs.) If we limit our attention to constant-elasticity demand schedules, a proportional shift in marginal cost will always cause a shift in price by the same proportion. At the maximum-profit output, $MC = P(1 - 1/e)$. If we hold e constant, we will find that $kMC = kP(1 - 1/e)$. With a demand schedule having a price elasticity of 2, we found that $P = 2MR = 2MC$ in equilibrium. A rise of MC by 10 percent of its original level would raise P by 10 percent of its original level. Of course, the *amount* of price increase will tend to be larger than the *amount* of the increase in MC.

However, the effect on quantity will depend on the elasticity of the demand schedule. The higher the demand elasticity, the larger will tend to be the reduction in quantity associated with a given proportional increase in MC and P. The closer demand elasticity approaches unity, the smaller will be the influence on quantity of a given proportional change in cost and price.

price discrimination

It may be advantageous to the monopolist to charge different prices to different buyers, if he can do so. However, price discrimination is possible only when the monopolist can prevent his customers from reselling his product among themselves. If arbitrage can take place, those customers permitted to buy at a low price may resell to those for whom the monopolist's price would be higher. Discrimination can only be effective if there are barriers to transfer among the customers.

Such barriers exist where the monopolist sells a service. The buyer who is permitted to obtain his doctor's attention or have his hair cut at a low price cannot resell these services to someone else. Sometimes arbitrage in a product is impeded by geography. Favored customers may be at a different location, and transport or other costs may stand in the way of resale. Arbitrage may also not occur if the buyers do not realize that the product is the same. Perhaps the monopolist uses different brand names and different packaging. Buyers who are charged a high price do not try to obtain the product from more favored buyers, since they do not know it is the same.

Why should the monopolist want to charge different prices anyway? The answer is that different buyers are likely to have differing elasticities of demand for the product. The monopolist can make more profit if he can charge a lower price for buyers with a higher elasticity of demand. By doing this, he can gain the benefit of selling them a larger quantity. The buyers with lower demand elasticity can be charged a higher price, since this will not result in a very great loss of sales volume.

For each separable market sector, there is a separate demand schedule and a marginal revenue schedule to correspond. To identify the most profitable output, we can combine these sector marginal revenue schedules into a synthetic MR schedule and find the output at which MR on this schedule is equal to marginal cost. (This synthetic MR schedule will not necessarily be the same as the marginal revenue derived from the demand schedule for the product as a whole, since that demand schedule presupposes that a uniform price is charged to all buyers.)

The monopolist allocates to each submarket an output such that the marginal revenue in that submarket is equal to the marginal cost of the total output of the firm. (Thus the firm will equate MR received from one submarket with MR from each of the others.) The most profitable price in each submarket is determined by the quantity of output allocated to it and by the demand schedule of the buyers in that submarket.

Figure 20-5 illustrates a situation where a monopolist can deal with two separable submarkets. Their demand schedules are expressed as follows:

$$Q_1 = 1,000 - P_1 \qquad \text{(therefore } P_1 = 1,000 - Q_1)$$
$$Q_2 = 1,200 - 5P_2 \qquad \text{(therefore } P_2 = 240 - 0.2Q_2)$$

Corresponding marginal revenue schedules will be

$$MR_1 = 1,000 - 2Q_1 \qquad \text{(therefore } Q_1 = 500 - 0.5MR_1)$$
$$MR_2 = 240 - 0.4Q_2 \qquad \text{(therefore } Q_2 = 600 - 2.5MR_2)$$

We need to add together the marginal revenue expressions given in terms of Q.

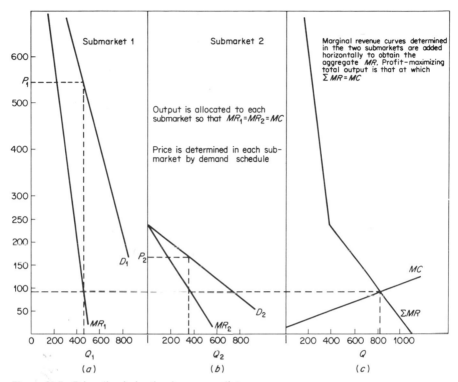

Figure 20-5 Price discrimination by monopolist.

However, in doing this we must remember that the functions are only economically meaningful for values of MR consistent with positive or zero quantities of output. The equation relating Q_2 and MR_2 will not be valid for values of MR_2 greater than $240, and our equation relating Q_1 and MR_1 will not be valid for values of MR_1 greater than $1,000. For marginal revenue between $240 and $1,000, the firm's aggregate marginal revenue schedule will simply be the expression for MR_1 from above. For marginal revenue of $240 or less, however, we add together the two MR expressions, using the form in which quantity appears on the left. This gives us the sum of Q_1 and Q_2 corresponding to any level of MR and corresponds to adding the two MR curves horizontally on the graph. Specifically, we have

$$Q_1 + Q_2 = 500 - 0.5MR + 600 - 2.5MR = 1{,}100 - 3MR$$

Letting $Q_1 + Q_2 = Q$, we have

$$Q = 1{,}100 - 3MR \quad \text{or} \quad MR = 366.6 - \frac{Q}{3} \quad \text{(for } 0 < MR < \$240\text{)}$$

Given the marginal cost schedule, we can find the profit-maximizing total output for the firm, at which marginal cost will equal this aggregate marginal revenue. If we assume that $MC = 10 + 0.1Q$, profit-maximum output will be where

$$366.6 - \frac{Q}{3} = 10 + 0.1Q$$

Thus $Q = 823.2$, at which MR and MC both equal \$92.30.

Next the firm must determine how much of this output to sell in each of the submarkets. The allocation is determined by finding values for Q_1 and Q_2 at which MR_1 and MR_2 are equal to \$92.30 (and consequently are equal to each other).

$$Q_1 = 500 - 0.5MR_1 = 500 - (0.5)(92.30) = 453.9 \text{ units}$$
$$Q_2 = 600 - 2.5MR_2 = 600 - (2.5)(92.30) = \underline{369.3}$$
$$823.2$$

We identify the prices in the two submarkets by substituting these Q values into the respective demand schedules, as follows:

$$P_1 = \$1,000 - Q_1 = \$546.10$$
$$P_2 = \$240 - 0.2Q_2 = \$166.14$$

Figure 20-5a indicates the submarket involving Q_1 and Figure 20-5b the submarket involving Q_2. The aggregation of the marginal revenue schedules appears in Figure 20-5c, where it is related to marginal cost to identify the appropriate total output and the equilibrium values of marginal cost and marginal revenue. The latter are traced back to the submarket diagrams to identify final values of quantities and prices.

government regulation of monopoly price

We have seen that economic conditions tend toward monopoly if the optimum size of the firm is large relative to the size of the market in which it operates. In extreme cases, it might be potentially more efficient to have the entire market supplied by a single firm rather than to divide the output among several. Such a case would pose two problems for public policy: how to assure that the entire output would in fact be supplied by one firm, and how to protect the public against monopoly pricing by such a favored firm. The latter problem would be acute if demand had a low price elasticity. Both problems have been elements in the government regulation of public utilities, a practice relatively unique to the United States. In other countries, outright public ownership of such natural monopolies has been more often employed. American public utility regulation has been most commonly applied to industries supplying energy (electric power, gas), communications (telephone, telegraph), and some forms of municipal transportation.

The entry problem is solved simply by a government franchise or certificate of convenience and necessity which prevents new firms from entering the industry in the particular locality. The pricing problem is attacked by forbidding the firm from charging prices (rates) which exceed cost plus a fair return on a fair valuation of the firm's capital. Although defining the fair return has posed many problems for regulators, its essential meaning is close to the normal return on capital which we have included in our economic definition of cost. As a first approximation, we can say that public utility regulation involves average cost pricing. Firms are forbidden to charge rates above average cost and usually have no economic incentive to charge less.

However, average cost is not ordinarily a single number but a function of output. In the absence of price discrimination, the equilibrium rate under regulation would be identified by the intersection of the demand curve with the average cost curve. Figure 20-6 shows two possible versions of this rate. In Figure 20-6a, we assume that the demand curve intersects LAC at an output below that of minimum LAC. This result can easily occur, for instance, in electric-power generation where economies of scale are very extensive.

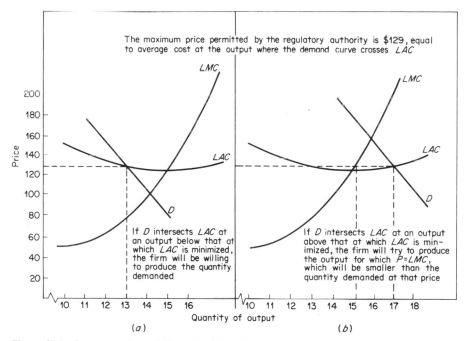

The maximum price permitted by the regulatory authority is $129, equal to average cost at the output where the demand curve crosses LAC

If D intersects LAC at an output below that at which LAC is minimized, the firm will be willing to produce the quantity demanded

If D intersects LAC at an output above that at which LAC is minimized, the firm will try to produce the output for which $P=LMC$, which will be smaller than the quantity demanded at that price

(a)   (b)

Quantity of output

Figure 20-6 Government regulation of public-utility monopolist's price.

Will the firm supply all the market demands at the regulated price of $129? In Figure 20-6$a$ it probably will. For outputs short of 13 units, the implicit marginal revenue schedule of the firm is the same as the price. The firm cannot raise the price above $129; therefore changes in output below 13 do not affect the price. To sell more than 13 would require that the firm reduce the price below $129. If demand is inelastic, marginal revenue beyond 13 would be negative. Even if demand elasticity were greater than unity, marginal revenue might still lie below MC. Observe that output 13 is smaller than that at which price would equal marginal cost; however, the deviation is less, the lower the elasticity of demand in this range.

If cost and demand conditions approximate those in Figure 20-6b, however, the firm will have an incentive not to supply the entire quantity demanded at price $129. Here the demand curve intersects LAC at an output larger than that which minimizes LAC. Thus LMC lies above LAC in this range, and the demand curve intersects LMC at a smaller output than LAC. Given the inability to charge a price higher than $129, the firm will make larger profits if it produces 15.2 units, at which $LMC = \$129$, even though customers demand 17 units. There will be a shortage of the product at price $129, so that some customers must go without or settle for quantities less than those desired.

To be sure, the outcome is not really an equilibrium, since the firm is making more than a normal return on its capital. The regulatory authority may observe that LAC is lower at output 15.2 than at output 17 and insist that the firm reduce its rates. However, at any regulated rate above minimum LAC, the firm will continue to have an incentive to produce less than the quantity demanded. If the regulatory process is slow, as it usually is, the firm can continue to receive excess profits for quite a long time. And the tendency for regulated rates to fall may worsen the shortage.

In practice, the regulatory authorities have become increasingly concerned about the adequacy of supply; they might be able to put pressure on the firm to expand output to 17, perhaps by threatening it with a rate reduction if it does not comply or with loss of its monopoly position if that threat fails. In some cases, however, government production or subsidy has been used (for instance, in the rural electrification programs) to meet the fact that mere regulation of monopoly price does not always solve the problem of inadequate quantity supplied.

As a means of protecting the public, however, rate regulation on the average-cost-plus basis has more often run into another problem. Since firms are, in effect, guaranteed an opportunity to cover their costs, they may lose the incentive to keep costs down. Worse, there may be ways that management can benefit by deliberate inflation of costs. The regulated firm may simply decide to pay all its employees at levels above the competitive rates of wages and salaries. The opportunities for cost inflation have been exploited in the past through the device of the holding company. This is a supercorporation which may own regulated utility companies and also other unregulated companies which supply inputs used by the utilities, such as equipment. By inflating the prices charged for such equipment, the unregulated member of a holding company may reap huge profits, while utility rate increases pass the costs along to the consumers. Regulatory authorities have attacked these problems directly by maintaining some surveillance over utility costs and by direct restriction on the use of the holding-company device.

Even in the absence of these problems, there remains the question of what incentive exists for the firm to improve its service or put into effect cost-reducing innovations, if rates never yield more than a fair return. Of course one answer is that the fair return itself can be defined to include an incentive element. In practice, however, the more effective answer has been relatively ineffective regulation! By this we mean that although rates tend to be held equal to average cost, they are not adjusted except after a time lag. In the short run the firm stands to gain by cutting costs, even though rates will eventually be reduced in response. Perhaps the firm must, in the short run, absorb rising costs out of profits, even though ultimately higher costs (if bona fide) will lead to higher rates.

Regulated public utilities commonly make use of price discrimination. This means that the simple principle of average cost pricing does not apply. The issues involved are far too complex to explore here, but one idea is worth noting. Suppose a firm is initially in a situation like that of Figure 20-6a. If there exists a submarket for the product with a high demand elasticity at output 13, it might be advantageous to the firm to make a discriminatory rate reduction to that submarket. The initial price $129 exceeds marginal cost at 13 units of output, and thus it is conceivable that marginal revenue in the high-elasticity submarket would intersect marginal cost beyond 13. This sort of situation is sometimes cited to indicate that rate discrimination may mean lower rates to some customers, rather than higher rates, as compared with the alternative of rate uniformity to all customers.

selling costs

When we analyzed pure competition, we concluded that the individual firm had no incentive to incur expenditures for advertising and related sales-promotion activities. The individual competitive firm is only one small supplier among many, all furnishing a homogeneous product. Even if advertising increased market demand for the product as a whole, the individual firm would receive so little benefit from this that the selling costs would not be worthwhile.

For the monopolist, by contrast, selling costs may be a means of adding to profit. Sales-promotion activities might shift the demand schedule to the right. They might decrease the price elasticity of the demand curve. Either or both of these tendencies could increase the profits of the firm.

Full analysis of selling-cost strategy involves far more complexities than can be considered here. Selection of optimal sales-promotion activity involves a range of managerial decisions similar in some ways to the choice of the least-cost input mix. There are infinitely many ways of spending a given sum of money on sales promotion. We must assume that the firm chooses among these in such a manner that each sum is spent with optimal effectiveness. However, identification of the effectiveness is not simple as in the theory of production, where we could specify that maximum output be gained from each chosen combination of inputs. Here we merely assume that firms manage somehow to choose the optimum utilization of each possible level of selling cost, even if we don't know how.

The next problem is, what functional relation exists between selling expenditures and demand for the product? This is a problem in consumer psychology rather than technology. However, it is not unreasonable to assume that an increase in selling expenditures will tend to increase demand for the product but that there will be a sort of (eventually) diminishing return, in the sense that the marginal stimulus to demand tends to fall, per dollar of selling cost, as total selling expenditure increases.

We could make this notion a bit more precise by measuring the impact of selling expenditures either on the quantity demanded at some specific price or on the price buyers would be willing to pay for some specified quantity. If we let TSC stand for total selling cost at each possible level of output, presumably $dP/dTSC$ is positive but decreases as TSC increases.

If this is so, we can revert to orthodox marginal analysis. At each output, the firm will presumably carry selling expenses up to the point where the last dollar of selling cost adds just one dollar to the total revenue of the firm. Note this is not a marginal revenue situation in the orthodox sense. We are looking at a comparison of $dTR/dTSC$, where $TR = PQ$, where Q is given, and where P is a function of TSC. To illustrate, suppose that at 10 units of output, the price were equal to $10 + \sqrt{TSC}$. With no selling costs, price is $10; with $1 of selling cost, price is $11; with $4 of selling cost, price is $12; and so on. A total revenue function would have the form $TR = Q(10 + \sqrt{TSC})$ and its derivative with respect to TSC would be

$$\frac{dTR}{dTSC} = \frac{Q}{2\sqrt{TSC}} = \frac{5}{\sqrt{TSC}}$$

Carrying TSC up to the point where the last dollar spent would raise total revenue by just one dollar would require TSC of $25. A similar calculation can be made (conceptually) for each other level of output.

Having determined the appropriate level of selling expenditure for each level of output, we could then find the most profitable output–selling-cost combination by several routes. One would be a simple confrontation of total cost and total revenue. However, it seems preferable to choose an approach which stresses the difference between selling cost (which is aimed at affecting demand) and production cost (which is necessary to production). We can do this by identifying the total net revenue (TNR) from selling any quantity of output as being equal to the total revenue minus total selling cost at that output: $TNR = PQ - TSC$.

Given a demand schedule for the product which reflects the influence of selling cost, we can determine TNR for each output level. Suppose the demand function can be written in this form:

$$P = 10 + \sqrt{TSC} - Q \quad \text{and} \quad TR = 10Q + \sqrt{TSC}\, Q - Q^2$$

If optimal selling cost is used at each level of output, we will find that

$$\frac{dTR}{dTSC} = 1$$

$$\frac{dTR}{dTSC} = \frac{Q}{2\sqrt{TSC}}$$

Thus, optimal $TSC = Q^2/4$. To obtain TNR, we substitute as follows:

$$TNR = TR - TSC$$
$$TNR = 10Q + \sqrt{TSC}\, Q - Q^2 - TSC$$
$$TNR = 10Q + \frac{Q}{2}Q - Q^2 - \frac{Q^2}{4} = 10Q - \frac{3}{4}Q^2$$

Taking the derivative of this expression with respect to output gives us a measure of marginal net revenue (MNR), as follows:

$$MNR = \frac{dTNR}{dQ} = 10 - \frac{3}{2}Q$$

The optimum output is that at which this marginal net revenue is equal to marginal production cost. As a simple example, if marginal production cost were constant at \$5, the profit-maximizing output would be where $10 - \frac{3}{2}Q = 5$, which would be at $3\frac{1}{3}$ units. Total selling cost would be $Q^2/4 = \$2.78$. The selling price would be $10 + 2.78 - 3.33 = \$9.45$.

It can be shown that marginal cost will equal marginal revenue at this output if we include both selling and production costs in marginal cost. (Both MC and MR have values of \$6.67 in this example; see if you can derive this.)

The more cumbersome MNR approach is preferable, however, because it more adequately reflects the fact that the firm is making adjustments along two margins. One is change in the level of selling cost per unit of output, and the other is change in the quantity of output itself. Inequality between marginal cost and marginal revenue would be a symptom of disequilibrium, all right, but if selling cost is included in MC the disequilibrium does not necessarily call for a change in output; it may signal need to change selling effort instead.

Of course the individual firm operates under great uncertainty in identifying the influence of selling costs on demand for the product. Our analysis does set forth the logic of determining optimum selling costs, but only on the assumption that most of the really difficult problems have already been solved.

We have introduced the theory of selling costs here because a monopolist could benefit from using them. To the foregoing, we might add that an insecure monopolist might use selling costs as a method of helping to prevent entry of new firms, even if his short-run profits might be impaired in the process. However, the incentive to incur selling costs may be greater when the firm is subject to competition from producers of close substitutes. Thus much of the analysis may have even greater relevance to the next chapter, in which we discuss market structures falling between pure competition and pure monopoly.

summary

Monopoly refers to a market situation in which there is only one producer of a product for which there is no close substitute. The market demand schedule for the product is also the demand curve confronting the monopolist, who can control the selling price. Since the demand curve is downward sloping, the marginal revenue curve associated with it will lie below it. Maximum profit for the firm is obtained (in the absence of price discrimination) at the output where marginal cost equals marginal revenue. The higher the demand elasticity, the closer price will be to marginal cost at the profit-maximizing output. An upward shift in costs will tend to lower the equilibrium output and raise the equilibrium price. However, an increase in demand may either raise or lower the price, depending on whether marginal cost is rising or declining in the equilibrium range.

The monopolist may find it advantageous to employ selling costs. And if the firm can separate its customers, it may be able to gain from price discrimination, taking advantage of different demand elasticities in different submarkets.

There is no guarantee that a monopolist will be profitable. If no entry is possible by new firms, however, any profits he succeeds in making can persist for a long time. If entry is possible, the monopolist may keep the price somewhat lower than the short-run profit-maximizing level to deter prospective newcomers.

Efforts to regulate monopoly price in so-called public utilities have often called for the equivalent of average cost pricing. Such regulation raises problems: whether firms have an incentive to keep costs down, whether quantity is adequate to meet demand at the regulated price, and similar issues.

TERMS AND CONCEPTS

1. Marginal revenue
2. Monopoly
3. Marginal net revenue

QUESTIONS AND PROBLEMS

1. A monopolist can produce a product at a constant marginal cost of $10 per unit. Find the most profitable price and output corresponding to each of the following demand schedules confronting the monopolist; prove that your solution does yield maximum profits (assuming no fixed costs):
    (a) $Q_D = 100 - P$
    (b) $Q_D = 100/P$
    (c) $Q_D = k/P^n$ (where k and n are positive constants $n > 1$)

2. A monopolist can divide his customers into two groups. Group I has a demand schedule for his product expressed by $Q_D = 100 - P$. Group II has a demand schedule expressed by $Q_D = 900 - 5P$. Marginal cost is constant at $10. Find the most profitable output and determine the appropriate price and quantity for each of the submarkets. Explain why it would not be advantegeous for the firm to transfer 1 unit of output from the lower-price market to the higher-price market once the so-called equilibrium position is achieved.

3. How can a monopolist benefit from sales-promotion activities if there are are no close substitutes for his product?

monopolistic competition
and oligopoly

Neither pure competition nor pure monopoly represents a very realistic image of a
normal product market. Typically, industries fall somewhere in between. The two
market-structure types we examine in this chapter can be regarded as intermediate
situations. Each is to be regarded merely as a simplified representation of an even
greater variety of detailed market-structure conditions.

monopolistic competition

There are many industries in which the number of firms is large, their average size
small, and entry easy, but where the product or service of one firm is somehow differentiated from that of the others. The awkward term *monopolistic competition* is
used to describe such a condition. The term may be defended on grounds that the
analysis incorporates some features taken from the theory of monopoly (downward-
sloping demand curve, marginal revenue less than product price) with some features taken from the theory of pure competition (easy entry tends to eliminate
excess profits).

In product markets, situations of monopolistic competition are associated with branded products, but paradoxically, consumer brand loyalties are likely to be relatively weak and there may be little awareness of which brands come from which producers. The whole complex of industries engaged in processing and marketing of packaged foodstuffs in the United States provides a good illustration. The number of firms is large, technical economies of scale do not make large size essential for efficient operation, and it is not difficult for new firms to enter the industry. Canned, frozen, or otherwise packaged food products are typically branded, but customers typically regard one brand as a close substitute for another.

Many of the products one finds in the drugstore or variety store are also produced under conditions of monopolistic competition. Drugs and cosmetics can often be produced efficiently even on a small scale. However, customer awareness of brand differences is probably greater, and readiness to shift brands somewhat smaller, in drug and cosmetic products than in packaged foods. Many consumers find it easy to evaluate the quality of food products, but judgments on drugs and cosmetics are not always so easy to make.

Retailing and service business may also be areas of monopolistic competition. Again, technology does not dictate that a firm must be large to be efficient, so entry may be potentially easy. However, location differences typically establish a basis for differentiation in the minds of consumers. In services rendered by individuals (such as lawyers or doctors) the personality variable may be an important basis for differentiation. So is the fact that a doctor or lawyer can serve a customer better if he deals with him repeatedly over time.

The market structure of an industry is reflected in the demand schedule confronting the individual firm. Because of differentiation, the firm in monopolistic competition has some control over its price. If the firm raises its selling price, it will not lose all its customers. For the same reason, the individual firm cannot be certain of selling any desired quantity at an unvarying price; increased quantity placed on the market will tend to lower the price for the individual firm. Thus the individual firm's demand curve is downward sloping. However, since one firm's product is a close substitute for those of other firms, the elasticity of demand for its product will tend to be relatively high.

If we take the demand schedule for the firm's product as given, we can analyze its price-output decisions in the same manner as we did those of a monopolist. From the demand schedule we determine a total revenue schedule, which in turn yields a marginal revenue schedule. The profit-maximizing output of the firm will be that at which marginal cost equals marginal revenue, and the corresponding price is the one for which that quantity of output can be sold, as measured by the height of the demand curve at the chosen quantity. The higher the elasticity of demand, of course, the closer this price will be to marginal cost.

However, we have assumed that entry into the industry is easy. If existing firms in the industry are receiving more than a normal profit—if price exceeds average cost—new firms will be attracted into the industry. The added output supplied by new entrants will tend to reduce the demand for products of the older firms, each of which may find its own demand curve shifting to a lower level. Perhaps the purchases of the new firms will raise input prices as well. In any event, easy entry will tend to bring price and average cost into equality with each other.

This sounds like the same equilibrium condition we obtained in the case of pure competition, but it differs in detail. One important difference is shown in Figure 21-1. Industry equilibrium requires that price equal average cost, while equilibrium for the firm requires that marginal revenue equal marginal cost. These two conditions are simultaneously fulfilled only in the situation shown in Figure 21-1b, where the demand curve is tangent to the average-cost curve. Observe that the tangency occurs on the downward-sloping portion of AC, so the profit-maximizing output is somewhat smaller than that at which average cost would be minimized.

Can we be certain that MC will equal MR at the output where the demand curve is just tangent to AC? Yes, we can. Tangency between average cost and average revenue means both curves have the same slope at that point and the

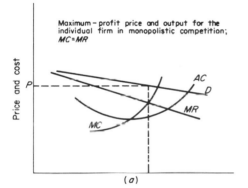

(a)

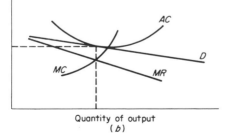

Quantity of output
(b)

Figure 21-1 (a) Maximum-profit position of firm in monopolistic competition; **(b)** the firm in industry equilibrium: monopolistic competition.

underlying functions have the same derivative. If average cost and average revenue have the same derivative at that point, the derivative of total cost (marginal cost) will be equal to the derivative of total revenue (marginal revenue) at that same output.

Another difference from the long-run equilibrium of the purely competitive industry lies in the fact that, with product differentiation, firms in monopolistic competition will be likely to incur selling costs and other expenses for nonprice competition. In addition to advertising and other sales efforts, firms may experiment either with variations in the quality and style of the products themselves, or variations in packaging, or in such service aspects of the business as delivery times, advice to customers, credit terms, and trial and return privileges.

The selection of a profit-maximizing strategy of nonprice competition will tend to follow the same logical lines which we outlined for the monopolist. The individual firm must attempt to identify the most effective way of spending any given sum on selling effort or other nonprice competition. Once that has been determined, an appropriate expenditure for each level of output can be identified, by carrying such expenditure up to the extent that the last dollar of expenditure adds just $1 to revenue received for that quantity of output. Then we can derive a schedule of total net revenue, deducting selling and related costs from total revenue, and find the most profitable output at which marginal net revenue equals marginal production cost.

In practice, since firms in monopolistic competition are producing products which are close substitutes, the individual firm may feel that the potential impact of selling costs and quality variations on its demand curve is great. If all firms engage in extensive nonprice competition, however, the results may be largely self-defeating for the industry as a whole. Costs of nonprice competition may consume a large part of total revenue and may be an important element in the elimination of excess profits, as described by Figure 21-1b. Average cost rises to equal price, as firms step up expenditures for nonprice competition, a process quite different from that in a purely competitive industry.

The higher the elasticity of the demand schedule confronting the individual firm the smaller will be the excess of price over marginal cost. However, the gap of price over marginal production cost may be quite large if firms incur heavy expenditures for nonprice competition.

There is no necessary reason for all the firms in a monopolistic-competitive industry to charge the same price. Indeed, there may be some tendencies toward a systematic stratification of prices. Some product lines will be of higher quality than others, and the higher quality is likely to cost the customer more. Even if products do not differ much, one firm may succeed in creating a strong and inelastic demand for its product and charging a high price. This creates an opportunity for other firms to sell a similar product at a much lower price even without extensive selling expenditure. This condition is easy to observe in drug and cosmetic products; chain stores often handle high-priced nationally advertised brands but also offer, right beside them, cut-price varieties carrying their own private brand labels.

responses to changes in data

What would be the long-run response of output and price in a monopolistic-competitive industry to a shift in product-demand or input-supply conditions? Suppose the supply of an input decreases, so that the industry must now pay a higher price for any specific quantity than was previously necessary. Firms' cost curves shift upward, leading them to reduce output and raise price. If the industry was initially in equilibrium with $P = LAC$, firms will now be making losses and some will drop out of the industry. This will tend further to reduce output and raise product price; however, decreased demand for inputs will tend to bring costs down somewhat. Ultimately adjustment in the number of firms will restore equality between product price and LAC, and this will normally occur where output is less and product price greater than in the original equilibrium. The higher the elasticity of market demand for the product, the greater the curtailment of output relative to the rise in market price.

Suppose the market demand for the product were to increase. Existing firms might raise their prices; but even if they did not, each could benefit from lower average cost by sliding down the average cost curve to a more efficient level of operations. Thus the industry would be receiving more than a normal profit, and newcomers would be attracted into it. Entry would continue until equality was restored between product price and average cost. Output would tend to be greater than before. But what about price? As in the purely competitive case, analysis of the long-run equilibrium price change requires consideration of what happens to industry costs as output increases. To the extent that input prices are bid up by the expansion of industry output, each firm's average cost curve will shift upward and the equilibrium price will be correspondingly higher.

However, there are two complications we did not encounter in the competitive case. One is that the shift in demand may alter the optimum pattern of selling costs, which will be a component of equilibrium average cost. The other is that the reshuffling of industry population and output may move firms closer to the minimum point on their average cost curves, absorbing some of the cost-increasing pressure from rising input prices. This could occur if increase in the number of firms made the demand schedule for each firm's output somewhat flatter, thus bringing the tangency point at which $P = AC$ closer to the bottom point on AC.

In the real world, the excess profits of existing firms are not always eliminated by the entry of new competitors, if the products of the older firms are sufficiently unique and differentiated. The soft drink industry is relatively easy to enter, but new firms have not been able to duplicate the successful chemical combination of Coca-Cola. New firms can easily enter the production of aspirin, but customers buy Bayer aspirin at a price which is probably ten times its production ......n implicit faith that it is somehow unique, even though its chemical content is the same as the less expensive brands.

It is also true that industries which appear characterized by monopolistic competition sometimes contain situations where one firm is in close competition with only a few other firms. Retailing in a large city may contain many firms, each relatively small. However, the individual retailer may be primarily in competition with his close neighbors for the business of those people who live or work in that particular neighborhood. Where one firm is most intensely competing with only a few others, we have elements of oligopoly rivalry, and the analysis of monopolistic competition may not be adequate in itself.

oligopoly

Oligopoly refers to a market structure where the number of firms is relatively small and the individual firm is relatively large, but not so large as to be a monopoly. Details of the oligopoly situation may differ substantially depending on the precise number and size of firms—whether one firm is substantially larger than the others, or whether the industry contains a fringe of relatively small firms as well as the giants, for instance. Our concern is to identify the intrinsic logic of the oligopoly relationship, rather than its details, and we will concentrate on a relatively simple case where there are several firms of relatively equal size.

Oligopoly is a situation commonly encountered in heavy industry, where technological economies of scale may lead individual firms to become very large in pursuit of production efficiency. However, many of the largest firms are much larger than mere production efficiency would require, typically bringing under common ownership many plants at different locations which may be completely independent of one another in the technological sense. There are strategic advantages to large size, as well as technological advantages, and often the strategic advantages account for the extremes of size and concentration.

On the other hand, oligopoly may also exist where the market is small. Local retail and service businesses, outside of large cities, may come closer to oligopoly than to monopolistic competition.

The unique element in oligopoly situations is the element of rivalry, the fact that each firm as an individual is self-consciously competing with each of the others in the industry as an individual. It is this awareness of who one's competitors are that makes oligopolists feel that their situation is one of more intense competition than is found in other market structures.

In particular, rivalry confronts the individual firm in oligopoly with a kind of demand situation we have not encountered before. Because each firm is large, its actions tend to have a substantial effect on the condition of each other firm. Each other firm may change its own policies in response, and this may have a substantial effect on the original firm. Because of this *circularity* or *feedback*, the rational firm will try to anticipate what its rivals will do before making a change in its own policies. The demand schedule confronting the individual firm becomes determinate only on the assumption that some specific reaction pattern will be forthcoming from the rivals.

What firms expect of each other may be a matter of experience. The oligopoly relation may tend to pass through a sequence of stages in which the firms change their expectations of each other, and consequently their behavior. We shall illustrate with a hypothetical sequence, showing how the oligopolists may learn from experience.

naive oligopoly and the price war

The first stage of oligopoly may be one in which each firm is ignorant of its potential influence on the others and of their potential responses. Perhaps technological change or merger has led to the recent emergence of a small number of large firms whose managers are accustomed to making decisions without worrying about the responses of competitors. In particular, we assume that the individual firm believes not only that it can change its selling price at will but that other firms will not change their prices in response. If the product is homogeneous, the individual firm may conclude that the demand curve for its own product has a very high elasticity. This may be especially true of an industrial product sold to skilled purchasing agents who are always on the lookout for a better price. A small price reduction may be sufficient to draw a lot of business from the other firms, and a small price increase may drive customers to the other firms. With a highly elastic demand curve, marginal revenue is not much below price, and the output at which marginal cost intersects this apparent MR curve may be a large output, to be sought by reducing the price.

If firm A reduces its price, it will gain some increase in sales from the fact that the industry demand schedule is downward sloping. The more elastic the market demand schedule for the product, the more sales firm A will gain in this way. If the market demand schedule is inelastic, however, as it is for many industrial products, a price reduction will reduce the total industry revenue. Firm A need not consider this, for its price reduction will also take business away from the other firms, and ordinarily that will be its chief effect. The smaller the number of firms, the larger the potential impact on each one individually of such a disturbance. If firm A had only two rivals, each would lose one customer for every two gained by firm A. If firm A had twenty rivals, however, each would lose only one customer for every twenty gained by A. The fewer and larger the firms, therefore, the less likely they can ignore the disturbance caused by firm A's price reduction.

Rather than lose so much business, the other firms are likely to reduce their prices. And they may reduce them to a level below that of A in hopes of winning back their lost customers. This may induce A to cut prices still further, and so on.

Thus a price war may break out among the oligopolists. How far it goes, and how it affects the belligerents, will depend on several circumstances. If the elasticity of market demand for the product is high, price reduction will lead to substantial increase in total industry output. Firms may find themselves producing at capacity and thus lose the incentive for further price reduction. However, if market demand for the product has a low elasticity, the increase in output is not very great and there is less tendency to halt the warfare. Further, the damage to the price cutters is potentially greater with inelastic demand, since total industry sales revenue is reduced by the price reductions.

The relative magnitude of fixed and variable costs may also affect the outcome. A firm will not ordinarily cut price below average variable cost; it would lose less money by closing. Further, if a firm did set a price below average variable cost, its rivals might ruin it by purchasing output from it themselves. If variable costs are a relatively large part of total cost, therefore, tendencies toward price cutting may be choked off fairly rapidly. In heavy industry, however, variable costs may be a relatively small part of total cost, and thus the degree to which price may be cut is potentially much greater.

From these considerations we can conclude that the potential extent of a price war and the potential damage it may do the industry tend to be the greater (1) the more nearly homogeneous the product, (2) the lower the elasticity of market demand for the product, and (3) the smaller the proportion of variable costs to total cost. Industries such as steel and petroleum refining have a high-risk rating in all three of these categories.

The price war may take a predatory turn. If one firm has a strong financial and technical position, it may decide to try to drive its rivals out of business. It may offer to buy out the rival firms, after convincing them that their future is otherwise not a bright and promising one. Or it may stop short with inflicting painful wounds which will make the rivals unlikely to undertake independent competitive actions in the future. Predatory adventures of this sort in nineteenth-century American industry provided much of the impetus for the adoption of antitrust legislation.

In any event, the price cutting will ultimately cease, and firms will learn from the experience. Each is likely to perceive that the industry as a whole is damaged by price cutting and that each firm may be better off in the long run if it voluntarily relinquishes some of its independence, provided that its rivals follow suit. Historically, the next step is likely to go to an opposite extreme—from extreme independence, the firms are likely to turn to some form of combination or collusion.

cartels

The oligopolists might decide on a complete consolidation, or one firm might succeed in buying out or driving out all of the others. Thus one outcome of oligopoly warfare might be monopoly. Suppose, however, that the individual firms are unwilling to relinquish all of their identity and independence. They may still join together in some sort of collusive agreement, a *cartel*. It is characteristic of a cartel that some decisions are made collectively by the firms as a group. One cartel may differ quite a bit from another, depending on how extensive the decisions are over which group decision-making is extended.

At first glance, it might appear that a cartel of several firms would act just like a monopoly. After all, the firms have a common interest in maximizing the profits of the group as a whole. However, there remains something on which they are not agreed—the division of the profits among the members. Conflict of interest over the division of the spoils may interfere with the ability of the cartel to behave like a monopoly, because individual firms may be unwilling to submit to extensive group decision-making. To insure itself of a satisfactory share in the cartel's profits, not just now but in the future, the firm must retain some bargaining power. A complete pooling of operations, appropriate for joint profit maximization, might well put some firms in a position where their bargaining power was lost. At some future time, the other firms might simply vote to reduce (or eliminate) the share of a weak firm, and it might have no satisfactory recourse.

Suppose, for instance, that one of the firms joining the cartel has relatively old and inefficient facilities. A profit-maximizing, cost-minimizing monopolist might decide to shut down firm A's facilities entirely and produce the entire cartel output with the facilities of the other firms. Firm A's personnel might be dismissed, or absorbed by other firms. Firm A might then cease to exist as a physical production unit, even if its ownership structure persisted. Lacking productive facilities, firm A would also now lack bargaining power. As long as it retains productive facilities, it can always threaten to produce and sell outside the cartel, potentially reducing the profits of cartel members. Lacking facilities and personnel to operate them, it is much less likely to be able to rebuild a productive unit as a bargaining device.

Suppose, on the other hand, that the constituent firms have formerly sold differentiated products with different brand names. If all the branded products came under the control of a monopoly, it might decide to withdraw the less effective brands and concentrate production on the stronger ones. Each constituent firm in a cartel will wish to retain some of its traditional brands, however, in case it needs to threaten to withdraw. It may be much more difficult to resuscitate an old brand, after several years of dormancy, if the firm tries to return to an independent role.

If the cartel were to be operated as a profit-maximizing monopoly, it would surely pool and coordinate its advertising and other nonprice competition activities. Its total advertising expenditures would certainly be less than those which the individual oligopolists would tend to make in the absence of collusion. However, the individual cartel members are unlikely to be willing to give up control over their selling efforts, though they may agree to restrict them somewhat.

Other limitations on full monopoly action are more easily apparent when we look at the specific policy decisions a cartel must make. Suppose it concentrates attention on price. Some kind of marginal cost and marginal revenue calculations might be estimated for the cartel members as a group, and an estimate of the profit-maximizing price might be derived. In a highly centralized cartel, actual marketing may be consolidated in the hands of a joint selling agency, which can of course maintain the profit-maximizing price. In such a case, however, the cartel will still have to decide how to allocate output among the firms. The profit-maximizing allocation would be the one which would minimize costs. This would give larger output to the lower-cost firms, who may feel they should receive a commensurate share of the profits; the higher-cost firms will be reluctant to accept such a system, but may insist on a pooling of revenues and a sharing of profits on a basis unrelated to output quotas. Such disagreement may make it impossible to establish a joint selling agency. Instead, the cartel may simply assign an output quota to each firm, leaving it to the firm to find buyers, and of course assuming that the cartel-determined price will be maintained. The profit of the individual firm will now be the difference between its own revenue and its own costs (although some firms may develop the practice of "selling" part of their output quota to other firms). If the cartel has estimated the market demand for the product properly, there should in fact be enough customers to go around.

It may be impossible to get the firms to accept output quotas as well as agree on a price. In that case, individual firms may still compete with each other through nonprice methods. Such an arrangement is vulnerable, however, because the individual firm will have a large incentive to cut its price slightly below the cartel-fixed level, if it can pick up a lot of highly profitable sales. One firm's opportunity to gain by cheating on the agreement depends on the fact that the other firms are keeping the agreement. If one firm can negotiate secret price concessions in deals with individual customers, it may be able to avoid provoking retaliation from rivals. But each firm has the same incentives to cheat, and if all yield to temptation, the cartel agreement soon breaks down.

Even if the cartel arrangement is faithfully upheld by its members, it may be undermined by the entry of new firms attracted by the high cartel price. However, the cartel may be a powerful instrument for punishing outsiders and interlopers. Cartel members may agree to use discriminatory price cuts in the particular locations or product specialties important to the outsiders, with the cartel members sharing the possible costs of such action. If the cartel members are an important part of the market for certain inputs, they may try to use their bargaining power to induce suppliers to cut off supplies from the outsiders. If a supplier refuses, the cartel members may cease to buy from him. Similar pressure may be put on distributors or other customers, cartel members refusing to sell to anyone who deals with the outsider. In some countries, business firms have enlisted the aid of government to make cartel membership compulsory, to make cartel policies legally binding on member firms, and to restrict entry of new firms. By contrast, cartel agreements in interstate commerce are illegal under United States anti-trust laws—although the government itself has imposed cartel-like arrangements in some sectors such as agriculture and transportation.

implicit collusion

Even if outright agreement among rival firms is prohibited, the firms in an oligopoly are likely to fall into behavior patterns which have some of the attributes of collusion. This is particularly true if they have had a bad experience with price cutting, so that a defensive attitude weighs heavily in their minds.

If a group of oligopolists has just emerged from a bout of price warfare and are still somewhat in a state of shock, unwilling or unable to join formally together, each one may find it easiest to adopt a policy of not instigating any price changes. Such a situation is reflected analytically by the "kinked" demand curve illustrated in Figure 21-2. We must assume that there exists a price for the product and that it covers average costs for most of the firms. Firm A fears that if it were to initiate

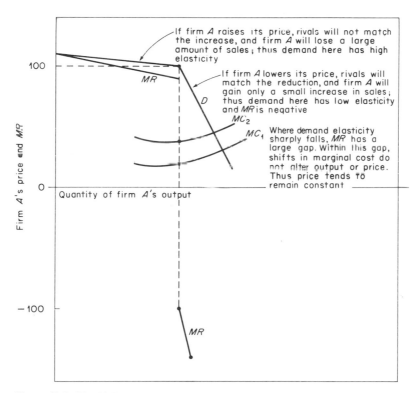

Figure 21-2 The kinked demand curve: oligopoly.

a price increase, rival firms would not increase their prices and firm A would lose a lot of business. The demand curve for its product thus appears highly elastic for prices above the existing level. By contrast, firm A fears that if it initiates a price reduction, the rival firms *will* match it and firm A will not gain very much in total sales by such a reduction. Its demand curve below the existing price may have a much lower elasticity.

If we derive the total revenue and marginal revenue schedules associated with this kind of demand curve, we will find that total revenue is typically maximized at the existing price and output and that the marginal revenue curve is discontinuous. To illustrate, Figure 21-2 shows the firm producing an output of 10 units at a price of $100. The demand schedule for higher prices is assumed to be $Q = 110 - P$. The demand schedule for prices below $100 is assumed to be $Q = 15 - 0.05P$. Table 21-1 shows the total revenue and marginal revenue calculations for prices near $100.

Using arc values for marginal revenue, the discontinuity is apparent in the big jump from a large positive value to a large negative value. The marginal revenue schedules will be as follows:

$$MR_1 = 110 - 2Q \qquad \text{(for quantities less than 10)}$$
$$MR_2 = 300 - 40Q \qquad \text{(for quantities greater than 10)}$$

The elasticity of demand for the firm's product at prices below the existing level will tend to be the same as the elasticity of market demand for the product of the entire industry. If the latter is greater than 1, then the firm's marginal revenue will be positive even for a price reduction. But there may still be a large

TABLE 21-1

Price	Quantity	Total Revenue	Marginal Revenue ($\Delta TR/\Delta Q$)
$103	7	$ 721	
			$ 95
102	8	816	
			93
101	9	909	
			91
100	10	1,000	
			−101
99	10.05	994.95	
			−103
98	10.10	989.80	
			−105
97	10.15	984.55	

gap in the MR schedule. So long as marginal cost at output 10 is somewhere in the gap, the firm has no incentive to change the price. In our example, the marginal cost curve might undergo large shifts up or down without causing the firm to change price and output. Over time, of course, the kinked demand curve might shift to right or left, changing the output which the firm could sell at the existing price. But such shifts would not tend to alter the price.

Such a pattern of price stabilization has sometimes occurred. The theory behind it is deficient, however, in that it does not really explain why the price is where it is. And the pattern itself will not necessarily bring the industry as a whole anywhere near profit maximization. In particular, it immobilizes the industry against price increases which might be an appropriate response to an increase in demand or an increase in costs. Ultimately the firms will become aware of this. They may shift from the essentially defensive posture of immobility to a more aggressive behavior pattern which enables them to cope more effectively with changing conditions.

One such arrangement is *price leadership*, a probable outcome where rival firms produce a homogeneous product and where one firm is larger than the others. After the firms have coexisted for a time, there may develop a tacit understanding among the firms that price changes will be initiated only when the change appears desirable to increase total industry profits. Price is thus not used as an instrument of competitive rivalry among the firms. The price leader accepts a role of "industrial statesmanship," trying to estimate cost and demand conditions for the entire industry and making price changes accordingly. The leader must have some confidence that the other firms will follow him, particularly if he initiates a price increase. Such confidence may be warranted if the other firms have learned from experience that the leader is acting on behalf of all of them and that his judgments have in the past proved sound.

For price leadership to succeed, firms must be able to follow the leader. They must have information on the price he charges. Price leadership is difficult to maintain in situations where the number and variety of products is large, or where frequent price changes are needed to cope with seasonal or other fluctuations in demand or supply conditions.

Even if firms follow a price leadership pattern, they may continue to compete strenuously by nonprice methods. And just as in the cartel situation, the individual firm may have a strong incentive to make price concessions to individual buyers if these can be kept secret to avoid retaliation.

Even if firms do not maintain actual price leadership, an oligopolistic modus vivendi may emerge around some form of *market sharing*. This refers to some tacit understanding about the appropriate output share or sales territory of each firm. Each firm may consistently purchase the same proportion of some crucial input, such as leaf tobacco or beef cattle. Firms may respect geographic spheres of influence, each one expecting to be left alone in its own territory and in turn refraining from invading the territories of the others. Or each firm may limit the range of its own products, concentrating on certain specialized types and qualities and leaving the rest to other producers.

Over time, a group of firms in oligopoly may develop a harmonious pattern of implicit collusion which enables them to approximate the price-output patterns which would maximize their joint profits. However, their costs are likely to be higher than those of a profit-maximizing monopolist, for reasons already noted. Such a monopolist would tend to concentrate production in the most efficient facilities. The individual oligopolists are likely to spend more money on sales-promotion activities, directed at one another, than would a profit-maximizing monopolist. Product price and average cost may therefore both tend to be some-what greater under oligopoly.

Entry possibilities will also influence the oligopoly price situation. If there are no artificial barriers to entry but the individual firm needs to be large in order to achieve sufficient efficiency to survive, entry may proceed in a somewhat dis-continuous fashion. Even if a potential newcomer has access to substantial capital and skilled technical and managerial personnel (a common enough situation for a firm already operating in other sectors of the economy and considering diversi-fication), it may feel that its entry would reduce the product price sufficiently that any existing excess profits would be transformed into losses. Should demand increase or costs decline, however, the potential gains may be sufficient to attract a large newcomer, whose entry would be marked by a considerable dislocation for the older firms. The more readily small firms can enter the industry and survive, perhaps in spite of initial cost disadvantages, the stronger will be the long-run tendency for price not to exceed average cost.

oligopoly price discrimination

Price discrimination is common in oligopoly situations. However, it may have different purposes and results under different circumstances. For example, price discrimination may be used as a form of cutthroat competition. A firm which sells many products, or reaches many geographic areas, may make heavy price reductions for those products or regions where it encounters competitors. This may be a way of driving competitors out, or forcing them into a merger or cartel. At the opposite extreme, however, price discrimination may develop as part of a pattern of implicit collusion, a pattern designed to minimize price competition. For many years, the steel industry in the United States has followed a pricing pattern which emphasizes *delivered prices*—that is, the price of the product delivered to the point of use. The delivered price to any point tends to be the one set by the nearest steel producer. Steel producers who are further distant are often willing, however, to match the delivered price, trying to win a customer's business by more vigorous nonprice competition. On such sales the more distant steel producer "absorbs freight" by paying the higher transport cost and must be content with a lower net price. Since different customers pay, in effect, different net prices (after transport costs), the use of freight absorption tends to result in price discrimination. Competition in this form may lead to cross-hauling, since there is no guarantee that a steel producer will win all the business closest to his mill. Thus this style of competition does not minimize costs or maximize profits for the steel producers. They follow it because it minimizes the danger of outright price competiton without violating laws against outright collusion. The practice does not result in price reductions to individual customers.

Finally, price discrimination may arise in oligopoly as the breakdown of a cartel or price-leadership pattern. The firm which decides to cheat on the high public price in order to expand its own sales is likely to do so by secret price reductions extended only to large buyers whose demand elasticity appears high to the prospective cheater. By keeping his price cut secret and limiting it to a few buyers, the cheater hopes to delay discovery and retaliation by his competitors.

A relatively large member of an oligopoly may also be able to put his competitors at a disadvantage by inducing suppliers to sell more cheaply to him than to his competitors. A large retail chain in the United States allegedly threatened to undertake production of some items for itself unless suppliers of those items would make price reductions which they did not give to other buyers. Large auto manufacturers allegedly were able to obtain lower steel prices by threatening to build their own steel mills.

other elements of oligopoly strategy

The more effectively a group of oligopolists succeed in avoiding price competition and keeping selling price above average production cost, the greater is likely to be the incentive for the individual firm to try to increase its sales at the existing price level. This will tend to be reflected in intensive nonprice competition through advertising and other selling effort. Nonprice competition does not raise the same dangers of mutual disadvantage as does price competition. Price changes involve a one-dimensional, unequivocal impact on other firms, whereas nonprice competition can proceed along many dimensions. One objective of nonprice competition may be to increase the effective differentiation of products in the minds of consumers, thus making each firm somewhat less sensitive to price changes made by rivals. Stress on product innovation may be very beneficial to the consuming public. But heavy expenditures on advertising may add substantially to costs and indeed go far beyond the level which a rational monopolist would spend. Such emphasis may help to protect the existing firms against entry.

The individual oligopolist may attempt to protect himself against his rivals, and indeed to gain the edge on them, by "vertical" relationships involving supply sources or distribution outlets. In the extreme case, a firm may engage in vertical integration, bringing under its ownership and control the production of important inputs such as raw materials, or distribution outlets for reaching the final buyers. Such integration may appear desirable for defensive reasons if there is danger that rival firms will do the same. Individual firms in steel and aluminum production, for instance, own most of the reserves of the metal ores they require. There may be no particular technical or cost advantages in such ownership and control, but each firm is at least spared the risk of becoming dependent on its rivals for a crucial raw material. If the inputs are supplied by a competitive industry with low concentration and little danger of centralized control, there may be no incentive for the oligopolists to acquire direct ownership and control. The cigarette manufacturers have little incentive to enter directly into production of leaf tobacco; no firm need fear that its rivals will be able to control the leaf supply directly.

Since wholesale and retail trade are typically competitive activities, easy to enter, individual manufacturing firms have little incentive to acquire direct ownership of distribution outlets. However, they may employ strategic devices which give them a competitive advantage in dealing with nominally independent wholesale and retail firms. Auto manufacturers do not own their dealerships, but they do employ a franchise system which restricts the freedom of the dealer to handle competing models. Most gasoline stations are nominally independent, but the major brand-name refiners typically lease the physical facilities to the service station operator and in turn impose restrictions on the products he can handle. More broadly, manufacturing firms may employ tying contracts or exclusive dealing arrangements to influence relations with distributors or other customers. In a tying contract, the manufacturer may agree to sell or lease a product only on condition that the customer buy something else from the same supplier. Manufacturers of business machines used to require that customers buy punch cards from the same manufacturer; a major photographic firm required buyers to purchase film processing services along with the film, etc. Exclusive dealing contracts bind a distributor not to handle the products of competing producers.

Such devices may offer a fertile field for one firm in an oligopoly to gain an advantage over the others. They tend particularly to confer a strategic advantage on the large and diversified firm, regardless of whether it is more efficient or not. And they may make it very difficult for new firms to enter an industry, because crucial supply sources or distribution outlets may all be controlled by the firms already in existence.

In the United States, the freedom of large firms to employ such strategic devices is severely limited by the Clayton Antitrust Act. This law prohibits price discrimination, mergers, intercorporate stock ownership, tying contracts, and exclusive dealing arrangements when such practices lessen competition or tend to create a monopoly.

broader aspects of business strategy

The firm in a purely competitive industry may have very little choice whether to try to maximize profits or not. Its major problem is to survive and yield a normal return to its owners, and the competitive environment may provide only a limited area within which it can operate and survive at all. It is when we move away from situations of small firms and easy entry that the range of managerial discretion becomes larger. In situations of big business oligopoly, where entry may be difficult, the firm has a much wider range of policies which are compatible with its survival. Economists and students of business administration have suggested that the mere assumption of profit maximization may be either insufficiently precise or simply incorrect as an analytical basis for explaining the behavior of firms. Some of the proposed modifications are very complex, and we will content ourselves with a brief listing and identification.

1. Time, expectations, and present value. Our conventional theory of the firm plays down the fact that the benefits of present decisions will come some time in the future. Of course this becomes explicit when we consider capital investment decisions, and we have seen how the firm must form some expectations about future productivity, revenues, and costs to estimate the present value of the marginal net revenue product of a capital asset. A similar emphasis is needed, however, in dealing with more commonplace questions such as a response to a change in input or output price. Production decisions are usually made in advance of actual sales, and the firm's output decisions should therefore be related to expected price, not merely the present price. Indeed, the distinction between long-run and short-run behavior may turn on the length of time over which price expectations are extended. To make decisions about capital assets lasting ten years, the firm must have some expectations about product (and input) prices extending over ten years also.

To say that decisions must be based on expected prices may leave everything hanging in thin air unless one has some idea about how expectations are formed. Presumably expectations are based on past experience in some fashion. Precisely what the relationship is has been a field for active empirical inquiry in recent years.

The firm's objective must also be qualified; presumably it should be treated as the maximization of expected future profits. However, future profits constitute a stream of revenue spread out over time. The firm may be regarded as trying to maximize the present value of the expected profit flow; this permits us to extend the time horizon indefinitely into the future. This present value is hardly a precise magnitude; the individual revenue and cost expectations going into it are uncertain, and there is also a problem of identifying the appropriate discount or interest rate to convert the expected flow into a present value.

On the other hand, emphasis on maximizing the expectation of long-run profit flow helps to deal with situations where the firm may appear to sacrifice short-run gains. A monopolist who refrains from charging the most immediately profitable price because he does not want to provoke entry of new firms or some sort of government intervention may be acting in a manner consistent with long-run profit maximization. So might a firm which sustains a damaging strike rather than yield labor concessions which might add substantially to future costs.

2. Risk and uncertainty. Because future events are uncertain, decisions made on the basis of expectations are risky. It may be helpful to assume that the firm estimates not merely the most probable outcome of a given decision but also the range of possible outcomes, with some estimate of the profit or loss associated with each, and an assessment of the relative probability or likelihood of each outcome. The range of possible outcomes may be crucial, since the firm may feel that certain outcomes are so disastrous that all possibility of their occurrence should be avoided. More likely, however, the firm may be willing to accept some risk of disaster provided the probability is below some threshold level. To do this requires some estimate of the probability of the disastrous event. The firm's behavior would depend in part on how its management formed their estimates of probability (business conditions do not ordinarily lend themselves to purely actuarial calculations) and in part on how they respond to a given probability configuration. Some firms might behave more as "risk avoiders" than others, and resulting differences in behavior might not be easy to infer merely from the assumption that they try to maximize expected profits.

Problems of risk and uncertainty are particularly relevant to oligopoly strategy, where the individual firm may be very much concerned with how rival firms will react to any change which it innovates. A mathematical-economic approach oriented towards problems of this sort is called the *theory of games*. Applications of the theory differ importantly depending on whether there are only two players (e.g., firms in an oligopoly) or a larger number and whether the total potential winnings of the players constitute a fixed "pot" (so that the larger one player's winnings, the smaller the winnings of the others) or can vary. Much of game theory deals with two-participant, zero-sum games, in which the two players' winnings add to a constant sum. Each player is assumed to have a choice among several strategies. Associated with each strategy chosen by player I will be various payoffs, measured in profit, total revenue, or some other medium valued by the participants. The payoff for each strategy of player I will reflect the strategy chosen by player II. For each player, one could imagine a table of expected payoffs, associated with each possible combination of strategies. In Table 21-2, for instance, we assume there are three possible strategies available to each player. Numbers in the table represent expected payoffs to player I; the corresponding values for player II are obtained by subtracting player I's gains from some constant (say $200 to make the example symmetrical).

It is assumed that each player knows the data in the payoff table, acts accordingly, and knows that his opponent will do likewise. Under such assumptions, it is easy to prescribe prudent conduct for each player: be prepared for the worst. If player I adopts strategy I, he can expect player II to choose his strategy III, leaving player I with zero profits. If player I adopts strategy III, his rival will counter

TABLE 21-2

Player I	Player II		
	STRATEGY I	STRATEGY II	STRATEGY III
	(Expected gains to player I)		
Strategy I	$200	$100	0
Strategy II	$100	$100	$100
Strategy III	0	$100	$200

with strategy I. Player I is well advised to find the strategy with the "least-worst" minimum value, and that is strategy II. This kind of solution, called a *minimax solution*, is one of the distinctive contributions of game theory. It would not be difficult to apply this approach to the case described by the kinked demand curve. The theory is readily extended to situations where the elements in the payoff table are expressed as probability distributions rather than as single numbers.

Extensions of game theory into cases with more than two players permit analysis of *coalitions*, in which some players gang up on others. On the whole, however, the assumptions required to make game analysis determinate have been too restrictive to give it much value as an analytical device.

3. Does the firm maximize profit? Large corporations are typically managed by people who do not necessarily own a large proportion of the firm. The owners—the stockholders—may in fact have relatively little knowledge or control over the detailed operating decisions of the firm. Under such circumstances, why should a rational management seek to maximize profits? Will there not tend to be other considerations relating more directly to their own welfare? A clear conflict of goals may arise in cost minimization. Management salaries and expense perquisites are elements of cost: they are also costs the appropriate magnitude of which cannot be established precisely. Evaluation of the marginal revenue product of executive talent may be imprecise, and often there is not a competitive market from which a going price of such talent can be inferred. Chances are that top management may be overpaid, relatively to the level of remuneration which would maximize stockholder profits.

For similar reasons, a management-controlled firm may demand somewhat less in the way of managerial effort, be somewhat slower to replace waning talents, and provide a bit more job security than stockholder interests would warrant. In more extreme cases, incumbent management may practice favoritism toward their own family members, old school chums, or members of a particular cultural, religious, or nationality group.

At a different level, management control may lead to an aversion to risk-taking; incumbent management may see little potential personal gain from the success of a risky undertaking but a large potential personal loss if it fails.

The potential conflict of interest between management and ownership is not in dispute. How far it extends in practice is another question. Many firms use stock ownership or stock options to stimulate management incentives. If incumbent management flagrantly neglects stockholder interests, the value of the stock may fall to the point where energetic outsiders can buy a controlling interest and oust the offending management group.

One particular line of argument holds that management goals may be more involved with the output or sales of the firm rather than its profits. Professor William Baumol has argued that the large firm's objective may be to maximize sales, subject to the condition that some minimum level of adequate profit is also achieved. Such a policy might dictate a somewhat lower price and higher output than under profit maximization, but it might also dictate a larger volume of selling expenditure.

Description of actual pricing methods in large firms often focuses on methods of cost-plus pricing, where product price is determined by adding some conventional markup to the average cost of the product. At least two conceptual problems are raised by such methods. First, if average cost depends on quantity produced and if quantity produced depends on how much the customers will buy at each possible price, the firm can only obtain a determinate average cost figure by making some assumptions about output and about the demand schedule for the product. Second, one is left wondering about the size of the markup employed. Perhaps it too represents some inferences about demand elasticity and related matters. Average-cost-plus pricing techniques do not seem to have much to recommend them as methods of maximizing profits. However, if all firms in an oligopoly have similar costs, the technique may be an effective way of harmonizing pricing practices by the various firms in a kind of generalized price leadership pattern.

oligopoly response to changes in data

How firms in an oligopoly respond to changes in demand or in costs may depend on the precise status of their interrelation and also on what managers are in fact trying to maximize. It is probably true that price changes are always somewhat traumatic for oligopolists and that oligopoly situations may consequently display somewhat less price flexibility, at least in the short run, in response to changes in demand or cost. If firms are in the uneasy kind of truce characterized by the kinked demand curve, they may keep price unchanged in the face of very large shifts in demand or costs.

If oligopoly firms are in outright collusion or in some implicit counterpart such as price leadership, they are more likely to make the same sort of responses which a monopolist would make to changes in costs. An upward shift in costs would tend to provoke price increases, particularly when the cost increases relate to an input used by all firms. Response to a demand increase might depend on managerial goals and pricing techniques. For instance, use of average cost pricing, or a managerial goal stressing sales maximization, would tend to operate against raising product price even if an increase in market demand for the product made such a price increase potentially profitable. Such conditions might make firms willing to lower price in face of rising demand if they were moving along downward-sloping average and marginal cost curves.

Conditions of entry and exit of firms will be reflected in the response patterns of the industry. A rise in input prices might be sufficient to cause a large firm to withdraw from the industry altogether; this might in turn be sufficient to place the remaining firms in a position to receive more than a normal profit. A rise in market demand for the product might initially improve industry profits sufficiently to induce a new firm to enter the industry operating at a fairly large scale; its entry might push the entire industry into a position of receiving less profit than before the initial demand increase occurred.

summary

Monopolistic competition is the term applied to a market structure where there are many firms, each relatively small, and easy entry, but where the product of each firm is somewhat differentiated from that of the others. Because of differentiation, the demand curve confronting the individual firm tends to be downward sloping and marginal revenue is less than price. Profit-maximizing output for the firm will tend to be that at which marginal cost equals marginal revenue, but pressure from entry of new firms will tend to eliminate excess profits and bring price equal to average cost for each firm. This equilibrium will be represented by a point of tangency between the demand curve confronting the firm and the downward-sloping portion of the average cost curve. Because of efforts to accentuate differentiation, firms are likely to spend heavily for sales-promotion activities and other forms of nonprice competition.

Oligopoly is a market structure in which the number of firms is small and some or all of the firms are relatively large relative to the market demand for the product. Details differ depending on whether the product is homogeneous or differentiated and whether entry is easy or difficult. But in each case, the individual firm must try to anticipate reactions of rivals before undertaking a change in pricing or related policies. The demand schedule confronting the individual firm is determinate only if there is some unique potential response pattern forthcoming from rivals. Because of this interdependence, the oligopoly situation cannot be summarized in a single tidy equilibrium description.

Relations among firms in an oligopoly may move through a sequence of stages. Initially, each firm may assume that it can change its price without provoking retaliatory price changes from the rivals. A price cut initiated on this basis may set off a price war, which can work to the disadvantage of all firms. They may then react to an opposite extreme of outright consolidation or of collusion. In the United

States, both of these possibilities are limited by antitrust laws. In addition, effective collusion is limited by the fact that, although the firms may agree on the desirability of maximizing their joint profits, they are not in agreement about how the profits should be shared.

Lacking the possibility of collusion, firms may emerge from a price-war experience in a state of shock, pathologically fearful of making any price change, in a manner described by the kinked demand curve, with its discontinuous marginal revenue curve. Such an outcome does not give the firms any means of adjusting to changes in cost or demand, however, and is likely to be superseded, over time, by some form of implicit collusion which comes closer to achieving a profit-maximizing result for the firms. The strongest form may be price leadership, where the price leader tries to approximate the decisions a monopolist would make. Less extreme forms may involve some degree of market sharing. Whatever the precise pattern which emerges, individual firms may attempt to protect their position by vertical linkages with suppliers or distributors. Oligopoly firms are likely to channel most of their competitive energies into *nonprice* competition through sales-promotion activities and through changes in quality and style of product.

TERMS AND CONCEPTS

1. Monopolistic competition
2. Oligopoly
3. Price leadership
4. Tying contract
5. Vertical integration
6. Cartel
7. Collusion

QUESTIONS AND PROBLEMS

1. The market structure in which a firm sells its product is reflected in the product demand schedule confronting the individual firm. Explain the relationship as it arises in each of the four market situations we have analyzed.

2. An industry operated by a rational monopolist is likely to yield higher profits than the same industry operated under conditions of oligopoly even if the oligopolists charge the profit-maximizing price. Give at least two reasons for this.

3. Identify conditions under which a group of oligopolists might end up charging a price higher than the one which would maximize their joint profits.

4. What conditions determine whether entry into an industry is easy or not? What can existing firms do to make entry of newcomers more difficult?

imperfect competition
in factor markets

Conditions of pure competition are often absent in the markets for factors of production. The firms employing one factor may be sufficiently few in number and large in size that each affects the price of the factor. Price may also be controlled on the selling side, for instance by a strong labor union. It is also true that factor-market activities are affected by imperfections in product markets. In this chapter we consider these aspects of imperfect competition.

monopsony

It is often the case that an individual firm purchases a sufficient quantity of one factor to have an influence on the price of that factor. We will use the term *monopsony* to apply to such a situation, even though, strictly speaking, that term might mean a firm which is the *only* purchaser of a factor. The monopsonist is confronted by an upward-sloping supply schedule of the factor. The shape of that supply schedule depends on how much of the factor is employed elsewhere in the economy and what its marginal productivity is in those other uses.

The monopsonist is sometimes also a monopolist in the product market, but this is not a necessary condition. Indeed, it is possible that a firm might be a monopsonistic buyer and yet be selling in a perfectly competitive product market. This might result if producers are numerous, yet are geographically dispersed so that each dominates the market for labor in a local area.

A monopsonist is in a position to consider the influence which his purchases have on the price of the factor. We will assume that he pays the same price for all units and does not discriminate. Under these conditions, the more he purchases, the higher the price per unit he must pay.

marginal outlay

To analyze this situation, we make use of the concept of *marginal outlay*, defined as the change in the firm's expenditures on one factor associated with a change in the quantity of that factor. Under pure competition, the marginal outlay for a factor is equal to its price. Under monopsony, it is higher than the price.

Suppose a monopsonist is confronted by a factor supply schedule expressed by the equation $Q_a = 100P_a - 1,000$. Table 22-1 illustrates the relation between marginal outlay and factor price for the initial integral values of P.

Marginal outlay can be calculated between two points on the supply schedule. It is then expressed as $\Delta TO_a/\Delta Q_a$, letting TO_a stand for total outlay. Suppose the firm is employing 100 units of a. If it were to increase its employment to 200 units, this would push the price up from $11 to $12. Total outlay on this factor would thus be increased from $1,100 to $2,400, an increase of $1,300. Thus the marginal outlay per unit of a would be $13.

TABLE 22-1

Price of a	Quantity of a Supplied	Total Outlay on a	Δ Outlay on a	ΔQ_a	Marginal Outlay (between Points)
$10	0	0			
			$1,100	100	$11
11	100	$1,100			
			1,300	100	13
12	200	2,400			
			1,500	100	15
13	300	3,900			
			1,700	100	17
14	400	5,600			
			1,900	100	19
15	500	7,500			

Marginal outlay can also be calculated at a single point on the supply schedule. We construct a schedule expressing total outlay on a as a function of the quantity of a. The derivative dTO_a/dQ_a of this total expenditure function is the marginal outlay at any point.

We can rewrite our supply schedule in terms of P_a as follows:

$$Q_a = 100P_a - 1,000$$
$$100P_a = Q_a + 1,000$$
$$P_a = \frac{Q_a + 1,000}{100}$$

To obtain total outlay, we multiply price times quantity

$$TO_a = P_aQ_a = \frac{Q_a + 1,000}{100}Q_a = \frac{Q_a{}^2 + 1,000Q_a}{100} = \frac{Q_a{}^2}{100} + 10Q$$

$$\frac{dTO_a}{dQ_a} = \frac{Q_a}{50} + 10$$

This last expression gives us the marginal outlay schedule, which shows marginal outlay increasing as the quantity of a is increased.

The relationship of marginal outlay to price is determined by the elasticity of supply, in accordance with the following:

$$MO_a = P_a\left(1 + \frac{1}{e}\right)$$

To illustrate this, we find that our derivative formula indicates marginal outlay is 12 when Q_a is 100. Using the formula for elasticity of supply, $(dQ/dP) \cdot (P/Q)$, we find that supply elasticity at that output is 11. Since $P = 11$, we find that $1 + 1/e = 12\frac{1}{11}$ so that $MO = 12\frac{1}{11}$ of 11, which is 12. Test your understanding of this relationship by calculating marginal outlay and elasticity of supply at the point where $Q_a = 500$.

profit-maximizing input

The monopsonist will maximize his profits if he employs factor a up to that quantity at which the marginal outlay on the factor is equal to its marginal net revenue product. The marginal net revenue product measures the change in the total revenue of the firm, minus changes in expenditures for other inputs, associated with the change in the quantity of factor a employed by the firm. $MNRP$ is calculated in the assumption that the production function, demand schedule for the product, and supply schedules of other inputs are given.

As the quantity of factor a employed increases, its $MNRP$ tends to decline. If the monopsonist is selling in a purely competitive market, the decline of $MNRP$ results from the diminishing marginal rate of substitution between a and other inputs and from decreasing returns to scale. If the monopsonist faces a downward-sloping product demand curve, this accentuates the downward slope of the $MNRP$ schedule.

If the firm is operating at a point where the $MNRP$ of factor a is greater than the marginal outlay for it, the firm can increase its profits by increasing the quantity of a which it employs. As it does so, however, $MNRP$ falls and MO rises. Eventually the firm reaches a point where they are equal. To employ additional units of a beyond this point would cause profits to decline.

Figure 22-1 illustrates the profit-maximizing input situation of a monopsonist. The supply schedule is the one we used in the illustration above: it is

$$P_a = \frac{Q_a}{100} + 10$$

and the marginal outlay derived from it is $MO_a = Q_a/50 + 10$. The schedule of total net revenue product is assumed to be expressed as

$$TNRP_a = 20Q_a - \frac{Q_a{}^2}{200}$$

From this we obtain $MNRP = 20 - Q_a/100$.

Marginal outlay and $MNRP$ are equal at a quantity of 333 units of input. To find the profit-maximizing price, we note from the supply curve the price which must be paid to obtain 333 units of the input. This is \$13.33. The solution is shown numerically

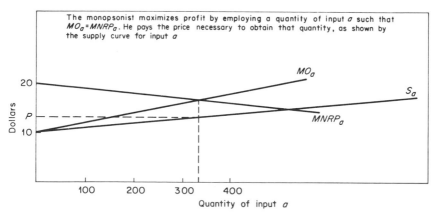

Figure 22-1 Profit-maximizing input for monopsonist.

TABLE 22-2

Quantity of Input a	Price of a	$MNRP_a$ $20 - \dfrac{Q_a}{100}$	MO_a $10 + \dfrac{Q_a}{50}$	$TNRP_a$ $20Q_a - \dfrac{Q_a{}^2}{200}$	Total Outlay on a $\dfrac{Q_a{}^2}{100} + 10Q_a$	Profit
200	$12.00	$18.00	$14.00	$3,800.00	$2,400.00	$1,400.00
300	13.00	17.00	16.00	5,550.00	3,900.00	1,650.00
333	13.33	16.67	16.67	6,111.11	4,444.44	1,666.67
350	13.50	16.50	17.00	6,387.50	4,725.00	1,662.50
400	14.00	16.00	18.00	7,200.00	5,600.00	1,600.00

in Table 22-2. The total net revenue product of input a represents total revenue of the firm minus expenditures on other inputs. When we subtract expenditures on input a from $TNRP$, therefore, we obtain a measure of the profits of the firm. As Table 22-2 shows, these are highest when the firm buys 333 units of a.

factor proportions

The monopsonist's decision about least-cost input combinations will be affected by concern for his influence on the prices of inputs. When we analyzed the choice of input mix under competitive conditions, we compared the firm's isoproduct curve with a set of isocost lines, based on some given set of input prices. We concluded that the least-cost input combination was identified at the point where the marginal rate of substitution between inputs was equal to the (inverse) ratio of their prices.

If a firm is a monopsonist, however, the isocost curves cease to be straight lines, and their slope is no longer equal to the ratio of input prices. Figure 22-2 illustrates the influence of monopsony on factor proportions. Input a, measured horizontally, is available in perfectly elastic supply at a price of $10. However, input b, measured vertically, has an upward-sloping supply schedule, assumed to take the form $b = P_b$. The typical isocost curve can be expressed as follows:

$$TC = a \cdot P_a + b \cdot P_b$$
$$TC = 10a + b^2$$
$$a = \frac{TC}{10} - \frac{b^2}{10}$$

In Figure 22-2, isocost lines are drawn for $20, $40, $60, $80, and $100. These display two striking features. First, the isocost curves are not straight lines, but bend, reflecting the change in the price of input b as its quantity purchased varies. Second, the curves are parallel horizontally, but not vertically, and their vertical

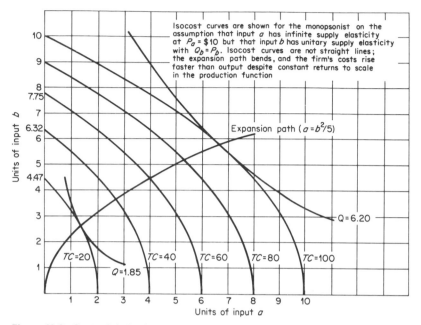

Isocost curves are shown for the monopsonist on the assumption that input a has infinite supply elasticity at $P_a = \$10$ but that input b has unitary supply elasticity with $Q_b = P_b$. Isocost curves are not straight lines; the expansion path bends, and the firm's costs rise faster than output despite constant returns to scale in the production function

Expansion path $(a = b^2/5)$

$Q = 6.20$

$TC = 20$ $TC = 40$ $TC = 60$ $TC = 80$ $TC = 100$

$Q = 1.85$

Units of input a

Units of input b

Figure 22-2 Cost minimization and input mix: monopsony.

intercepts become increasingly close together as one moves upward. The precise shape will of course depend on the specific values chosen for the input supply schedules. The outward bulge will be typical since each input's supply schedule will tend to slope upward, as a higher price is associated with a higher quantity. (Had we given both input supply schedules in the form $b = P_b$, each isocost curve would have been the arc of a circle.)

The least-cost input combination for each level of output is still at the point where the appropriate isoquant is tangent to an isocost curve. However, the slope of the isocost curve is no longer equal to the inverse ratio of the prices of the inputs. Rather, it is equal to the inverse ratio of the marginal outlays for the inputs. In our illustration, the marginal outlay for input a is equal to its price, and is \$10. The marginal outlay on input b can be obtained as follows:

$$TO_b = b \cdot P_b = b^2$$

$$MO_b = \frac{dTO_b}{db} = 2b$$

We know that the typical isocost curve can be expressed as follows:

$$a = \frac{TC}{10} - \frac{b^2}{10}$$

The slope of the isocost curve will be the derivative $da/db = (-)b/5$. Ignoring the minus sign, this will be equal to the ratio

$$\frac{MO_b}{MO_a} = \frac{2b}{10} = \frac{b}{5}$$

Thus a general condition for cost minimization would be to select an input combination such that the marginal rate of input substitution (along an isoquant) is equal to the inverse ratio of the marginal outlays on the inputs. This condition will include as a special case the situation where the firm is buying inputs in a purely competitive market and the marginal outlay on each is equal to its price.

The elasticity of supply of an input provides the relationship between the price of the input and the marginal outlay on it. The lower the elasticity of its supply, the greater the excess of marginal outlay over input price. If the inputs have different elasticities of supply, the monopsonist will tend to substitute against the one with the lower elasticity and use relatively more of the other, compared to the competitive case. In our example, input b has a lower elasticity of supply, and the firm tends to use less of it and more of a for each level of output than it would it if were merely equating MRS with P_b/P_a.

When the inputs have differing supply elasticities, the expansion path is likely not to be a straight line, so the least-cost proportions will not be the same at each level of output. To illustrate, we consider the simplest Cobb-Douglas production function in the form $Q = \sqrt{ab}$. We know that the marginal rate of input substitution da/db is equal to a/b. Setting this equal to the ratio of marginal outlays, we obtain

$$\frac{a}{b} = \frac{b}{5}$$
$$b^2 = 5a$$
$$a = \frac{b^2}{5} \quad \text{and} \quad b = \sqrt{5a}$$

Either of the last equations identifies an expansion path of least-cost input combinations drawn in Figure 22-2. The expansion path is not a straight line. As output expands, the price of b is bid up and the firm uses relatively more of a per unit of output.

shape of cost functions

Existence of a monopsony position in buying inputs also changes the relationship between a firm's cost functions and the prices of the inputs. Since the firm must pay a higher price for an input as its employment increases, the firm's cost functions will tend to be more sharply tilted upward than if the input price were constant. To illustrate, we consider short-run cost schedules involving only one variable input. Assume that two firms have identical short-run production functions expressed by $Q = 4b^{1/2}$ and that each has fixed cost of $160. One firm is a monopsonist, confronted by a supply schedule of input b expressed by $b = P_b$. The other firm (perhaps in another location) can buy all it desires of input b at a price of $9. From the production function, we determine that $b = Q^2/16$. For the monopsonist, cost schedules are derived as follows:

$$TC = 160 + b \cdot P_b = 160 + b^2 = 160 + \frac{Q^4}{256}$$

$$MC = \frac{Q^3}{64}$$

For the competitive buyer, however, cost schedules are as follows:

$$TC = 160 + b \cdot P_b = 160 + 9b = 160 + \frac{9Q^2}{16}$$

$$MC = \frac{9Q}{8}$$

If both firms produce 12 units of output, they will buy 9 units of b at a price of $9 per unit and incur the same total cost, namely $241. However, the monopsonist's marginal cost could be $27 compared with $13.50 for the competitive buyer. It takes a higher product price to induce the monopsonist to produce 12 units of output than it would take to induce the competitive buyer to produce at this level.

Observe that the monopsonist's marginal cost is below that of the competitive buyer at low levels of output. In this range, the monopsonist is benefiting from his ability to obtain input b at a relatively low price. In our example, the monopsonist's MC is lower for outputs less than about 8.5 units.

The general effect of monopsony is to give the monopsonist a larger exponent for the Q term in his cost functions than would be the case under comparable competitive conditions. Beyond some level of output, therefore, his MC curve will slope up more steeply; beyond some other level of output, it will be higher than the MC curve of a comparable competitive buyer.

Thus the existence of a monopsony position affects both the input proportions and the output which the firm finds most profitable. Our analysis of the two separately tends to confirm our earlier proposition, to the effect that the monopsonist tends to buy less of any input at any given price than would an otherwise similar competitive firm. And the reduction of purchases will be more drastic, the lower the supply elasticity of the input.

price discrimination

A monopsonist may be able to discriminate in the price he pays for inputs. He may be able to obtain some units at a lower price than is required for the others. This can only occur if there are obstacles to resale; otherwise, more favored sellers will tend to buy the input from less favored sellers and resell it to the monopsonist at the more favorable price.

The monopsonist tends to discriminate on the basis of different elasticities of supply. If a portion of input supply has a very low elasticity, the monopsonist may be able to buy it at a very low price while being willing to pay more to obtain desired quantities with a higher elasticity.

The significance of supply elasticity can be illustrated by discrimination in paying labor. Workers already employed by a firm are likely to have a relatively low elasticity of labor supply, at least in the neighborhood of the existing wage. Some would not leave their present employment even if their wage were reduced somewhat. However, if the firm desires to hire additional workers, it may find their elasticity of supply is quite high. None are available at wages below the going rate, but by raising its offer somewhat, the firm can obtain a large number.

Under these circumstances, the firm may choose to offer higher wages to the newcomers while at the same time not increasing the wages of those already employed by the firm. Such discrimination is aided if each person's wage is kept secret from the others; otherwise the firm may suffer from discontent among the senior workers.

monopoly in the product market

The state of competition in the product market affects the demand for inputs. In this section we consider the situation of a firm which is a monopolist in the product market but buys its inputs under competitive conditions.

Conditions in the product market show up through differences in the manner in which the marginal revenue product or the marginal net revenue product is determined. This can most simply be illustrated by considering the marginal revenue product, calculated on the basis of short-run considerations. The firm is operating with some given quantity of a fixed input a and bases its decision concerning the employment of the variable input b on the marginal revenue product of b. The marginal revenue product of b is defined as the change in total revenue associated with a change in the quantity of b employed. If the firm is selling in a purely competitive product market, MRP_b is simply equal to the marginal physical product of input b, multiplied by the price of the product. We have referred to this as the value of the marginal product, or VMP. But suppose the firm is a monopolist in the product market. An increase in output tends to decrease the price of the product. Marginal revenue is less than price. Consequently, the marginal revenue product is less than the VMP. We determine MRP by multiplying the marginal physical product times its marginal revenue.

The relationships among MPP, MR, and MRP are illustrated in Table 22-3. We assume that the long-run production function can be expressed by the equation $Q = 10\sqrt{ab}$ and that the quantity of a is fixed at 9. Thus the short-run production function is $Q = 30\sqrt{b}$. By taking the derivative of this, we obtain an expression for the marginal physical product of b, which is $dQ/db = 15/\sqrt{b}$. The demand schedule confronting the monopolist we will assume to be expressed as $P = 15 - Q/10$. From this we can determine the total revenue schedule $15Q - Q^2/10$ and the marginal revenue schedule $15 - Q/5$.

In Table 22-3, the marginal relationships are shown in two ways: as differences in totals between separate points, and as derivatives at a single point. In each case, note that the value of MRP is equal to the product of MPP times MR. We can also illustrate this relationship with the values of the derivatives. We can obtain an expression for the MRP_b directly if we construct a total revenue product function in terms of b. This is derived as follows:

$$P = 15 - \frac{Q}{10} = 15 - 3\sqrt{b}$$
$$Q = 30\sqrt{b}$$
$$TRP_b = PQ = (30\sqrt{b})(15 - 3\sqrt{b}) = 450\sqrt{b} - 90b$$
$$MRP_b = \frac{dTRP_b}{db} = \frac{225}{\sqrt{b}} - 90$$

We have already established that

$$MPP_b = \frac{15}{\sqrt{b}} \qquad \text{and} \qquad MR = 15 - \frac{Q}{5} = 15 - 6\sqrt{b}$$

When we multiply $15/\sqrt{b}$ times $(15 - 6\sqrt{b})$, the result is also $225/\sqrt{b} - 90$.

Remember that we are dealing with a firm which is a monopolist in its product market, but buys its input in competitive markets. The most profitable amount of input b for the firm to purchase will thus be that at which the MRP of the input equals the price of the input. Suppose the price of b were \$22.50. The most profitable amount for the firm to employ would be 4 units, producing an output of 60 and selling it at a price of \$9.

At any given price for the product, the MRP_b as the monopolist sees it is lower than would be the MRP_b seen by a competitive firm with the same production function. To the competitive firm, MRP_b at that price-output situation would be \$9 times 7.50, or \$67.50. The competitive firm would thus purchase more of b than just 4 units. (How much would the competitive firm buy? Try to figure it out, using the

TABLE 22-3

Units of Input b	Output	Product Price	Total Revenue	Between Points MRP_b	MPP_b	MR	Derivative MRP_b	MPP_b	MR
1	30.00	$12.00	$360.00	$360.00	30.00	$12.00	$135.00	15.00	$9.00
2	42.43	10.76	456.55	96.55	12.43	7.77	69.10	10.61	6.51
3	51.96	9.80	509.21	52.66	9.53	5.53	39.90	8.66	4.61
4	60.00	9.00	540.00	30.79	8.04	3.83	22.50	7.50	3.00
5	67.08	8.29	556.39	16.09	7.08	2.27	10.62	6.71	1.58

schedule for MPP_b). This conclusion is a general one; the monopolist tends to buy less of an input than the quantity at which the price of the input would equal the value of its marginal physical product. This is simply a reflection of the fact that he does not produce up to the output where marginal cost equals price, but stops at the smaller output where marginal cost equals marginal revenue, MR being less than the product price. Thus the VMP of the input remains higher than the price of the input.

We have stated our example in terms of the MRP calculated in the short run. The same principles would apply to the marginal net revenue product calculated for the long run. $MNRP$ is the change in the firm's revenue, minus the change in expenditures on other inputs, associated with a change in the amount of one specified input. For the firm selling in a competitive market, the change in revenue is proportional to the change in output. For the product monopolist, the change in revenue is proportionately less than the change in output. Consequently, at any given price-output situation, the specific value of the marginal net revenue product of each input as seen by a monopolist would be lower than the value of $MNRP$ as seen by a firm selling in a competitive market. Thus the product monopolist would tend to buy less of each input.

Suppose the product monopolist were also a monopsonist in buying inputs. We could depict his situation by combining our two previous sections. The firm's maximum-profit input position would be where the $MNRP$ of each input was equal to the marginal outlay for that input. The quantity of the input purchased at any given price would be even less than if the firm held a monopoly position on only one side of its operations.

impact on input price and allocation

We have seen that industries buying an input under monopsony conditions tend to buy a smaller quantity of it than would a competitive buyer under otherwise equal circumstances. Similarly, a firm selling in a monopolistic product market would tend to employ less of the input than a competitive industry with otherwise similar conditions. Such monopsony and monopoly purchase curtailments would tend to reduce the total market demand for an input below the competitive level and would therefore also tend to lower its market price. The lower price would in turn encourage use of the input by competitive industries to a somewhat greater extent than if a purely competitive price prevailed.

bilateral monopoly

An interesting special case arises when a monopoly seller confronts a monopsony buyer. The situation is likely to allow an area for bargaining and strategy between the two. Of course, the monopoly seller will not sell unless the price covers his costs, and the monopsony buyer will not buy unless the price he pays is less than the average revenue product of the input. Between these two areas, however, there may lie a range of indeterminacy.

The situation contains elements similar to that of oligopoly. The two firms have a potential common interest in maximizing their combined profits but a conflict of interest concerning the division of the profits. Typically each has incomplete knowledge of the cost-profit conditions of the other. Each is therefore able to threaten the other with possible dire consequences if the other's demands are fully met. The seller may plead inability to cover cost and stay in production; the buyer may complain of inability to pass high costs along to customers without heavy loss of sales. As in oligopoly, each firm is influenced by the reactions it expects from the other. Thus there is no unique equilibrium outcome.

monopoly in sale of factor service

We now turn to the selling side of the factor market and consider the possible operation of monopoly in sale of factor services. The most interesting cases of this sort concern the activities of labor unions, so we will confine our attention to that subject.

It has been correctly noted that a labor union is not ordinarily a monopolist in the strict sense, since it does not literally sell the services of its members. However, unions sometimes act like monopolists and may have monopoly effects. Union power may rest on some method of controlling the supply of labor. In some cases, such control results because all practitioners of a skilled craft are members of the union, and sell their services only on terms influenced by the union. In other cases, union power rests on the possibility of disrupting employer operations through strikes, boycotts, or other forms of harassment. The potential influence of a labor union is always weakened, however, to the extent that it is easy for employers to hire qualified workers who are not union members.

We consider first a labor union formed among the present employees of a single firm in a competitive industry. Such a union has very little potential for raising the wages of its members. On one hand, the firm may find it easy to obtain nonunion workers, and the union members may be invited to leave their jobs if they do not care to continue working for the former wage. If the firm cannot make such a substitution, it will still have little freedom to grant a wage increase to the union. Such an increase would tend to raise the firm's costs. If other firms are not granting similar concessions, this firm's higher costs will mean less than normal profits, or outright losses, and it will close down if this condition persists.

For this reason, workers in such an industry may attempt to form a union covering all firms in the industry. Then wage concessions can be extracted equally from all firms, and no individual firm is singled out. Even so, the firms are likely to resist granting wage increases, since they may initially be making only a normal profit, and a wage increase may inflict temporary losses. Admittedly, the price of the product will tend to rise in response to any increase in wages. However (in the absence of collusion) the price rises only as industry output is curtailed, and part of the reduction in output is brought about by the departure of unprofitable firms.

Let us suppose that the union succeeds in obtaining a higher wage rate for its workers. What will happen to employment opportunities and the total wage income of the union members? The effect on employment opportunities will depend on the substitution effect and the output effect of the wage increase. If it is easy for the firms to substitute against the union members, their employment may decline substantially. Such substitution might come through greater employment of non-union workers. Or it might come through substitution of capital goods for labor.

The higher wage rate will tend to raise costs and cause the output of the industry to decline. The price of the product will tend toward a higher level, equal to the new minimum long-run average cost. At the higher price, consumers purchase less of the product than they formerly did. The higher the price elasticity of demand, the greater the decline in quantity sold for a given rise in product price. And the rise in product price itself depends on how large the wage increase is and how large union wage costs are in relation to total costs.

If union wage costs are a small part of total costs and if consumer demand for the product has a low elasticity, then the output effect of the wage increase will tend to be slight. The larger the influence of union wage costs on total cost, however, and the higher the price elasticity of consumer demand for the product, the greater the reduction in output—and, therefore, the greater the reduction in job opportunities.

We can ordinarily assume that there will be some loss of job opportunities in the industry as a result of the wage increase. However, this need not mean that any present union members are thrown out of work. Suppose, for example, that the demand for the product is growing from year to year and that a certain number of workers leave voluntarily because of retirement or transfer to other employment. The higher wage rate causes job opportunities to be less than they otherwise would have been, but there may still be enough for all present union members who want to remain. What happens is that the industry adds fewer workers to its payrolls than it otherwise would have.

What happens to the total wage income of the union members? This depends on the elasticity of demand for labor, reflecting the substitution effect and output effect. If demand elasticity is greater than 1, the loss of job opportunities will be so extensive that total wage income of union members will be reduced. If demand elasticity is less than 1, the higher wage rate predominates over the loss of employment, and the total wage income of the union members increases. If a union were behaving like a monopolist, it would try to maximize the wage income of its members, seeking a point of unitary demand elasticity. However, such a maximization postulate does not seem warranted. Indeed, the union resembles a cartel in that the members retain their separate identities. They share common interests in

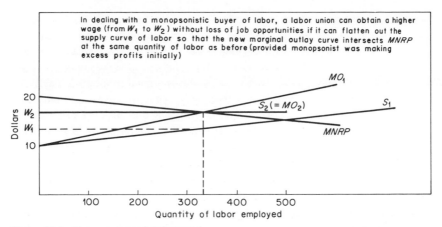

In dealing with a monopsonistic buyer of labor, a labor union can obtain a higher wage (from W_1 to W_2) without loss of job opportunities if it can flatten out the supply curve of labor so that the new marginal outlay curve intersects $MNRP$ at the same quantity of labor as before (provided monopsonist was making excess profits initially)

Figure 22-3 The monopsonist thwarted.

maximizing the income of the group but have conflicting interests regarding its division.

An interesting special case of the influence on unions on employment can arise if the union deals with a firm which is a monopsonist in its labor market and is sufficiently powerful in the product market to be making profits above normal. The union may be able to gain a higher wage without loss of job opportunities and without causing a higher product price. This peculiar possibility is shown in Figure 22-3.

We assume initially the conditions shown in Figure 22-1. The monopsonist is employing 333 men at a wage of $13.33 per day. Next we assume that a union is formed which effectively demands a wage of $16.67 per day; this happens to be the value of the marginal net revenue product of labor when 333 men are employed. In addition, the union undertakes to find additional workers for the firm at that wage if needed. The result of the union's action is to flatten the supply curve. Formerly, the firm could lower the wage by reducing the number of men employed and had to raise the wage to obtain more men. Now the union has eliminated both sources of slope. The union wage holds regardless of the number of men employed.

The firm is now faced with the same sort of perfectly elastic labor supply which it would face in a purely competitive market for labor. When the elasticity of supply becomes infinite, the marginal outlay and the wage become identical. The marginal outlay curve becomes identical with the supply curve. The new supply and marginal outlay schedules have the constant value of $16.67. The firm will employ a number of men such that the marginal net revenue product of labor is also $16.67. This is the same quantity, 333, which it employed before.

But what about the output side? Won't the higher wage rate cause the firm to have higher costs and thus reduce output and raise price? The answer is that the firm's costs are changed, but in such a manner as to leave output and price unchanged. The reason is that the marginal cost of the firm at the original output is not increased. So long as the firm held a monopsony position, its marginal cost schedule reflected the fact that an expansion of output would push up the wage rate. Marginal cost was originally based on a marginal outlay higher than the wage. With a horizontal supply curve, the firm calculates marginal cost on the basis of a marginal outlay equal to the wage. Since the marginal outlays are equal, before and after, the marginal costs are also equal. Thus output and product price do not change. Of course, the firm has higher average costs, and its profits are reduced. In this case, the union's actions have operated purely as a transfer mechanism, shifting income from employer to workers.

This case does appear rather esoteric, however, and one may doubt that it is very common. More generally, we would expect that unions could successfully gain higher wage rates for their members but that this would tend to reduce job opportunities in the sectors where union strength is great. One result may be to increase the supply of workers seeking employment in the sectors where union influence is weak. Wages in the nonunion sector may therefore tend to be lower than they would be if unions were less strong. Another consequence is that the value of labor's marginal product may be higher in the strong-union sector than in the weak-union sector. And we know that failure to equalize marginal products is associated with a failure of the economy to maximize the value of its output. A transfer of workers from the weak-union sector to the strong-union sector could raise the value of total output. But such a transfer cannot occur as long as the union wage scale is above the competitive equilibrium wage.

nonwage aspects of union activity

Analysis confined to the wage effects of labor unions tends to give an inaccurate picture of union interests and effects. Much of labor-union attention is directed towards problems of fairness and justice in the treatment of individual workers. In the case of wages, this leads to a concern for the wage structure—for pay differentials associated with different jobs and other variables. It leads also to concern for justice and fairness in such policies as hiring and firing, promotions, and disciplinary actions. Often the union presses for the adoption of definite and well-known rules by which such actions are guided. That which is expected in advance and is customary often seems fair to the people involved.

Unions also often seek to participate in the making of decisions which affect the workers directly. One might say that they seek some sort of democratic process. Sometimes the results are adverse to efficiency and productivity. Workers may resist changes in job specifications and thus impede technological progress. But sometimes union participation in management decisions can increase efficiency. The union may facilitate communication of productive ideas from workers to management. Worker participation in decisions may improve morale and promote better understanding of the need for efficiency and profitability if good wages and working conditions are to prevail.

In an industrial country, a person's happiness may depend as much on the way he is treated at work as it does on the income he receives. The chief benefit of labor unions in Western industrial countries has been the reduction of opportunities for arbitrary treatment of one worker in relation to another and the increase of opportunity for workers to share in decisions affecting their well-being.

summary

We classify as a monopsonist any firm which is a sufficiently large buyer of an input to have an appreciable effect on the price of that input. The monopsonist is confronted by an upward-sloping input supply curve. The most profitable amount of the input for him to purchase is the quantity at which the marginal outlay for that input is equal to the marginal net revenue product of the input. The least-cost input mix is that for which the inverse ratio of marginal outlays equals the marginal rate of input substitution.

A firm's input purchases are also affected by the state of the market in which it sells its product. The schedules on which the firm's demand for an input are based (MRP and $MNRP$) reflect the elasticity of demand for the firm's product. The lower that elasticity, the lower the elasticity of the MRP and $MNRP$ curves also.

A labor union may act like a monopolist in the market for labor services. If the union succeeds in raising the wage rate, there is likely to be a decline in job opportunities available for the union workers. The higher wage will set off a substitution effect against union workers and will also tend to reduce the output of the industry. If the total demand for the union workers is inelastic, however, their total wage income may increase. The possibility exists, however, that formation of a union to deal with a monopsonist may raise the wage rate without reducing job opportunities.

TERMS AND CONCEPTS

1. Monopsony
2. Marginal outlay

QUESTIONS AND PROBLEMS

1. The marginal cost schedule of a monopsonist is not the same as the marginal cost schedule of a competitive firm with the same production function

paying the same prices for inputs. Illustrate by calculating the long-run cost schedules for the firm used in connection with Figure 22-2 above and comparing them with the type of cost schedule one would obtain for a competitive firm under comparable conditions. Explain the reasons for the difference and the consequences.

2. According to the American economist John Kenneth Galbraith, a labor union may exercise countervailing power to reduce the potential damage to the public resulting from the existence of giant business firms. Analyze the probable effects of the formation of a strong labor union on product price and output if the initial situation were as follows:

   (a) Originally a large monopoly firm was purchasing labor under competitive conditions.

   (b) Originally the large monopoly firm was also a monopsonist in the labor market.

3. Assume that the supply schedule of an input to a monopsonist is expressed by $Q = 100 \sqrt{P} - 10$. Calculate the total and marginal outlay schedules associated with this supply schedule. Explain how marginal outlay figures in the monopsonist's calculation of the optimum quantity of the input to purchase. Illustrate the profit-maximizing decision on the assumption that the $MNRP$ schedule of the input is $30 - Q/50$. Prove that profit is maximized where $MNRP = MO$.

4. Explain the determinants of the supply schedule of an input to a monopsonist.

imperfect competition
and economic welfare

In the English language the word "imperfect" usually suggests inferiority. The terminology of economics creates a tendency to regard "pure" competition as some sort of welfare optimum, to regard the real world as less happy than it might be if "perfection" were more nearly achieved. This is an unfortunate verbal tendency for two reasons. First, many so-called imperfections in markets are inevitable. Inherent qualities of human beings produce a world in which there are only imperfect knowledge, less than perfect mobility of productive resources, and tendencies for disequilibrium to persist.

The particular kinds of market imperfections with which this chapter is concerned are those which confront individual firms with downward-sloping demand curves for their products and upward-sloping supply curves for their inputs. Such situations arise if the individual firm is large relative to the size of the market in which it buys or sells, or if the market is small relative to the size of individual firms. The apparently redundant second phrasing is very useful, because many markets are small, and sellers are usually differentiated from one another, if only by location and personnel. Much of the "imperfection" of this sort is also inevitable.

Even if pure competition were feasible, one should not assume that it would be desirable in all respects. More probably it would be desirable in some ways and undesirable in others. At any rate, the problem needs to be analyzed explicitly and not left for only an implicit or semantic solution.

structure, behavior, and performance

We have distinguished between various situations of (product) market structure differentiated in terms of such characteristics as the number and relative size of firms, the extent of product homogeneity or differentiation, and the ease of entry. It is possible to associate certain patterns of behavior with certain conditions of market structure. Judgments about the goodness or badness of these behavior patterns enable us to evaluate the performance of various market situations. Such analysis may suggest forms of structure or behavior which should be promoted or prohibited by public policy.

We will examine the relationship between conditions of market structure and the following aspects of behavior:

1. Relation of price to cost
2. Extent to which costs are kept to a minimum
3. Extent and forms of nonprice competition
4. Degree of collusion
5. Degree of coercive or cutthroat forms of competition

price and marginal cost

Under pure competition, price tends to equal marginal cost, an equality sought by the firm in finding the output of maximum profit. When the demand curves facing individual firms are downward sloping, however, price is higher than marginal cost. The firm's profit-maximizing output is identified at the point where marginal cost equals marginal revenue. Since marginal revenue falls below price to an extent related to the elasticity of demand, price tends to exceed marginal cost more, the lower the elasticity of demand at that output.

A firm in monopolistic competition is likely to face competition from close substitute products. Consequently, its demand curve is likely to have a high elasticity, and the price will tend therefore not to be very much higher than marginal cost. For a monopolist, however, price may be substantially higher than marginal cost if elasticity is not much greater than unity. (Since marginal revenue is positive only at outputs for which demand elasticity is greater than 1, the monopolist tends to operate at an output for which demand elasticity is greater than 1.) If demand elasticity were 1.25 at the profit-maximizing output, the monopolist's profit-maximizing price would be five times his marginal cost, since $MR = P(1 - 1/e)$.

What difference does it make whether price is close to marginal cost or not? The importance lies in the effects on the composition of total output. When products are priced at marginal cost, each pair of product prices stands in the same ratio (taken inversely) as the marginal rate of transformation between the products along a production-possibilities function. Since consumers equate their subjective marginal rate of substitution to the price ratio, the optimum composition of output is achieved at the output for which that price ratio is equal to the marginal rate of transformation.

If some prices are above marginal cost and others equal to marginal cost, the composition of output will be distorted. The monopolized products will be produced in relatively insufficient quantity, and the competitive products will be produced to (relative) excess. This can be illustrated by assuming an economic system which starts from competitive equilibrium. The two products A and B are priced at marginal cost, and the output of the economy is represented by the point E in Figure 23-1. At that point there is tangency between the production-possibilities curve and community-indifference curve, reflecting the existence of equality between P_A/P_B and MC_A/MC_B.

Now assume that production of product B becomes monopolized. To maximize profits, the monopolist reduces output and raises his price. The curtailment of output reduces the money prices of factors, which brings about a fall in the price of product A and an increase in its output. As production of B is cut, output moves to the left from point E. As displaced factors are absorbed in increased output of A, output moves up. With all factors employed, output will be on the production-possibilities curve, but at a point "northwest" of E. A new price line

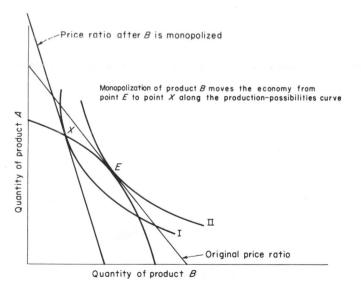

Figure 23-1 Effect of monopolization in output and prices.

will come into existence, steeper than the original. Consumer demand will push output to some point X, where the slope of the community indifference curve is equal to the (inverse) ratio of the product prices at the point of intersection with the production-possibilities curve. Point X lies on a lower indifference curve; thus the new composition of output is not so well adapted to consumer preferences as the old one.

Note that the optimum composition of output can be achieved even if individual product prices do not equal marginal cost provided that all prices exceed marginal cost by the same proportion. So long as $P_A/P_B = MC_A/MC_B$, the conditions for optimum composition of output are met.

By the same token, there is no virtue in having one industry produce an output where marginal cost equals product price, if a substantial sector of the economy does not conform to this criterion. The ideal output of one industry can only be judged in terms of the relative absorption of resources there and in alternative uses. This emphasis is neglected by economists who advocate marginal cost pricing for public utility services without considering that, on the average, firms in other sectors produce somewhat less than the output at which marginal cost equals price.

price and average cost

If entry into an industry is easy, the long-run equilibrium price tends to be equal to the average cost (including a normal return on owners' investment). If price is above average cost, more firms will be attracted. If price is below average cost, firms will leave the industry.

Equality of price with average cost is important chiefly in relation to the distribution of income. Costs arise from payments to factors of production for services. The excess of revenue over cost results in "excess" profits—that is, income to the owners which exceeds the market value of the services rendered by their labor and property. Whether this sort of profit is good or bad is a matter of value judgment. Such profit has been criticized on grounds that it is parasitic and is not a reward for productive activity. In many societies, such profit goes largely to a small group of wealthy people and may make income distribution more unequal. But such profit could be defended if there were reason to believe that it acted as an incentive for productive enterprise or if the income from profit were largely used for productive investment.

the level of costs

Economic efficiency is served when costs are kept to a minimum. The cost of any product reflects the amount of scarce resources used in making it. The lower the unit cost of a product, the greater the amount of it which one can obtain with a given amount of resources, and the smaller the sacrifice of other products required for any given amount of that product.

In a purely competitive industry, firms are under strong pressure to keep costs down. Price is continually being forced toward the average costs of the industry generally. A firm can make profits by being more efficient than its rivals, but it may easily be forced out of business if it falls behind them. Such competitive pressure encourages firms to choose technically efficient methods of using any given combination of inputs and to select economically efficient input combinations. Such pressures may be equally strong in an industry characterized by monopolistic competition.

A monopolist protected against entry has somewhat more freedom to be inefficient, although he still has the profit incentive spurring him to reduce costs. But monopoly does not provide the scope for variety, for trial and error, which is likely to exist in an industry with many firms and easy entry.

An oligopoly in which there is some degree of collusion (explicit or implicit) but not complete pooling of activities may be even less efficient than a monopoly. A monopolist owning several plants would allocate production among them in a manner suitable for minimizing costs. But if each plant is under separate owner-ship, oligopoly collusion may allocate production among them in a manner which is unrelated to their efficiency. Some plants may be kept in service despite costs so high that a profit-maximizing monopolist would close them down. On the other hand, if the spirit of rivalry is strong in the oligopoly, the existence of several decision-making units may promote more experimentation and variety and out-perform a comparable monopoly.

An important problem in keeping costs down is effective management of people. However, a constant emphasis on efficiency and economy is not always pleasant to the people in a firm, management or subordinates. If a firm is not hard pressed by competition, the temptation to maintain a more relaxed, but more costly style may win out. The existence of family firms may give rise to this problem. The head of the firm may feel it is more important to keep peace in the family than to try to get maximum efficiency from everyone. And it may be difficult to recruit outsiders, however efficient, and to dismiss family members, however inefficient. Such cases reflect the fact that management really has other goals besides profit maximization. A firm may fight much harder when its very survival is at stake.

The level of costs depends also on the scale of output. In pure competition, entry or exit of firms creates pressure for existing firms to operate at the scale at which average cost is lowest. However, if the industry is subject to free entry but firms are faced with downward-sloping demand curves, the firms tend to produce at an output level below the point of lowest average cost. Individual firms tend to be smaller than the optimum size.

It is not easy to generalize about industries not subject to easy entry. The monopolist seeks the most profitable output, and this is not automatically the output of lowest average cost. Firms in an oligopoly may be striving for greater power and influence relative to rivals or to suppliers and customers. This may lead them to a size which is greater than the optimum. The formation of the United States Steel Corporation through merger in 1901 illustrates this tendency.

It does appear, however, that costs per unit are relatively constant over a broad range of outputs for many firms. Under such conditions, there may be little difference in efficiency between firms operating at different scales.

nonprice competition

Not all costs are production costs. Firms may incur costs for advertising and other sales-promotion activities or for other forms of nonprice competition such as variation in quality and style of the product. In pure competition, the individual firm has virtually no incentive to advertise, for it has no way of gaining for itself very much of the benefit of any increase in the sales of the industry's homogeneous product, and it can already sell all it desires at the market price.

A monopolist may have some incentive for advertising and other sales-promotion activities. Such activities may help reduce the likelihood that new firms will enter his industry. Sales promotion may shift his demand curve to the right or make it less elastic.

However, the most fertile areas for nonprice competition are those in which competition is vigorous but not perfect. The firm which confronts competition from close substitutes may be very eager to increase the apparent differentiation of its product and to create in the minds of the customers the idea that it is superior.

Competition through changes in the quality and style of the product is also likely to be more vigorous when each firm is obliged to compete with close substitutes and when the number of firms is not small. Successful action largely pays off through diverting business away from rivals. The larger the share of the industry business which the firm holds already, the less additional gain it can hope for.

Nonprice competition activities add to the costs of firms. Taking consideration of the economic system as a whole, are these costs justified? Or would the economy function better if all resources were used for necessary operations of production and distribution?

Consider first expenditures on advertising and other related selling costs, such as the employment of salesmen. Such expenditures are not negligible in modern industrial economies—they run to about 2 or 3 percent of the gross national product in the United States. Two major arguments can be advanced in favor of such expenditures. First, they are informative. Imperfect knowledge is a chronic problem in a world of change. Advertising communicates information about what things are available, where they can be obtained, and (sometimes) what they cost.

Further, in many countries advertising provides a subsidy to information media generally—newspapers, radio, television. Trained salesmen can be a valuable means of transmitting information about technically complex products. Firms selling industrial equipment often provide valuable service to their customers through their sales personnel.

Second, advertising may encourage and support other forms of competition. Price competition among stores can be made more effective when price reductions are advertised. Advertising provides a method of calling to the attention of buyers innovations and improvements in products.

Against these claims, several counterarguments may be advanced. Advertisers are prone to assert that their products embody innovations even when they do not. If everyone makes such claims, the resulting "noise" may be so loud that no one can hear anything. A genuine product improvement may be unable to gain proper attention. Advertising may make claims which simply are not true. Producers of drugs and medicines have often been tempted to claim therapeutic results not warranted by evidence. Cigarette manufacturers have only recently ceased to claim that smoking is beneficial to the health. Government action to prohibit false advertising may benefit both the public and the ethical business firm.

Much modern advertising can be criticized because of some of its side effects on the consuming public. There is a tendency to appeal to everyone's latent sense of guilt and inadequacy, to create psychological needs and concerns which the products advertised cannot really satisfy. American-style advertising, which is rapidly spreading across the rest of the world, has also a strong tendency to glorify the consumption of material goods as *the* means to happiness. An unwholesome obsession with income and consumption may result.

To be sure, partisans of advertising argue that advertising is necessary, in high-income societies, to keep the aggregate demand for goods at a high level. No one knows what would happen to consumer spending in an economy like that of the United States in the absence of advertising, although there is an understandable tendency among advertising people to exaggerate their influence on consumer spending. There is certainly no indication that the marginal desire for economic goods and services is small, judging by the willingness of even relatively high-income people to seek gainful employment. Willingness to work is, after all, a measure of people's desire for consumption. If people's desire for additional income and consumption did weaken, it should not be difficult to make a corresponding reduction in the normal amount of time which they spend at work. If public opinion appears to prefer, government financial policies can be managed in such a way that additional output is directed into capital formation or into government programs. The idea that people's desires should be manipulated conflicts with the economists' general feeling that the economy—and particularly the business community—should adapt to people's desires.

The existence of advertising does create a problem for economic analysis. Conventional welfare economics evaluates the extent to which the pattern of production matches up with the pattern of consumer desires. But if those desires are themselves constantly being changed by advertising, how can one use them as bench marks for welfare judgments? Only if we had some ulterior criterion of "better" or "worse" tastes and preferences could we pass judgment on the results.

It is also true that the allocation of resources into sales-promotion activities such as advertising, and into communications media generally, tends not to follow the criterion of orthodox consumer demand. There seems to be no meaningful way of identifying a consumer demand for advertising services as such. When advertising underwrites the costs of radio or television broadcasting, neither the quantity nor quality of the resulting product bears any necessary relation to what the consumers of such media services would demand if such products were sold at a price reflecting their economic costs.

innovation

Other forms of nonprice competition can best be evaluated in relation to the important process to which they are related—the process of developing and introducing new and improved products and methods of production. Competition through variations in the quality and style of products may be trivial and wasteful, but it sometimes leads to real improvements. Very possibly the efficiency of the economy could be increased in the short run by holding constant existing standards of quality and style and eliminating trivial and costly variations. But in the long run, producers do stand to benefit if they do a better job of meeting consumer desires. A forced elimination of variations in quality and style might do more harm than good.

Is there any general relationship between market structure and innovation performance in an industry? To deal with this question, it is useful to divide the innovation process into two aspects: the willingness and ability to introduce innovations when they become known, and the willingness and ability to think up new ideas and to experiment with them to render them commercially feasible. Looking at the introduction of innovations, an industry characterized by pure competition is likely to show up well. Firms stand to gain a temporary advantage by introducing some measure which will improve the product or reduce costs, even if rivals ultimately imitate it. And the penalty for failing to keep up with innovations introduced by others may be severe. Actually, any industry where entry of new firms is easy should be receptive to innovation. If existing firms are unwilling to introduce the new idea, there will be an incentive for new firms to spring up to introduce it—or firms already operating in other sectors of the economy may diversify their operations to carry innovations from one product sector to another.

One might feel that any firm, whether competitive or not, would have an incentive to innovate if the novelty were to the liking of customers. Certainly even a sheltered monopolist can increase his profits by accepting cost-reducing improvements. The difference is that he is not under the same life-or-death urgency about it. Moreover, a monopolist might prefer to avoid certain innovations which would increase the durability of his product and reduce the total potential sales volume over time.

On balance, it would appear that a relatively atomistic market structure, with easy entry, would be more favorable to the introduction of innovations. How does it happen, then, that in many areas farming is slow to adopt known improvements? Such reluctance has its roots in the whole pattern of the psychology of particular farmers, and we cannot explain it. We can observe, however, that reluctance to innovate will tend to prove fatal (commercially, that is) to the laggards, unless a large portion of their costs are the implicit costs of the owners' labor and property. If most costs are explicit, money-payment costs, laggard farms will be driven out of business.

What about the willingness and ability of firms to think up improvements in products or methods of production and to make the developmental efforts required to make them commercially feasible? Some economists argue that firms in a monopoly or oligopoly position are favorably situated to carry on the research and development activity, often risky and expensive, upon which much of technological advance depends in a modern industrial economy. This view was particularly associated with the late Professor Joseph Schumpeter. Such a view reflects the conviction that the firm must be relatively large, in the absolute sense, and must be protected to some degree against over-rapid imitation by rivals. Large size permits diversification in research activity and allows a certain pooling of risks. Further, a firm which is enjoying "excess" profits to begin with may find it much easier to finance research out of current income than would another firm which had to use other sources of finance.

Such a priori reasoning can be supported by the evidence of a good record in research and development by such concentrated industries as chemicals. However, a broader examination of innovation dispels any notion that a simple generalization can be drawn. There are oligopolies with poor records in innovation (cement and cigarettes in the United States). There are industries with a relatively good innovation record which are not highly concentrated and in which individual firms are not huge in absolute size (electronics and drugs in the United States). Within individual industries it is often not the largest firm which is the most progressive (e.g., the steel industry in the United States).

Even in the modern industrial world, not all inventions are products of giant industrial research laboratories. Such major twentieth-century inventions as television, the jet aircraft engine, and the self-developing photographic process originated outside the halls of giant business. Important improvements in manufacturing techniques still come forth from suggestions of rank-and-file industrial workmen familiar with existing processes and able to spot ways of improving things.

Efforts to explain why one heavy industry made a good innovation record and another did not (as one might observe in comparing the American auto and steel industries between 1900 and 1930) often fall back on ad hoc factors of entrepreneurial personality. Certainly no simple relationship exists between market structure and innovation.

In any case, the profit motive alone is not likely to lead business firms to spend as much money on research and development activity as would be optimal for the economy as a whole. The individual firm is inhibited in such expenditures by the risk that other firms will find out and utilize the technical information which results, without having paid for developing it. In addition, research activity often produces side effects in the general advance of knowledge which may benefit the public generally but not be useful to the firm which finances it. We have here a clear case where the social benefit of an activity is potentially greater than the private benefit. In some countries, patent law attempts to deal with this discrepancy by giving an inventor exclusive control of his invention for a limited period of time. This may be better than nothing, but it has many difficulties in practice. A more desirable approach may be for government to give financial promotion to research and development activity. Government agencies themselves can carry on research and distribute the results (as is widely done with agricultural techniques). Government can subsidize business research expenditures, either directly or through tax concessions, and it can give encouragement to nonprofit institutions such as universities and foundations, which may perform research and disseminate the results.

collusion and coercion

It is easy to show a connection between market structure and the likelihood that firms in an industry will act collusively with each other or will attempt coercive measures designed to damage a rival. Such actions arise chiefly in oligopoly situations. An industry with many firms and easy entry is not likely to produce collusion, because it is too difficult to get all firms to join and conform. The incentive for one firm to remain outside a collusive group increases as the proportion of the other firms in the agreement grows. Similarly, industries with large numbers of firms do not give rise to the sense of direct rivalry with one other particular firm which may easily develop when oligopoly prevails. Coercive or punitive actions designed to drive a rival out of business or to force him to refrain from aggressive competition are most common where the number of firms is small.

market structure and public policy

From the standpoint of static economic analysis, it appears that a good case can be made in favor of market structures with a large number of small firms. Since differentiation may be a good thing, we need not specify pure competition. However, there are two important reservations about seeking to achieve such a structure as a goal of policy. The first arises because of economies of scale. In many industries, the technically optimum size of firm is so large that the industry is bound to be concentrated and oligopolistic. The second reservation arises because in some cases, at least, large firms and concentrated structure may help to promote innovation. This consideration is less important if government or nonprofit institutions sponsor a large amount of research and development activity.

On the other hand, there seems no reason for government to encourage large size and small numbers of firms in particular industries. Firms have an incentive to grow large for the sake of the greater power and security they gain, even after they pass the point of minimum costs. Such desires do not automatically coincide with economic efficiency for the system as a whole.

market behavior and public policy

There have been times when economists believed there was a clear connection between market structure and good or bad economic performance and were willing to urge the government to make market structures purely competitive. Such a conviction is no longer widespread. Instead, emphasis has shifted largely to suggestions about forms of business behavior. In general, it appears desirable that government restrict the opportunity for business firms to profit by actions which are not beneficial to the public, while at the same time trying to maximize the opportunity of firms to compete freely in the areas regarded as legitimate. Specific applications of this idea are as follows:

1. **Entry.** Easy entry into an industry or occupation is a way of keeping prices and costs down, and encouraging variety and innovation. It can also be regarded as a good thing in itself, since it gives people a wider range of occupational opportunity. Government can promote entry in a positive way by helping firms obtain credit and technical information. It can protect them against unfair competitive tactics from rivals. In a negative sense, government can refrain from erecting arbitrary barriers to entry, often undertaken to protect the incomes of people already in a business. Competition from imports can be regarded as a form of entry. There is little danger that domestic consumers will be overcharged by a domestic monopoly if substitute products can be imported without heavy tariffs or other import restraints.

2. **Collusion and coercion.** Firms are more likely to act independently of each other if they are forbidden to enter into cartel arrangements or other forms of collusion. Individual firms which want to compete independently, perhaps to

introduce innovations, will be better able to do so if they are protected against destructive competitive attacks from established rivals. Such attacks may take the form of direct physical violence or slanders of a company's products or personnel. They may take more subtle forms such as price discrimination (a large, well-established firm may reduce its selling price in a geographic area served by the victim, while refraining from reductions elsewhere). Established firms may harass a newcomer by pressing their suppliers not to sell to him or urging their customers not to buy from him. Some of these unfair actions can be prevented by government.

3. **Size of firm.** Government might directly restrict the size of firms, although this may be costly if it prevents achievement of the optimum scale of operation. Alternatively, government may limit the manner in which large firms may grow: in the United States, large firms are relatively free to grow by purchasing newly produced capital goods, but are restricted in their freedom to buy out other companies or merge with them. Government may restrict the freedom of large firms to utilize the strategic advantages of size by preventing them from engaging in price discrimination or tying and exclusive-dealing arrangements with suppliers and customers.

4. **Government competition.** There may be situations where private monopoly is so strongly entrenched, or where the standards of private entrepreneurship are so poor, that the government itself may undertake production. However, monopoly by government is just as liable to abuse as private monopoly. Yet if there are private firms in an industry, competition from government enterprise can be very destructive to their initiative and needs to be used with restraint lest it worsen the deficiencies which it is intended to remedy.

imperfect competition in labor markets

From the standpoint of narrow economic analysis, it is easy to find fault with monopoly in the labor market such as might be exercised by a strong trade union. To the extent that labor monopoly raises wage rates above the competitive level, several adverse consequences may result. One is that the output of the product will tend to be reduced, which is likely to create (or aggravate) the output distortion we described in connection with Figure 23-1.

However, the effects on output need to be considered in context. Formation of a strong union in the competitive sector of an economy which already has a monopolized sector could improve the composition of output. The union might tend to push resources back into the monopolized sector and thus undo the sort of distortion described in Figure 23-1.

Unfortunately, the strongest unions in industrial economies seem to be found in highly concentrated industries. When one adds a strong union to a closely-knit industrial oligopoly, as in the steel industry, the result is to aggravate output distortion.

To the extent that a trade union succeeds in raising the wage rate above the competitive level, it is also likely to reduce job opportunities. Often this reduction takes concealed forms. Present union members are not necessarily dismissed, but opportunities are reduced for newcomers to the labor force, or for workers seeking to transfer out of other sectors of the economy. A further consequence is that the supply of people seeking work in the nonunion sector may be increased, and thus the wage rate prevailing in the nonunion sector may be correspondingly reduced.

Would not some of these difficulties be eliminated if strong union organization extended to all sectors of the economy? For a full analysis of this, we would have to bring in moneyflow analysis, which is out of place in this book. However, two important considerations will help analyze the problem:

1. It is probably inconceivable that *all* labor—meaning all human effort devoted to economic production—could be organized into unions. Likely to remain outside would be business managers and self-employed persons such as farmers, storekeepers, and professional people.

2. The essential method by which labor unions achieve higher wage rates (if they do) is by restriction of supply. This means that any gains by union members come at the expense of someone else in the system, either nonunion labor or recipients of nonlabor incomes (rents, interest, profits). And the restriction of supply measures the number of people who would like work at the going wage and cannot find it.

defense of unions

The foregoing considerations relate mainly to efforts of unions to raise wage rates above the competitive level. But we have already noted that much of the potential benefit of unions may arise through influence on the wage structure, or nonwage aspects of the job. These need not have harmful consequences to outsiders.

There is, however, a dilemma. To perform their beneficial functions, unions require some degree of power and security. Yet the more power they possess, the more harm they may inflict through excessive wage demands. There is no simple way out of this conflict of objectives. In particular, it would be undesirable to take the extreme position that unions should be prohibited or that they should be assisted by government to gain great strength.

summary

Certain patterns of business behavior tend to arise under certain conditions of structure in product markets. Atomistic markets usually mean high or infinite demand elasticity confronting the firm, which in turn means that price is close or equal to marginal cost. A monopoly, however, may operate with price far above marginal cost, with potential distortion of output resulting. Easy entry keeps price close to average cost, while difficult entry makes it possible for existing firms to enjoy profits for a long time, with resulting effects on the distribution of income. Different market structures are associated with differences in willingness to use nonprice competition. Nonprice competition involves extra costs, which may be an economic waste but can in some circumstances be beneficial—particularly if they enhance price competition and promote innovation. Collusion and cutthroat competition are chiefly encountered under conditions of oligopoly. Monopoly in the labor market can produce harmful effects on composition of output and on the relative incomes of union members and nonunion members. However, potential benefits of unions on wage structure and on nonwage conditions of employment may compensate for some economic harm they may do.

QUESTIONS AND PROBLEMS

1. It has been suggested that the ratio of price to marginal cost could be used as a measure of the degree of monopoly in an industry. Explain the logic and limitations of this measure.

2. From a theoretical standpoint, oligopoly might be the best or the worst of all possible market structures. Describe patterns of oligopoly conduct which could qualify for each of these extreme classifications.

3. "Firms in a situation of monopolistic competition are likely to be too numerous and too small." Explain the theoretical basis for this generalization and give some illustrations from observations of retailing and service businesses.

economic role of government in a market economy

Our emphasis throughout the bulk of this book has been on the functioning of a market economy. We have attempted to explain and to evaluate the behavior of the economic system first under conditions of pure competition and then under conditions of imperfect competition. We have seen that even under pure competition, the functioning of the economy would not be ideal. Further, pure competition is not feasible for all markets.

By observing areas in which the performance of private enterprise is likely to be deficient, we can form one basis for determining a potential economic role for government. We ask, in effect, what functions government *might* beneficially perform. However, this approach is not sufficient to define an optimum economic role of government. We must also have some idea of limitations on the effectiveness of government activities. These limitations may cause unsatisfactory government performance in some areas where, on purely abstract grounds, one might have hoped for beneficial government action. One asks, in effect, what functions is government *competent* to perform? An optimum role for government can be defined for those areas where there is need for government action and where government competence can be expected. We begin by noting areas in which economic performance, in the absence of government, is likely to fall short of potential. Later we consider the likelihood that government action will in fact prove to be competently undertaken.

the legal framework

A market economy cannot function properly without a system for the maintenance of order and the settlement of disputes. The whole notion of a market economy rests on the idea that people can acquire income only by performing productive services. This implies that people must not be free to take things from other people by force. Preserving the security of persons and property against violence and disorder is therefore one of the potentially beneficial functions of government. To preserve such security, government itself may have a near monopoly on the use of force and may be obliged to provide a means of settling disputes (through a system of judicial institutions) as an alternative to private use of force.

The market economy also requires an extensive legal code dealing with such matters as property, contracts, and the structure and functioning of corporations and other organizations. Some set of practices respecting property and ownership is essential for a market economy. Ownership links the power to control the use of something with the opportunity to enjoy the income which may result. Thus the prospect of income directs the use to which the property is put. Without some link between power and reward, the incentive function of the factor-pricing system would be undermined.

Government must not merely protect property; it must define what is to be regarded as property and establish precisely what rights are associated with each kind of property. For example, is it proper to treat human beings as property, through some form of chattel slavery? Large questions arise in treatment of such forms of property as patents, copyrights, and shares in the ownership of a corporation or partnership.

Similarly, the institution of contract contributes to the efficiency of a market economy. Contracts provide for continuing relationships between firms or individuals, in which there will be a balance of performance and reward. It is not sufficient that government enforce contracts; government must define what kinds of contracts are to be tolerated or encouraged. Shall it be legal for two firms to make a contract agreeing to fix the price of a product they both produce? Or to refuse to sell to some other firm? Concern for contracts involves the government in a concern for debt contracts, promises to repay loans on certain terms. The institution of debt is a valuable one in relation to saving and investment, but it requires a delicate balancing of the interests of creditor and debtor to achieve fairness and to be functional.

The corporation, a creature of the law, has proved a highly functional institution for economic efficiency. The corporation is well adapted to promote specialization by permitting the detailed management of a business to be handled by persons other than the owners, by formalizing the delegation of power and responsibility among the management, and by separating the ownership of "the corporation" by the stockholders from the ownership by the corporation of the specific assets used in the business. To design corporation law which will contribute to efficiency and fairness is a challenge to government policy.

Government must also concern itself with the punishment of fraud and related forms of unfair dealing. Some degree of trust and confidence is essential in a market economy. If consumers cannot have any confidence in the products they buy, the whole process of specialization and exchange may break down. Advertising practices may come in for particular concern.

Historically, governments have at times been themselves a threat to the security of persons and property. Predatory governments, perhaps dominated by powerful military figures, have at times singled out wealthy businessmen for blackmail, extortion, or expropriation. Adam Smith and his followers typically blamed government interference with personal freedom and private property as a principal reason why some regions did not develop economically.

money and the money-flow

Instability in the flow of total expenditure was for a long time one of the most serious deficiencies of the private-enterprise economies of the United States and Western Europe. This instability culminated in the devastating economic depression of the 1930s, which was a major cause for the rise of Hitler and the coming of World War II. Since the 1930s, it has been recognized that government has the power, through monetary and fiscal policies, to control the flow of total expenditures for production in the interests of high output and employment and relative stability of prices.

Government can stimulate more rapid increase in the money-flow by increasing the quantity of money itself. This may be done through a central bank, or through direct currency issues. Government can also stimulate the flow of aggregate expenditures by spending more, at given tax rates, or by reducing tax rates relative to expenditures. Conversely, government can slow down the expenditure flow by reducing the quantity of money or by shifting its tax and expenditure position toward a smaller deficit or larger surplus.

There are difficulties in the timing and magnitude of such policies. Nevertheless, control of the money-flow by monetary and fiscal means has been carried out effectively in major countries since World War II. There has been no repetition of the disastrous depression of the 1930s.

collective services

We noted in Chapter 19 that a competitive economy would tend to underproduce certain collective services, benefits of which could not or should not be restricted to those paying for them in market purchase. Many of the normal activities of modern governments involve such services. National defense is one; provision of aids to transport and navigation is another. Much research activity comes into this category. As a good illustration, governments in the United States have carried on extensive research work on agricultural products and methods, making the results available to all. The result has been a rapid rise in productivity, benefiting both farmers and consumers. Yet one farm acting alone would have had difficulty gaining enough extra income for itself through such activity to pay for it.

Highways are another example of this sort of service, an example which also contains other elements relevant to defining the proper role of government. It would be possible that highways be privately owned and that each user be charged a toll. To apply this principle to all roads and streets would have several disadvantages. First, it would be expensive to collect the tolls; much labor would be required for that purpose. Second, the marginal cost of permitting an extra trip on a highway would be very small, in terms of the speed at which the highway would deteriorate. If the toll were higher than that low marginal cost, there would be a social loss to the extent that peoples' use of the highway would be unduly reduced. In this respect it would be similar to the lighthouse example noted in Chapter 19.

An additional consideration appears in relation to constructing the highway. By its nature, the highway requires the use of certain specific adjoining tracts of land. It might be very difficult for a private firm to acquire all the needed land in the open market. Once the firm had most of the land it needed, the owners of the remaining tracts could demand exorbitant sums; they would enjoy the position of a monopolist confronted with an inelastic demand schedule. Governments deal with this problem by using their coercive powers to force the sale of property. In principle, the owners are compensated on a reasonable basis, although it is hard to prescribe rules for such action. Water supply and sewage disposal, electric power and telephone service are all examples where the power of government may be needed to permit physical connections of service facilities. Government may use its powers of eminent domain to assist privately owned companies which perform the actual services.

equating private with social costs and benefits

Where private costs or benefits differ from social costs and benefits, the competitive market will not necessarily produce the optimum output. Where there is some clear notion of what the social costs or benefits are, government may be able either to improve the allocation or to bring prices into line with the social magnitudes. For example, a social cost may arise from the smoke damage or water pollution resulting from industrial activity. Government might require that individual firms maintain adequate air- and water-purification facilities, thus bringing private costs up to social costs. Or government might conduct a program of water purification itself and assess the cost on the firms responsible for the original pollution.

Very often, however, the social costs and social benefits are not subject to precise measurement. Even then, government can provide a means for public opinion to alter the patterns of activity which would exist in a purely private-enterprise situation.

distribution of income

There is no objective, scientific way of identifying an optimum distribution of income. However, there may be considerable agreement among the people in a society about income-distribution elements which they regard as good or bad. For example, most people seem to agree that extreme poverty is bad; that people should, if possible, have enough to eat and enough to avoid extremes of physical discomfort in life. Poverty is unpleasant for adults, but it is particularly adverse for the children born and raised in such an environment. Their health and education are likely to be neglected, and their own future productivity and income prospects prejudiced thereby.

There are several ways in which government may act to alter income distribution. The first is through taxation and transfer payments. Taxes must be levied in any event, and the government can simply choose a tax system which yields a less unsatisfactory income distribution. Or it can go further and make income payments to poor people to raise their level.

Instead of cash payments, governments often try to aid the poor by providing them with services free or below cost. Housing is one illustration. However, public housing offered below cost raises several problems. One is fairness: usually there is not nearly enough public housing for all poor people. How shall the scarce supply be rationed among those who want it? If occupancy is contingent on a low income, the family may lose incentive to improve itself, if that entails a risk of being dispossessed. In addition, economic analysis suggests that people will generally gain a greater degree of utility if permitted to allocate their incomes for themselves instead of receiving one particular consumption service free or below cost. Thus an equal sum of money distributed in cash might be expected to yield more utility than if it were spent for low-cost housing. However, a major goal in assisting low-income families may be to improve life for their children; some government restriction on freedom of consumption may be appropriate to insure that government assistance is in fact used in ways which benefit the children.

Other kinds of services provided to poor people may be a form of "investment in human capital." Programs to improve health and education increase the opportunity for children to become productive when they grow up. Aside from their effect on income distribution, health and education services are likely to yield social benefits greater than private; thus there is a case for government influence to augment the quantity produced.

Government may also aid low income families by helping them to reduce their birthrates, which are typically high among low-income groups. Reduction in the number of children per family directly raises per capita income and reduces the number of people who will in the future be coming out of poverty environments. And lower birth rates help to ease problems of family health and education.

Sometimes concern for income distribution leads to government intervention in the functioning of particular markets. Import duties or farm price supports are used to protect certain workers or property owners against decreases in income which might result from changes in factor supplies, technology, or consumer taste. Governments have restricted entry into particular industries or occupations and have at times fostered cartel arrangements within them as income-supporting measures. In the long run such measures tend to harm economic efficiency and may discriminate unfairly in favor of a limited group of beneficiaries. In the short run, however, it may sometimes be advantageous to slow down the pace of economic change. There is a limit to the speed with which workers can transfer their employment out of farming or some high-cost industry which is being undersold by imports. Some government intervention to ease transitions may be preferable to a laissez-faire outcome. However, it is not easy to ensure that government measures to prop up a "sick" industry or occupation will not be permanent impediments to efficient long-run adjustment.

market structure and business behavior

From the viewpoint of static equilibrium analysis, the existence of monopoly or tightly knit oligopoly is likely to cause distortion in the composition of output, as compared to the Pareto-optimum position. However, one cannot demonstrate that an atomistic market structure would be superior if considerations of economic growth were brought into the picture. There may be times when it would be both economically desirable and politically feasible for government to subject large firms to literal "trust-busting," dividing them into larger numbers of smaller firms, but it is clearly not an easy policy to follow. More defensible are government measures to maintain ease of entry and to restrict the freedom for existing firms to act in collusion with each other, to employ cutthroat tactics, or otherwise to take advantage of the strategic advantages arising from size.

Assuming that the harm resulting from monopoly or bigness is excessive prices, governments have sometimes tried to impose price controls on such firms.

However, as we noted in Chapter 20, American cost-plus regulation of public utilities may have adverse effects on firms' incentives to keep costs down and may require detailed surveillance of firms' expenses, technology, and service.

Economists stress the fact that if one sector of the economy is monopolistic and another competitive, the composition of output will be biased. Relatively too little will be produced by the monopolistic sector and relatively too much by the competitive. One possible solution is to enforce marginal-cost pricing on the monopolistic sector. It is not clear how this could be done consistent with cost control incentives. Marginal cost pricing does not yield optimum output for one industry taken in isolation if a substantial segment of the economy keeps price above marginal cost. Conceivably optimum output composition could be more closely approximated by enforcing output reduction and price increases on the formerly competitive sector, but this raises a host of other problems. Another possibility would be forming government enterprises in formerly monopolized sectors to compete and thus force prices down and output up.

Such proposals for bringing monopoly conduct closer to the optimum are largely hypothetical. They require a degree of knowledge and precision which is seldom at the disposal of government. In any event, the real world displays few cases of outright monopoly except those resulting from deliberate government action. The practical problems largely arise in situations of oligopoly and related markets, where elements of competition are blended with elements of monopoly. Experience in the United States suggests that government can perform a useful function if it prevents collusion, limits the ability of large firms to grow by merger or to use their powers oppressively, and helps preserve opportunities for entry. Direct regulation of prices or profits has not been conspicuously successful.

government enterprise

Socialist and communist ideologies developed in the nineteenth century blamed many social evils on private ownership of the "means of production." Marxists were convinced that injustice in the distribution of income, recurrent crises of unemployment, and irreconcilable conflicts between socioeconomic classes were all rooted in the private ownership of productive enterprise. Socialists and communists of varying stripes have urged public ownership of productive enterprises, perhaps by the state, perhaps by less highly centralized organs, as a necessary step toward ameliorating the alleged evils of capitalism. Such ideological conviction is largely responsible for the prevalence of government enterprise in modern-day communist countries; it also explains some situations of government enterprise in Western countries such as Great Britain.

Time has not dealt kindly with the Marxian analysis of capitalism. The expected impoverishment of the working class did not materialize. Government measures to deal with poverty, monopoly, and business depressions have all been developed along lines which do not require government ownership and operation of productive enterprises. Further, actual experience with government enterprise, particularly in Russia, has made evident the fact that it provides no automatic solutions to problems of industrial society. Government enterprise appears neither necessary nor sufficient to remedy the ills traditionally cited by ideological critics of capitalism.

To be sure, government enterprise has been undertaken in the United States and in the other noncommunist countries for pragmatic reasons having little to do with ideology. The term *government enterprise* is generally used to refer specifically to forms of government production which are or can be sold in the market. The post office is a government enterprise; so is electric-power production by TVA. In many countries transportation and communications systems are operated by government enterprises.

In present-day underdeveloped countries, a case for government enterprise has developed which differs substantially from traditional socialism but builds partly on Russian experience. This reflects the conviction that their underdeveloped condition is a reflection of inadequacy of private entrepreneurship in their particular cultural setting. Certainly the quality of entrepreneurship is crucial to the functioning of a market economy. Whatever its other results, government enterprise in Soviet Russia has been an instrument for a high rate of economic growth. Even in many Western countries, similar growth-promoting results can be observed, from nineteenth-century railway building in France and Germany to modern experimentation with atomic energy. Government enterprise may be employed where there are extensive economies of scale, where initial capital requirements and risks are substantial, and where the activity may be related to social goals such as national security. To be sure, government efforts to promote economic growth may show up in many other forms besides government enterprise.

Most underdeveloped countries do not lack entrepreneurs as such. Indeed, typically a large proportion of the urban population are entrepreneurs—shop keepers, vendors, craftsmen. However, many of these countries do experience a shortage of the kind of entrepreneurship required for industrial operations beyond the small scale. Industrial entrepreneurship requires many qualifications besides energy and a desire to make profits. First, it tends to require much more familiarity with technology than is required for commercial activity. Second, the entrepreneur is much more likely to need investment in durable capital, with attendant risks and need for a long-term view. Third, the industrial firm requires a larger labor force and consequently more skill in handling large numbers of employees— not just the owner's family.

It is easy to understand that governments in underdeveloped countries might seek to remedy entrepreneurial shortages. However, the qualifications which are lacking among private entrepreneurs may not be more abundant among government officials. The government does possess superior ability to draw on foreign resources—capital, technical advice, and even management personnel. And a government enterprise need not be deterred by financial risk in the same manner as private capital. By the same token, unfortunately, a government enterprise may give less consideration to the productivity of an investment and the efficiency of continuing operations.

problems of government enterprise

Government faces many problems in the management of public enterprises. One is the difficulty of ensuring efficient operation. In the private economy, competition presses individual firms to keep costs down. The larger the number of firms, the greater the scope for variety and experimentation in production methods. Government often enjoys a monopoly position. It can set its own price. Moreover, the costs need not be less than the price; deficits may be subsidized out of the budget. Within a single enterprise, there may be little scope for variety and experiment— and indeed, little motivation for it either.

Good administrators can succeed in instilling a concern for efficiency in their subordinates. The government enterprise can also benefit by checking its methods of operation against those used in other countries. The technology of railroading, or electric-power generation, can be kept technically efficient by such comparisons. Sometimes it is possible to permit private competitors to operate in areas of government enterprise, although they may not wish to do so. Private firms may provide a cost comparison to judge the efficiency of government.

Similar considerations relate to the quality of services rendered by government enterprises. Competition helps keep each private firm sensitive to consumer goodwill; quality of service is sustained for fear of losing business. Government monopoly may be indifferent to such matters. In a democratic country, the political system generally provides a method whereby consumer complaints can be heard and made effective. But this may not be sufficient to make an industry improvement minded.

Government enterprises face difficult problems in deciding the appropriate prices to charge. Merely encouraging a government enterprise to maximize its profits is not appropriate if it holds a monopoly position. Setting price equal to marginal cost may not be easy to carry out (long-run marginal cost may be hard to ascertain); further, there is no assurance that marginal cost pricing will insure optimum output, if price exceeds marginal cost in parts of the private sector. Some form of average cost pricing may be better than the feasible alternatives. Average costs may be easier to calculate; the implied guidance for output is not far off target, and the enterprise gains the autonomy which comes with financial self-sufficiency. However, any cost-based pricing system is only as good as the effectiveness of underlying control of costs and efficiency.

There may be good economic reasons for selling some services below full cost, perhaps because of external benefits or income-distribution effects. This may require subsidy, however, and there is the danger that the subsidy will not be sufficient to enable the enterprise to produce all that is demanded at the official price. Resulting discriminations in distribution may undermine the social benefits of the program. Public housing quite typically encounters this difficulty.

A related problem concerns the appropriate scale of investment in a government enterprise. Ideally, public investment decisions should be guided by some calculation of expected rate of return, modified where appropriate by an allowance for social benefits or costs. Capital outlays by government enterprises should yield as much as the market rate of interest, otherwise scarce capital may be drawn into low payoff uses in the public sector at the expense of higher payoff projects in the private sector. Access to interest-free funds from the government budget may encourage wasteful investment by government enterprises.

In recent years economists have devoted much attention to criteria for public investment decisions, under such headings as "project evaluation" and "cost-benefit analysis." Such procedures typically are aimed at estimating the anticipated rate of return from a project. From such estimates officials can presumably rank alternative public projects in order of priority. In addition, by setting some cutoff rate of return, they can determine the total volume of public investment during a given period, thus affecting the allocation of capital between public and private uses. Such estimates typically begin with the same considerations that a private firm would study in its investment decisions. These would include the initial cost of the investment, its technical productivity, and the size and time-shape of the revenue increases which would flow from it. However, government projects may also allow for estimated benefits beyond actual revenues generated. Formal cost-benefit evaluations usually require that a price tag be put on these "external," nonrevenue benefits, even if the estimating procedures are not very precise. A multipurpose water-control project might generate revenues from the sale of electric power, but might also provide recreational facilities for which users would not be required to pay. Estimates of such nonrevenue benefits may be somewhat arbitrary, but at least they could be applied with relative consistency to different government projects, helping to allot public investment to the higher-benefit projects.

Even if consistent cost-benefit standards are applied, and a meaningful rate of return estimated for each potential government investment, there remains the question of the appropriate cutoff rate to use in determining the total volume of public investment in a given period. Private firms are likely not to carry investment to the point where marginal efficiency equals the interest rate but to allow themselves a couple of extra points margin for protection against risk. Further, the interest rate for private funds may be higher than the one government must pay, reflecting the government's special credit status as a sovereign authority with powers to tax and create money. If the government were paying 5 percent interest on its securities, it might appropriately require that public projects yield 6 or 7 percent for better allocation between public and private uses of capital.

Much of the success of government enterprise depends on the image of government itself possessed by its employees and by the general public. In Western countries, the ideals of democratic utilitarianism have helped spread the idea that government is a functional form of social organization, intended to perform services and guided by public opinion. Government employees are servants of the people, not their masters. However, in many parts of the world, a much older conception prevails. Traditions of monarchy and of a hereditary ruling class reflect an image of government as a system of power and status for those who control it, with emphasis on the incomes and prestige they receive, rather than the functions they perform. Government may still appear as a relationship between rulers and ruled, with the rulers being implicitly recognized as superior and meritorious persons. Even where formal civil-service systems have been installed, they may serve largely to ensure that everyone has fair and equal access to the coveted government positions, rather than to provide means to spur government employees to efficient performance of useful services.

the problem of goals

A private competitive economic system gives considerable scope for variety in the goals of individuals. Diversity in tastes for consumer goods can be accommodated; it is not necessary that everyone consume the same things. Differences in individual occupational preferences are not merely acceptable, they may be very desirable to enhance efficiency through specialization. It is characteristic of the market economy that people are often able to weigh the relative cost of choosing one line of consumption or employment rather than another, although not everyone enjoys being reminded of the cost of his choices.

There are, as we have seen, certain types of goals which private enterprise will not succeed in meeting. Certain functions and services, collective in nature, can only be provided if government undertakes them (or, as sometimes happens, if nonprofit private organizations and enterprises perform them). To say this does not, however, give us an easy guide to whether the public wants such services sufficiently that government should provide them.

One criterion is whether the public, collectively, is willing to tax itself sufficiently to pay for the service. This is a reasonable criterion but encounters several difficulties. Ordinarily, some people will not desire the service, whatever it may be. Yet it may be impossible to exempt them from taxation. Secondly, the taxation required to support the particular service may not be isolated so that citizens have the opportunity to approve or disapprove of that marginal amount separately. Third, some people may desire the service intensely, yet have no way of making their desire effective.

The truth is that the same considerations which make collective services difficult to provide through the market also make them difficult to provide, on a rational and efficient basis, through government. The problem is complicated if the prospective beneficiaries of a service are able to avoid carrying much share of the tax burden for it. One must then compare the cost to one group with the benefit to another, which is not easy to do.

Democracy provides a political means for dealing with the problem of goals of government action. By democracy we mean a structure of government in which individual citizens are able to campaign for political office, in which (some) office-holders are elected by the people in competitive elections, and in which governmental actions are undertaken in an environment of public scrutiny and discussion within a legislative body and in public media generally. Democracy provides a method of making government officials sensitive to the desires of the public. To make this effective, there must be competition for elective offices, and the electorate must have some basis for evaluating the past and potential performance of candidates.

Experience in the twentieth century has indicated, however, that merely establishing the forms of democracy is not sufficient to insure its effective working. In many underdeveloped countries especially, governments are more likely to be authoritarian, lacking the formal apparatus of democracy and representative government. Even an authoritarian government cannot be indifferent to public opinion. But officials can be much more free to substitute their own values for those of the public. Perhaps this will work out all right. Sometimes "father knows best." But the characteristics which enable a man to obtain and keep power do not necessarily equip him with a superior moral sense or with the ability to prescribe for his people policies which, after the event, they will be grateful for.

conflict of goals

The goals which government pursues, whether derived from public opinion or those of a ruling elite, are likely to contain conflicting elements. Conflict of goals is rooted in the economic fact of scarcity itself. There are many commodities we would like more of but haven't enough resources to produce. We would like more leisure *and* more income, more consumption now *and* a more rapid rate of economic growth. Income distribution in particular embodies conflict of goals; it is not possible for each of us simultaneously to increase his proportional share of the national income.

Collective services may be particularly subject to this problem. There is no ready manner to identify the benefit received by each beneficiary or to assign the tax burden associated with paying for the service. The situation is made to order for disputes over whether a given service should be performed, what amount of resources should be devoted to it, and how the burden should be assessed.

The market economy does not eliminate conflict of goals. But it does permit different individuals to make different adjustments rather than enforcing uniformity. The price system is geared to variations involving a little more and a little less and to multilateral variations among numerous variables, such as the commodities consumed by a family. The political system, even in a well-functioning democracy, is not well geared to such adjustments. Much political decision-making is based on the binary choices represented in voting for or against a particular candidate or legislative proposal. And many political decisions must involve uniformity of treatment of various citizens—in the assessment of tax liability, for instance.

One may also ask how the political system weights the desires of various members of the community. We already know that the economic system weights them on the basis of the income and wealth of the household. The political system weights them on the basis of power and influence. Even in a democracy, not all persons are equal in political power and influence. Some groups which lack wealth and economic power may be able to wield political influence. However, political power may simply gravitate toward existing centers of economic power. Neither the form of political democracy nor that of competitive capitalism guarantees that every individual will have a fair shake.

Some social critics argue that economic discourse itself is biased; that it concerns itself with only a limited range of human needs and desires—those perhaps not very important ones. The economist looks at people's desires for goods and services and for occupational activities. But what about each person's preferences about the kind of society he wants to live in, the kind of people with whom he wishes to live? What about people who want to escape from dog-eat-dog competition for personal, social, and economic advancement, from relentless upward-mobile status-seeking and compulsive conspicuous consumption? What about people who want a sense of solidarity with their fellows, an opportunity to submerge private differences and work together for the common good? Such questions cannot be dismissed lightly. They suggest that one might be dissatisfied with the market economy, even if it performed its chosen tasks well, on grounds that it focuses on secondary or trivial objectives.

A free society may permit considerable scope for some of the latter goals. The person who is eager to join with others in unselfish common pursuit of some important objective may find the opportunity through such voluntary organizations as churches, clubs, political parties, or in some cases even business firms. What he will have a more difficult time assuring is that his fellow workers will be in fact high-minded and unselfish.

Desires for solidarity and moral uplift have repeatedly surged into political action over the past two centuries. Efforts to promote them through government actions, however, have been disappointing at best and alarming at worst. Each of us understandably wishes that his fellow men would behave in certain ways, but it is hard to defend either the feasibility or propriety of utopian programs of social engineering designed to make people better in character and personality when such programs are backed by the coercive authority of government.

the choice of means

Even if there is agreement on objectives of government policy, there may remain difficult problems in the choice of means. However, this is an area in which technical advice can help the government. Economists as such have no particular qualifications to prescribe what the objectives of government should be, but they can help to identify efficient policy procedures to achieve given objectives. A good illustration is in the technical analysis of monetary and fiscal policies to promote economic growth and full employment without inflation.

There is insufficient space here to attempt a complete catalog of possible methods of government action. However, a few useful distinctions can be noted. One is the distinction between actual performance of an economic service by the government (which thereby incurs the burdens of acquiring resources and trying to use them effectively) and actions by the government to influence private persons to provide the service. The direct approach may be necessary where the service is one for which payment cannot be required from the beneficiaries. The indirect approach may be suitable where some of the service would be provided by the market, but for some reason the quantity (or quality) would not be adequate. By a subsidy (or tax concession) the government can provide an incentive for the quantity of output to be increased and perhaps, if necessary, for the quality standards to be altered. The indirect approach raises problems of supervision and control, but it also offers substantial advantages. In particular, it may retain the advantages of competition in the industry, with its pressure for efficiency and its opportunity for diversity.

Government may be able to achieve positive results by negative methods—that is, by veto, prohibition, or punishment. Traffic regulation may order people to drive on one side of the road, to signal for turns, and to stop for red lights, but such orders become effective only when contrary behavior is punished. (However, voluntary compliance will be fairly good to the extent that each individual realizes he is safer when he and others conform to the rules.)

The negative approach is not always suitable for economic objectives. For example, it has been traditional in industrial countries to regard payment of low wages as bad and to try to raise wage rates by minimum-wage laws which prohibit paying wage rates below a certain standard. One possible result, however, is that employment opportunities are reduced and some people receive no wages at all. Another example can be observed in slum-clearance programs in many cities, where the emphasis is on the destruction of old run-down buildings, with much less attention given to the provision of good housing for the people displaced by the destruction. It is very difficult for government simply to compel people to do something; it gets much better results when it provides a potential reward rather than merely a potential punishment.

power and responsibility

Typically government has a virtual monopoly on the instruments of force and coercion in society. Its opportunity to inflict injury on individuals gives it the power to raise revenue by compulsion; this is in contrast with private business firms, which are dependent on voluntary expenditures. The coercive authority of government is essential for its functions of maintaining internal order and national defense. To be sure, most governments possess legitimacy in the eyes of the public, so that the actual use or threat of coercion does not come into use very often.

The greater the power of a government, however, the greater the harm it may bring about by misguided actions. One of the traditional arguments against a large economic role for government has been based on the conviction that government would use its authority unwisely in the economy. Adam Smith urged limiting the role of government because he feared that politically powerful businessmen would turn the policies of an interventionist government unduly to their private advantage and to the detriment of the general public. Some modern critics have gone further and raised the alarm that centralized control of economic life by government might lead to totalitarian control over all aspects of individual activity. The latter fears have not generally materialized in Western societies. However, even if government economic policies do not infringe on prized individual freedoms, there remain problems of competence and responsibility.

If government is to conduct economic policy efficiently, there must be some method to ensure that individuals who exercise power have some competence and an incentive to use it. Within the administrative system this requires that some system of performance evaluation be possible and that performance be defined in terms of policy objectives rather than deference to superiors or number of pieces of paper handled. In a democracy, pressure for competence in pursuit of policy goals comes from the desire of elected officials to be reelected. The system can only work well if the electorate can evaluate the performance of candidates and if elected officials can in fact effectively influence the conduct of administration. Neither governments nor their scholarly critics have done very much toward systematic evaluation of the effectiveness of past programs, in a manner which would improve the process of learning from experience.

pressure-group bias

One of the sovereign powers of government is the power to make mistakes. It is nearly as important to identify things the government should not do as to extend its positive agenda. Even where government activity does not transgress against any generally accepted moral standards, it may be economically counter-productive. Economists need to consider whether there are systematic tendencies toward such adverse effects.

In the United States and other industrial countries, there typically exist producer groups which are relatively self-conscious, organized and vocal, and consequently able to influence the government. The logic of profit maximization certainly implies that if business firms can influence government actions, it is logical to try to improve their profits by this means. Nor is this inherently wicked. The question is, does such influence, in the aggregate, worsen the performance of the system? Sometimes it does.

Any producer group stands to gain private benefit if it can behave more nearly like a monopoly. Existing members of the group can gain (or be protected against loss) if entry is restricted, supply curtailed, and price increased. To permit a single group to do this may yield a tangible benefit to the rather small number of members. The group's restrictive actions tend to inflict a somewhat larger burden on the remainder of the society, but the burden is much more widely distributed and may therefore be unnoticed. Once government actions on this basis begin, however, they generate demands for similar assistance by other producer groups as well. Perhaps the efforts to provide such aid will merely cancel out. But they may have some tendencies which are cumulatively contrary to maximum economic efficiency and welfare.

The traditional illustration in American history has been the protective tariff against imports. An individual producer group could often see clear potential gain to itself from tariff protection. By the principle of logrolling, however, tariff laws tended to include protection for a great variety of industries. In some cases the benefit an industry's members received from the tariff on their output was canceled by tariffs on their inputs. But the cumulative tendency toward protecting everyone was to discriminate against export industries and consumers and to move the system away from the sort of optimality described in Chapter 18. Yet the individual producer group is rational to seek a higher tariff. The other groups are going to do so anyway; a decision by the pickle packers to refrain will not deter other groups. In our own time the federal income tax displays the results of a similar process of competitive pressure-group influence.

If a country's political system is subject to a producer pressure-group bias, there may be a systematic tendency for government to undertake counter-productive actions. Under such circumstances, well-intentioned policies may end up being captured by clientele groups who divert them to their own goals. One is not then surprised if regulation of transport media becomes chiefly a means for protecting railroads and truck companies against competition, if urban renewal becomes chiefly an instrument for enriching local construction firms and real estate dealers, if postal policy is dominated by a concern for the postal employees, or if national defense is under the influence of a vaguely defined military-industrial complex. Such considerations suggest a skeptical attitude toward extensions of the economic role of government into activities which involve detailed involvement with particular industries and producer groups.

the overloaded circuit

As the size of government increases, so does the difficulty of coordinating its operations. Government is subject to diseconomies of large-scale operation. Layers of supervisory workers increase, and the problem of communication between top officials and the rank and file of operative employees grows.

This creates a serious problem of responsibility. There can be only a limited number of truly top-level government officials: a prime minister or president, a cabinet, a legislature. The function of top officials involves evaluating the performance of existing government programs and deciding what to do about their continuation. This process comes to focus particularly on the operation of budgeting. A government budget brings together for comparison the projected expenditures for the various government activities. A major task of top officials is to achieve an efficient allocation of resources among these various programs, present and projected. They can only do this if they know what is currently being done, and particularly only if they can compare activities in one program with those in another. Budgeting calls for a marginal analysis; would it be better to allot an additional million to defense, or to education, or to highways, or perhaps to keeping taxes lower or reducing the government debt?

The larger the government becomes, the more difficult it is for its leaders to control and evaluate its activities. The same is even more true of the citizens as a whole. In the United States, the average citizen can have no idea even of all the activities which the federal government performs, much less whether they are well done or worth doing at all.

In this view, the top-level political leadership in government can be regarded as a scarce economic resource. The problem is how to use it to maximum advantage. With such a fixed factor, expansion of the scale of government activity is subject to diminishing returns. Enlarging the government reduces the efficiency and accountability not merely of the marginal activity but probably of its other activities as well.

At the same time, one can assign priorities to the various possible activities of government. At one end of the scale, there are activities which are urgently needed and can only be performed by government. Such are the maintenance of order and justice, national defense and foreign policy, and the management of monetary and fiscal policy to influence the flow of aggregate expenditures. Beyond this, we enter a range of policies less urgent but still potentially beneficial. As we move along such a priority listing, we have something like a principle of diminishing marginal utility. At some point, the declining advantages and the declining efficiency of operation will eliminate any further net gain from extension of government.

The magnitudes involved are hardly measurable, and individual members of the society may well differ in their evaluations; but some such explicit weighing of costs and benefits seems as good a method of trying to determine the optimum scale of government as any feasible alternative.

summary

Even in a world of competitive equilibrium, the private economy might fail to produce optimal results: desired collective services might fail to be produced, and divergence between social and private costs and benefits might lead to distortions in the pattern of output. Further, a real-world laissez-faire economy is likely to be confronted with problems of monopoly, instability, and inequality in the distribution of incomes. The shortcomings of the private economy provide one element in a possible agenda for government economic activity. However, it is also necessary to consider what functions government is competent to perform.

Government can improve the environment for the private economy by providing an appropriate legal framework and by preventing serious instability in the flow of aggregate demand. A considerable array of collective services may be appropriate, ranging from traditional services such as defense and highways to the expansion of research activities. Various methods are available for eliminating discrepancies between social and private costs and benefits. External costs such as those associated with air or water pollution can be internalized by forcing business firms to maintain purification facilities or by taxing them to finance government antipollution programs.

Government influence on income distribution may be exerted directly, through transfer payments, indirectly by efforts to raise the productivity of low-income families or by providing free or subsidized services to some families.

Government may attack monopolistic market structures directly, trying to increase the number and decrease the size of firms, or it may restrict the ability of large firms to abuse the strategic advantages of their size.

For reasons of ideology and power, or to promote economic growth, important products or services may be provided by government enterprises, which may sell their output in the market. Such enterprises are confronted with problems of how to ensure efficient operation, what prices to charge, and what criteria to follow for investment. The criteria used by private profit-seeking firms are not always appropriate but frequently contain elements that need to be considered. For instance, government investment projects can better be undertaken if some estimate of expected rate of return is calculated, but this rate of return may properly include an allowance for social benefits which do not yield revenue to the government.

Although technical economic analysis can help identify appropriate means to pursue given goals, the selection of goals of policy requires a suitable political process by which public opinion can make itself felt. Because of the potential coercive power of government, its mistakes may be potentially more harmful than those made by private firms or individuals. A particular problem in a market economy is the potential policy distortion arising from the strength of producer pressure groups which may be able to use government to protect themselves against competition and change.

Government operations appear subject to diseconomies of large-scale operation. Further, there are some government activities which are more important than others. Government policy may be more effective in the high-priority areas if some restraint is used in the extension of scale and scope of government activity. The fact that the private economy displays shortcomings is not a sufficient condition for government action; there must be some reason to expect that government is competent politically and administratively to do things better.

QUESTIONS AND PROBLEMS

1. Imagine you are involved in preparing estimates of the prospective rate of return on a government program of investment in a multipurpose water-control project involving dams and hydroelectric power facilities. The project will provide recreational facilities on new-formed lakes—camping, boating, fishing. Flood damage downstream will be reduced. However, some private homesteads in the area to be flooded must be sold to the government whether the owners wish it or not. Illustrate how calculations of the social benefits of such a project might be performed. What problems arise?

2. Some people believe that the undesirability of a government policy can be demonstrated if that policy restricts people's freedom. How would that criterion apply to each of the following areas:
   (a) Government restricts people's freedom to drive as fast as they wish.
   (b) Government restricts the freedom of business firms to cooperate with each other in determining output and prices.
   (c) Government restricts the freedom of business firms to hire only white Anglo-Saxon protestant workers.
   (d) Government restricts the freedom of landowners in a given area to use their properties for glue factories, garbage dumps, rendering plants, drag strips, and jet airports.
   (e) Government subjects young men to involuntary service in the armed forces.

3. Explain why education services would probably be underproduced if provided only by business firms charging market prices to their customers. How could government cure such underproduction without furnishing the services itself? What criteria should determine the proper quantity and types of education services?

nswers to selected
end-of-chapter questions

2. (a) $dy/dx = 10$
   (b) $dy/dx = 10$
   (c) $dy/dx = 10 - 5/x^2$ (The last term can also be written $-5x^{-2}$.)
   (d) $dy/dx = 1.581/\sqrt{x}$ (or $1.581x^{-\frac{1}{2}}$)
   (e) $dy/dx = 15x^2 - 24x + 4$

3. (a) $dy/dx = 10$ when $x = 10$. From this we may estimate that an increase in x by 0.1 will raise y by ten times as much, or 1.0. Check this by calculating the value of y for $x = 10$ and $x = 10.1$.

$$
\begin{array}{ll}
\text{if } x = 10 & \text{then } y = 100 \\
\underline{10.1} & \underline{101} \\
\Delta x = 0.1 & \Delta y = 1.0
\end{array}
$$

(d) $dy/dx = \frac{1}{2}$ when $x = 10$. From this we may estimate that an increase in x by 0.1 will raise y by one-half as much, or 0.05. Check this by calculating the value of y for $x = 10$ and $x = 10.1$.

	if $x = 10$	then $y = 10$
	10.1	$\sqrt{101} = 10.499$
	$\Delta x = 0.1$	$\Delta y = 0.499$

Unless the underlying function is linear, the change in y estimated from the derivative will not be precisely identical with that obtained by calculating the two separate values for y and subtracting. The smaller the change in x, the closer the results of the two methods.

(e) $dy/dx = 1{,}264$ when $x = 10$. From this, we may estimate that an increase in x by 0.1 will raise y by 1,264 times as much, or 126.4. Check this by calculating the value of y for $x = 10$ and $x = 10.1$.

	if $x = 10$	then $y = 3{,}838.0$
	10.1	3,965.8
	$\Delta x = 0.1$	$\Delta y = 127.8$

chapter 3

1. One implication of outward-bulging indifference curves is that the consumer would be better off to consume all of one or all of the other, rather than a combination of both. Tangency between budget line and indifference curve would represent the most expensive way of reaching a given indifference curve.

2. $dB/dA = (-)(2 + B)/A$. The demand function for B can be expressed as

$$B = \frac{Y}{2P_B} - 1 \quad \left(\text{or} \quad \frac{Y - 2P_B}{2P_B} \right)$$

5. The indifference curve would become parallel to the axis. If additional units of a commodity are positively undesirable, the curve might bend away from the axis.

6. Since the substitution effect always works to decrease the consumption of a product which has risen in price, the situation postulated can only occur if the income effect works in the other direction and is sufficiently strong to overpower the substitution effect. The situation (called the *Giffen paradox*) is alleged to arise in low-income countries having a low-cost high-calorie staple foodstuff, such as potatoes in nineteenth-century Ireland, rice in modern Asia. People are already spending a large proportion of their income on it. Raising its price forces them to cut down consumption of other products in order to survive.

chapter 4

2. **(b)** $e = \frac{1}{2}$
   (d) $e = 0.48$

6. **(a)** $e = 100/Q - 1$
   (b) $e = 1$
   (c) $e = 2$

7. A rise in the price of A will tend to have a negative income effect on consumption of other commodities. Substitutes and complements are usually identified without reference to this income effect.

chapter 5

1. **(b)** $e = 2$
   (d) $e = P/(P - 5)$. As P rises, e declines, but approaches unity as a limit.

2. **(b)** $P = \$10$
   $Q = 20$
   (c) $e_s = 3$
   $e_d = \frac{1}{2}$

chapter 6

1. **(d)** $MPP_b = dQ/db = 5b^{-\frac{1}{2}}$ (or $5/\sqrt{b}$)

3. **(a)** 2
   (b) $\frac{2}{3}$
   (c) If $a = b$, the elasticity of output reduces to $(20 - 3a)/(10 - a)$ which takes different values depending on a, decreasing as a increases.

chapter 7

3. At the equilbrium wage of 62, 150 workers are available and are hired. The output and income pattern is as follows:

Grade	Number of Tracts and Owners	Hired Workers	Output per Tract	Total Output	Income per Owner	Total Income
A			0		62	4,960
B			0		62	4,340
C	50	50	136	6,800	74	3,700
D	(10)	20	227	2,270	103	2,060
	(10)	30	289	2,890		
E	10	50	462	4,620	152	1,520
	80	150		16,580		16,580

5. **(c)** At a wage of 75, there are only 100 jobs available. If the union is either powerful or lucky it will reserve those for workers from land of category A, forcing owners of B and C tracts to return to self-employment. The union need not compensate owners of C land, who earn 70, but must pay out 720 to owners of B land. The 100 employed workers receive total income of 7,500, but retain only 6,780 after the assessment to compensate those who withdrew. Thus their average wage is only 67.8, which is less than the free-market equilibrium wage. The best round-number wage under this compensation system is 71. Jobs can be found for 170 workers, leaving only 10 to be compensated at a total cost of 90. After paying their assessment, hired workers are left with about 70.5 as their wage. The compensation works better the lower the elasticities of demand for and supply of hired labor.

(d) Owners of E land would continue to employ their former number of workers, earning more than their self-employment income of 90. Owners of D land would hire no workers.

chapter 8

1. **(a)** The isoquant is $ab = 25$. $MRS = da/db = 25/b^2$, which is $25\!\!/\!16$ when $b = 4$.

   (b) Least-cost input combination is 7.071 units of b and 3.535 units of a, involving a total cost of \$141.42.

   (c) $MPP_a = dQ/da = 2.5(b/a)^{\frac{1}{2}}$
   $MPP_b = dQ/db = 2.5(a/b)^{\frac{1}{2}}$
   $[2.5(b/a)^{\frac{1}{2}}]/10 = [2.5(a/b)^{\frac{1}{2}}]/5$
   $b = 2a;\ a = b/2$
   $25 = 2a^2;\ 25 = b^2/2$
   $a = 3.535;\ b = 7.071$

   The $MRS\ da/db$ is equal to the ratio of marginal products:
   $MPP_b/MPP_a = [2.5(a/b)^{\frac{1}{2}}]/[2.5(b/a)^{\frac{1}{2}}] = a/b$ (from ratio of MPP terms)
   $da/db = Q^2/25b^2 = a/b$ (from MRS)

   (d) $b = 2a$. After price of a rises, $b = 4a$.

2. The marginal rate of substitution between a and b is always a linear relationship in a function of the general form $Q = a^m b^n$. Raise all terms to the power $1/m$ to eliminate the exponent on a; thus
   $Q^{1/m} = ab^{n/m}$
   $a = Q^{1/m}/b^{n/m} = Q^{1/m}b^{-n/m}$
   $da/db = (-)(n/m)(Q^{1/m})(b^{-n/m-1})$

   Substituting the first equation in place of $Q^{1/m}$ yields
   $da/db = (-)(n/m)(ab^{n/m})(b^{-n/m-1})$

   This simplifies to
   $da/db = (-)(n/m)(a/b)$

Setting $da/db = P_b/P_a$ (and dropping the minus sign) we obtain

$(n/m)(a/b) = P_b/P_a$

$a = (m/n)(P_b/P_a)b$

which is linear when m, n, P_a and P_b are given.

chapter 9

1. **(a)** $Q = 10$; $ab = 125$

   $Q = 20$; $ab = 1,000$

   (b) 9.1 units of a and 13.7 units of b

   $a = \frac{2}{3}b$ identifies output-expansion path

   (c) $TC = 1.732Q^{3/2}$ $(= (3Q^3)^{1/2})$

   $LAC = 1.732Q^{1/2}$

   $LMC = 2.6Q^{1/2}$

2. $STC = 32 + 0.125Q^3$

4. **(b)** $AFC = 100/Q$

   $AVC = Q/2 + 100$

   $AC = 100/Q + Q/2 + 100$

   $MC = Q + 100$

   (d) To find minimum AC, set $dAC/dQ = 0$. $dAC/dQ = \frac{1}{2} - 100/Q^2 = 0$, where $Q = 14.14$. Substituting this value for Q indicates that $MC = AC$ = \$114.14 at this output.

chapter 10

1. **(a)** $ab^2 = 100,000$ for $Q = 10$

   $ab^2 = 3,200,000$ for $Q = 20$

   (b) $e = 0.6$

   (c) $a = \frac{5}{4}b$

   (d) $TC = 13.92Q^{5/3}$

   (e) $Q = 89.44$ units, using 2,075 units of input a and 1,660 units of input b.

   (f) $SMC = 0.55Q^{3/2}$. At a price of \$500, output in the short run maximizes profit at about 94.07 units, in the long run at about 99.73 units.

   (g) The increase in P_b shifts SMC to $0.6585Q^{3/2}$. At a product price of \$464, profit-maximizing output would be about 79.36 units. The new value of LMC is $26.25Q^{2/3}$. At a product price of \$464, profit-maximizing output would be about 74.32 units.

chapter 11

1. $TNRP_a = 20a^{4/5}$. Demand schedule for a is $a = (16/P_a)^5$. When $P_a = 8$, $a = 32$, $b = 64$, and $Q = 320$. The MRS da/db along this isoquant is

$\frac{5}{4}a/b = (\frac{5}{4})(\frac{32}{64}) = \frac{5}{8} = P_b/P_a$. The total cost function is $TC = 0.945Q^{1\frac{9}{6}}$, yielding $MC = 1.05Q^{\frac{1}{6}}$. When $Q = 320$, $MC = \$2 =$ product price.

2. $MPP_a = 12/a^{\frac{3}{6}}$
   $MRP_a = 60/a^{\frac{3}{6}}$

   With $P_a = \$7.50$, the most profitable quantity of a is 32 units, producing 120 units of output. The relevant SMC function is $0.003805Q^{\frac{3}{2}}$, which equals \$5 when $Q = 120$.

chapter 12

3. $dQ/dP = 3P^2$
   $P/Q = P/P^3 = 1/P^2$

   Thus $e = 3$.

5. Total revenue = total cost + profit

   $TR = TC + \pi$
   $TC = a \cdot P_a + b \cdot P_b$
   $TR - b \cdot P_b = a \cdot P_a + \pi = TNRP_a$

   If $ANRP_a = P_a$, then $TNRP_a = a \cdot P_a$, and $\pi = 0$. At this situation total cost equals total revenue and $AC = P$.

chapter 13

3. $dQ/da = 133.33/a^{\frac{1}{3}}$
   $W = \$4.44$

   Total output would be \$180,000. Labor receives $(27,000)(\$4.44) = \$120,000$, and input b receives $(8,000)(\$7.50) = \$60,000$. The MPP of input b is $3,000/b^{\frac{2}{3}} = \$7.50$ in equilibrium.

4. $e = 3$

chapter 14

1. Setting up the solution in ordinary present-value form yields an equation $2r^3 + 5r^2 + 3r - 1 = 0$. We can approximate a solution by letting $r^3 = 0$ and solving the resulting quadratic, which yields $r = 23.85$ percent. The true value will be slightly smaller. By approximation we find $r = 23.4$ percent.

2. $V = \$2,723$

3. Let d represent the marginal efficiency of capital, meaning the internal rate of return on the marginal investment. By definition, d takes a value such that

$$\sum_{x=0}^{n} \frac{Y_x}{(1 + d)^x} = P$$

where P represents the price of the capital good and Y is the expected stream of future income. In equilibrium, $d = r$, the rate of interest. By definition, the discounted $MNRP$ of a capital good is the present value of expected future income discounted with the interest rate. Thus

$$MNRP = \sum_{x=0}^{n} \frac{Y_x}{(1+r)^x}$$

In equilibrium, this equals the price of the capital good. When $d = r$, the two expressions are interchangeable.

chapter 16

4. The equilibrium input ratio is $a_1 = 125b_1/(1,125 - b_1)$. Some points on the production-possibilities curve are approximately these:

Q_A	Q_B
0	1,000
121	927
334	777
419	715
516	623
630	507
777	334
1,000	0

Since the function is symmetrical in A and B, it represents an arc of a circle with its center in the negative quadrant. The general formula for a circle is $(x - h)^2 + (y - k)^2 = R^2$, where h and k are the coordinates of the center and R is the radius. In this example, $h = k$. The circle can be derived by substituting Q_A for x and Q_B for y. From the first point we obtain $(0 - h)^2 + (1,000 - h)^2 = R^2$. From the fifth point we obtain $(516 - h)^2 + (623 - h)^2 = R^2$. Multiplying out and setting the two equal to each other eliminates R and enables us to determine that $h = -1,243$. We obtain $R^2 = 1,243^2 + 2,243^3 = 6,576,098$. Substituting these values back into the original equation, we obtain $Q_A^2 + 2,486Q_A + Q_B^2 + 2,486Q_B = 3,486,000$, which does approximate the production-possibilities curve we are looking for.

chapter 17

1. $MCOR = b$. Since dQ/dK does not decrease with increased capital, the function does not display diminishing returns.

2. Assume the production function takes the form $Q = aK^xL^{1-x}$, where a represents a scale constant. The $MCOR$ derived from this function is $dQ/dK = ax(L/K)^{1-x}$. As long as capital and labor increase at the same proportional rate, the ratio L/K remains constant and the entire expression is also a constant. This is equivalent to the Harrod-Domar postulate that $dQ/dK = b$.

3. Capital receives one-fifth and labor four-fifths of total income. Changes in factor supplies are always offset by changes in factor prices; the real demand schedule for each factor has unitary elasticity.

chapter 18

1. A trader starting in Japan with 1,000 yen could purchase 100 units of cloth which he could sell in Thailand for 1,000 baht. With this he could buy 50 units of rice which would sell in Japan for 1,500 yen. Thus Japan would tend to export cloth and Thailand rice.

4. Draw the two production-possibilities curves so they intersect at the original no-trade output positions of the two countries. The two curves will then overlap. The area of overlap represents a potential for increased joint production by moving to a position where the two curves are tangent to each other. The tangency point cannot be identified from production-possibilities curves alone, however, since it depends on demand conditions as well.

chapter 19

4. If medical services are to be provided without direct cost to the recipients, the first problem would be how to raise the money to pay for the necessary factor services; the second, what quantity of services should be offered. If government undertakes to supply the entire quantity demanded at a zero price, the service will tend to be overproduced (compared with alternative uses of factors of production). If supply is less than demand at the zero price, there is the problem of how to ration the available supply among the prospective customers.

chapter 20

1. (a) $P = \$55$; $Q = 45$
   (b) With unitary elasticity of demand, $MR = 0$. The monopolist should produce the smallest possible (positive) output and charge the appropriate price.
   (d) $Q = k[(n - 1)/10n]^n$
   $P = 10n/(n - 1)$

2. $Q_1 = 45$; $P_1 = \$55$
   $Q_2 = 425$; $P_2 = \$95$

   Shifting one unit of output from Q_1 to Q_2 would lower total revenue from $42,850 to $42,848.80.

chapter 22

1. The monopsony data used for Figure 22-2 yield these cost functions:

   $$TC = 8.77Q^{\frac{2}{3}}$$
   $$MC = 11.69Q^{\frac{1}{3}}$$

   At output of 5 units, the monopsonist uses 5 units of b, so its price to him is $5. He uses 5 units of a costing $10 each. With those same input prices, a competitive buyer would have these cost functions:

   $$TC = 14.14Q$$
   $$MC = 14.14$$

   At output of 5 units, the competitive buyer would have total cost of $70.70, while the monopsonist's total cost would be $75. The competitive buyer would use 3.535 units of a and 7.07 units of b. If the monopsonist used this combination, it would cost him about $85, since he would have to pay a price of $7.07 for that quantity of input b. At an output of 5 units, the monopsonist's marginal cost would be $20, compared to $14.14 for the competitive buyer. Observe that the monopsonist's marginal cost is less than that of the competitive buyer for outputs less than 1.77 units.

3. $Q = 227$ units of the input.

index

454